The Last Days of Hitler

The Last Days of Hitler

The Legends, the Evidence, the Truth

ANTON JOACHIMSTHALER

Translated by Helmut Bögler

Brockhampton Press

Arms and Armour Press
An Imprint of the Cassell Group
Wellington House, 125 Strand, London WC2R 0BB

This book was originally published as *Hitlers Ende* by F. A.
Herbig Verlagsbuchhandlung GmbH, Munich, and translations of
quoted matter may therefore not precisely accord with the original
texts on which they are based.

British Library Cataloguing-in-Publication data:
A catalogue record for this book is available from the
British Library

Edited and designed by Roger Chesneau/DAG Publications Ltd

Printed and bound in Great Britain by
Creative Print and Design (Wales), Ebbw Vale

This edition published in 1999 by Brockhampton Press,
a member of Hodder Headline PLC Group

ISBN 1 86019 902 X

Contents

Preface

On 30 April 1995 it was fifty years to the day since Hitler put an end to his life. Seldom before in history has the death of one man, who in his day dominated most of Europe, given rise to so many legends, lies and half-truths. The Soviet authorities, who were the only people in a position to conduct investigations, did far more to confuse the issue than to clarify it, and what their findings actually amounted to has still not been made public. (I do not count the Russian journalist Lew Bezemensky's publications—*Der Tod des Adolf Hitler*, C. Wegener Verlag, Hamburg, 1968, and 'Hitlers letzte Reise', *Der Spiegel*, No. 30, 1992, p. 110 *et seq.*—as official Russian investigation reports.) There were witnesses to Hitler's death and the cremation of his body, and these witnesses were interrogated in the West. Hitler's body was never found, however, and so the rumours started—and they have been with us in innumerable versions for fifty years.

I would like to cite just one example of many which, together with Bezemensky's publications, made me decide that I would investigate Hitler's fate more thoroughly. In his biography *Adolf Hitler*, the German historian Werner Maser writes, on page 523:

> 'The charred body [Hitler's]—there was nothing left of the face and only a horribly burnt remnant of the shattered skull—was pushed on to a tarpaulin, lowered into a shell crater in the vast graveyard around the Chancellery and, under heavy Soviet artillery fire, covered with earth, which was then stamped down with a wooden stamper,' reports his personal adjutant Otto Günsche . . .

Maser cites Günsche's[1] testimony as a 'statement to a friend and *Dr* Giesing. Reported by *Dr* Giesing on 8.6.1971.' I questioned Otto Günsche about this on 14 October 1994 and he said, 'I do not know this gentleman [meaning Maser] and I never said this to anyone.'

The German journalist Joachim C. Fest, who used much of Maser's material, had already written the following on page 1023 of his biography *Hitler*:

> Shortly before 2300 the remains of the almost completely burned body were pushed on to a tarpaulin and, according to Günsche's report, 'lowered into a shell crater in front of the bunker entrance, covered with earth and stamped down with a wooden stamper.'

As his source, *Herr* Fest cites Maser on page 1152 with the following words: '124, statement by Otto Günsche, cit. W. Maser, *Hitler*, p. 432 . . .' Fest is already quoting the 'statement by Günsche in Maser'. This example demonstrates how myths and legends are born and perpetuated in literature by reputable historians and journalists.

For a long time now I have been concerned with Hitler's fate. I have spoken with actual witnesses—Albert Speer,[2] Christine Schroeder,[3] Hermann Giesler,[4] Otto Günsche, Walter Frentz,[5] Adolf Dirr[6] and many others—and, in arduous research, compiled statements by other historical witnesses. I have only taken into account the testimonies of witnesses who were directly involved in the events. There is much material by other people whose knowledge is based on second-hand accounts, and we all know the problems associated with hearsay.

The basic material which I have relied on—testimonies, interviews, written reports, photographs, plans etc.—originated with the following institutions: the Berlin Document Centre; the German Federal Archives in Koblenz; Files of the Denazification Tribunal, Special File 'S', Munich; Witness Reports (designated 'ZS') and the David Irving Collection in the Institute for Contemporary History, Munich; the testimonies of people in Hitler's immediate entourage in the National Archives, Washington DC (Historical Interrogation Commission, War Department General Staff G – Historical Branch; Third Army Intelligence Center and Headquarters US Forces; European Theater, Military Intelligence Service Center); the so-called 'Musmanno papers';[7] and testimonies by witnesses heard during the 1952 proceedings at the Federal Court in Berchtesgaden to declare Hitler dead and to determine the exact time of his death.

The last requires some explanation. On 2 July 1948 the records office of Berlin-Mitte notified a Munich lawyer concerning Hitler's death in connection with proceedings before the Denazification Tribunal:

> With reference to your enquiry of 21.6.1948 I inform you that Hitler's death has not been recorded by the Records Office at Berlin-Mitte. Our attempts to find any positive records on the death of Adolf Hitler, which would permit the recording of same, have been without result.

In other words, three years after Hitler's death there was still no official declaration of death in any of the three records offices of Hitler's official places of residence (Berchtesgaden, Munich and Berlin). The Records Office in Berlin, which supposedly held jurisdiction, refused to record Hitler's death officially. Hitler's chauffeur, Erich Kempka,[8] and the former Reich Youth Leader of the NSDAP, Artur Axmann,[9] had both testified under oath in Nuremberg that on 30 April 1945 they had seen a body being carried out of the *Führerbunker* which was wrapped in a blanket and was dressed in Hitler's trousers, shoes and socks. Nevertheless, the Berlin Records Office did not consider this to be proof that Hitler was dead, maintaining that this could have been any corpse dressed in Hitler's trousers and shoes.

The question whether Hitler's death could be officially registered was of importance to the denazification hearings. If Hitler's death was not conclusively proven, then proceedings against him *in absentia* would have to take place and the court could sentence him to a maximum of ten years in a labour camp as a 'chief offender'. On the other hand, if Hitler *were* dead, then only the confiscation of his property would be necessary.

In October 1948 hearings were begun by Denazification Tribunal I in Munich against the defendant, the 'former Chancellor of the *Reich*, Adolf Hitler', and on 15 October a decision was arrived at, classifying him as a 'chief offender'. Despite the fact that the tribunal was not shown a death certificate, the proceedings also settled Hitler's estate. After a short deliberation the tribunal decided to confiscate all the property belonging to the former *Führer*, comprising a house at 16 Prinzregentenplatz in Munich, several houses near Berchtesgaden (which were greatly reduced in value owing to bomb damage) and a claim of roughly five million marks against the publishing firm of Eher in Munich. A claim by Hitler's sister, Paula Hitler,[10] who called herself Wolf, that she should be granted the legacy left to her in Hitler's personal will was denied.

Dr Wilhelm Motzet, who had been appointed trustee of the estate by the court, declared Hitler's will to be invalid. One can read in the files on the proceedings:

> Adolf Hitler's will is invalid; it lacks the proper legal form. According to his own will, the estate falls to the State since the NSDAP no longer exists. The value of the estate cannot be determined at this time. The portion of the estate of Adolf Hitler lying in the State of Bavaria is confiscated. The costs of these proceedings are to be paid from the estate. The amount in dispute will be decided upon later.

Hitler's sister, Paula Hitler-Wolf, then took up residence in Berchtesgaden on 1 December 1952 in order to promote her claims based on Hitler's personal will. She applied for a certificate of inheritance, which, however, could not be issued without Hitler's death certificate.

Meanwhile legal proceedings had also been initiated in Austria. These originated from a claim by the German-Bohemian *Graf* Jaromir Czernin-Morzin, a former landowner in the Riesengebirge with an ancestral castle at Hohenelbe, who had been forced to sell the bulk of his property to the German State in 1938 because of debts. He had subsequently moved to his sole remaining residence, a hunting lodge in Marschendorf, from which, like all other Germans, he had been expelled by the Czechs after the war. Included in the property sold by Czernin-Morzin had been an oil painting by Jan Vermeer, *The Artist in his Studio*, which Hitler had bought for 1,600,000 Reichsmarks for his *Führer-Museum* in Linz. In the early 1950s Czernin-Morzin declared in Munich that he had been coerced into selling the painting and demanded restitution from the Austrian State. This led to a legal investigation, which resulted in a court action being brought against Hitler in order to confiscate his private property in Austria. On 29 July 1952 *Dr* Herbert Eggstein of Vienna, who meanwhile had been appointed trustee *in absentia* for Hitler's property in Austria, applied for the issue of a death certificate in order to secure the rights of the Austrian government to the Vermeer painting. As far as the painting was concerned, the Austrian government simply declared that 'as Hitler's private property, this painting is now the property of the Austrian State'. The painting was sent to Vienna and is probably still there. The issue of a death certificate was, however, denied, for reasons based on a law dating from the reign of Charles V (!) which stated amongst other things that a criminal sentence could be carried out against a person who was deceased. *Dr* Eggstein thereupon applied in Germany for proceedings to be initiated to declare Hitler dead.

After a dispute about jurisdiction between the courts in Berchtesgaden and Berlin-Schöneberg, Hitler's two principal places of residence, the decision was reached that the Federal Court in Berchtesgaden held jurisdiction, and the local Federal Judge, *Dr* Heinrich Stephanus, began proceedings towards the end of 1952 which lasted until early 1956. In his painstaking and conscientious investigation, Stephanus heard 42 witnesses, of which thirteen had only returned from Russian prisoner-of-war camps in 1955 and 1956, and studied all the surviving German files as well as all the available foreign literature. He concluded:

> There can no longer be the slightest doubt that on 30 April 1945 Adolf Hitler put an end to his life in the Chancellery by his own hand, by means of a shot into his right temple.

The file attached to Hitler's death certificate—which was issued on 25 February 1956—is over 1,500 pages thick and includes witness statements, some of which fill more than 50 pages. During the course of the investigation experts from the State Criminal Investigation Department of Bavaria were brought in as advisers. These experts, who took part in the interrogation of witnesses, contributed their specific expertise in the fields of chemical and medical toxology, forensic medicine, weapons, pyrotechnology and general scientific criminology to help Judge Stephanus frame his questions and evaluate the answers. It subsequently became apparent that a reconstruction of the actual events was required, leading to an 80-page report on Hitler's death being presented by these experts on 1 August 1956.

On 31 December 1956 readers of the *Süddeutsche Zeitung* (No 313) were able to read the following final account:

Registration Office certifies Hitler's death.
Berlin (SZ)—As of Friday 28 December 1956 Hitler is legally dead. His name is now entered under No 29,050 in the 'Register of Declared Dead', which Records Office I in Berlin-Dahlem maintains for the Federal Republic and West Berlin. According to the still valid registration law of 1937, Hitler is entered in the records as '*Führer* and Reichs Chancellor'. His demise is entered as an 'assumption of death' permanently since none of the more than 40 witnesses interrogated ever saw his body [this is not true]. The declaration by the Federal Court of Berchtesgaden dated 25 October 1956 has been legally binding since 3 December.

The excellent work by *Dr* Stephanus and the various experts carried out 43 years ago during their four-year investigation continues to deserve our admiration. However, the proceedings regrettably had one serious flaw: the Hitler case was conducted behind closed doors! One asks oneself 'Why?' The reason given was to prevent the witnesses from influencing each other's testimony. Unfortunately this left much room for speculation and wild fantasies, as the many books and articles published over the ensuing 43 years amply prove. Despite the Federal Court in Berchtesgaden having ascertained all the facts and published them on 26/27 October 1958 in a six-page press release containing all the details, nobody seemed to believe it. The results were not evaluated and recognised internationally to the degree they deserved to be.

The German and international press repeatedly complained about the secrecy of the proceedings, and quite rightly so:

If such proceedings [went the *Berchtesgadener Kurier* on 27 November 1954] as in the case of Hitler take place behind closed doors, then one could at least expect the court to keep the local press informed. What reason at all is there for this exaggerated secrecy in the declaration of death case of this criminal of violence?

On 15 October 1954 the *Berchtesgadener Anzeiger* reported:

Berchtesgaden—As we announced in our last issue, yesterday the interrogation of a major witness, Fritz Echtmann, a dental technician from Berlin, took place in the Berchtesgaden court. Representatives of the national and international press as well as of radio and television, who had come to Berchtesgaden expressly for this event, were very disappointed that the interrogation took place behind closed doors, allegedly so that other witnesses would not be influenced. The reporters . . . waited from 0800 to 1300 in front of the court building. Some of them even entered the garden of the court, only to be evicted . . .

To this day we do not know the reason for this exaggerated secrecy.

I have included acknowledgements of sources in the narrative and have attempted to restrict the number of notes. Quotations that are not explicitly acknowledged are taken from the records of the court proceedings in Berchtesgaden 43 years ago. Many of the eyewitnesses were between 25 and 35 years old in 1945 and have died in the meantime, so I have only been able to interview a few of them personally.

I would like to thank the members of the BDC (Federal Document Centre) in Berlin, the BA (Federal Archives) in Koblenz and the Institute for Contemporary History in Munich, who helped me with my research in the 1980s. My thanks also goes to *Dr* Hans Brunschlik and *Frau* Erna Baar of the Special Registry 'S' in Munich for their assistance. I am very grateful to *Herr* Otto Günsche who, despite the fact that he was 'not very pleased' about my numerous questions, still gave me much information which helped to round out the picture. My special thanks go to *Frau* Christa Gschwendtner, Director of the Federal Court in Laufen, for her permission to read and evaluate the files.

Anton Joachimsthaler

Translator's Note

The text of this book contains some terms in German, many of which are either words invented by the Nazis or words that received a specific meaning during the Nazi era, as well as other terms and abbreviations with which not every reader will be familiar. In order not to burden the text with translator's notes of explanation, such terms are explained below.

Ardennes Offensive: Hitler's final major offensive in December 1944 in the Ardennes mountains on the border between Germany and France/Belgium, better known in the West as the 'Battle of the Bulge'.

Bendler Block: The German Armed Forces Supreme Command and its administrative staffs were housed in a huge complex in Bendlerstrasse in Berlin, and this was commonly referred to as the Bendler Block.

Berghof: Hitler bought an old farmhouse, the Berghof, on the Obersalzberg—a mountain near Berchtesgaden in one of the most scenic regions of the Bavarian Alps—and then put Martin Bormann in charge of 'acquiring' most of the rest of the mountain. This was done by coercion, threats and intimidation, until all the local farmers had sold out, naturally at a 'very reasonable price'. The old Berghof was then torn down and a huge new Berghof erected, together with various outbuildings, houses for guards, underground garages, a private cable car etc., where Hitler went for relaxation but where also he received important foreign dignitaries.

Brandenburg Infantry Regiment: An élite unit whose members did not fight as regular troops but were used in commando and special forces type assignments.

Brown House: From the very early days of the Nazis, brown had been their symbolic colour, viz. the brown shirts of the SA. The houses in each city in which the NSDAP had its offices were therefore colloquially referred to as 'brown houses'.

***Bruderschaft*:** Literally, 'brotherhood'. The Germans, being a particularly formal people, make a ceremony of the occasion when they decide to offer another German the use of christian names. It requires that each person raise a glass of some alcoholic beverage, link arms and then drink. With men this is followed by a handshake and the annunciation of one's first name. With women, the handshake is replaced by a kiss on the cheek. It is known as 'drinking brotherhood'.

Chancellery: The Chancellery (*Reichskanzlei*) was the seat of the Chancellor. The original building dated from the time of Bismarck. Hitler, who suffered from megalomania, had the Chancellery rebuilt and extended to more than double its original size. The two main buildings were then referred to as the New and the Old Chancellery.

Front: The Russian equivalent of an Allied or Germany Army.

***Führer* bodyguard:** This consisted of men and officers of the *Führerbegleitkommando* (Command accompanying the *Führer*) and the *Reichssicherheitsdienst* (Reich Security Service). To keep things simple, the term normally used throughout this book for these two organisations is 'bodyguard'. For more details on both services, see Note 36.

***Gauleiter/Gau*:** True to their passion for all things 'Germanic', the Nazis structured their party administration in the Reich into *Gaue*, because this had been the term used by the ancient Germanic tribes for tribal subdivisions. Each *Gau* was headed by a *Gauleiter* or party boss.

Gleichschaltung: Literally, 'same-switching'. This was the Nazi euphemism for the step-by-step process of bringing all aspects of public life under total Nazi control. In the case of the media, it went far beyond mere censorship and resulted in their being forced to publish verbatim what they were told to say.

Grossadmiral: Dönitz, like his predecessor Raeder, held the rank of *Grossadmiral*—literally, 'Great Admiral'—and his duties, in Anglo-American terms, combined those of the First Sea Lord/Chief of the Naval Staff with those of the senior fleet commander. Germany did not have a Navy Ministry with a political appointee at its head.

Leibstandarte: In SS terminology the *Standarte* was a regiment comprising from 1,000 to 1,300 men, commanded by a *Standartenführer* (colonel). Several élite units, called *Leibstandarte* (literally, 'body regiment') were named after prominent Nazis. During the war the *Standarten* were increased in size and became divisions of the *Waffen-SS* which fought mainly in the East.

NKVD: The Soviet Secret Service.

NSDAP: *Nationalsozialistische Deutsche Arbeiterpartei* = National Socialist German Workers' Party, i.e. the Nazi party.

Obersalzberg: See Berghof.

Ordensburg: Literally, 'Castle of the Order'. The Nazis built several neo-romanesque and neo-gothic castles to house their various pseudo-religious 'orders'.

OKH: *Oberkommando des Heeres* = Army Supreme Command.

OKW: *Oberkommando der Wehrmacht* = Armed Forces Supreme Command.

Old Fighters: Hitler's companions from the early days of the Nazi movement before the Nazis came to power, particularly those who had taken part in Hitler's abortive, so-called 'beer hall *putsch*' on 9 November 1923 in Munich, were later dignified by the title 'Old Fighters'.

OT: Commonly used abbreviation for *Organisation Todt*, which consisted of workers' battalions organised and led by the first Reich labour leader Todt. These workers were mainly used in building fortifications like the *Westwall*, the defences along the Franco-Belgian coast and the German autobahns.

Reichskriegsflagge: Literally, 'Reich War Flag', this was a small political and paramilitary group that later on merged with Hitler's Nazi party.

Reichsmarschall: The highest military rank bestowed during the Third Reich. Hermann Göring was the only person to hold it.

Rossbach Organisation: One of several extreme right-wing paramilitary organisations, consisting mostly of former Army officers, which were formed during the Weimar Republic. Named after their leaders, these private armies 'fought' against the 'liberal-socialist-communist traitor governments' who had accepted the Versailles Treaty, disarmament and reparations. The most famous of these was the Kapp organisation, which attempted a *putsch* in Berlin in 1923 and had to give up when the unions called a general strike.

SS: Many of the people mentioned in this book were members of the SS and their ranks are given according to the titles invented specifically for the SS. Most of these terms are virtually untranslatable and 'jawbreakers' to boot.

Tiergarten: Literally 'zoo', the Tiergarten is a district in central Berlin which, while containing the Berlin zoo from which it takes its name, is a very extensive park. The government district lies on its eastern boundary.

Volkssturm: Literally 'national storm', the *Volkssturm* was a sort of militia levied in the final phase of the war. It consisted of units made up of men over military age, civilians previously exempt from military service and boys under age, who were given a rifle and a handful of cartridges, sometimes grenades or anti-tank rockets, and then sent to fight. This was truly scraping the bottom of the barrel and their military value was nil.

Waffen-SS: Literally, 'Weapons SS'. As opposed to the 'Police SS', the 'Concentration Camp SS', the 'Political SS' *et al.*, the *Waffen-SS* consisted of armed formations—infantry, armour and artillery—which fought as regular soldiers. It was a 'private' army (and a rival of the regular Army) which grew enormously in size as the war progressed, finally fielding whole corps.

Westwall: Better known in the West as the Siegfried Line, this was a 250-mile (400km) long system of about 15,000 bunkers, tank traps and gun positions that stretched along Germany's western frontiers from Aix-la-Chapelle (Aachen) to the Swiss border at Bale. When the Anglo-American forces, enjoying almost complete air superiority, reached it in 1944–45, it proved to be of very limited value.

Wolfsschanze: Literally, 'Wolf's Fortress', this was the code-name for Hitler's military headquarters near Rastenburg in East Prussia where he spent the greater part of his time from 1941 on and from where he directed the war personally. The complex was very elaborate and housed several hundred people in a park-like area surrounded by several rings of fences and guard posts. It was here that Hitler was almost assassinated on 20 July 1944.

Zossen: A village outside Berlin and the last headquarters of the German Army.

1. Legends, Lies and Half-Truths

Legends are invented or reported events that are born or occur where truth, for whatever reason, has lost its credibility. And legends feed with an insatiable appetite on the lust of audiences for the stories told by rumourmongers, pompous asses and psychopaths. This applies particularly to Hitler's exit from the world stage in April 1945.

As came to light later, Hitler gave specific instructions on how his corpse was to be dealt with: it was to be burnt immediately. These orders were carried out by Hitler's adjutant Otto Günsche and Hitler's valet Heinz Linge.[11] On the morning of 2 May 1945 the 301st and 248th Infantry Divisions of the Russian 5th Army had stormed the Chancellery. The Russians had already heard that Hitler was supposed to be dead, but, being suspicious people, they fostered a cheap propaganda trick to the effect that Hitler had escaped.

In the gardens of the Chancellery, near the exit from the bunker, the Russians found thirteen to fifteen burnt corpses in various states of disintegration. But there was no identifiable corpse attributable to Hitler. Thereupon the Russians prepared 'Hitler's body' and on 4 May 1945 laid it down among the ruins of the Chancellery, permitted photographers and cameramen to take pictures and presented it to an admiring world as 'the deceased Hitler!' And when Russian television presented a 'sensational picture by the KGB' of this same 'body' as recently as 15 September 1992, the commentator said, 'Hitler's corpse was probably the first surprising find by the Russian soldiers.' But even back in 1945 this nonsense had been too blatant for the most hardened Russians and they later declared the man to be a double, and still later simply a 'fake'. One wonders just who it was who made that poor unfortunate up to look like Hitler, laid him out in the Chancellery, surrounded him with finger-pointing Russian soldiers and allowed him to be filmed and photographed. When the deception came unstuck, the Russians suddenly 'discovered' a further corpse:

It lay on a blanket that was still smoking. The face was charred, the skull drilled through by a bullet, but the horribly disfigured features were undeniably those of Hitler. The Russians made no secret of their find, but they did not however announce it officially for the time being. They wanted to be very cautious, in order to prove the identity of the corpse beyond any doubt. Furthermore, the question of what to do with it also required careful consideration . . .[12]

One can continue reading from Bezemensky, who describes years later how 'the Russian soldier Ivan Tzurakov dragged the pathetically disfigured corpse of Hitler out of a bomb crater by one leg'. There is not one word of truth in any of this, despite the fact that in May 1945 Russian officers informed the Americans, including General Eisenhower, that a body had been found which was 'most assuredly attributable to Hitler'.

The international press now also assumed that Hitler was dead and that his remains had been found by the Russians. On 6 June 1945 the Soviet Military Administration in Berlin, commanded by Stalin's deputy Marshal Georgi K. Zhukov, held an 'unofficial' press conference with Allied war correspondents. An officer from Zhukov's staff gave details of the 'search for Hitler's body'. Before that, on 26 May 1945, Harry Hopkins, Averell Harriman and Charles Bohlen had met Stalin in Moscow. At this meeting talk also turned to Hitler's death. Stalin said he did not believe that Hitler was dead: more probably he was in hiding somewhere. 'The whole thing is curious,' Stalin remarked, adding, 'All this talk about burials and disposals appears very doubtful to me.'[13]

In the eyes of the ageing Stalin, Zhukov was not the saviour of Russia but rather his deputy and rival, whom, according to later reports by various Russian historians, he feared even more than Hitler. As Harry Hopkins had already noted (see Harry Hopkins, *White House Papers*, 7 June 1945), Stalin declared in Moscow that 'Zhukov will have very little influence on policy in Berlin . . .'

After the press conference of 6 June, Stalin immediately sent Andrei Vyshinsky (later prosecuting attorney at Nuremberg) to Marshal

Zhukov in Berlin as his 'political representative to the Chief of the Soviet Military Administration'. And then, at a major press conference on 9 June 1945, the legends surrounding Hitler were born: 'The new "official Russian version" was announced to the world by no less a personage than Marshal Zhukov . . .' According to this new Stalinist doctrine, Russian experts *had not* succeeded in identifying Hitler's body and one therefore had to assume that Hitler had left Berlin at the last possible moment. This statement by Zhukov was not based on provable facts but solely on the unpredictabilities and ambitions of Stalin, to which everyone kowtowed. While Zhukov was holding his press conference, Vyshinsky sat next to him like a shadow. As Stalin's representative, he was there to ensure that Zhukov spoke his lines exactly as ordered (see *Pravda*, 10 June 1945). Zhukov told the international press:

> The circumstances are highly mysterious. We did not identify Hitler's body and I cannot say anything about his fate. He may have left Berlin by air at the very last moment. In any case, the condition of the landing strip would have permitted this . . .

The next day Zhukov travelled to Frankfurt, still closely shadowed by Vyshinsky, in order to parrot the same text from his 'Supreme Commander' (as Zhukov invariably called Stalin) to General Eisenhower and his staff.

When, during the talks in Moscow, Hopkins had referred to the disappearance of a large German submarine, Stalin had said that 'maybe Hitler escaped to Japan in such a boat'.[14] Later on Stalin also suggested Argentina and particularly Spain, where Hitler could have found refuge with Stalin's arch-enemy General Franco. All of these hints were now in place for fomenting legends: an aircraft, a submarine, various countries of the world . . . what more do imaginative people require for inventing stories?

In the meantime, in Berlin, Marshal Zhukov was still chairman of a committee of (allegedly seven) NKVD officials charged with the further investigation of Hitler's fate. But this authority was also soon taken away from him and Lavrenti Beria, the head of Stalin's Secret Service, had all the Western witnesses brought to Moscow. By mid-

September 1945 the investigation committee in Berlin and Moscow had supposedly completed its task (it did not actually finish until May 1946). Its final report was never published. Instead, a document is alleged to have been presented that did not add anything important to Stalin's statement to Harry Hopkins four months earlier. The document reportedly stated that

> Not a trace was found of the bodies of Hitler and Eva Braun.[15] Nor was there any trace of the petrol-drenched grave in which the bodies of Hitler and his companion were allegedly cremated according to statements by some of the witnesses. Some witnesses have now confessed to swearing an oath to Hitler that, if they were captured, they would claim to have seen Hitler's and Eva Braun's bodies being burned on a pyre in the Chancellery garden.
>
> All the witnesses have now admitted to the investigation committee that they did not see a pyre, nor Hitler's or Eva Braun's bodies.
>
> It has been determined that Hitler attempted to cover his tracks with the help of false witnesses.
>
> There is irrefutable evidence that a small aeroplane took off from the Tiergarten in the direction of Hamburg. It is known that there were three men and one woman aboard. It was also determined that a large submarine left Hamburg harbour before British forces arrived. On board were mysterious people, including a woman.[16]

In other words, Stalin's previously reiterated statements were based on three claims—that all the witnesses who stated that they had seen the funeral pyre were lying, that a light plane took off from the Tiergarten (on the East–West Axis) on the morning of 30 April 1945 and that a submarine left the port of Hamburg a few hours later.

Despite the fact that many senior Soviet officers in Berlin and Moscow knew of Hitler's death from statements by witnesses, and that Hitler's identity had been established beyond doubt, this knowledge had to be kept officially secret and the German witnesses (the so-called Chancellery Group) had to disappear in Russian prisons and labour camps for ten years. The Russian investigators had not investigated but rather covered up, because that was what Stalin demanded.

Even after Stalin's death on 5 March 1953 the Soviet government maintained its official silence, and in the fifth volume of the *History of the Great Patriotic War*, published in 1963, the storming of the

Chancellery and Hitler's bunker is mentioned only very briefly, while nothing at all is said about Hitler's fate.[17]

From then on story after story appeared about Hitler's fate. As early as June 1947 a book edited by Herbert Moore and James W. Barrett entitled *Who Killed Hitler?* was published in the United States (Booktab Press, New York). In the introduction W. F. Heimlich, the former Chief Intelligence Officer of the US Army in Berlin, wrote the following:

> I was assigned to find Adolf Hitler or his body immediately after the entry of US forces into Berlin. I can positively state that I found neither Hitler nor his physical remains. Despite a thorough search in the area, I was unable to discover any proof that his body had been burnt, nor was I able to find persons who were eyewitnesses to Hitler's final days in the Chancellery . . . I can only stress the fact that I was not successful in finding reliable eyewitnesses for Hitler's activities after 22 April 1945— nine days before his alleged suicide . . . My own personal conclusion is, that as far as Hitler's fate is concerned, everything after 22 April 1945 is a mystery . . .

In like vein, authors have piled story upon story, legend upon legend. In Chapter 11, 'The Double in the Führer's Kitchen' (p. 59), one reads:

> Whoever the man might have been, he was never seen outside the heavily guarded kitchen under the Chancellery where Hitler's meals were cooked and then carried to the bunker via an underground passage [Hitler's meals were cooked by *Fräulein* Constanze Manziarly[18] in the kitchen of the air raid shelter of the Old Chancellery]. He was never allowed on the surface, not even at night . . . Himmler knew about Hitler's double: he had suggested the idea to Hitler . . .

In Chapter 12, 'Eva Braun's Underground Boudoir' is described. We see a 'weeping Hitler' whom everybody has betrayed and abandoned, distributing poison ampoules. In Part II of the book, we learn 'the truth about Hitler's death', nicely ordered according to private American investigations, the official British report by Major H. R. Trevor-Roper and secret Russian reports. There we learn, for example, that Hitler and Bormann withdrew into the Alps after the double had been shot. Or we see Hitler and his gold treasure being transported by submarine to Japan, Argentina or elsewhere in South America. He is sighted all over the place. 'It is also possible that he was shot by his own people.' Everything is possible. The final sentence of the book states: 'In consequence, the death of Adolf Hitler is probably the most perfect mystery story of all time—a mystery without an ending.' The only 'mystery' about Hitler's fate was created by the authors of the book!

During those years one newspaper article after another appeared: 'Hitler's Fake Suicide', 'Hitler's Argentinian Connection', 'Did Adolf and Eva Die Here?', 'Hitler is Alive', 'Is Hitler Really Dead?', 'Hitler and Bormann in Monastery in Tibet' and 'Farmer in the Brazilian Jungle'. Witnesses who claimed to have spoken with Hitler even appeared. 'In December 1946,' Trevor-Roper reports, 'a German aviator who called himself Baumgart testified in Warsaw that he flew Hitler and Eva Braun to Denmark on 28 April 1945. This story is pure invention.' And Trevor-Roper continues: 'Despite the fact that Baumgart was subsequently committed to an institution, those who wish to believe him (and others) will certainly do so . . .' How right Trevor-Roper was.

The aeroplane story could simply not be scotched. From 1945 right through to 1995 (!) irresponsible journalists, and lunatics, continued to invent new stories about Hitler's escape from Berlin. Musmanno, for example, wrote about the German aviatrix Hanna Reitsch,[19] who was captured on 9 May 1945, interned and interrogated by the Americans in the prisoner-of-war camp at Oberursel from October 1945 to the autumn of 1946:

After the war Hanna Reitsch was arrested und interned by the Allies under suspicion of having flown the *Führer* to Argentina. After she was able to prove the falseness of these allegations, she settled in the town of Oberursel near Frankfurt/Main and that is where she told me her story.[20]

During the proceedings conducted by the court in Berchtesgaden between 1952 and 1956 to declare Hitler dead, piles of mail were received about Hitler's whereabouts. People claimed to have seen Hitler somewhere and to have spoken to him, but were naturally not permitted to divulge his place of refuge etc. Even a letter to the court by Hitler himself is filed among the documents: 'I am alive and I will return. Adolf Hitler.', someone wrote the court on 7 October 1954!

The *Süddeutsche Zeitung* (No 16, 21 January 1953) reported:

Munich (SZ)—In connection with the efforts of the court in Berchtesgaden to officially declare Hitler dead, the Bavarian Justice Department has received announcements by former party members in which they claim that Hitler is still alive. These ominous missives even claim 'meetings with Hitler'. To divulge his place of refuge however, is impossible before a general amnesty is declared . . .

Even worse, witnesses appeared who, without any apparent ulterior motive, testified in all seriousness how Hitler managed to escape from Berlin. The following two reports stand as examples for many others:

During the summer of 1946 I recognised a fellow Bavarian by his accent in the POW camp in Charkov. I struck up a conversation with him and learned that he was from ——. During our conversation he told me that he had been the *Kommandeur* [*sic*] of Hitler's bodyguard. He had been awarded the Knights' Cross; his name was —— or ——. I asked him if he knew anything specific about Hitler, where Hitler was, if he was still alive or if he was dead. At the time I did not believe that Hitler had been cremated. —— told me the following. He had been present on 20 or 21 April 1945 when Hitler had boarded an aircraft with another person and flown out. I did not ask where the airstrip was located nor who the other person had been, because I assumed it could only have been an airstrip near Berlin and that the other person had been Eva Braun. —— continued: Hitler had not returned because, if he had, then he would have known about it, since with the rank of *Major* he was responsible for Hitler's protection . . .

Another statement of 31 August 1955:

In January 1952 I was visiting one of my suppliers of fir trees in ——. This was the farmer —— in —— He told me the following. He had recently been in possession of a German periodical. As far as he could remember, its title was *Triumph*. This periodical was allegedly printed in a place near Weinheim on the Bergstrasse. In the periodical there were photographs that a German explorer had taken during an expedition to Tibet. The pictures showed Adolf Hitler. Furthermore, there was also a report by the explorer about a conversation with Hitler. During this conversation Hitler explained that during the collapse in 1945 he had flown out of the capital to the Baltic, from where he had continued his journey by submarine. Later on he travelled by mule. He and his entourage had taken about two million dollars in gold with them. He was now in Tibet and fighting against Bolshevism. At the appropriate time he would again place himself in the hands of the German nation and render account. For the time being, however, the prevailing form of government in Germany was a democracy. He would have to wait until democracy had disappeared, as it had done once before. When the explorer asked whether he could publish Hitler's statements, the latter answered the question in the affirmative . . .

'The desire to invent legends and fairy tales,' wrote Trevor-Roper as early as 1946, 'is a far more typical characteristic of man—and perhaps particularly of the Germans—than the love of truth . . .' Anyone who has taken the trouble to investigate the circumstances surrounding Hitler's fate can only confirm this statement.

As already mentioned, Stalin kept insisting that Hitler had found refuge with the Soviet leader's arch-enemy General Franco in Spain. To round this off, the following article, entitled 'Hitler's Archives Stored in Spain', appeared in the *New York Times* on Wednesday 27 June 1945 (p. 4, col. 3):

Last night radio Moscow reported that Hitler's personal archives were hidden in Palencia in northern Spain, where they were being guarded by a special Falangist garrison. The report, which NBC recorded, went on to state that a squadron of German airplanes had flown the archives to the Balearic Islands, from where Spanish government aircraft had transported them to Madrid and later to Palencia.

On 25 May 1952 the former US Chief of Intelligence, who had allegedly conducted an official investigation into Hitler's disappearance, stated that he had found no proof, only rumours, of Hitler's death.[21] Heimlich roundly declared that his investigations had shown that Hitler's body had not been burnt in the Chancellery as everyone assumed: 'The investigation of the stains on the couch, where Hitler allegedly killed himself according to the reports, showed that the stains were human blood, but not of the blood groups of either Hitler or Eva Braun.' Heimlich went on to say that his investigations had also shown that the report of Martin Bormann's[22] death had proved to be false. It was, however, futile to continue to speculate about what had become of Hitler. His results had never been published officially, because there was a fear that they could fuel the rumours circulating that Hitler was still alive. Particularly in South America, such a conclusion would have fanned the belief that Hitler was living in some remote part of the world and waiting for his chance to return, as Napoleon did from Elba. In a further statement by the Colonel, he claims that his people conducted an intensive search of the ground surrounding the Chancellery:

> Two enclosures were constructed, one of wire mesh like a chicken coop and beyond that a second one of finer mesh. Every shovelful of earth was first thrown through the wider net and then through the finer one, in the hope that one would thereby quickly discover even the smallest piece of evidence of the remains of a human body.

It must be noted that this is exactly what the Russians actually did do, and Heimlich is possibly 'confusing' his own work with that of the Russians. This is precisely how the Russians discovered the dentures of Hitler and Eva Braun. It was never reported that American experts conducted the same kind of investigation in the garden of the Chancellery.

> The digging produced pieces of uniforms, scraps of a woman's dress, a man's hat with the initials 'A.H.', suitcases, books, periodicals and other minor items such as the remains of a switchboard from the bunker. But after two days of digging, even further afield, we found no traces of any human bodies and, what is even more significant, no traces of any burning.

The former Chief of Intelligence concluded his final report to Washington with the statement that 'no proof of Hitler's death in Berlin in 1945 has been found'.

How this man, who had already made similar statements in the introduction to the book *Who Killed Hitler?*, came to make such claims will forever remain a mystery. I assume he got this information from a Russian officer, because the procedure that he describes as having been conducted by the Americans was in fact only carried out by Russian investigators. Heimlich died in 1964 and can no longer be questioned. In any case, all of his statements belong to the realms of legend. As far as is known, the Russians did not allow any American investigators into the Chancellery to conduct searches in the gardens.

As already mentioned, there are hundreds of articles about Hitler's disappearance or demise. One need only look into the *Subject Guide to Books in Print* or the *Reader's Guide to Periodical Literature* or study the indices of newspapers like the *New York Times* from 1945 to 1947 or German papers of the same period. There is a vast welter of printed matter, mostly full of untruths and completely worthless.

And writings on the subject continue in the same vein to the present day. In the course of my researches I came across a particularly repulsive example which forces one to question the mental state of the author who dreams up such nonsense, how, in 1969, a publisher, Wesermühl in Wels in Austria, could print such a concoction, and who reads the outpourings of such a deranged mind. In this book, *Flight from Nuremberg*, the author, Werner Brockdorff, writes on page 175:

> . . . still of decisive importance is Bormann's escape, the various stages of which I was able to trace precisely, and his own description of Hitler's escape and subsequent salvation . . .

On page 153:

> Martin Bormann was the first person to enter Hitler's living room on 30 April 1945 after the already legendary shot. And he—together with *Dr* Stumpfegger—is probably the only one who could have claimed with any certainty whether the two bodies were really those of Adolf Hitler and his wife . . . Neither Hitler's driver Erich Kempka nor his valet Linge saw the bodies so clearly that they could have identified them under oath [*sic*] . . . When the others came into Hitler's living room the heads of the corpses had been swathed and the bodies covered by dark-coloured army blankets . . .

On page 198:

> On 30 April 1945, towards 1600, when the 'death of the *Führer*' had been announced and the ensuing consternation was at its height, Hitler and his wife, accompanied by four SS men, slipped out of the Chancellery in the confusion—both 'corpses' were still burning!—and shortly thereafter went to ground in the underground garages in Hermann-Göring-Strasse.
>
> Hitler was dressed in a plain soldier's overcoat with raised collar and the cap of a mountain trooper. Eva Braun had disguised herself as a man;

the four SS men wore civvies. Each of the fugitives had a poison ampoule ready that could be crushed between the teeth in an emergency . . .

On page 199:

Hitler and his companions made good progress through the Tiergarten to the Victory Column. At the Tiergarten railway station they were forced to rest for some time, because Hitler was very exhausted by the unusual exertions. In the late evening they succeeded in breaking through the Russian lines in front of Pichelsdorf and reached the Scharfe Lanke on the Wannsee. Below the lighthouse opposite Weinmeisterhorn a boat was waiting, and in this they crossed the Havel river, landing on the eastern shore north of Schildhorn. The following day, 1 May 1945, a Bv 138 flying boat landed very near the fugitives' hideout . . . On the very same day the fugitives then transferred to the well-known submarine in Flensburg Bay, which changed station on the day of capitulation and waited for Bormann near Waabs in Eckernförde Bay . . .

On page 200:

. . . the route had been fixed precisely beforehand and Bormann had prepared Hitler's safe disappearance well. Two agents from Counter Intelligence II and three former *Brandenburger*, two of whom came from Argentina, were involved. It was only shortly before Christmas 1945 that the submarine finally landed about five miles south of the southern Argentinian port of Puerto Deseado . . .

Hitler was very incensed about the poor coordination and put all the blame on Bormann. When he then inspected his future home, two weeks later, he was reconciled with his secretary. Based on maps and photographs, Bormann had chosen a landscape that was very similar to that of Berchtesgaden. On top of that, Bormann had ordered the construction of a 'Berghof' in miniature, provided an adequate security system, had remembered to install greenhouses for the vegetarian Hitler and had built a house for himself very near the 'Berghof'. A communications centre with the latest available equipment permitted reception of any radio station on earth. Furthermore, there was a private generator which was driven by water. This Argentinian 'Berghof' was surrounded by fake farms in which the bodyguards were quartered. By now, most of the men have married and raised families. They cultivate the land assigned to them and supply the colony with food . . .

One is permitted to ask oneself whether Werner Brockdorff should not be committed!

The American book *Hitler: The Survival Myth* by Donald M. McKale (Stein & Day, New York, 1981) cannot be taken seriously either. In essence the book is a compilation of the various stories about Hitler's escape from Berlin. The number of variations is incredible!

With great regularity the ensuing years continued to produce articles in newspapers and magazines about Hitler's fate and disappearance. For example, *Bild Zeitung* said on 7 May 1993 (No 105/18, p. 24):

Did Adolf Hitler survive the Second World War?
The fantasies about the Nazi monster Adolf Hitler (he would be 104 today) refuse to abate.
- Hitler is alleged to have survived the Second World War by two years. This is the claim made by historian Fred McKenzie in his book.
- The Hitler found in the *Führerbunker* was one of three doubles.
- The real Hitler shaved off his moustache and fled through an underground tunnel to a three-engined Ju 52 equipped with floats.
- He flew to Spain and was hidden in the presidential palace of fascist Franco. Code name: 'Adilupus'.
- He allegedly died on 1 November 1947—heart failure.

On 24 May 1994 readers of the Munich *Abendzeitung* and the *Münchner Merkur* (p. 4) were able to read:

British claim: Hitler wanted to blow himself up in an airplane.
London—During the final days of the Second World War Adolf Hitler allegedly toyed with the idea of blowing himself up in an aircraft. This is what *The Times* claimed last weekend based on recently released secret files from the British radio surveillance service . . .
The recordings now add to the speculation about the fate of Hitler shortly before the end of the war by claiming that Hitler wanted to board a plane loaded with explosives and blow himself up somewhere over the Balkans. By one last spectacular act, the *Führer* intended once again to impress his adherents.

Gregory Douglas, an American, described Hitler's escape from Berlin in several articles in *The Military Advisor* (Vol. 3 Nos 11 and 12 and Vol. 4 No 1, 1992/1993) which are supposed to be followed by a book entitled *Flight of the Wolf— Berlin 1945*. His information supposedly stems from the Chief of the *Gestapo* Heinrich Müller,[23] who allegedly worked for the CIA in Switzerland in 1948 (officially Müller has been listed as missing in Berlin since 1945). Douglas reports that the various theories about Hitler's death, whether from the British or the Russian side, are all rejected by Müller, and Hitler's double, who was allegedly discovered in Breslau in 1941, suddenly appears. With the exception of a few minor instances, however, this man was not seen in public after 20 July 1944. In March 1945 Hitler had a meeting with Heinrich Müller—from which Bormann was excluded—on the subject of his own future:

> Then Müller suggested to Hitler that he leave Berlin without prior announcement and only accompanied by a small staff, in order to await the expected falling out between East and West in a safe place . . .

According to Müller, Hitler's double was kept under control with sedatives and isolated as far as possible. Those who knew him only saw him for brief moments. In the end he was killed in April 1945 by a shot in the head from a pistol, wrapped in an army blanket and buried near a pond at the foot of the terrace of Hitler's Chancellery. To the CIC's question why the Russians never found the body of Fegelein[24] after his alleged execution, Müller replied:

> Obviously because there was nothing there to find . . . We created a double, dressed him in Hitler's uniform and buried him in a spot where he was sure to be found.

As far as the double was concerned, the Americans asked Müller who else knew about him, and he answered:

> Naturally myself, Linge, Rattenhuber[25] and *Dr* Goebbels.[26] I strongly assume that Otto Günsche had his doubts, in other words that he suspected that he was not dealing with the real Hitler in the final days.

Douglas then continues:

> The SS was completely loyal to Hitler and none of his personal SS men deviated in the slightest from their personal loyalty to Hitler. Even if one of the SS men in the bunker had his doubts, he kept silent, despite the fact that Günsche testified in Russian captivity, 'I did not see the dead *Führer*. Those things were all done without including us.'

To summarise Douglas, Heinrich Müller is supposed to have survived the war—like Gehlen—and to have possessed interesting documents and microfilm from Hitler's personal state papers. In 1948 Müller allegedly lived in Switzerland and testified that Hitler fled on 22 April 1945 by plane together with Eva Braun, Hewel,[27] Burgdorf[28] and Fegelein. The pilot was Georg Betz[29] and the first stage of the flight ended at Hörsching airport near Linz. (Douglas even published a flight plan which is obviously fictitious.) From Hörsching the flight continued to Barcelona on 26 April 1945 on board a Ju 290A-6. Heinrich Müller himself allegedly escaped from Berlin on 29 April 1945 and, instead of spending the ensuing years on the unemployment list, found work with the CIA; his former deputy Globocnik allegedly worked for the British. It is worth noting that the plane on which Hitler is supposed to have left Berlin was listed as a total loss by the *Luftwaffe* towards the end of May 1944! The plane in which Hitler then supposedly flew on to Barcelona had been grounded in Barcelona since the beginning of April! Hitler's 'special seat', which was allegedly installed in this plane, was actually installed in an aircraft that was destroyed by bombs on the Munich Riem airstrip on 24 March 1945! These facts have been researched and proved.

Let me close this topic with a 'sensational' report by *Bild* of April 1995, which demonstrates that, even half a century after Hitler's death, the manufacture of myths is still continuing:

Controversial topic from England.
Hitler strangled by his valet? Hitler was too much of a coward to commit suicide and he was therefore strangled by one of his SS men, according to British pathologist Dr Hugh Thomas.
   And this is what really took place on 30 April 1945 at the demise of the dictator: Hitler's valet, SS man Heinz Linge, picks up the cyanide ampoule and tries to force it into the *Führer*'s mouth from behind. He forces open the mouth . . . Despite his greatly weakened state, Hitler succeeds in freeing his head from the powerful grasp . . . With brute force Linge turns the prematurely aged Hitler around and strangles him. Hugh Thomas continues: Then the body of a dead woman is brought in and Linge forces Eva Braun's dentures into the body's mouth. Both bodies are then carried outside and burned. What happened to the real Eva Braun remains Hugh Thomas's secret. If Thomas's version is correct, then Hitler did not die as previously assumed. Historians are of the opinion that he withdrew into his living room in the bunker together with Eva Braun and there shot himself with his pistol.

2. The Bunker

According to the dictionary, a bunker is 'a stone or reinforced concrete emplacement for one or several weapons', or 'a bomb or shell-proof accommodation, usually made of reinforced concrete'. Why Hitler's last refuge is consistently called a 'bunker' is not clear, but it is possibly because this is a less cumbersome term than 'air raid shelter'. What it was in actual fact was just that, an air raid shelter specifically designed as such and meant only for temporary occupation during an air raid.

It has become generally accepted practice to speak of 'the bunker in the Chancellery'. This, too, is incorrect. In the complex of buildings comprising the Chancellery there were several air raid shelters with many subsidiary rooms and alcoves, connected to each other by various passages. From the end of the war and up to the present day, one has constantly heard and read about 'secret passages' (which all sound very interesting) and 'escape tunnels'. To give just one example:

> Berlin—Has Hitler's secret escape route been discovered in Berlin-Kreuzberg? All indications point in this direction . . .
> Underneath the 66m high Kreuzberg, construction workers have discovered an extended system of tunnels and bunkers from the Second World War. Neighbours reported yesterday that the kilometre-long labyrinth was built by miners from the Ruhr district to plans drawn up by Hitler's chief architect Albert Speer. According to witnesses there is also an underground connection between the former Chancellery and Tempelhof, the former airport some two kilometres away . . .[30]

To come to straight to the point, there were no 'secret passages', and plans of the air raid shelter that show such passages are all imagined. They were first presented to the world by Trevor-Roper, who took a very cursory look around in 1945, and the American journalist Cornelius Ryan, and have been uncritically quoted by all other writers since—even by O'Donnell, Uwe Bahnsen and authors in the GDR who should have known better (or so they claim).

Let us attempt to get to the truth and let the facts speak for themselves. Without wishing to describe the complete history of the Chancellery, we must begin with Hitler's appointment as Chancellor on 30 January 1933, when he moved into the Chancellery in Wilhelmstrasse. Right at the start he allegedly said that the Chancellery was much too small and needed to be rebuilt. Initially Hitler was not able to move into the residential wing at 77 Wilhelmstrasse because since October 1932 the rooms were being used as a temporary residence by President Paul von Hindenburg while his palace was being refurbished. Hitler therefore occupied the rooms of the State Secretary in the Chancellery. When Hitler was finally able to move into the residential wing in the autumn of 1933—Hindenburg had moved out because his palace was now ready—he immediately commissioned Paul Troost,[31] a Munich architect, to refurbish his apartments on the first floor. Hitler had his new office installed on the garden side and next to it a reception room for ambassadors, with a room *en suite* for his adjutants. The former conference room was enlarged and refurnished to serve as the cabinet meeting room. Adjacent to the cabinet room a smaller private office, a living room, a bedroom with a connecting bathroom and a roof terrace were built for Hitler's private use. A number of smaller guest rooms facing on to Wilhelmstrasse were added (two of which Eva Braun later used during her infrequent visits to Berlin).

The ground floor of the Chancellery was also extensively rebuilt. The entry hall with its main door leading to Wilhelmstrasse was remodelled and an annex to the salon on the garden side converted this into an imposing reception hall. On the right, or street, side there were two living rooms, the banqueting hall and the winter garden; on the left, or garden, side two film projection rooms were added together with a cloakroom and a room for guards. Hitler commissioned a young architect, the 29-year-old Albert Speer, to supervise the works. This was the beginning of Speer's career as Hitler's favourite architect and later on as his Minister of Armaments and Munitions.

Hitler, who in less than sixteen months had managed to concentrate all executive power in his own hands (he was Chancellor, Head of State, Commander-in-Chief of the Armed Forces and Leader of the NSDAP), required further rooms, for example a large reception room (to accommodate at least 200 people) for state functions. To provide for these, a new two-storey wing was added to the Chancellery in the garden on the south side, joined to the private apartments by a winter garden. On the side of the Foreign Office, two two-room and two three-room apartments for staff were added. According to the new ordinance requiring all newly constructed public and military buildings, factories and railway stations to be furnished with air raid shelters, the new extensions to the Chancellery received such a shelter, which was based on Hitler's own plans. Because of his experiences during the First World War, Hitler considered himself to be an expert on the construction of shelters. Speer and others report that Hitler seized upon any occasion when the conversation turned to bunkers to hold forth on their architecture. The records of the conferences between Hitler and Speer between 1942 and 1945 are full of Hitler's proposals, orders and detailed instructions (for example, the thickness of roofs). There are many sketches and drawings in Hitler's own hand which demonstrate his strong interest in the planning and construction of various types of shelters and bunker systems.

As can still be seen from the original plans of 1935,[32] a concrete block measuring 21.2m square was built beneath the cellars. The shelter had a ceiling 1.6m thick; together with the 0.75m thickness of the floor of the banqueting hall, the total thickness was 2.35m. The walls were 1.2m thick. Hitler's adjutant Julius Schaub[33] and the chief machinist Johannes Hentschel[34] reported after the war that when a deeper air raid shelter was added in 1944—the so-called *Führerbunker*—the floor of the banqueting hall (i.e. the roof of the original air raid shelter) was strengthened by 1m, the resulting total thickness of 3.35m having taken the heaviest British and American bombs into consideration.

The ceiling level of the air raid shelter was 1.6m under the cellar floor (not, as O'Donnell stated, 4.56m) and the shelter could be reached by three entrances with eight steps down from the cellars under the banqueting hall and the winter garden. The entrances all had gasproof steel doors. The air raid shelter was completely self-sufficient, containing a 40kW diesel generator supplying electricity for lighting, ventilation, heating, water pumps and a small kitchen. There were also toilets and a washroom.

The shelter was divided by a central hallway. To the left of the entrance were the washroom and the toilets and, adjacent to these, the kitchen with larder and pantry, then two bedrooms with closets and luggage cubicles. On the opposite side there were further bedrooms, in which *Frau* Goebbels[35] lived later with her six children. Counting the generator room, the toilets and the washroom, the shelter contained sixteen rooms in total, all of which were quite small, averaging 3.5m by 3.2m.

The main entrances to the shelter were from the pantry in the banqueting hall or the kitchen on the ground floor of the Chancellery. Eighteen steps led down into the cellar underneath the banqueting hall. Several witnesses have reported that the steps were covered with a red carpet and that the route was well lit. Later on—between February and April 1945—armed guards, either from the *Führerbegleitkommando* (Command Accompanying the *Führer*) or the *Reichssicherheitsdienst* (Reich Security Service[36]), guarded the entrance.

According to a statement made on 13 March 1948 by *General* Hans Krebs'[37] adjutant, *Major* von Loringhoven,[38]

> . . . nobody was allowed into the bunker without being searched for weapons. For example, every time I went into the bunker I always carried a large briefcase full of maps and documents. We all had to hand over our coats and sidearms. The briefcase was thoroughly searched by the SS guards.[39]

When Musmanno asked von Loringhoven to describe the security procedures in the bunker in more detail, the latter said:

> A: Yes, but I am not an expert on security; that was none of my business. All I can say is how I got into the bunker myself and what I observed in the way of security. I believe it was a very carefully designed system, but I do not know how many guards there were in and around the Chancellery nor how many guards covered the various entrances. We normally entered the *Führerbunker* from the garden side.

Q: Was that the so-called emergency exit?

A: Yes, but it was a very wide, albeit deep, stairwell that led far underground. I have already told you yesterday that Hitler's bunker had a roof 8 metres thick.

Q: How did you approach the bunker if you were already underground?

A: We normally came by car over a narrow roadway in the garden of the Chancellery and then walked along a narrow path to the garden entrance. The path was very uncomfortable and when it was dark we had to be very careful because there was lots of debris and many bomb craters. Outside the emergency exit there was an SS guard post. We then went down the stairs into a room with a coat stand in which two guards— SS officers— were on duty. We had to take our coats off, lay down our pistols and hand over our briefcases to be searched. Only then were we allowed into the conference room.

Q: One moment please. Are you describing normal entry procedures during the early part of March?

A: Yes, before 22 April. Later on, when we—I mean Boldt and myself— went to the bunker through the connecting tunnel from the bunker in Voss-strasse, we were very carefully controlled by two heavily armed SS guards in the cellar under the banqueting hall at the end of the passage and had to hand over coats and pistols there. At the top of the circular staircase leading from the outer bunker to the *Führerbunker* there was another SS guard and a further one in the hallway of the *Führerbunker*, who had to be passed before going into the waiting room of the briefing room . . .[40]

From the cellar under the banqueting hall, a 4m long passage led to eight steps leading down to the first airlock of the air raid shelter (5.2m below ground level). Through a second airlock, which later on was also guarded, one reached the central hallway of the shelter already described. Long wooden tables stood in this hallway and during March and April 1945 it served as a canteen for the members of Hitler's staff (bodyguards, secretaries, stenographers, telephone operators etc.) and also for the Goebbels family and their children. Going straight on from the second airlock one reached a third airlock and from there eight steps again led up to the cellar under the banqueting hall. Via an emergency exit that was added later on, one could climb out of this cellar into the garden of the adjacent Foreign Office.

At the other end of the central hall of the air raid shelter one could also climb up into the cellar of the banqueting hall by either of two stairwells on each side. In other words, it was possible to walk completely around the concrete block of the air raid shelter in the vast cellars under the banqueting hall and the winter garden.

Because the space between the inner wall of the cellar and the outer wall of the air raid shelter was only between 2.75m and 3m wide, Trevor-Roper, in his book *The Last Days of Hitler* (1946), drew a 'plan of Hitler's bunker' showing a passage leading to the Foreign Office. Trevor-Roper also mistakenly forgot to include the machine room, the toilets and the washroom.

The next person to present a plan of the bunker was Cornelius Ryan in his book *The Last Battle* (1966). He simply took over Trevor-Roper's drawing with all its mistakes and added some more of his own. He forgot the three rooms missing from Trevor-Roper's plan and added imaginary 'passages' to Trevor-Roper's 'passage'—a further one leading to the Foreign Office and one leading to the Propaganda Ministry on the other side of Wilhelmstrasse. To this day nobody seems to have noticed that there were no 'passages' at all and that one was simply walking around in the cellar under the banqueting hall. But why do research when it is far easier to copy someone else? Ryan also made a number of other mistakes. The sizes of the rooms and the placing of the doors and stairwells are incorrect, as is the passage leading to the New Chancellery; most importantly, for some strange reason he showed the ceiling of the *Führerbunker* to be 2.8m thick when it was really 3.5m thick. Over the following years everybody copied Ryan's mistaken plan, including James P. O'Donnell in his books *The Bunker*, *The Berlin Bunker* and (in German with Uwe Bahnsen) *Die Katacombe*. In this last book O'Donnell and Bahnsen write (p. 58):

Both from the adjacent Foreign Office as well as from the Propaganda Ministry on the other side of Wilhelmstrasse, underground passages led into the cellar of the Old Chancellery and from there into the *Führerbunker*. And since all the other Ministries were connected to the Foreign Office and the Propaganda Ministry by similar underground passages, one can say that the *Führerbunker* actually formed the centre of a subterranean labyrinth of government. Officials and messengers could negotiate whole city blocks underground until they finally reached an entrance to the *Führerbunker*.

As already stated, such passages to the Propaganda Ministry and other places existed only in the imagination of Ryan, O'Donnell and Uwe Bahnsen. Hans Fritzsche,[41] who worked on Goebbels' staff, told Musmanno in Nuremberg on 5 February 1948:

> . . . on 1 May the telephone lines were out and so I ran across Wilhelmstrasse from cover to cover in order to obtain information in the *Führerbunker* . . .

Schaub stated in Garmisch on 22 March 1948 that 'there were no passages; that is another one of these lies . . .'

Hitler's growing megalomania began to express itself early on in his need for ever more grandiose buildings and apartments. The Old Chancellery was, in his words, 'in no way suitable any more'. By 1935 Hitler had ordered the purchase of all the houses in Voss-strasse and on 11 January 1938 he commissioned Albert Speer, who on 30 January 1937 had been created a professor and appointed to the post of General-Superintendent for the Reconstruction of the Capital, to plan and build a new Chancellery on Voss-strasse under the overall supervision of the Chief of the Chancellery Hans-Heinrich Lammers.[42] Prior to that, a first stage of the project had begun in early 1937 with the conversion of 2–5 Voss-strasse into apartments for secretaries and Hitler's bodyguards and their families, and underground garages and repair shops for Hitler's cars. This project was completed in December 1937.

After Speer—who was responsible for the rough draft and the artistic elements, the technical details and the supervision of the building work being handled by his colleague Carl Piepenburg—had presented Hitler with his concept (estimated costs were 28 million Reichsmarks) and obtained his approval, the remaining houses on Voss-strasse between Wilhelmsplatz and Hermann-Göring-Strasse were torn down. In January 1938 construction was begun, starting with a large air raid shelter with a ceiling 2m thick. As the detailed drawings were not yet ready and Piepenburg worked from rough sketches, the result was a huge, confused labyrinth with hundreds of rooms, hallways, alcoves, garages and so on that in 1945 housed several hundred civilians and over 100 soldiers of Hitler's bodyguard. In Voss-strasse, for example, there were goods lifts by means of which trucks with trailers and cars could be brought 4.5m below ground and then driven to the places were they were unloaded or parked. Well into the last weeks of the war, the Generals and their staffs used this system to drive their cars to meetings with Hitler. This huge shelter had its own emergency power supply, a 100kW diesel generator for lighting, ventilation and pumps. There was also a complete hospital and dental clinic, two kitchens and the storage rooms for Hitler's Supply Officer, Arthur Kannenberg.[43]

At the beginning of the war Hitler had ordered a part of this shelter to be put at the disposal of the public, and up to 250 children from Berlin families who had no air raid shelters in their own houses were taken in overnight and fed under the supervision of two doctors and several kindergarten nurses. Fifty to sixty pregnant women were treated in the hospital and gave birth there. The administration of the whole complex was the responsibility of Hitler's personal adjutant, Alwin-Broder Albrecht.[44] In February 1945 these public facilities were moved to the *Reichstag* because the shelter was needed for military staffs, guards and dignitaries. Room had to be made for *Generäle* Burgdorf and Krebs, important Nazis like Fegelein, Voss[45] and Hewel and adjutants such as von Loringhoven, Boldt and Weiss[46] as well as secretaries, stenographers and servants. On 4 February 1945 Martin Bormann also moved into the shelter with his greatly reduced staff and was given a small room to sleep in. Finally, in April 1945 a company of SS guards was added. During the final weeks the hospital was extended to include a field hospital under *Dr* Werner Haase,[47] *Dr* Ernst-Günther Schenk[48] and *Dr* Ludwig Stumpfegger.[49] Hundreds of civilians and soldiers filled the halls and passageways as well as the garages, and the overcrowding became hopeless. The lighting was poor and kept flickering, the water pressure sank and the toilets were blocked. Everywhere puddles formed and poisoned the air with their stink of urine. And still more people seeking shelter came in, until every room, all the hallways and even the stairwells were stuffed with human beings. When finally the ventilation broke down and the temperature rose, the stench became intolerable. The worst thing, however, was that there was no more water. Drinking water had to be rationed and there was still not enough to go around. It is not difficult to imagine the chaos and suffering in the shelter, which was never designed to house such a large number of people permanently. Many died, particularly the wounded. Their bodies were carried out into the garden of the Chancellery, thrown into shell craters and burned or simply covered with dirt. If the shelling was too heavy, the dead were stacked in the exits until it abated. Of course, none of this was perceived in the hermetically isolated Chancellery and Hitler's bunker.

Because the storage rooms assigned to Arthur Kannenberg for his supplies of food, beverages and tobacco, from which Hitler and his entourage were supplied, were located in the opposite side of the shelter facing Wilhelmstrasse and everything would have had to be carried to Hitler's kitchen above ground over a fairly long distance, construction of an underground passage connecting the cellar of the New Chancellery with the cellar in the winter garden of the Old Chancellery was begun in 1939. From there the servants could carry supplies directly upstairs to the kitchen via eighteen steps. This passage was, according to von Loringhoven, between 70 and 80m long, 2.3m high and 1.2m wide. The roof was only about 1m thick and the passage lay 1.2m under the ground level of the garden. Although the passage was originally designed to serve only as a supply route—people referred to it as the 'Kannenberg Passage'—it was later also used as a protected route by visitors coming from the shelter in Voss-strasse to the old bunker and on to the *Führerbunker* to meet Hitler.

As mentioned earlier, because of his experiences during the First World War, Hitler considered himself to be an expert in the design and construction of bunkers. The Hitler–Speer conferences between 1942 and 1945 bear witness to his numerous ideas and demands, and one must concede that he did actually possess some expertise. It is quite hard to understand today that, up to the very last years of the war, he continually had extensive bunker systems built to serve as his various *Führer* headquarters. As late as 20 June 1944 Speer reported that

. . . approximately 28,000 [!] workers were employed in building the various *Führer* headquarters, despite which—because of the overall dispersion of effort—the danger existed that none of these sites would provide quarters of sufficient size and strength within a foreseeable time frame. As a result of the meeting, during which the *Führer* had himself briefed in detail, the following was minuted:

(a) The work in Rastenburg is to be completed without delay. The Mauerwald complex for the OKW is to have an underground shelter for all the staff added. Furthermore, the communications bunker under construction is to be completed. [Five months later, on 20 November 1944, the 'Wolfsschanze' *Führer* headquarters was abandoned and blown up.]

(b) In the 'Riese' complex only Block I and sections A, B, D, and G of Block II are to be completed for the time being. The rest of the system is to be completed at a later date. Furthermore, the completion of the complex in Fürstenstein is to be given priority so that it can be ready by 1 November 1945.

(c) The 'Lothar' complex is also to be given priority, starting with sections I and II. Limited underground quarters in concrete blocks are to be provided as quickly as possible. The *Führer* stresses that the interior finishings of the bunkers are to be kept simple; in particular, he does not want wooden panelling installed . . .[50]

Up to the end of 1944 three *Führer* headquarters with various ancillary installations were still being built by the *Organisation Todt*, 'Wolfsschanze' near Rastenburg (total cost, according to budget, 36 million Reichsmarks), Hagen (13 million Reichsmarks) and the 'Riese' complex near Charlottenbrunn (150 million Reichsmarks). These three bunker systems alone cost almost 200 million Reichsmarks, not to mention the materials and labour they tied up.

When war broke out Hitler's interest in bunkers turned into a mania. There is extensive documentation demonstrating his involvement in minute details such as the thickness of ceilings and the proper way to insulate layers of concrete. With the development of increasingly heavier Allied bombs, which reached a weight of between 3,500kg and 6,000kg by 1944–45 (the maximum was 10,000kg), Hitler kept insisting on increasing the ceiling thicknesses of both military and civilian bunkers. In a revealing discourse during the evening briefing on 23 March 1945 he stated:

Naturally, nothing is completely safe, that is clear. But the bunkers here in the Chancellery are generally safe against bombs of up to 1,000kg. So a section can be housed here. I can always kick some sections out [referring to staff departments]. One can do that. A section can then be housed here. Zossen out there is not safe, not because it could not be theoretically safe but because it was built by the Army and not by a contractor. If the OT and a competent construction company had built it, then 1m thick concrete walls would hold inasmuch as they would not easily fall apart underground. But I saw where a bomb had penetrated on the side and immediately burst through 1m underground. And I also saw the reinforcements on the outside, reinforcements with only two layers and on the inside also only two layers. That is a joke. All that means is that one built concrete buildings. The earlier buildings by Speer are not up to scratch either: this has to be made clear. Even the buildings here [in the Chancellery] are massive only because of the huge buildings above which give some protection . . . But truly safe they are not . . .[51]

Later on Hitler even lost confidence in his own bunker, built and reinforced in 1944:

Every time there was a heavy air raid [said Schaub on 12 March 1947], Hitler had himself woken up, dressed and immediately went into the plotting room where he followed the air raid on a map of Berlin. He said little and no one knew what was going on inside his head.[52]

Hitler feared that a hit would cause flooding in the bunker. In a letter of 19 April 1945 Eva Braun wrote her friend Herta Schneider:

. . . we already have artillery fire from the Eastern Front and naturally air raids every day. From the east and the west, just as they please! Unfortunately I have orders [Hitler's] to stand at the ready at every alarm, because of the possible danger of flooding . . .

Christine Schroeder, one of the secretaries, later reported:

Every time a bomb went down near the bunker, the whole block, down to the ground water, shook perceptibly. 'That was close,' Hitler said on one occasion. 'The bomb could have hit us.'[53]

Albert Speer later also remembered air raids he had experienced in the bunker, and he confirms *Frau* Schroeder's statement:

When heavy bombs detonated nearby, the whole mass of the bunker shook due to the rapid transmission of the shock waves in the sandy subsoil of Berlin. Each time Hitler would start in his chair . . .[54]

The origins of the *Führerbunker* date back to 1943. On 18 January Hitler commissioned Albert Speer to build a new, reinforced air raid shelter in the garden of the Old Chancellery. Hitler told him:

> Since the air raid shelter in the Old Chancellery only has a ceiling 1.6m thick, a bunker must immediately be built in the garden according to the new dimensions [ceiling 3.5m, sides 3.5–4m thick] but with the same internal dimensions as the existing bunker. Piepenburg is to supervise the construction.[55]

Speer immediately charged Piepenburg to begin the planning and was able to submit a first draft after only nineteen days, on 6 or 7 February 1943. The plan, which showed the same arrangement of rooms as in the existing shelter but included Hitler's wish for a small bathroom with a toilet, an emergency exit leading to the garden with an observation tower and a connecting way to the old air raid shelter,[56] was approved by Hitler. However, he demanded that the walls and roofs be strengthened, even if this meant a reduction in height and space, and that the angles between ceiling and walls be reinforced by steel girders as in the bunkers of the *Westwall*.[57]

Detailed plans were then prepared over the following months, but it was only in April 1944 that work finally began. A pit approximately 10m deep was dug. The outer wall of the banqueting hall on the garden side was pierced at the floor level of the old air raid shelter and 1.2m thick reinforced concrete walls were erected to form a protected passage leading from the emergency exit of the old shelter to the outer wall of the new shelter. From there a left-hand circular staircase with twelve steps led down (7.6m below ground level) to a gasproof steel door leading into the 16m long central hallway of the new *Führerbunker*. The bunker itself rested on a 2m thick concrete foundation slab. The walls were 3.6m thick (the interior height after deducting the space for piping, heating and ventilation ducts etc. was 2.85m) and the ceiling measured 3.5m, with steel girders at the angles resting on the walls as Hitler had specified. Because the foundations were deep in the ground water, special concrete was used, and the whole block rested in a concrete pan from which seeping water had constantly to be pumped out. After the war, about 5cm of water seeped into the bunker during the summer months in 1945 and, as numerous photographs indicate, Russian soldiers and American journalists could only reach the hallway, Hitler's quarters and the conference room on dry feet by walking on cushions and other objects.

Many strange claims have been made about the thickness of the ceiling. It ranges from 11m (!) according to one of the secretaries, *Frau* Junge,[58] to 8m and 5m according to von Loringhoven and Schaub respectively, and even Speer, who should have known better, claims 5m. Cornelius Ryan speaks of only 2.8m. The only person to give the correct figure, 3.5m, is Erich Kuby, the editor of *Der Spiegel* magazine, in his 1965 book *Die Russen in Berlin*.

The 3.6m wide central hallway of the bunker was divided by a 0.5m thick concrete wall with a steel door—guarded by an officer of the bodyguard—into a 7.5m long corridor and an 8m long waiting room. The walls between the various rooms were of reinforced concrete and also 0.5m thick.

If one entered the bunker by coming down the circular staircase from the old shelter and going through the steel door into the corridor, the following description shows the picture presented at the time. The stairs and the corridor had stone tile floors covered with a red carpet. Along one wall of the corridor there were cabinets with air raid and fire protection equipment; against the opposite wall stood a long, narrow table above which hung a clock. Several chairs and a telephone for the guards completed the furnishings.

The first room on the right was the machine room. This room was completely taken up by a diesel generator, ventilation equipment, various pumps, air conditioning equipment and drums of fuel (according to machine-minder Hentschel, ten to twelve drums). All this machinery created a high level of noise, as several witnesses have testified. On 24 November 1954, for example, Maximilian Kölz, a former member of the Reichs Security Service, stated:

> I saw Adolf Hitler shaking each person's hand [after midnight on 30 April 1945] . . . If anything was said, I could not have heard it in the constant noise created by the machines. The generator and the ventilation equipment were running simultaneously, both driven by diesel engines . . .

Next to the machine room was the air plotting room. Here, according to Schaub, maps of Germany and Berlin hung on the walls, covered with cellophane. Five members of staff received notices of approaching Allied bomber formations by telephone and drew the direction of flight and probable target areas on the maps. 'During major air raids,' Schaub testified in Garmisch on 12 March 1947, 'Hitler came into the room and silently followed the development of the air situation.'

Behind the plotting room was the telephone exchange, where *SS-Oberscharführer* Rochus Misch sat at the switchboard. There was also a telex, which during the final days was mostly used by Martin Bormann's secretary *Fräulein* Else Krüger.[59] Opposite the machine room were toilets and a washroom. In the washroom there was a small wooden kennel for Hitler's dog Blondi and her five pups. Continuing on through the guarded dividing door in the corridor, one came into the waiting room.

The waiting room also had a stone tile floor with a red carpet. According to the secretary *Frau* Johanna Wolf,[60] eight paintings by old masters hung on the wall opposite Hitler's private rooms. The paintings were mostly landscapes but also included a Madonna with Child. Below the paintings stood ten to twelve fine old armchairs and against the opposite wall stood an upholstered sofa, a rectangular table and two upholstered easy chairs. This was the room in which the attendants to the daily briefings assembled and where visitors were asked to wait until called into Hitler's presence by an adjutant or servant. The furniture and the paintings came from Hitler's apartments in the Old Chancellery.

On the right was a door leading into a complex of four rooms, two rooms each side by side. This single entry proved to be very inconvenient when the bunker was in constant occupation and overcrowded. The first room served as the day room for the staff in attendance. The next two rooms were the bedrooms of valet Heinz Linge and the orderly officer. The rearmost room, which was slightly the largest (4m by 3.2m) served as an infirmary and dressing station and contained the most immediate medical equipment. *Dr* Morell[61] and later on *Dr* Stumpfegger also slept here. When *Dr* Goebbels and his family moved into the bunker on 22 April 1945, he was given this room as his living-cum-bedroom.

On the left a door led into an antechamber. This was furnished with a small table, a chair, a stool, a grandfather clock and a coat stand, on which hung Hitler's field-grey trenchcoat, his cap with its broad peak, his light suede gloves and Blondi's leash. Hitler's servants also used this room to put things down when serving or to wait on his pleasure. Linge referred to it as the 'serving and writing office'.

From the antechamber a door on the left led into Eva Braun's bedroom (after mid-March 1945), which was connected to a bathroom via a narrow closet. Straight ahead from the antechamber a door led into Hitler's living room, which also served as his office. This room was also connected to the bathroom. From Hitler's living room, a door on the right led into his bedroom.

The last door on the left in the waiting room led to the military briefing room. This was larger than the other rooms in the bunker (4m by 3.6m). In the middle of the room stood a large table with maps, and there were benches and a few chairs ranged around the walls. During briefings up to twenty people stood shoulder to shoulder around the table in order to report to Hitler, who sat at the table.

At the end of the waiting room section of the corridor a gasproof steel door led into an airlock with a guard post. From the guard post a further gasproof door on the right gave into a 3m wide stairwell with 38 steep steps (the step width was 1.5m) leading up into the garden of the Chancellery. The exit was formed by a massive square concrete block (6.6m by 6.6m and 4.6m high) with a strong steel door. A few yards to the right-hand side of the exit stood an 8.3m high round concrete observation tower 4m in diameter, which was not quite finished. The tower—which was *not* designed for the defence of the exit—was constantly occupied by a guard, who was able to observe the surrounding area through three armoured steel slits. Construction had also begun on a second observation tower on the other side of the exit but this was never completed. The circular staircase giving access to the observation tower from the interior was also not ready in January 1945, so that the guards had to climb into the tower from outside over scaffolding and ladders. On the left of the airlock and guardroom was a room with bunk beds for the guards and behind that a shaft which led up into the unfinished observation tower.

It is worth noting that, until Hitler's return from the Ardennes offensive on 16 January 1945, work on the bunker continued with the highest priority until the last possible moment. The terrain around the outside of the bunker resembled a huge construction site which, because of the deteriorating military situation, was never cleared up after the workforce was withdrawn in January.

The distribution of space and the size of the rooms were exactly like those of the upper air raid shelter, as Hitler had specified. The new complex was, after all, only a reinforced air raid shelter and not designed for constant occupation as occurred in the final weeks until April 1945. And, like its predecessor, the bunker was completely self-sufficient with regard to power and water supply.

There are many descriptions of the bunker and its furnishings by the secretaries as well as by Linge, Schaub and others. The most detailed descriptions were given in Nuremberg by Julius Schaub on 12 March 1947 and secretary Johanna Wolf on 25 February 1948.[62] Schaub, for example, stated that the room which Eva Braun used later on as her bedroom was originally intended as Hitler's dressing room:

> It was not until February 1945 that it was furnished with Eva Braun's furniture from her room on the first floor of the Old Chancellery, so that she could sleep there after she unexpectedly appeared in Berlin against Hitler's orders and refused to return to Munich.

Eva Braun's room contained a bed, a small table, an armchair, a small dresser and a slightly larger sideboard, and the floor was covered by a multi-coloured rug. Hitler's bedroom had a bed with a bedside table, a wardrobe, a dresser, two chairs and oxygen apparatus. Günsche testified that Hitler already had an oxygen bottle in his bedroom in the bunker of the 'Wolfsschanze' *Führer* headquarters because he believed he was not getting enough oxygen in the room. Hitler felt much better with the additional oxygen, so when from February 1945 onwards he slept in the bunker because of the constant air raids, he had oxygen installed there as well. At the foot of the bed stood a safe, and there was a carpet on the floor. Next to the bed there was a bell button with which he could summon his valet Linge (formerly Schaub) at any time of the day or night.

Johanna Wolf described Hitler's living room-cum-office as follows:

It was a small room. Against one wall stood a two-and-a-half-seater blue and white brocade sofa with a wooden frame. There was a small occasional table in front of the sofa. To the right of the door leading in from the antechamber there was a small desk and on a small side table next to the sofa stood a radio. The sparse furnishings were completed by three armchairs in the same pattern as the sofa and two stools. Above the desk hung the painting of Frederick the Great by Anton Graff and above the sofa a still life by a Dutch master with fruit in the foreground and a landscape in the background. The stone floor was covered by a fine, soft, patterned carpet.

After Hitler's suicide on 30 April and the unsuccessful attempts by Goebbels, Bormann and Krebs to conclude a cease-fire with the Soviet leadership (Chuikov and Zhukov) on the morning of 1 May, the bunker emptied rapidly. Almost all the members of Hitler's entourage had their personal effects stored in the shelter in Voss-strasse. Now, as if a great weight had been lifted from them, everyone was only concerned with himself and with saving his own life, with the preparations for the planned break-out and getting through to the West. The commander of the 'Citadel', *SS-Gruppenführer* Wilhelm Mohnke,[63] announced at 1900 on 1 May that from 2100 onwards the break-out from the Chancellery was to take place in several groups.

Towards 1700 *Dr* Goebbels had withdrawn to the upper rooms of the old bunker with his family. Their inner thoughts and what they discussed there will never be known. It was certainly not easy to be together with the six beautiful children, knowing that *Dr* Stumpfegger would soon come—as Günsche stated on 21 June 1956—to kill them. As Goebbels' adjutant, *SS-Hauptsturmführer* Günter Schwägermann[64] testified later,

. . . with a grey face, *Frau* Goebbels came into the room where the dead children lay. She could hardly speak . . . Then Magda Goebbels broke down completely . . .

Towards 1900 Schwägermann conducted her to the antechamber of the briefing room where a pale but composed *Dr* Goebbels waited. As Schwägermann testified in Munich on 4 February 1948,[65] Goebbels then informed him that he and his wife intended to shoot themselves.

He charged Schwägermann with the burning of their corpses, having already ordered Hitler's adjutant Alwin-Broder Albrecht to get hold of some petrol. On 7 February 1956 *SS-Hauptsturmführer* Karl Schneider[66] testified:

> During the morning of 1 May 1945 I again sent petrol to the *Führerbunker* after receiving an order by telephone. The order came from Albrecht. I sent along four cans, which was all I could manage from the final reserves. I was not informed this time, either, what the petrol was for . . .

Schwägermann testified in detail[67] concerning the deaths of *Dr* Goebbels and his wife:

> . . . it was about 2030 when the Minister and his wife came out of the room. He very calmly went over to the coat-stand and put on his cap, coat and gloves. He then offered his wife his arm and they both left the bunker via the emergency exit into the garden without saying a word.
>
> I waited in the stairwell, listening for the shots. After these had sounded, Goebbels' driver, *SS-Ordonnanz* Alfred Rach, and another SS man whose name I do not recall carried the petrol cans into the garden. Following Goebbels' express wish to make sure that he was dead, I told the soldier that he was to shoot him. We then left the bunker and stepped out into the glare of the houses burning all around us and I saw the bodies of the Minister and his wife lying dead in the garden a few metres away.
>
> As agreed, the soldier then fired once or twice at the body of *Dr* Goebbels. Neither of the bodies gave any sign of movement. We then poured the petrol that had been brought up over the bodies and lit it. The bodies were immediately enveloped in flames.
>
> We returned to the bunker. Downstairs we encountered *SS-Gruppenführer* Mohnke, who was the *Kampfkommandant* of the Chancellery. He ordered us to set fire to the *Führerbunker*. We emptied one or two cans of petrol in the antechamber of the briefing room and ignited it. Suddenly the draught caused by the fire made the heavy steel door leading into the corridor slam shut. While this prevented the spreading of the fire, we were now surrounded by a sea of flames. We ran to the steel door. We were in luck. The bolt had slipped, so that the lock had not snapped shut. All three of us applied our full strength, managed to open the door and reached the shelter in Voss-strasse. Here we learned that, in the meantime, the break-out from the Chancellery had been decided upon . . .

SS-Hauptsturmführer Karl Schneider, who had seen the corpses of Goebbels and his wife lying in the garden, stated on 7 February 1956:

After I had fallen into the hands of the Russians on 2 May 1945 I was taken to the garden exit of the *Führerbunker* that same afternoon together with Lange, the cook. Two bodies were lying there, one male and one female. The male corpse, which was readily identifiable, was that of *Dr* Goebbels. His face was singed black-brown. The hair was completely singed off. His lower right arm was pointing upwards. The hand, including the wrist, was completely burned away. The body was almost completely naked. Parts of the clothing lay next to the body. The female corpse was so badly burned as to be unrecognisable. It obviously belonged to *Frau* Goebbels. The bodies lay about 1m in front of the garden exit from the bunker. Scattered about were twelve empty petrol cans.

Lange and I were then immediately taken from the Chancellery to Tegel by truck, and the body of *Dr* Goebbels was taken with us. The body of *Frau* Goebbels was fetched later . . .

Despite the fact that accounts by several witnesses and reports by American journalists clearly state that Schwägermann and Rach only set fire to the antechamber to the briefing room with petrol, one can read the following statement, allegedly attributable to Johannes Hentschel, on pages 366 and 367 of O'Donnell and Bahnsen's book *Die Katacombe*:

. . . one of them, Schwägermann or Rach, poured petrol into Hitler's office [*sic*] and then threw in a torch or a burning cloth. They must have slammed the steel door in great haste. Fortunately I had shut down the ventilators in Hitler's rooms, otherwise we would all have been blown up . . . and investigated the door to Hitler's office. It was hotter than a grill. The red rubber insulation in the door frame was melting and running down like molten lava . . .

I cannot imagine that a technician like Hentschel would make such a statement. In any case, he does not mention these events in the testimony he gave in November 1954. Apart from the fact that, with the door closed, the fire would have quickly gone out on account of the lack of oxygen, the reporter Percy Knauth and the photographer Vandivert, who visited the bunker in July 1945, gave a comprehensive description of Hitler's completely undamaged living room-cum-office in *Life* magazine (23 July 1945). Their photographs, for example, show the sofa and the other furniture. In this report Percy Knauth wrote:

. . . lighting our way with candles and flashlights, we descended the many steps to the *Führerbunker*. Debris lay about on the stairs—papers, gas masks, ammunition and parts of German uniforms. From the darkness below a smell of dampness and cold smoke rose towards us. In the light of our flashlights we then saw a half-open steel door. Behind it were beds with damp mattresses that had fallen out, and all kinds of rubbish. We turned left, passed another door and found ourselves in the large waiting room (to the briefing room) of the *Führer*'s suite. The smell of fire and cold smoke was now very strong and it was clear that the room had been set on fire by SS soldiers. Charred pictures with sooty frames hung on the walls and partially burned furniture lay all about. The floor of the room was about 5cm deep in water and the soggy carpets squelched as we carefully made our way through. Turning right in the waiting room, we came into a small room [the antechamber to Hitler's living room-cum-office] that had also been burned and then into Hitler's living room. Here there had been no fire. Against one wall stood a sofa with a light wooden frame and thick brocade cushions. This was where Hitler and Eva Braun— his bride of 48 hours after she had been his mistress for sixteen years— had shot themselves, if the story told by Hitler's driver, Ernst Kempke [Kempka] is true. We held our lights close to the sofa. There were blood-stains on the light-coloured armrest of the sofa. Blood had dripped down and collected in small coagulated stripes in the corner. Blood was also to be seen on the outer side of the sofa on the brocade cloth.

There appeared to be no doubt. Eva's body must have fallen over the armrest. Hitler, who sat next to her, had shot himself in the temple and must have fallen forward with his head resting on his knees. We did not see any blood there, nor any on the floor, because of the water washing round our feet. The debris and rubbish present in the bunker defied description . . .

After 2200 the break-out of the so-called 'Chancellery Group' under the leadership of Mohnke and his adjutant Klingemeier then took place, followed at short intervals by other groups under Rattenhuber and others. Security guard Hermann Karnau,[68] for example, stated on 13 November 1956:

I thereupon returned into the bunker to pack my belongings that were in the guardroom next to the garden exit. In the bunker I met Director Högl[69] of the Criminal Police. There was no one else to be seen. Högl told me that the break-out would take place under the leadership of *Brigadeführer* Mohnke and ordered me to supply myself with weapons and food. I then packed my belongings and made my way through the central hallway and the main entrance of the bunker to the New Chancellery in order to learn the hour of departure. The departure of the 'Chancellery Combat Team' then actually took place on 30 April 1945 at 2215 with a total of 450 people, including many women and children, and made its way across Wilhelmsplatz and from there via the subway tunnels in the direction of Friedrichstrasse–Schönhauser Allee . . .

As early as about 0200 on 2 May 1945, many people died at Weidendamm Bridge. Director Högl, pilot Betz, *SS-Hauptsturmführer* Lindloff,[70] servant Wauer and many others were killed there. Later, at about 2000, Mohnke's group was taken prisoner by the Russians in the cellar of the Schultheiss-Patzenhofer brewery on Schönhauser Allee. Martin Bormann and *Dr* Stumpfegger met their fate on Sandkrug Bridge near the Lehrter railway station by committing suicide with prussic acid ampoules. Only a very few succeeded in making their way to the West—Kempka, Axmann, Schwägermann, *Frau* Christian,[71] *Frau* Junge, Zander, *Fräulein* Krüger, von Loringhoven, Boldt, von Below,[72] Johannmeier, Lorenz,[73] Karnau, Mansfeld[74] and Poppen. Most were captured by the Russians.

And so, after the various groups had left the Chancellery by midnight, only a few soldiers from the *SS-Leibstandarte Adolf Hitler* and the overcrowded field hospital with *Dr* Haase and the nurses remained. In the bunker lay the bodies of the six Goebbels children and that of *General* Krebs. In the machine room of the bunker Johannes Hentschel was still on duty. Telephone operator Misch had already left the bunker during the early morning of 2 May.

It remains a mystery why, in his book, Bezemensky displays a photograph of the 'charred body' of *General* Krebs, whereas in the autopsy report which he reproduces on page 341 there is no mention of any burns. Soviet General M. J. Katukov, who visited the bunker on 3 May, saw Krebs' body lying in one of the rooms dressed in full uniform. When he was taken prisoner, *General* Weidling announced Krebs' death. On 9 June 1945 the Russians issued a report on his death, despite the fact that in Moscow Stalin claimed that Krebs had hidden himself somewhere. What can one say to all this? On the other hand, the bodies of *General* Burgdorf, of Schädle,[75] Commander of the *Führer*'s Bodyguard, of adjutant Albrecht and many others were never found in the Chancellery and have remained lost without trace.

The last of the many occupants to remain in the empty *Führerbunker* was machine-minder Johannes Hentschel. He still tended his machinery, which he allegedly kept running in order to be able to supply the field hospital in Voss-strasse with water. Inside the bunker he did not notice that meanwhile Russian troops had stormed the Chancellery against only sporadic and feeble resistance. Then suddenly, as Hentschel testified on 22 November 1954, he was faced by Russian soldiers:

> ... On 2 May 1945 I was taken prisoner by the Russians. It was 9 o'clock in the morning. I was in the machine room of the bunker. I was then interned in the Home for the Blind in Oranienstrasse until 12 May, where I was interrogated several times. On 12 May I succeeded in joining a large group of captured soldiers, with whom I then went to Posen and later to Russia, where I was held captive until 4 April 1949.

According to this statement by Hentschel it is clear that the first Russian soldier entered the *Führerbunker* towards 9 a.m. on 2 May 1945, 42 hours after Hitler's suicide. The following statement by Marshal Zhukov is incorrect inasmuch as he refers to the evening of 2 May:

> On the evening of the same day, the 301st and 248th Rifle Divisions of 5th Attack Army conducted the final engagement for the Chancellery. The major resistance was encountered on the approaches and in several rooms of the buildings. In one attack group of the 1050th Rifle Regiment, Major Anna Vladimirovna Nikulina, instructor of the Political Department of the 9th Rifle Corps, displayed great bravery in that she raised the Red Flag on the Chancellery together with officers I. Davidov and F. Zhapovalov. After the capture of the building, Colonel V. Y. Zhevzov, Deputy Commander of the 301st Rifle Division, was appointed Commander of the Chancellery.[76]

Naturally, the Soviet generals enjoyed the triumph of their victory and they immediately inspected Hitler's last refuge, the Chancellery and the bunker. On 3 May 1945 Marshal Zhukov and his staff visited the Chancellery. A detailed account was later given by Soviet General M. J. Katukov:

In those days one question kept being asked: what had become of Hitler? The story that he had committed suicide was not convincing. The opinion was that his entourage had set this rumour going in order to cover his tracks. Everybody was governed by the desire to lay hands on Hitler and bring him to public trial. I kept hearing that the soldiers were constantly proposing various ways of executing him. But even the most horrible methods did not satisfy them. It would appear that there was no form of revenge on this fiend that could satisfy the common soldier.

Naturally, we also discussed where Hitler could be. Nikitin suggested we visit the *Führerbunker* in the Chancellery.

'Where is Hitler? Show him to us!' we demanded of Colonel Zhevzov, Commander of the Chancellery.

'He has escaped, the dirty pig. Into the hereafter, but still escaped. Only his charred body is left,' he answered.

We descended the steep steps into the bunker. Stale air met us. We came to a long corridor, turned left and then right and finally reached a massive door like that of a strongroom.

'This is where he lived,' he said, and stepped aside so that we could pass. We inspected Hitler's reception room, the bedroom, the dining room and the bathroom. Zhevzov told us about a gigantic steel reinforced concrete slab that lay directly over Hitler's apartment to protect him from bombs and shells.

All these years we had sworn that we would enter the very den of Fascism and now we had reached our goal. And it was in fact a den: to call it accommodation would have been misplaced.

In an adjoining room lay the body of a man in the uniform of a general. 'The Chief of Staff of the Army, General of Infantry Krebs,' explained Zhevzov.

It was the same man who, on the morning of 1 May, had brought the message to the bunker that the Soviet Supreme Command insisted on unconditional surrender and refused any negotiations with the Fascists. This announcement had led to several suicides in the bunker.

We thanked Zhevzov for his efforts and left the Chancellery.[77]

The stream of visitors continued unendingly and Colonel Zhevzov was kept busy in the ensuing weeks, guiding all the prominent visitors. Besides journalists from all parts of the world, Winston Churchill also visited the Chancellery on 16 July 1945. True to his motto, 'No sports', however, he only went down a few steps of the bunker and then turned back. In his book *Churchill: Taken from the Diaries of Lord Moran* (1966), Moran reports on page 291:

His guide, a Russian soldier, took him across the courtyard outside the Chancellery to the hideout where Hitler, like a wounded animal that crawls into a hole, allegedly died. The PM followed him down some stairs. When he learned that there were two more sets of stairs to come, he abandoned his idea of exploring the bunker and slowly climbed back up the stairs. When he reached the top he sat down on a gilded chair and wiped the sweat off his brow.

'Hitler,' he said, 'must have come up here to catch some air, and he must have heard the firing coming closer and closer.'

I returned to the hole in the ground. I breathed the damp, fetid air and felt my way down over several steps into a room where, as far as I could make out in the light of a torch, clothing, gas masks and all kinds of other stuff lay about. I picked up a burned glove. I then returned to the PM and we silently drove back past the endless files of Russian soldiers . . .

Allied Generals, on 21 August 1945 Prime Minister Mackenzie King of Canada, diplomats and many others visited Hitler's bunker over the following weeks and months. Permanent Under-Secretary of State Sir Alexander Cadogan noted in his diary on 17 July 1945:

This time it was somewhat better as we descended into Hitler's bunker from the garden. Unfortunately the electric light was not working and it was not easy to get a good view with only the light from a flashlight. We were shown a room in which Hitler supposedly died. Behind the next door there was a further room that allegedly belonged to Eva Braun. A vase stood on the table with a twig in it that had obviously been a flower.

At the exit from the bunker there was a shallow crater in which, we were told, Hitler and Eva Braun had been buried and later dug up and cremated. That is also a rumour, of which there are many, and nobody knows the truth . . .[78]

There were still documents, papers and other objects lying about in the Chancellery and the bunker, which shows in how disorganised a fashion the Russians were acting. As late as 10 September 1945 (!) Lieutenant-Colonel J. L. McCowen found the notes of Hitler's daily routine (from 14 October 1944 to 28 February 1945) kept by his valet Linge lying in an armchair. They have been stored with the following note:

This document was found on 10 September 1945 in the Reichs Chancellery in Berlin, by Lt. Col. J. L. McCowen, in the presence of Brigadier S. G. Galpin.[79]

In his book *Hitler's Final Days*, Trevor-Roper refers to this and writes on page 27:

> . . . the [Russian] investigations in Hitler's bunker, for example, were surprisingly incomplete: they left Hitler's diary—a thick volume, 35 x 17.5cm—lying on a chair for four months until an English visitor discovered it . . .

Linge, questioned about the matter, stated on 10 February 1956:

> During my service with Hitler I kept a diary, in which I recorded the daily events (meetings, visits, visitors etc.) . . .

Linge's later records, from 29 February to 30 April 1945, were probably found by the Russians, since Marshal Zhukov described the final days in the Chancellery (Hitler's marriage etc.) at a press conference in Berlin on 9 June 1945. As Zhukov explained, his knowledge of the events was based on 'the diaries of Hitler's adjutant which had fallen into Russian hands' (Günsche never made such recordings). When it became known that the British had taken notes by Linge, the Russian military government forbade any further visits to the Chancellery and the bunker by Allied officers and journalists in September 1945. Going even further, according to Trevor-Roper's statement in 1946, they accused the British of hiding Hitler and Eva Braun-Hitler in their zone of occupation. This accusation led, according to Trevor-Roper, to his being asked by British Intelligence to reconstruct Hitler's demise.

And once again the bunker witnessed an eerie scene. In April 1946, exactly one year after Hitler's death, the Russians, as a sort of finale to their investigations, re-enacted Hitler's suicide and the burning of his corpse. For this reconstruction they brought all those people in their hands who had formerly been involved to Berlin from their various Moscow prisons. The scenes of Hitler's and Eva Braun's suicides and the burning of their bodies were recreated, photographs were taken and extensive film footage was recorded. The American journalist Marguerite Higgins, who happened to be visiting the Chancellery, reported on the event, even though she was immediately evicted from the premises by the Russians. Where the photographs, film and interrogation reports from this event in 1946 are stored today in Moscow is probably known only to a few. Sooner or later they will probably appear—in exchange for hard currency. Hitler's valet Linge made the following statement about this event on 10 February 1956:

> Towards the end of April 1946 I was taken to Berlin together with Günsche, Baur,[80] Henschel, Hofbeck, Misch and a radio operator who had served in the Chancellery. I do not recall the name of this radio operator. Prior to this he had been a complete stranger to me. This radio operator had transmitted Bormann's final messages on Hitler's death. During the journey and in Berlin we were kept strictly apart. Commissar Klaus, whom I mentioned earlier, was also present; this Commissar held the rank of *Oberstleutnant*. In Berlin I was required to draw exact plans of the rooms in the bunker and to describe their furnishings. I was then also closely questioned during a visit to the bunker. The furnishings were mostly still there, although they were badly damaged. I was required to demonstrate the sequence of events leading up to the suicide. During this, the walls were examined for damage. No such damage was discovered. The bloodstains on the side of the sofa and on the wall were still there. I was also taken into the garden, where I had to point out the spot where the burning had taken place. Furthermore, I was questioned about the location of the burial of the remains, about which I was not able to give any exact information. During this session there were several senior Russian functionaries present. Based on pictures I have seen in the meantime, I believe that I recognise one of these functionaries, who was treated as a special authority by the others, as having been Marshal Sokolovsky . . .

From then on, the complex of the Chancellery, the structure of which was still largely preserved as contemporary photographs show, and the bunker, into which ground water had already seeped in June 1945, remained largely undisturbed. In February 1949 the Soviet occupation forces decided to eradicate the last vestiges of Hitler's power and residence. The rubble was intended for use in the construction of a Russian victory monument. From 21 February 1949 onwards the Chancellery was blown up and demolished, the usable material was taken away and the ground was levelled. Despite several attempts using heavy charges, the *Führerbunker* could not be blown up and so further efforts were spared. The observation towers and the concrete block of the emergency exit had already been blown up in 1947 and the debris lay about in the other ruins. The stairwell was still there.

The stonework, particularly the marble, of the Chancellery was then used as building material for the massive Russian Memorial in Treptow Park and for the Kaiserhof underground station (renamed Thälmann-platz Station in the GDR). The remains of the bunker were covered with earth and for many years only a widely visible mound, covered with grass and only 325m away from the Berlin Wall, marked Hitler's former underground residence. This desolate grass-covered area near the Wall remained unchanged until 1985. When I visited the site in 1985 the remains of the bunker were again being brought to light. The mound had been removed and the observation towers were being broken down into transportable chunks. The concrete block of the emergency exit had already gone. Subsequently the 3.5m thick ceiling was removed layer by layer, the bunker was filled in and a roadway and apartment buildings were built over the top. Today nothing remains to remind us of the dramatic events which took place deep underground here during the last days of April 1945.

3. The Final Months, Days and Hours

In 1943–44 Hitler was already a broken man. He knew that Germany could no longer win the war and he also knew that he was gravely ill. But he was a fanatic who believed in himself and his mission, and he was able, through his incredible willpower, to continue to drive himself and others until the bitter end.

That Hitler knew the war to be militarily lost in 1944 can be clearly seen from some of his own statements, and also from statements by the Commander of the Armed Forces, *Generalfeldmarschall* Wilhelm Keitel,[81] and the Chief of the Military Command Staff, *Generaloberst* Alfred Jodl.[82] According to Jodl's testimony, the catastrophic situation in Russia during the winter of 1941–42

> . . . caused Hitler to be probably the first person to begin worrying that the war on two fronts could crush him and that the war could be lost . . .[83]

Jodl also stated that Hitler already knew towards the end of 1942 that the war could most probably no longer be won and that the best that could be expected was a stalemate. In his testimony in Nuremberg in 1946 Jodl said:

> . . . then, when towards the end of the year [1942] Rommel, beaten at the gates of Egypt, also fell back on Tripoli, when the Allies landed in French North Africa [7–8 November 1942], not only the key soldiers, but Hitler as well, were clearly aware that the God of war had turned his back on Germany and gone over to the other side. Hitler's activities as a strategist were now mostly over. From this time on he increasingly interfered in operational decisions, often down to the local tactical level, in order to enforce what he believed the Generals were unable to comprehend, namely that one had to stand or fall, that any voluntary step back was for the worse. Opinions are divided whether he shortened or extended the war in so doing. One thing, however, is certain: he never again took a strategic decision. Perhaps there were none left to take . . .

But his military advisers—one hears it so frequently being said to-day—should have made it clear to him that the war was lost. What a naïve idea! Long before any other person on earth, Hitler presumed and knew the war to be lost . . .[84]

The Commander of the Armed Forces, *Generalfeldmarschall* Wilhelm Keitel, also reportedly came to the conclusion in 1943–44 that Germany could no longer win. On 17 June 1945 Keitel testified in Bad Mondorf:

For me, the course of the war was characterised by three decisive events:
—our defeat in central Belorussia
—our defeat in Romania
—the Allied invasion in the West
which made me conclude that Germany could no longer win the war militarily . . . Furthermore, I reached my own conclusion that our troops on the Eastern Front would not only not be able to defend themselves, but would also not be able to stop the development of an attack. The Allied invasion in Normandy forced us to wage war on two fronts . . . The conclusion I drew from the events in 1944 was that the war could now only be won politically: a military victory was no longer possible . . .[85]

But Hitler was no longer able to play politics, nor was he willing to. And after the conference at Casablanca (14–26 January 1943) there was no longer anybody among the Allies willing to talk with him. According to *Generaloberst* Jodl,

Hitler was a statesman. He was a dictator. He was C-in-C of the armed forces and, from 1941 on, even of the Army. He had started the war, he alone and no one else, and he actually waged it . . .[86]

In 1918 Hitler the soldier had become Hitler the politician. In 1939 the politician had reverted to being a soldier who could not turn back and he remained a soldier until the end, because he had himself blocked any other alternative for ending the war.

From 1943 onwards Hitler was a sick man. In the autumn of 1943, from September to November, and again in April 1945 he was in fact acutely ill. On 23 February 1944 Hitler travelled by special train from his 'Wolfsschanze' headquarters to Berchtesgaden, in order to take a few days' rest—insofar as the conduct of the war permitted this. During this interval the concrete ceiling of his bunker was to be reinforced to a thickness of 8m and other building work was to be carried out. When in July 1944 the East Prussians started to panic and flee because the Russians had reached the eastern frontiers of the province, Hitler once again returned to the 'Wolfsschanze' in the hope that this would have a calming effect on the civilian population and on the troops. He and his immediate staff flew to the 'Wolfsschanze' on 14 July 1944, and within a few days of his arrival the assassination attempt by *Oberst Graf* Schenk von Stauffenberg took place.

In a briefing on 31 July 1944 in the 'Wolfsschanze'—only eleven days after the assassination attempt—Hitler made some revealing remarks about the state of his health:

I will not be able to board a plane in the coming week at least because of the condition of my ear. [The explosion on 20 July damaged both of Hitler's eardrums and ear-ducts. This damage only healed after a long stay in bed. He also had a burn on his right leg, haemorrhaging in his right elbow and a bruise on his back, caused by a falling beam.] With the other one [ear], the issue is in doubt, but if only one heals completely I won't give a damn—I'll take the risk. But if I were to board a plane now, with the ringing and the changes in pressure, it could lead to a catastrophe. And what would happen if I were suddenly to contract an inflammation of the middle ear! I would have to undergo treatment. As long as the wound does not heal, the danger of infection remains. This did not simply pass my head without any effect whatsoever . . .

Naturally I can stand and I can also talk for a certain time, but then I suddenly have to sit down again. Today I would not dare to speak in front of 10,000 people. I would not risk a speech such as the one I delivered recently on the Obersalzberg [Hitler had spoken in front of about 100 armaments experts on 22 June 1944] because I could easily suffer an attack of vertigo and collapse. Furthermore, when walking, a moment can occur when I have to pull myself together, so as not to go off on a tangent . . . Actually I should have stayed in bed for ten to fourteen days, but in fact I worked for at least eight hours a day all told, and I am not even counting the reading of reports—I spent at least eight hours reading reports, memoranda and other things. In other words, in my present condition I am doing at least the same amount of work as our fine gentlemen in their arduous posts in Paris and elsewhere. But as long as it does not become absolutely necessary, I do not wish to force myself to the limit, which could possibly cause a breakdown under certain circumstances— and it is actually not necessary. Otherwise, the miracle is that the blow has caused my nervous problem to disappear almost completely. My left leg still trembles slightly when meetings go on for too long, but, before, this leg even trembled in bed. This has almost completely disappeared because of the blow . . .[87]

One can only presume that Hitler's nervous disorder, which became much worse later on in Berlin, was Parkinson's Disease, a degenerative illness affecting certain parts of the brain which results in serious organic damage to the nervous system and can also influence both willpower and emotional control. In 1942 Hitler experienced serious attacks of vertigo for the first time—probably because of the heavy psychological pressure resulting from the catastrophe of the first winter in Russia. In addition his stomach disorders, about which Hitler had been complaining for some time, increased. Probably also during that year, but certainly no later than early 1943, the left side of his body began twitching—initially the leg and later on the arm—and this continued to worsen, except for a short period of improvement obviously due to the shock caused by the explosion on 20 July 1944. But Hitler's relatively good state of health after the assassination attempt did not last long. He soon began complaining of pain in his ears and in his back, where a falling beam had hit him. It took all his willpower to conduct his daily briefings and read the dispatches brought by Linge. In addition to the damage to his ears, he had a festering infection in his left maxillary sinus, which was being treated by *Dr* Erwin Giesing[88] and *Dr* Carl von Eicken.[89] For a time the evening briefings had to be cancelled every second day. Hitler had to lie down frequently, his walk was unsteady and he suffered severe headaches. On 18 September 1944 he collapsed with massive stomach pains and had to go to bed. In addition he contracted jaundice, allegedly after an altercation with Göring.[90] It was almost three weeks before Hitler felt better again. Christine Schroeder later described Hitler's condition at the time:

During his illness in September 1944 I frequently visited Hitler in the small room in the bunker. I saw that he was at the end of his physical capacity. In a tired voice, he spoke of the terrible pains caused by his stomach cramps. 'If these spasms continue,' he said, 'then my life will have become senseless. I will then take the quick way out . . .[91]

Martin Bormann also drew a picture of Hitler's existence underground in a letter to his wife of 1 October 1944:

> . . . During the three days since the *Führer* fell ill, he has not been outdoors at all. He still has to keep to his bed: apparently he is greatly weakened by the effect of the castor oil and his stomach cramps.
>
> I at least now have a large room, almost 6 by 7 metres, with four large windows and lots of light, and can sleep with the windows open. The *Führer*, however, lives down below in his room in the bunker, only has electric light, only the stale air in the room—where the air pressure is constantly too high because fresh air has to be pumped in—and it is as if he had to live in a cellar without any light at all. To live in a cell like that is unhealthy in the final analysis and becomes unbearable in the end for any living being. Any normal plant would die because of the lack of air and light. Schaub is of the same opinion, and *Dr* Morell has pointed it out several times, but the *Führer* does not want to change his quarters for the time being. He is also constantly complaining about our huts with their brick walls, which, he says, will be destroyed by the first heavy air raid, and then we will all have to make do with much less space! I am very unhappy because of this attitude and the illness of the *Führer*. After all, everything depends on his health! And he of all people, who normally thinks in terms of biology, of the laws of nature, refuses to accept these laws for his own person! It is really an eternal shame, because it does effect the *Führer*, even though there is a lot of nonsense being bandied around about this. Today the briefings had to be cancelled for the third day in a row.
>
> Last night the *Führer*, who is feeling somewhat better although he is still far from well, called me in for a talk. I was with him for one and a half to two hours, until 1.15 a.m. Today at lunch he also kept me by his side in order to discuss a lot of confidential matters. His continuing trust in me always makes me very happy![92]

From 1936, when he cured Hitler of eczema on his leg from which he had been suffering and improved the condition of an intestinal problem with a treatment called 'Multaflor', *Dr* Theodor Morell enjoyed Hitler's full confidence as his personal physician. When he was in pain, did not feel well or was suffering from a cold, Hitler appreciated Morell's rapid cures. However, Hitler's nervous disorders did not get better. On the contrary, towards the end of the war they continued to worsen, until he was forced to steady his left limbs—which twitched very badly—with his right in order to keep them still. On 2 April 1945 Morell noted:

> *Führer* had lots of aggravation and slept poorly . . . Military situation very bad! Therefore, tremors in left hand very strong . . .[93]

On 3 October 1944, *Dr* Karl Brandt,[94] together with *Dr* Erwin Giesing, an ENT specialist, and *Dr* Hans-Karl von Hasselbach,[95] accused Morell of having given Hitler a daily dose of sixteen anti-gas pills that contained so much strychnine as to come close to the maximum permissible. Morell replied that he had not prescribed this high a dose and complained to Hitler. Brandt tried to make Hitler realise that the treatment by Morell was, as von Hasselbach put it, 'poisoning the Head of State either by culpable negligence or with premeditation'.

Martin Bormann describes the situation in a vivid letter to his wife on 4 October 1944:

> The *Führer* is still far from well. Brandt and Hasselbach claim Morell's treatment to be completely wrong: they believe he is poisoning the *Führer* with his injections. I am not able to judge, I am not a physician, and the *Führer* still has complete confidence in *Herr* Morell. I am only very sad about the present weakened condition of the *Führer*. I have asked him whether he doesn't want to go and spend ten days to a fortnight at the Berghof as soon as his health permits him to travel, but the *Führer* believes a stay there to be impossible as long as the present war situation continues. He feels that people would not understand and take it the wrong way . . .[96]

Hitler was used to *Dr* Morell and depended upon him. On 8 October he decided against the doctors: he sent von Hasselbach back to the Army and told Brandt to go back to Berlin and his job as Reich Commissioner of Health. On Himmler's[97] recommendation Hitler added *SS-Arzt* Ludwig Stumpfegger to his staff as his attending surgeon. Bormann described the episode:

> Yesterday Hasselbach was dismissed as the *Führer*'s personal physician and *Dr* Stumpfegger, up to now Uncle H.'s [Himmler's] treating physician, is to replace him. The new man seems to be very nice. Brandt is also no longer in attendance. There was another quarrel between Morell on the one hand and Hasselbach and Brandt on the other, but now the problem which was so unpleasant for the *Führer* has been solved.[98]

Morell stayed on, even though Bormann himself later said of him:

> By God, I will be relieved when I no longer have to deal with *Dr* Morell and his work—he is a real pain in the neck . . .[99]

For Hitler, Morell's medical treatment was vital because he believed in him and was convinced of his abilities. He suspected that the accusations raised by Brandt and von Hasselbach against Morell were only designed to have Morell removed from his presence. And, so he went on to conclude, since the doctors knew that he could not live without Morell's treatment, they intended to kill him indirectly. He once said to *Frau* Schroeder:

> These stupid doctors have not been able to help me nor find me an internist. Morell in any case has helped me . . . They forget that I do not have the time to go to bed like other people every time I catch the 'flu. During all these years I have not even been able to take a holiday. When I was in the mountains, my work went on just as in Berlin. I simply do not have the time to be ill . . . There is actually no one at all I can depend on. That makes me sick.

And on 16 April 1944 he told *Frau* Schroeder over lunch:

> If I didn't have Morell I would be lost. And Brandt and Hasselbach wanted to remove Morell. They did not consider what would have become of me without Morell. If something happens to me, then Germany is lost, because I do not have a successor. The first [Hess] went mad, the second [Göring] has lost the support of the nation and the third [Himmler] is rejected by the people.[100]

When there was a crisis, Hitler was seized with stomach cramps, and every time he felt unwell, caught a cold, became over-tired or suffered from insomnia or vertigo he always called *Dr* Morell. And Morell always came with an injection, which gave Hitler relief, or pepped him up, or calmed him down and made him sleep. A typical example can be found in Morell's notes of 30 October 1944:

> 6 a.m.: I am to report to the patient [Hitler] immediately and bring some Eupaverin . . . *Führer* worked through the night and took a grave decision which caused him great inner turmoil. The agitation continued to increase until finally—as is always the case with great agitation—the cramps started . . .[101]

Apparently Morell applied increasingly more potent drugs and by doing so contributed to Hitler's poor state of health towards the end.

In early October 1944 Hitler also developed a bad toothache. On 14 October his dentist, *Dr* Hugo Blaschke,[102] was called to headquarters in order to examine the patient. He found a massive infection in tooth No 6 in the left upper jaw. Since this tooth formed part of a substantial bridge and Hitler refused lengthy treatment, Blaschke decided to cut off the section of the bridge with teeth 5 and 6 and extract tooth 6. At 2040 on 10 November 1944, ten days before Hitler's departure to Berlin, Blaschke carried out the operation.[103]

From late October/early November 1944 onwards, the reports reaching Hitler's headquarters from the fronts became worse and worse. On 16 October General Tchernjakovsky's 3rd Belorussian Front had launched an offensive towards Gumbinnen and Goldap and succeeded in breaking through to East Prussia. The stiff resistance offered by *General* Friedrich Hossbach's 4th Army (he had been Hitler's adjutant to the Army from 1934 to 1938) managed to bring the Russians to a halt after three weeks. Nevertheless, on 1 November 1944 the Red Army stood at Goldap, only 60km north-east of *Führer* headquarters.

At a meeting at Sonthofen on 5 May 1944 *Generalfeldmarschall* Keitel had given an indication of Hitler's strategic thinking when he referred to 'conducting a war to gain time while awaiting developments . . .'[104] Hitler and the OKW held to the concept of maintaining resistance in the East until—having defeated the Allied attack in the West, which would result in a greater willingness by America and Great Britain to make peace—they could then turn on the Soviet Army with larger numbers of troops. Various circumstances and the assassination attempt of 20 July postponed the military initiative in the West. Towards the end of September 1944, however, while he was still in bed with jaundice, Hitler had informed *Generaloberst* Jodl that he intended conducting a major strategic offensive in the West at the earliest possible date, employing newly created forces and with the main objective of destroying a substantial number of American divisions. Hitler, grasping at the desperate hopes of the fanatic, believed that success would be his and was sure that, after the destruction of large numbers of US troops, the American press would seize on the heavy losses and mobilise public opinion against prolonging the war, which would then enable Germany to come to an agreement with the US government. Hitler was convinced that he could hold his front against the Russians in the East while more easily gaining ground in the West by means of a rapid surprise attack. Because he had to withdraw the divisions needed for this from the Eastern Front (a move which would have bitter consequences), this final attempt by Hitler to regain the initiative depended on the Eastern Front being able to hold firm for as long as necessary. An evaluation of the chances for success also had to take Allied air supremacy into consideration. The operation therefore required a period of poor weather during which aircraft could not be employed, in other words a period of fog and rain in late November/early December. After weighing all the pros and cons, the Eifel and the heavily wooded Ardennes mountains— roughly in the centre of the Allied front—were selected as the point of attack.

Keitel and Jodl kept trying to make Hitler leave East Prussia and return to Berlin, both because of the proximity of the Russian front and because of the start of the Ardennes offensive, which had originally been scheduled for 1 December 1944. Hitler, however, was undecided and he hesitated, as Bormann reported to his wife on 25 and 26 October 1944:

It is still not clear when we will leave here. Because the *Führer* has declared that he will only leave if the military situation here in the east forces him to do so, we can only hope that we may and will stay here until the end of the war. On the other hand, we all wish for greater security for the *Führer*—60 or 80 kilometres is no great distance for tanks—and in any case we should go to a more pleasant place, in which the *Führer* can recuperate. But the *Führer* orders and we obey . . .

Yesterday, after my report, the *Führer* told me that he would not leave here in any case as long as the crisis in East Prussia continues . . .

He believes that his presence inspires many East Prussians with the necessary calm and confidence and compels the divisions to make the appropriate effort. And that is probably true. Without the *Führer*'s iron, decisive stance to support them, many officers abandon position after position, area after area, much too readily.

In any case, *Führer* headquarters here has already been 'dissolved', as the military expression goes—that is, everything that is not absolutely essential has been sent away. This applies both to equipment and to people . . .[105]

Hitler was now also being treated for acute inflammation of the nose and throat, which *Dr* Morell was the first to discover. *Dr* Carl von Eicken, who had been brought in from Berlin earlier, made several trips with Hitler and Morell to the field hospital in Rastenburg-Karlshof for x-rays. Several x-rays were taken—they are now in the National Archives in Washington DC—and on 18 November 1944 von Eicken diagnosed that Hitler was not suffering from cancer of the larynx but had a polyp on his vocal cords which needed to be operated on in Berlin. On 25 February 1955 von Eicken testified:

I first met and treated Hitler in 1935. I had to remove a large polyp on the vocal cords which had caused a major voice disorder. Some time between 1935 and the beginning of the war—I can no longer recall the date—I saw him once again during a consultation.

About four to five days after the assassination attempt on 20 July I was called to *Führer* headquarters in Rastenburg by *Dr* Morell to examine Hitler. There I discovered that a polyp had again formed on his vocal cords, which I removed by an operation some time in November 1944 in the Chancellery in Berlin [it was in fact on 22 November 1944, the day after Hitler's return to Berlin].

I must add that, during my examination of Hitler in July 1944, I discovered a rupture of both eardrums and a loss of balance, both being a result of the assassination attempt.

On 30 December 1944 I was once again called to headquarters, which at the time was located near Usingen, to examine Hitler. After that I never saw him again . . .

On 24 October 1944 the two Chiefs of Staff of Supreme Command West and Army Group B, *Generäle* Siegfried Westphal and Hans Krebs (Krebs had been promoted to General of Infantry and named Chief of Staff of Army Group B on 1 August 1944 to replace Speidel), were called to *Führer* headquarters. There Hitler informed them that he intended to regain the initiative and set in motion a 'change for the better' by means of an offensive in the West. After the successful defensive battles on the East Prussian–Lithuanian border and on the

Narev river in Poland, the Eastern Front was now largely stabilised. The attack in the West was to proceed from the area between Monschau and Echternach against the Ardennes.

On 10 November Hitler signed the *Führerbefehl*, i.e. the order of battle for the German armies. The main weight of the offensive was to be concentrated behind *Generaloberst* Sepp Dietrich's 6th SS Panzer Army, which was to reach the Meuse first and to cross the river between Huy and Liége.

The forthcoming operation on his vocal cords and the insistence of the Generals and also of Bormann then caused Hitler on 19 November to schedule his return to Berlin for 20 November 1944. As can be seen from Linge's notes, Hitler left his bunker at 1515 on 20 November and drove to the station in Görlitz, where his special 'Brandenburg' train waited. He never again saw the 'Wolfsschanze' headquarters, which were blown up shortly afterwards.

A beaten, broken, sick man left the headquarters from which he had directed the military fate of Germany for three years and four months. *Generaloberst* Jodl later said that Hitler had already asked himself whether he should not have brought things to an end:

> Could he not have made an end sooner in order to spare his nation unnecessary suffering? Indeed, this thought moved Hitler during the final days of his life. When on 22 April he informed me of his decision not to leave Berlin and to die there, he added: 'I should already have taken this decision, the most important of my life, in November 1944 and never have left my headquarters in East Prussia.'[106]

Hitler and his staff arrived in the still relatively undamaged Chancellery at 5.30 a.m. on 21 November 1944. Thereby the *Führer* headquarters was transferred to Berlin. The Armed Forces Command with its approximately sixty officers was quartered in Berlin-Dahlem. At 1630 Hitler had lunch with Eva Braun, who had arrived from Munich. The next day, at 1230, *Dr* Eicken removed the polyp from his vocal cords in the hospital in the Chancellery. For the next few days Hitler was only able to whisper, and he could still not speak loudly the following month.

The date for the start of the Ardennes offensive kept being postponed for various reasons. Then, at 1700 on 10 December 1944 Hitler left Berlin in his special train to go to the 'Adlerhorst' (Eagle's Nest) headquarters, built in 1940 near Ziegenberg west of Bad Nauheim. The train arrived at the station in Hungen at 3 a.m. and Hitler reached his bunker at 7.30 a.m. The Armed Forces Command moved to a camp in Friedberg/Hessia. That same afternoon, at 1740, Hitler addressed a group of about twenty or thirty Generals and other senior officers. Since he could still not speak loudly, he had to address a further group of army and divisional commanders the next day. Hitler's intention was to motivate the leading Generals and other key officers. After presenting a historical review and recapitulating the purpose of the war, he soon came to the heart of the matter regarding his planned offensive. Some of his important and revealing thoughts deserve being repeated here:

> . . . it is a war that can possibly last for many years, with high points and low points, and the victor in the end will be the one who survives all this with the greater determination . . .

> The war is naturally a great stress for all concerned. The longer the war lasts, the greater this stress will become. This stress will be borne absolutely as long as the slightest hope of success remains. The moment all hope of victory disappears, such stress is normally no longer shouldered with the same degree of willpower with which, for example, a fortress fights on as long as it can still hope for relief. It is therefore necessary from time to time to destroy the enemy's confidence of victory by demonstrating, through offensive blows, that the successful conclusion of his plans is impossible from the beginning. This will never be as effectively demonstrated by a successful defence as by successful offensive blows . . .

> In the final analysis, however, the war will be decided when one side realises that the war as such can no longer be won. To bring this realisation home to the enemy is therefore the most important task . . .

> If one has been forced into the defensive, it is all the more important to show the enemy from time to time by means of ruthless blows that he has not won anything after all, but that the war will go on interminably . . .

> To make it clear to the enemy that, regardless of what he undertakes, he can never hope for capitulation—never, never—that is the decisive factor. The slightest hint of capitulation will cause the enemy again to raise his hopes of victory . . .

> What will occur is what Frederick the Great was able to record as the greatest triumph of his life in the seventh year of his war. Let no one

claim later: yes, but the situation then was different. Gentlemen, the situation was no different. All of his generals, including his own brother . . . almost despairing of a possible success . . . The fortitude of one man alone made it possible to survive this battle and the miracle of a turning point occurred in the end . . .

We have just received the first official confirmation by the Americans that they lost 240,000 men in barely three weeks [the figure Hitler quoted was too high]. That number is simply gigantic, far higher than what we had believed they could lose. Therefore they are also shattered . . .[107]

In a further address after the offensive in the Ardennes had failed on 28 December 1944 which Hitler gave to twenty or thirty Generals and divisional commanders, who had been called to headquarters in connection with a new German offensive in Lower Alsace scheduled to begin at midnight on 1 January 1945, he again made some very revealing comments on his state of mind:

. . . bringing the action into context with the overall situation in which we find ourselves and the problems we face and which must be solved, and which, regardless of whether we solve them positively or negatively, will be solved, in the first case in our favour and in the other case to our destruction . . . it is simply a case of whether Germany wants to survive or if it is to be destroyed . . .

Only a few weeks ago you heard Churchill's statement and explanation in Parliament: all of East Prussia, parts of Pomerania and Upper Silesia—and possibly all of Silesia—are to be handed over to the Poles, who in their turn must give the Russians something in compensation. The seven or ten or eleven million Germans will have to be evacuated . . .[108]

The only nation about whose fate this war is being waged in the final analysis is Germany, which will either save itself or, if it loses this war, will go down. And I would like quickly to add, gentlemen: if I say this, do not take this to mean that I am even remotely thinking of losing this war. [Any psychologist will agree that, by using this turn of phrase, Hitler reveals that that was exactly what he *was* thinking about.] In all my life, I have never learned the meaning of the word 'surrender', and I am one of those men who worked his way up from nothing. For me, therefore, the situation in which we find ourselves today is nothing new. Formerly my situation was a very different one: it was far worse. I only say this so that you can understand why I pursue my objectives with such fanaticism and why nothing can wear me down. I could be really tortured by cares, and, as far as that goes, even my health could be shaken by cares: my resolution to fight on until, in the end, the scales tip in our favour would not be affected in the slightest degree . . .

And I wish to tell you something here and now, gentlemen: our forces are certainly not inexhaustible. It meant taking an incredible risk to mobilise these forces for this offensive and the coming blows, a risk that on the other hand also contains the greatest dangers. If you therefore read today that things are not going well on the southern sector of the Eastern Front in Hungary, you must appreciate that we naturally cannot be equally strong everywhere . . . But, despite all this, it was possible, by and large, to hold the Eastern Front . . .

The overall plan of the operation is clear . . . to liquidate the American divisions. The destruction of these American divisions must be the objective . . . exterminate division by division . . . Our only concern is to destroy and eradicate the enemy forces wherever we find them . . . We will then fight the third battle there, and there we will knock the Americans to pieces. That must be the fanatical goal . . .[109]

As Bormann reported to his wife on 26 December 1944, the stress caused by the situation aggravated Hitler's nervous disorders:

The Führer takes a short walk each day and this seems to do him good. I wish he could overcome these attacks of trembling—they began in his leg and have now spread to his left arm and hand. And everything depends on his health! The future of a whole nation . . . The first briefing of the day now takes place at 1700 and the second at midnight or half an hour after that . . .[110]

Let us return to the offensive in the Ardennes. The final reserves were being deployed in a hopeless attempt to launch an offensive. And when Hitler said, 'the objection that there comes a time when technical resources finally decide the issue is completely mistaken', he was wrong, because the Allied superiority in *matériel* was crushing.

The German offensive was again postponed several times. On 13 December a young *Luftwaffe* meteorologist predicted a period of bad weather and over the following three days the deployment of the final reserves took place. At 5.30 a.m. on 16 December 1944, a dark, foggy winter morning, Hitler's last major offensive of the war began. Roughly 250,000 German troops with 600 tanks and self-propelled guns advanced on a 100km wide front against four divisions of the American

8th Corps with 83,000 men, 242 tanks and 182 self-propelled guns. The murky weather prevented any Allied air activity and surprise was achieved, but the advance made only slow progress. One of the reasons was a lack of fuel for the heavily motorised German units. The Meuse was not reached. On 23 December the weather cleared up, and, day and night, the US Army Air Force attacked the German divisions, which had advanced about 60km. Flank attacks by General Patton from the south and Field Marshal Montgomery from the north brought the German advance to a halt. On 7 January 1945 *Generalfeldmarschall* Model recommended to Hitler that the front be pulled back. Hitler gave his consent, and with the order at 2 a.m. on 8 January to *Generaloberst* Dietrich to withdraw the 6th SS Panzer Army the Ardennes offensive had failed.

On 28 December 1944 Hitler had said to his divisional commanders:

> There can be no doubt that the brief offensive we have conducted has led to an immediate easing of the situation along the whole front, even if, unfortunately, it did not result in the great success one could have expected . . .[111]

How Hitler really felt at the time was later recounted by his adjutant to the *Luftwaffe*, *Oberst* Nicolaus von Below:

> During these days I remained in the bunker with Hitler when enemy aircraft were reported. The impression Hitler made on me was one of complete despair. Never before or afterwards did I see him in such a state. He now spoke of taking his own life, because the final hope of achieving a success had been destroyed. He made accusations against the *Luftwaffe* and the traitors in the Army. He said something like: 'I know the war is lost. The odds are too overwhelming. I have been betrayed . . . The best thing to do is to put a bullet through my brain . . .'[112]

Taken altogether, the Ardennes offensive was not only a tactical failure, it was a strategic mistake. The men and *matériel* deployed there were sorely lacking in the East. On 9 January 1945 *Generaloberst* Guderian[113] pointed out the dangers to the Eastern Front, particularly on the bridgehead at Baranov on the Vistula—as he had done once before on 31 December 1944. But Hitler and Jodl refused to listen. As he wrote later, Guderian had to return to Zossen with 'the insulting instructions from Hitler that the Eastern Front must help itself and make do with what it had.'[114]. Hitler and Jodl only began to reconsider their position four days after the big Russian Baranov offensive had begun, which would rapidly break through to Upper Silesia and the middle reaches of the Oder river in one drive. By then, of course, it was too late. Jodl testified later:

It was a desperate attempt in a desperate situation. In the East, the numerical superiority was too great to expect any kind of successful turnaround; in the West, it was the superiority in the air. One hoped, however, that this would not perhaps be so effective during the winter, given the right weather conditions. If the offensive were to succeed and therefore many English and American divisions be destroyed, then one could expect a halt for a period of time, enabling one to reinforce in the East on a generous scale and effectively stop the Russian advance, which by this time had reached the Vistula and Warsaw. Even the *Führer* was fully aware that it was just a desperate attempt in a desperate situation. After three days the offensive was recognised to have failed. Everything in the way of *matériel* and men that could still be brought east was brought there in order to try to meet the immediate greater danger, at least to some extent. However, this did no good either. Hitler probably now finally realised that the war was irrevocably lost. His conduct from then on, and many of his orders, can only be explained in terms of a shipwrecked man in the middle of the Atlantic who, without even the slightest hope of being rescued, still continues to swim as long as his strength holds out. The idea of sparing his nation the ultimate sacrifice and destruction by immediately calling a halt probably never entered his head, given the incredible sacrifices that had already been made to no avail and in the light of the complete collapse of all the hopes and endeavours which had been intended to lead his people to a pinnacle of greatness never before achieved—a people who were now assuredly facing terrible deprivation and endless horror and heading towards inevitable destruction. What he was probably contemplating was a heroic downfall, which would possibly inspire later generations to find the strength to surge back . . .[115]

On 12 January 1945 a further message of disaster reached Hitler in the 'Adlerhorst' headquarters: the Soviet Army had launched a major offensive out of the Baranov bridgehead in Western Galicia. On 12 January the 1st Ukrainian and on 14 January the 1st Belorussian Fronts advanced. Simultaneously, on 13 January, the 2nd and 3rd Belorussian and the 1st Baltic Fronts began their drive against East Prussia. The major part of the offensive, however, was the Vistula–Oder operation against a German eastern front that had been denuded of all reserves. Within only a few days it brought the Russians into the area between the River Memel and the Carpathian mountains and, after a rapid extension of the front, to Upper Silesia two weeks later and to the Oder river on 30 January. The direction of advance of the Red Army was clear—Berlin!

Hitler now tried in vain to bring in troops to the central sector of the Eastern Front, but the huge Russian offensive, with strong armoured forces and massive artillery support, rapidly broke through. Hitler realised that this was the beginning of the end, and at 1800 on 15 January he boarded his special train at Hungen station to return to Berlin, where he arrived at Grunewald station at 9.40 a.m. on 16 January. According to Linge's notes, he entered the Chancellery—which had in the meantime been hit by several bombs—at 10 a.m.

In the Old Chancellery the air raids had destroyed the cabinet room, the music room, the smoking room and the winter garden built in 1936. The second floor on the right, where Hitler lived, was still relatively undamaged. The shock of the explosions had shattered all the windows and plaster had fallen from walls and ceilings, but after some repairs the rooms were again serviceable. Hitler's office on the second floor garden side had also been damaged, but it was repaired, and, according to several witnesses, Hitler worked in this room until the middle of March 1945. This room was also used for the daily military briefings. Hitler continued to sleep in his bedroom on the second floor[116] until he moved into the bunker because of the daily (mostly nightly) air raids. We do not know the exact date on which Hitler moved into the bunker. Schaub and *Frau* Wolf claim he slept upstairs until 27–28 February. Christine Schroeder spoke of the first days in March 'when Hitler moved into the bunker completely enervated by the constant air raid alarms'.

The garden of the Chancellery had also been heavily damaged. The lawns were potted with bomb craters, the trees were torn and broken by shrapnel and the hitherto carefully tended paths could no longer be made out amongst the craters.

Between 15 and 17 January 1945 the Army Command moved into the 'Maybach I' camp near Zossen, which had housed the OKW at the beginning of the war, and the Army General Staff took up quarters in the neighbouring 'Maybach II' camp. Both camps consisted of barracks and some stone buildings that looked like country houses when seen from the outside or from the air but which had reinforced concrete roofs and bunkers going two floors deep into the ground. Hitler did not move into the house with a large concrete bunker which the OKW had reserved for him in Zossen because he did not believe it was safe enough. He preferred to stay in his familiar surroundings in the Chancellery. The others had to come to him! Meanwhile the new air raid shelter in the garden of the Chancellery had been finished in the nick of time and, if still damp, was habitable. Keitel and Jodl had to be quartered in villas in Berlin-Dahlem. This three-way split caused by Hitler greatly complicated the leadership of the German forces. The Generals and their staffs now had constantly to travel back and forth to and from Zossen, Dahlem and central Berlin in order to attend Hitler's daily briefings in the Chancellery.

The collapse of the German front in Poland and conflicting reports from the Army General Staff caused Hitler to become suspicious, particularly after he learned on 17 January that the last four weak battalions had evacuated Warsaw without his knowledge or permission. Against Guderian's protests, Hitler had the Chief of Operations of the General Staff, *Oberst* von Bodin, and two of his subordinates arrested, and shortly thereafter replaced the Commander of Army Group A, *Generaloberst* Josef Harpe, with *Generaloberst* Ferdinand Schörner and the Commander of the 9th Army, *General* Nikolaus von Vormann, with *General* Theodor Busse. But the superiority of the Russians along the whole of the Eastern Front was so overwhelming that no General could possibly obey Hitler's orders to hold on any longer.

Hitler suspected that the General Staff was not telling him the truth about the military situation. On 19 January 1945 he therefore issued a directive that from then on no commander, from divisional level on upwards, was permitted to order an attack or a withdrawal without having reported his intention to Hitler so far in advance that a counter order could still reach the front-line troops in time. Henceforward he would 'drastically punish' any ambiguous report reaching him, 'be it deliberate, or due to culpable negligence or because of lack of sufficient attention being paid'. As Army Chief of Staff, *General* Guderian had tried to convince Hitler in January that it was necessary to withdraw more troops from other fronts in order to build up a powerful reserve behind the Eastern Front. Hitler and the OKW were not willing to do so—at least, not at the time. That this decision had been a mistake became clear by the end of January. Bormann, for example, reports to his wife on 28 January 1945:

> We find ourselves in the same situation as 'Old Fritz' in the very worst phase of the Seven Years' War. In the East the fighting in Königsberg and Breslau continues, and the worst part of it is that our troops are showing signs of disintegration. Naturally we are doing everything possible to master the situation, but you can imagine the difficulties. We will have to withdraw more troops from the Western Front, and there, we are very well aware, the enemy is just in the process of mounting his next major offensive—and very soon at that![117]

Much too late the OKW, with Hitler's permission, now withdrew forces from the West and from other fronts and moved them to the Oder and Neisse rivers. Advance elements of the 1st Belorussian Front reached the Oder on 30 January 1945. The Soviet forces crossed the river on both sides of Küstrin and formed a bridgehead on the west bank. They were now only 70km from Berlin. But the offensive power of the Russian armies had suffered by the end of January 1945. Reinforcements and materials had to be brought up, supplies and the further advance had to be organised. The logistic requirements of the offensive were enormous. It was ten weeks after having reached the Oder before the Russians were able to mount their last big offensive, the battle for Berlin. This was to be Hitler's final battle—gigantic, bloody and senseless. Half a million people would die and a quarter of the Reich would be devastated. On 30 January 1945, the twelfth anniversary of the Nazis' seizure of power, Hitler's voice was heard for the last time in a recording played by the Greater German Radio Network. The gist of this speech was a warning to the Germans and the Western Allies about the dangers of Bolshevism.

If one believes Russian statements, then the attack on Berlin was being prepared by Soviet headquarters as early as the autumn of 1944. The Berlin operation called for simultaneous attacks by the 1st Belorussian Front from the Oder and the 1st Ukrainian Front from the Neisse. It is claimed that on 2 February 1945 Stalin ordered Marshal Zhukov to storm Berlin, 70km away, by a rapid advance on 15 and 16 February. According to Zhukov, Stalin cancelled this order on 4 February, which gave the Germans the time to build up their defences and bring in reinforcements.

On 3 February 1945 American bombers carried out a massive air raid on Berlin, during which the Chancellery was heavily damaged. Within half an hour 937 heavy bombers dropped over 2,264 tonnes of bombs on the capital; 58 heavy bombs detonated in the area of the Chancellery alone and caused extensive destruction. As Bormann noted in his diary, a serious attack directly on the Chancellery took place during the morning, destroying the New Chancellery, the façade of the *Parteikanzlei* (Party Chancellery), and, in the Old Chancellery, the *Führer*'s apartments, the entrance hall on the ground floor and the winter garden. Bomb hits destroyed the water and electricity supply to the Chancellery and knocked out the telephone lines and the heating system. The result was terrible chaos in the overcrowded rooms. It was not until the evening of 4 February that electricity was restored and the lights could be turned on. On 6 February 1945 Bormann wrote:

> This morning we again spent some time in the bunker but the main attack passed us by and hit Chemnitz and Magdeburg. Our life here is humble and fraught with risk . . . We are still sitting around in cold rooms and unfortunately it is still not possible to take a bath. On the other hand I am very grateful for my thick, fur-lined overcoat . . . The tables are covered with candle wax, glass shards and, naturally, dust. The *Parteikanzlei* still looks like a wilderness. There are repairs going on everywhere, but every carpenter who saws or hammers creates new dust and dirt . . .[118]

And on 26 February, after another heavy raid on the Chancellery:

> I have just heard that another three formations of enemy bombers are heading towards Berlin. Wireless reports have stopped but from time to time we can hear reverberating explosions in the distance. I ask myself what Berlin will look like when next I see it.[119]

The now almost daily air raids increasingly disrupted Hitler's routine. His secretary, Christine Schroeder, reported:

Frequently the last briefing only began after midnight and lasted two to three hours. After that the usual tea was served in Hitler's living room, accompanied by increasingly banal conversation. Hitler often played with the dogs. Then he excused himself and retired, which occurred between 5 and 6 o'clock in the morning during this time. There was not much time left for sleep because there were usually air raid alarms towards 11 a.m. Hitler did not stay in bed. He got up and dressed because he feared that a bomb coming down at an angle could hit the wall of the bunker and rip it open. After the alarm, which normally lasted until lunch time at 1400, Hitler held the afternoon briefing and supper was usually served towards 2100 or 2200.[120]

Secretary Johanna Wolf described Hitler's nightly 'teas' on 25 February 1948:

In the small room [Hitler's living room-cum-office] there were seats for only four to five people. Between 3 and 5 a.m. Hitler normally sat on the sofa drinking his tea and talking to us. Often there were only two of us present, *Fräulein* Schroeder and I. Eva Braun was only present occasionally; often she was not there.[121]

When asked why Eva Braun—who was apparently very sociable— did not take part, *Frau* Wolf answered that she probably had tea with him alone. When asked whether this was a daily occurrence, she said that

. . . it was a daily ritual and that either the adjutant or the servant summoned her by saying: 'Today the *Führer* would like to take his tea with such and such a person.' It was the same every day, the same routine as in Rastenburg. It was his way of relaxing and recuperating and it gave him the opportunity to think of other things. Yes, he talked about dogs a lot. He liked them . . .[122]

Frau Schroeder declared that the oppressive closeness of Hitler's room and the existing situation were very depressing:

If someone wished to cross the room, the armchairs had to be moved out of the way . . . Hitler's conversations became increasingly more one-sided and were only repetitions of the same old stories. Often he told the same ones at lunch, at supper and at night [i.e. in the early morning]

during tea. He, who formerly had talked on any and all subjects with such fervour, now only talked about dogs, the training of dogs, questions of diet and the stupidity and meanness of the world at large . . .[123]

The briefings in the *Führerbunker* are vividly described by *General* Krebs' adjutant *Major* von Loringhoven in his testimony of 13 March 1948:

In East Prussia the briefings were held daily in a special barracks and later in Berlin in the New or Old Chancellery—sometimes in Hitler's spacious office in the New Chancellery, which was actually a huge hall, then in Hitler's office in the Old Chancellery. But during the final weeks they took place down inside the *Führerbunker* in a very, very small room, because on account of the air raids there was often not enough time to bring all the maps etc. down into the bunker. That is why the briefings were finally only held in the bunker.

The people who gathered daily to discuss the military situation met there in a very small room. The room was about 3 by 4m. In contained a bench along the wall, two or three chairs and a small table on which two lamps stood and the maps were spread. Everybody stood around this table, at which Hitler sat on a chair. The older officers who attended the daily briefings could sit on the chairs from time to time because the briefings often lasted for hours. Everbody else had to stand, and that was terrible in that small room. One was tightly squeezed together—18 to 20 people stood in that small space—and the air in the room was very thick despite the air conditioning. And it was often a great strain to follow the discussion for a longer period. Against the back wall of the room stood a book case which contained writing paper, pencils and other office materials, which were occasionally used during the briefings, but there were no books. The room was lit by a light bulb hanging down in the middle.[124]

When asked whether the Generals or the person reporting talked openly during the briefings, von Loringhoven said:

Yes, although when a question was raised that Hitler did not like, then he normally started talking and the matter was not pursued. Hitler always sat on his chair and he was the only one who had a bit of room to move, because the maps were spread out in front of him so that he could actually see what had been drawn on them. The person reporting, that is, speaking about a military situation, normally stood on Hitler's left and could show him things on the map . . .[125]

During the night of 7 to 8 February 1945 the architect Hermann Giesler—the General Building Commissioner in Munich and since 1944 also charged with the rebuilding of Linz on the Danube—brought his completed model of the newly designed river frontage for the city to Berlin by lorry. It was then set up in a cellar of the New Chancellery. On the evening of 9 February, at 1915, Hitler inspected the model accompanied by *Dr* Robert Ley, Reich Organiser of the NSDAP and Leader of the German Labour Front, and *SS-Obergruppenführer Dr* Ernst Kaltenbrunner, Chief of the Security Police (who were Hitler's guests at the time), together with Hitler's cameraman Walter Frentz and Heinz Linge. Frentz took several pictures and one of them shows Hitler—who had only 79 days more to live—seated in front of the model in deep contemplation. One asks oneself what thoughts were going through his mind. The Soviet armies were taking up positions for their final offensive against the capital. Hitler knew that the war was lost and yet he gave detailed explanations to his companions about how he intended to rebuild Linz. As late as March 1945 he still spoke about the reconstruction of German cities and cultural monuments destroyed by the bombing:

> . . . for the culturally irreplaceable testimonials from the past have to be rebuilt and as close to the original as is humanly possible. With colour photography this is possible.[126]

As *Herr* Frentz himself told me, when the Allied bombing attacks began Hitler personally ordered him to photograph culturally important stained glass church windows. On Hitler's instructions, the colour photographs and diapositives were stored in the strongroom of the Chancellery in Voss-strasse. At the end of the war they were destroyed.

With his powers of persuasion, Hitler was able to convince his entourage—and probably himself as well—so that it is indeed likely that he himself also believed what he was talking about. His extraordinary self-confidence mesmerised the others: they believed him. Christine Schroeder later stated:

> As late as March 1945 Hitler spent endlessly long periods in front of a wooden model of the planned reconstruction and enlargement of Linz. In

moments like these Hitler forgot the war. He no longer felt tired and for hours he would elaborate on all the details of the new and refurbished buildings he had planned for his home town.[127]

From Linge's diary it can be seen that Hitler visited the model (which also contained his planned retirement home) time and time again and, as several witnesses report, spent long periods sitting silently in front of it:

9 February	1915:	Inspection *Prof.* Giesler
	0400:	Inspection model
10 February	0300:	Inspection model
13 February	1845:	Inspection model[128]

A further example of Hitler's powers of suggestion and his ability to convince was given by Christine Schroeder after the war:

The effect of Hitler's powers of suggestion on his long-time collaborators was particularly strong. I remember, for example, that on 19 March 1945 *Gauleiter* Forster of Danzig came to Berlin in complete despair. He reported that 1,100 Russian tanks were massed around Danzig, against which the *Wehrmacht* could only muster four Tiger tanks which, on top of everything else, didn't even have the necessary fuel. Forster was determined not to pull any punches and to confront Hitler with the whole terrible truth of the situation.

I supported him in his intention to tell the whole truth. He replied: 'You can bet on that. I will tell him everything, even at the risk that he will kick me out.'

You can imagine my surprise when he returned from his meeting with Hitler a completely changed man. 'The *Führer* has promised me nine divisions for Danzig,' he said with relief. When he saw my sceptical smile he said, 'Quite right, I don't know either where he will get them from. But he told me that he intends to save Danzig and there can be no more doubt about that.'[129]

As the final political event in connection with the 25th anniversary of the proclamation of the party programme, Hitler summoned his *Reichleiter* and *Gauleiter* to a reception in the New Chancellery at 1400 on 24 February. After lunch Hitler spoke to the dignitaries of his crumbling Reich. He spoke of an impending counter-offensive in the East (even though not a single prerequisite for such an offensive existed) and called on the party for a last great effort to achieve final victory. Hitler had known for a long time that the war was lost, but he spoke about miracle weapons and promised 'a historic turnaround this year'. At the end he also mentioned his poor state of health and said:

> . . . and were my whole left side to be paralysed, I would still continue to appeal to the German people not to surrender but to hang on until the end.[130]

There had been continuing differences of opinion between Hitler and *Generaloberst* Heinz Guderian, Chief of the Army General Staff, since 21 July 1944. When Guderian supported *General* Busse, Commander of the 9th Army, against Hitler's reproaches on 28 March, Hitler dismissed him with the words:

> Guderian, your state of health requires an immediate leave of absence. I believe your heart is again causing you problems. You will be back in six weeks.[131]

Guderian was given leave on 1 April and *General* Hans Krebs replaced him on this date. It is worth noting here that (as has become well-known since) Hitler always put the blame for reversals, failed offensives and lost battles on the Generals and senior officers. They were not obeying his orders or were not carrying them out as intended; they were lying to him and betraying him. On the other hand, as Supreme Commander, Hitler was not allowing them to develop initiative and conduct operations. But even so, mistakes were only being made by others and Hitler never admitted his own. As Jodl once said later, 'Hitler's convictions of his genius and his mission were much too great for that'.[132]

Out of seventeen *Generalfeldmarschällen* in the Army, in the course of the war ten were dismissed by Hitler, one was executed in connection with the assassination attempt of 20 July, two committed suicide and one was captured. Only three served until the end of the war without having been reprimanded by Hitler. Out of 36 *Generaloberste*, 26 were dismissed, including three executed in connection with 20 July and two dishonourably discharged. Seven *Generaloberste* were killed in action and only three stayed on without attracting Hitler's displeasure. This is a sorry balance sheet, particularly if one takes into account that these were highly qualified professionals who had proved themselves at the front during the war.

Hitler's military experience was mainly based on the First World War, which also accounts for his 'bunker mentality' and his fear of gas attacks. (As Linge noted in his diary, gas masks were distributed and tried out on 27 February 1945 and Hitler and his entourage also received gas masks.) The German Armed Forces Command and the Commander of the Army realised as early as November 1944 that the decisive battle in the East would take place along the Oder and Neisse. That is why Guderian speeded up the formation of a defensive barrier along the two rivers. A staggered system of defensive positions back to Berlin, Neustrelitz and Neubrandenburg was constructed. The three deep defensive lines along the rivers consisted of trenches and tank traps, gun emplacements and intermediate positions. The strongest defences were constructed on the Seelow Heights on the Oder, because these lay across the direct route to Berlin and the main attack was expected there.

On 9 March 1945 the *Kampfkommandant* of Berlin, *Generalleutnant* Hellmuth Reymann (who would be dismissed by Hitler on 21 April) issued an order on Hitler's instructions—the 'Basic Order for the Preparation of the Defences of the Capital of the Reich'. According to this order, the battle for Berlin was to be conducted with 'fanaticism, imagination, by all means of deception, deceit and guile' and from 'every block, every house, every storey, every hedge, every shell crater'. What was stressed most strongly in this order, however, was 'the fanatical will to fight'. Berlin now became a defensive area consisting of three concentric rings, the Outer Prohibited Zone and the Outer and Inner Defensive Zones. They included the government district with the Chancellery in the city centre, which was named the 'Citadel'. The construction of positions and tank barriers was speeded up and the population dug tank traps all around the city.

Contrary to his normal custom, on 3 March 1945 Hitler personally drove in a convoy of cars to 9th Army headquarters in Bad Saarow on Lake Scharmützel to discuss the defences with *General* Theodor Busse and to motivate the senior officers for the coming defensive battle. Afterwards Hitler also visited the command posts of two divisions of the 1st Corps, where officers and men from the ranks were introduced to him. In the evening Hitler returned to Berlin.

In a memorandum of 15 March 1945 Armaments Minister Albert Speer predicted the economic collapse of the Reich within the next four to eight weeks. Four days later Hitler issued his 'Nero Order': in case of a withdrawal anywhere within the Reich, not only all military installations but also all traffic and communications systems and industrial and supply installations as well as selected properties were to be destroyed. In their implementation instructions to this order of 30 March, Speer and Keitel toned things down and directed that installations should only be disabled, not destroyed.

Because the important airports of Gatow and Tempelhof were being bombed by the Russians from mid-March onwards, on 23 March Hitler ordered the immediate construction of a landing strip on the so-called East-West Axis (along the Charlottenburger Chaussee between the Victory Column and the Brandenburg Gate). In a briefing on that day, the following exchange took place:

> *Von Below*: If the Ju 52[133] has to land in the dark, this will be difficult due to the street lamps.
>
> *Führer*: Yes, the street lamps. But cut down the trees 20m to 30m on both sides—you don't need more than 50m in width.
>
> *Von Below*: I don't think 20m is necessary, but the removal of the street lamps is.
>
> *Führer*: He can remove the street lamps.
>
> *Burgdorf*: I will then give the order.
>
> *Führer*: It has just occurred to me. One could also have Me 163s and Me 262s [fighter aircraft] take off from the East-West Axis.
>
> *Hewel*: But not with the Victory Column in the middle.
>
> *Führer*: It is almost 3km to the Victory Column. That is far enough.[134]

The *Gauleitung* was then ordered to dismantle the street lamps immediately and to prepare the East–West Axis as a landing strip. Work was to be carried out at great speed because, reportedly, larger formations were expected. When the landing strip was ready, however, only a handful of Ju 52s with about 200 marines landed there.

On 4 April 1945 Hitler ordered the formation of a new fall-back line 'under the tightest leadership behind the 9th Army' and directed that the Eastern Front was to have priority in the delivery of mines. Continuing to insist on the rapid strengthening of defensive positions, Hitler declared as late as the end of March 1945: 'The battle for Berlin must and will then end with a decisive defensive victory.'[135]

After Hitler finally realised that the enemy armies attacking on two fronts could not be defeated by holding on to fixed positions and strongpoints—where they were supposed to bleed themselves to death—he grasped at the final straw: splitting the Allies, and possibly even a partial armistice or peace agreement. Following the progressive disintegration of the fronts, the defection of his allies, the collapse of armaments production, the destruction of Germany's cities and transportation systems by Allied bombing, the lack of fuel, the failure of the offensives in the Ardennes and the Vosges Mountains and the start of the Russian offensive against Berlin, Hitler's last remaining hope was a falling out between the Western Powers and the Russians. He clung to this hope of a miracle, similar to the one that had saved Frederick the Great when the Csarina had died, and in this belief he was propped up by his highly imaginative Minister of Propaganda, *Dr* Joseph Goebbels.

As early as 31 August 1944, at a briefing in the 'Wolfsschanze' in the presence of *Feldmarschall* Keitel and *Generäle* Krebs and Westphal, Hitler had declared his intention to continue to fight, at all costs and regardless of the consequences, in an endless monologue:

The time has not yet come for a political decision. It would be childish and naïve to assume that the time was ripe for political negotiations at a moment of the most serious military defeats. Such moments only come when one is successful . . . But the time is coming when the tensions between the Allies will have reached a point that will lead to a falling out. Every coalition in history has broken apart sooner or later. One has only to wait for the right moment, even if this is sometimes difficult to do. Since 1941 I have been at pains not to lose my nerve under any circumstances, but rather to find ways and means to save the situation whenever a disaster has occurred. I truly believe one cannot imagine a greater crisis than the one we have experienced in the East this year . . . If necessary, we will fight on the Rhine. I do not care in the least. We will continue this battle under any circumstances until, as Frederick the Great once said, one of our cursed enemies grows tired of fighting on. We will fight on until we can make a peace that will secure the survival of the German nation for the next 50 to 100 years.

But the moment will come when tensions between the Allies become so great that a rupture will become inevitable. Coalitions in the past have always failed at some point. One has only to wait for the moment, no matter how difficult this is. It has been my job—particularly since 1941—to keep my nerve under any and all circumstances and, whenever a disaster has occurred anywhere, somehow or other to find ways and means to recover the situation . . .

To continue the fight until the moment arises for a decent peace that Germany can accept and that will secure the survival of future generations. When this comes, I will make peace. I'm sure everyone can imagine that this war is far from agreeable for me. For five years now I have been cut off from the rest of the world: I have not attended the theatre, not been to a concert, not seen a movie. I live for one task only, to fight this war because I know that if there is not a person of iron will behind everything, then the war cannot be won. And I must blame the General Staff: instead of radiating this iron will, it has weakened the resolve of frontline officers who visit it; or, when officers of the General Staff have been sent to the Front, they have spread its pessimism . . .[136]

Two weeks earlier, Hitler had quoted Frederick the Great to Generals and senior officers at a meeting at the Platterhof on the Obersalzberg: 'I will continue to fight until our cursed enemies have finally had enough, until they are prepared to make peace with us'. He continued: 'That is exactly the situation today. We must fight on until that moment arrives . . .' And as late as 23 April 1945 Hitler said at a briefing:

I believe that the moment has come when out of sheer self-preservation the others will have to turn willy-nilly against this proletarian–Bolshevik colossus and Moloch which has grown out of all proportion. If I were to run away now like a coward, the others would only try to form some sort of new boundary line in southern Germany and that would be that. National Socialism would be gone and with it the German Reich. If I fight successfully here and hold the capital, then the English and the Americans might realise that it could be possible to face this whole threat together with Nazi Germany. And, in the final analysis, the only man for this is myself . . .[137]

The more desperate the military situation became, the more Hitler returned to this topic. He knew that, since their agreement on Germany's unconditional surrender as a war aim at the Casablanca Conference (14–26 January 1943), none of his enemies was prepared to negotiate. However, all of his life Hitler had been a fighter, and, true to type, he elected to continue fighting. His objective for quite some while had been to 'gain time'. Hitler's secretary *Frau* Schroeder told me that during the final weeks Hitler kept saying, 'It should be possible to drive a wedge between the Allies' and that he kept repeating, 'We must gain time'—or, as *Generaloberst* Jodl put it, 'We must continue to fight to gain political time.' This is what Hitler believed in and therefore the fight had to go on, without consideration for the suffering of the people, the hundreds of thousands of additional dead and wounded, displaced, tortured, captured—to gain time for the fantasies of a broken, sick, fanatical dreamer hidden in a bunker 7.6m underground.

On 6 April 1945 *Dr* Morell noted in his diary:

> The *Führer* generally only leaves the well ventilated and lit bunker for short periods of time . . . and goes into the garden of the Chancellery . . . He is very sensitive to light and dusty winds. Orderly treatment is very difficult because of the irregular way of living and the constant preoccupation with reports etc . . .[138]

Major von Loringhoven, who was in the bunker until 29 April 1945, also reported on 13 March 1948 that Hitler only left the bunker for short periods:

> Hitler's daily walk with his dog only lasted about half an hour and I sometimes saw him in the garden of the Chancellery. It was not a pretty sight. He only took very short steps, was bent over with his hunched back and could only move slowly . . .[139]

On 9 April Morell noted:

> *Führer* has not been outside for about ten days, only to an upper floor to eat, otherwise always in the bunker. The military briefings also take place in the bunker (reasons of safety) for some time now . . . This morning first briefing ended only at 5.30 a.m., then tea! Hopefully there will be no early morning air raid so that there will be time for some sleep . . .[140]

And on 10 April:

> *Führer* slept from 7.30 a.m. to 2 p.m. The military briefing last night lasted until 6 a.m., then tea until 7 a.m . . .[141]

When news of President Roosevelt's death was received during the night of 12–13 April, Hitler and Goebbels expected a turning point in the anti-Hitler alliance. On 14 April stenographer Gerhard Herrgesell reported:

> I believe it was on 12 April 1945, after the end of the nightly briefing. Besides myself there was another stenographer present, *Dr* Hager or *Dr* Buchholz. There were always two stenographers in attendance. Hitler was still with us in the briefing room. Suddenly Heinz Lorenz, a member of *Reichsleiter Dr* Dietrich's staff, came through the door and loudly proclaimed, 'My *Führer*, Roosevelt is dead.' Hitler, who had been sitting silently bent over a map for some time, suddenly became—how should I express it?—one can only say wild. He jumped up, walked several steps back and forth with great joy and then said, 'Didn't I always say so? I had a premonition.' I remember feeling embarrassed that a statesman could lose his composure in such a manner and jump up with such a display of childish joy . . .[142]

In his 'Order of the Day to the Soldiers of the Eastern Front' of 16 April, Hitler put his wishful thinking down in writing:

> At the moment when Fate has removed the greatest war criminal of all times [Roosevelt] from this earth, the turning point of this war will be decided . . .[143]

But Hitler and Goebbels were mistaken. The enemy's military operations on all fronts continued as if nothing had happened, because what had led to Stalin, Churchill and Roosevelt agreeing at Yalta to shelve their political differences for the time being had been Hitler and the Nazi system. Before everything else—and on this point the Allies were in complete agreement—the unconditional surrender of Germany had to be achieved. Until then other matters could wait.

On 2 and 3 April 1945 the 1st Belorussian Front (Zhukov) and the 1st Ukrainian Front (Konev) received their instructions for the final assault. The attack was to begin on 16 April 1945, although Hitler expected 'the major Russian attack against Army Group Vistula on

12 or 13 April', as *Oberkommando des Heeres* (OKH) informed General Heinrici's staff on 11 April.

On 14 April the Russians undertook a reconnaissance in force, during which they captured prisoners. And then, at 3.50 a.m. on 16 April, the Soviet offensive against Berlin was launched. With close to 750,000 men, 1,800 tanks and 17,000 guns, mortars and 'Stalin organs' (electrically fired rocket launchers), the 1st Belorussian Front under Marshal Georgi Zhukov opened a bombardment that could be heard 70km away in the eastern suburbs of the capital. At 5.30 a.m. the Russian armies began to advance, although they were initially stopped on the Seelow Heights. A short time later the 1st Ukrainian Front under Marshal Ivan Stepanovich Konev began its bombardment on a front running 350km south from the confluence of the Oder and Neisse rivers. Deploying seven armies—500,000 men and 1,400 tanks—the Russians crossed the Neisse. By 8.30 a.m. the Russian sappers had assembled twenty bridges and the tank armies had torn a 30km wide breach in the German defences.

The *Wehrmacht* report of 16 April 1945 stated:

> Furthermore, the enemy jumped off for a major offensive on the Oder. 3.50–6.30 a.m., artillery bombardment and bombing attacks, then enemy attack to the south and north of Frankfurt, where he advanced for several kilometres; secondly, on the Küstrin–Berlin highway, where he reached the high ground [Seelow Heights] (opposition by the 'Kurmark' Division); thirdly, to the north, direction of advance south-west . . .

Despite the fact that there were not enough German reserves to close off the break-throughs—a problem that was soon to lead to catastrophe—Hitler appeared to be optimistic that the battle for Berlin would end with a victory for the defences. In his 'Order of the Day to the Warriors of the Eastern Front' of 16 April—which was also published in all the newspapers still appearing in the Reich—and knowing the war to be lost, he still found rousing words, calling on his troops to hang on in order to gain time:

> For the last time the deadly Jewish-Bolshevik enemy has launched his masses in attack. He is attempting to destroy Germany and exterminate our people . . .

We have anticipated this attack and since January of this year every-thing has been done to build up a strong front. A huge mass of artillery will receive the enemy. Our infantry losses have been made up by count-less new formations. Reserve units, new formations and the *Volkssturm* are reinforcing our front. This time the Bolsheviks will suffer Asia's tra-ditional fate—i.e. they will bleed to death before the capital of the Ger-man Reich . . .

If every soldier on the Eastern Front fulfils his duty in the coming days and weeks, this final attack by Asia will fall apart, just as, in the end, the attack by our enemies in the West will also fail no matter what.

Berlin will remain German. Vienna will become German again and Europe will never become Russian . . . In this hour, the whole German nation looks to you, my warriors of the East, and only hopes that by your steadfastness, by your fanatism, by your weapons and under your initia-tive, the Bolshevik attack will drown in a sea of blood . . .[144]

From 17 April onwards the Russian superiority in men and *matériel* gradually began to gain the upper hand on the Seelow Heights. Zhukov concentrated his armour around the town of Seelow and near Wriezen on the northern slopes of the Heights, where the German defences were penetrated to a depth of 15 to 20km. On 18 April the Russians broke through. The Russian forces deployed around Seelow, includ-ing Chuikov's armies, advanced to within 30km of the Berlin city limits at Müncheberg. The picture now became clear: Marshal Zhukov's northern wing was in a position to encircle Berlin to the west and to link up with Konev's armoured forces advancing in the same direction from the south-west. If this were to succeed, Berlin would be enveloped and cut off. To the south, Marshal Konev had achieved a break-through on a broad front. The 1st Ukrainian Front had severed the link between Army Group Vistula (*Generaloberst* Heinrici) and Army Group Centre (*Generalfeldmarschall* Schörner) in Czechoslovakia. This was an even greater threat than Zhukov's penetration in the north, because if Konev's tanks could achieve the crossing of the Spree river, then they would meet only feeble opposi-tion on their way to Berlin.

The Russian spearheads reached the banks of the Spree at noon on 17 April, and within another three hours strong Russian advance units had crossed the river. Stalin gave Marshal Konev permission to advance on Berlin: 'Take your tanks to Berlin,' he cabled. Konev did so, following his advice:

Always forward, never look back; do not attack the enemy in his prepared defences. I do not want frontal assaults in any circumstances: bypass the enemy, deceive him, take care of your *matériel* and always remember that you must keep enough reserves for the final battle for Berlin.[145]

On 20 April Konev's 4th Armoured Guard Army advanced 45km against stiffening resistance. The Russians turned west, took the huge German supply depot and training camp at Jüterborg and reached Luckenwalde, 35km south of Berlin. General P. S. Rybalko's 3rd Armoured Guard Army further east found the going even easier and advanced 60km on the same day. The OKW at Zossen was now threatened. This caused *General* Krebs to ask Hitler for permission to abandon Zossen and to destroy everything of importance before it was too late. Permission was finally given, but by then it *was* too late. When the remaining staff fled Zossen ahead of the approaching enemy tanks, the telephone system was still fully intact and operations maps still hung on the walls. And while General Rybalko's tanks were taking Zossen and advancing to within 30km of Berlin, Marshal Zhukov was moving even closer to the city proper. His 2nd Armoured Guard Army took Bernau, only 15km to the north-east of Berlin, and from there advanced to Oranienburg, 30km north of the capital. Simultaneously an armoured column of Zhukov's left wing advanced to Fürstenwalde, 36km east of Berlin and in the rear of the German 9th Army.

This, together with General Rybalko's fluid advance to the north, threatened to cut off a major part of the 9th Army. *Generaloberst* Gotthard Heinrici, C-in-C of Army Group Vistula, therefore asked Krebs to obtain Hitler's permission to withdraw the 9th Army to positions closer to Berlin. Hitler, however, instructed Heinrici to order the Commander of 9th Army, *General* Theodor Busse, to hold his positions but to 'somehow' take care of his flanks.

In the meantime, in the north, beyond Zhukov's break-through, the 2nd Belorussian Front under Marshal Rokossovsky had joined the offensive and established several bridgeheads on the western bank of the Oder river between Stettin and Schwedt. In this way Rokossovsky intended to make his contribution to the encirclement of Berlin by occupying the plains of northern Germany. Russian armies were now enveloping Berlin from three directions.

After only four days of Russian advances, a deep breach opened up in the northern front of the 9th Army that had to be sealed by reserves hastily brought to Strausberg and Werneuchen. Simultaneously, however, the 1st Ukrainian Front with its two Armoured Guard Armies was advancing via Cottbus to the south of the 9th Army. With catastrophe looming ever closer, Hitler celebrated his 56th birthday on 20 April. Berlin itself hardly had time to commemorate the event, because from early morning until 2 o'clock at night more that 1,000 Allied bombers flew continuous waves of attacks and laid waste to whole swathes of the city. Moreover, for the first time Russian long-range artillery bombarded the city centre. The first shell exploded at precisely 1130 in Hermannplatz. Shoppers queueing in front of the Karstadt department store did not realise what was happening in time and the square was covered with dead and wounded.

Because Hitler did not rise until 11 a.m., the birthday reception for the Nazi dignitaries did not take place until the early afternoon, in conjunction with the military briefing. It was, however, more of a wake than a celebration. Albert Speer remembered:

> No one seemed to know what to say. In accord with the situation, Hitler accepted the congratulations in a cool, almost hostile manner.

This occasion was the last time the representatives of the Third Reich gathered together: *Generalfeldmarschall* Keitel, *Generaloberst* Jodl, *General* Krebs, *General* Burgdorf, *Grossadmiral* Dönitz,[146] *Reichsmarschall* Göring, *Reichsführer der SS* Himmler, Minister for Propaganda Goebbels, Foreign Minister von Ribbentrop,[147] Minister for Armaments Speer, Reich Youth Leader Axmann and Martin Bormann. All of them were extremely nervous and waited for Hitler's instructions as to when they would be permitted to leave Berlin and where they should go. Then the well-wishers dispersed, each in a different direction. The officials in the ministries did not fail to notice the exo-

A selection of newspaper articles which describe Hitler's 'escape and survival' in detail.

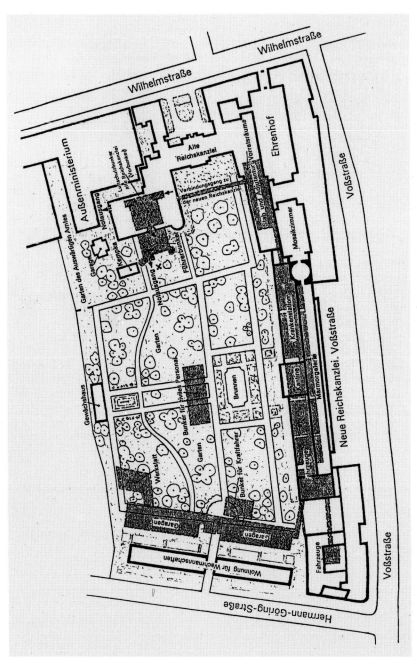

Diagram of the various air raid shelters within the Old and
New Chancelleries as in late 1944.

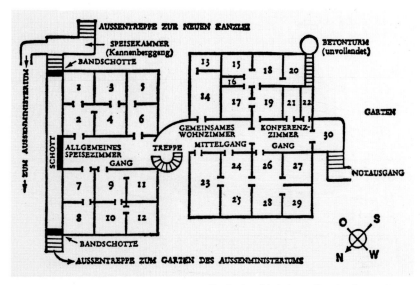

1946 drawing by H. Trevor-Roper of both air raid shelters (first bunker and *Führerbunker*): 1–4. Kitchen, pantry etc. 5–6. Storage rooms. 7–8. Servants' rooms. 9–12. Rooms of *Frau* Goebbels and children. 13. Electricity room. 14. WC. 15. Private bathroom. 16. Eva Braun's dressing room. 17. Eva Braun's bedroom/living room. 18. Hitler's office. 19. Antechamber to Hitler's private rooms. 20. Hitler's bedroom. 21.'Maproom' or small conference room. 22. 'Dog bunker' or dayroom for guards. 23. Machines (diesel generators). 24. Telephone and guard room (also used by secretaries). 25. Emergency telephone room and first aid station. 26. Living room. 27. Goebbels' bedroom (formerly used by Morell). 28–29. Stumpfegger's rooms. 30. Entrance and cloakroom.

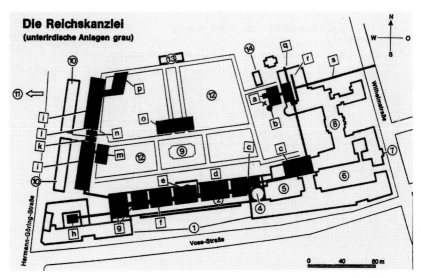

Plans of the air raid shelters in the Chancellery according to Cornelius Ryan (adopted by James P. O'Donnell and Uwe Bahnsen with non-existent 'underground passages'): 1. Hitler's Chancellery. 2. Marble gallery. 3. Hitler's office. 4. Round Room. 5. Mosaic Room. 6. Court of Honour. 7. Balcony. 8. Old Chancellery. 9. Fountain. 10. Apartments for guards. 11. To the Tiergarten (secret petrol depot; garages for twelve vehicles). 12. Garden. 13. Greenhouse. 14. Officers' quarters and Kempka's apartment. a. *Führerbunker*. b. Unfinished concrete tower. c. Bedrooms and duty rooms for adjutants and staff. d. Bunker for civilians. e. First aid room; surgery; dental surgery. f. Personnel. g. Washroom and canteen. h. Two cars and two armoured personnel carriers. i. Underground garages. k. Drivers' ready room. l. Hitler's Mercedes. m. Bunker for 80 drivers. n. Kempka's office. o. Underground shelter for ten vehicles. p. Workshops. q. To gardens of Foreign Ministry. r. Tunnel to Foreign Ministry. s. Tunnel to Propaganda Ministry.

Entrance to the Chancellery in 1940 as photographed by Hitler's personal cameraman Walter Frentz.

Entrance to the Chancellery, photographed by a Russian soldier in May 1945.

TIERGARTEN

GEWÄCHSHAUS

AUSSENMINISTERIUM

VERBRENNUNGSTELLE LINGE-
KEMPKA-HAUS

BUNKER-NOTAUS-
GANG FÜHRERWOHNUNG

FESTSAAL

WINTERGARTEN

ALTE
REICHSKANZLEI

NEUE REICHSKANZLEI WILHELMSTRASSE

An aerial view of the ruins and the terrain of the Chancellery in July 1945. Clearly
recognisable (circled) are the observation tower and the emergency exit from the
bunker in the garden.

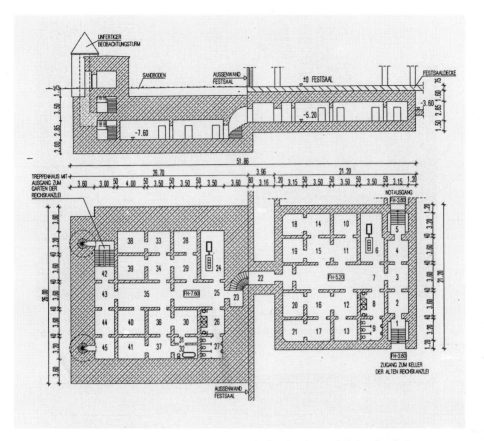

Plan and elevation of both air raid shelters (first bunker and *Führerbunker*):
1. Entrance. 2–4. Airlocks. 5. Emergency exit into the cellar. 6. Machine room. 7.
Canteen. 8–9. Toilets and washroom. 10–11. Bedrooms. 12–13. Kitchen. 14–15, 18,
19. Bedrooms (*Frau* Goebbels and children). 16–17, 20. Auxiliary apartments. 21.
Baggage room. 22. Passage. 23. Airlock. 24 Machine room. 25. Corridor. 26–27.
Toilets and washroom. 28. Telephone and telex. 29. Air plotting room. 30. Eva
Braun's bedroom. 31. Clothes closet. 32. Bath and toilet. 33. Bedroom. 34. Day
room. 35. Waiting room. 36. Antechamber. 37. Hitler's living room-cum-office. 38.
Doctor's room. 39. Bedroom (*Dr* Goebbels). 40. Briefing room. 41. Hitler's
bedroom. 42. Staircase. 43 Airlock and guardroom. 44. Guards' day room. 45.
Entrance to observation tower.

A photograph taken in July 1945 of the waiting room or antechamber in the *Führerbunker*. Schwägermann and Rach poured petrol on the furnishings and set them on fire.

In July 1945 the American GI John Shoemaker from Hattiesburg, Mississippi, visited Hitler's briefing room where the daily military briefings took place.

A view of Eva Braun's bedroom: the American GI Harvey Natchess takes a close look at the furnishings, 4 July 1945.

Hitler's sparsely furnished bedroom, July 1945. The American GI Shoemaker is standing in front of the bell-button on the wall with which Hitler could summon his manservant Linge whenever he wished. The safe has been opened by the Russians with a blow-torch.

Dr Goebbels with his six children in 1939. Goebbels had his children poisoned by Dr Stumpfegger on 1 May 1945.

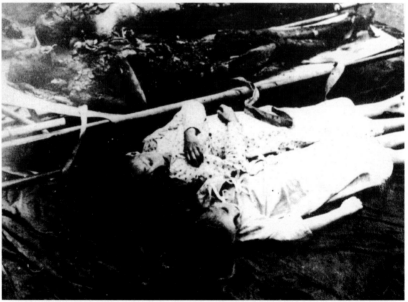

The bodies of two of the Goebbels children in the mortuary at the neurological clinic in Berlin-Buch in early May 1945. Behind them is the unrecognisably burnt corpse of Magda Goebbels and the body of *Dr* Joseph Goebbels.

A view of the Chancellery garden in the summer of 1948 showing the emergency exit and the observation tower in the foreground and the banqueting hall and the Foreign Ministry in the background.

This photograph, taken in mid-1949 at the corner of Wilhelmstrasse and Voss-strasse) shows the shattered remnants of the emergency exit from the bunker (circled) and the remains of the Chancellery after it had been blown up and demolished.

A 1988 photograph of the 3.5m thick reinforced ceiling of the *Führerbunker* which was dismantled piece by piece.

The former terrain of the Chancellery, showing the corner of Wilhelmstrasse and Voss-strasse and the location of the former *Führerbunker* (x) after the area was built up in late1994.

A July 1944 view of Hitler's bunker (*Führerbunker*) at the 'Wolfsschanze' headquarters. Between 23 February and 14 July 1944 the ceiling was reinforced to a thickness of 8m (!).

Hitler with Giesler and Ley on 9 February 1945 viewing the model of Linz in the bunker at the New Chancellery.

Hitler with Giesler, Kaltenbrunner and Linge viewing the model of Linz, 13 February 1945.

Hitler on 20 March 1945, on the way to greet members of the Hitler Youth who had distinguished themselves in the defence of Berlin. Left to right: Heinz Lorenz, Artur Axmann, Hermann Fegelein, Julius Schaub, Hitler, Otto Günsche (partly hidden), Wilhelm Burgdorf and Heinz Linge.

The last photographs taken of Hitler on 20 March 1945 in the garden of the Chancellery. Hitler is greeting Hitler Youth members who have been awarded the Iron Cross.

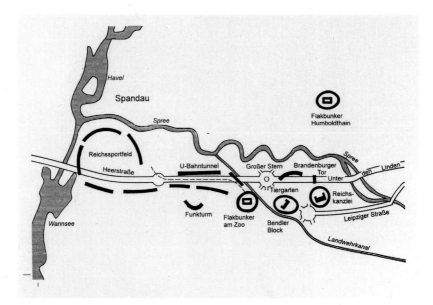

A drawing showing the last German resistance points in Berlin on 1 May 1945.

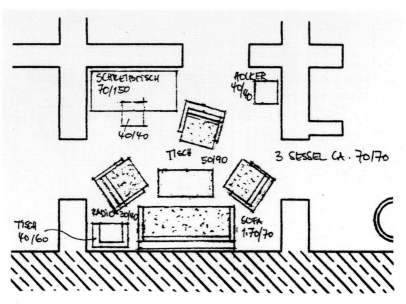

Furnishings of Hitler's living room-cum-office (3.5 x 3.2m) according to secretaries Wolf and Schroeder, showing furniture to scale.

dus of the Generals, but it was not until the evening that Bormann told Undersecretary Kritzinger that the senior administrative bodies of the Reich had to evacuate Berlin within two hours, otherwise the only remaining road south would be cut. On the morning of 21 April the Ministers of Finance (Ludwig, *Graf* Schwerin-Krosigk), Traffic (*Dr* Julius Dorpmüller), Justice (*Dr* Otto Thierack), Eastern Territories (Alfred Rosenberg), Education (Bernhard Rust), and Labour (Franz Seldte) left Berlin, as did *Dr* Otto Meissner, Chief of the Presidential Office. During the night of 21–22 April the road via Oranienburg was cut by the Russians. Only the road via Nauen was therefore still open to Hitler's fleeing ministers, but it too was under fire and was taken by Russian troops during the night of 22 April. With this, there was no road left leading west. Göring shook Hitler's hand and told him that he needed to leave to join Command Staff South in Berchtesgaden. Hitler allegedly only stared at him absent-mindedly and muttered a few trivial words. Albert Speer wrote later:

I was standing only a few feet away from them and felt I was experiencing a historic moment. The leadership of the Reich was parting company.[148]

Schaub testified on 27 October 1947 in Nuremberg that

Hitler was deeply disappointed, yes shattered, by the desire of his Paladins to abandon him now. He simply nodded his head and left the men he had previously elevated to such power without speaking a word.

The main topic of conversation during the afternoon briefing on 20 April had been how to maintain a unified political and military leadership if Russian and American troops were to split northern and southern Germany apart. As early as 15 April Hitler had ordered the creation of Command Staffs North and South if this were to come about. Now, on 20 April, the division of the Armed Forces Command into Command Staff A (North) and Command Staff B (South) ordered by Hitler came into effect. *Grossadmiral* Dönitz was to command in the north if Hitler were to be in the south, and *Generalfeldmarschall* Kesselring was to command in the south if Hitler were to be in the north. Hitler now made this directive partially operational and gave Dönitz far-reaching powers:

I charge the C-in-C of the Navy with the immediate preparation of the total mobilisation of all human and material possibilities for the defence of the Northern Area in case land communications in central Germany are cut. I empower him to issue all orders necessary for this purpose to all institutions of the State, the Party and the Armed Forces in this area.

[signed] Adolf Hitler[149]

With this, Hitler put Dönitz into a position of command, and it was also clear that the *Führer* would go south and take over command there. After the briefing Hitler left the bunker—probably for the last time—and went into the garden of the Chancellery. There he inspected a group of Hitler Youth who had been decorated for bravery in combat against the Russians. The scene was macabre: Hitler stroking the cheeks of children who had just barely escaped a senseless death, only to be sent back to the front so that the battle could go on for a few hours longer—the trusting faces of seduced and misused children, to whom he proclaimed that the battle for Berlin had to be won.

During the evening briefing it became clear that the defences on the approaches to Berlin had broken down. The closely concentrated spearheads of the Russian tank armies had torn the German front apart in several places. The 9th Army reported that the Soviet 1st Armoured Guard Army had advanced through Fürstenwalde to Highway 1 at Kagel and that the 2nd Armoured Guard Division had broken through from Prötzel via Werneuchen to Bernau. News of the capture of Bernau spread like wildfire through Berlin.

Towards 2200 on 20 April Hitler informed his personal staff, secretaries Wolf and Schroeder, adjutants *Admiral* Karl-Jesko von Puttkamer and Albert Bormann, six officers from the bodyguard, *Dr* Morell and *Dr* Blaschke, press attachés, stenographers, his favourite valet Wilhelm Arndt, cameraman Walter Frentz and others that 'the situation during the last few days has changed to such an extent that I am forced to reduce my staff'. Hitler also added that he would follow on to southern Germany. During the nights of 20 to 23 April three or four aircraft from the *Führer- und Kurierstaffel* flew a total of twenty flights to Munich, Salzburg and Ainring from the Berlin airports of Gatow and Staken (the last flight, at 3 a.m. on 26 April, took out Julius Schaub). One plane, a Ju 352 from the *Führerstaffel* piloted by *Major*

Gundelfinger, crashed near Börnersdorf during the night of 22 April with Hitler's servant Wilhelm Arndt, several men from the bodyguard, baggage belonging to secretaries Wolf and Schroeder, *Dr* Blaschke's baggage and the personal baggage of Hitler and Eva Braun on board. On 23 April Eva Braun wrote to her sister Gretl:[150]

> Did Arndt arrive with my letter and the suitcases? Here we have only heard that the plane is overdue. I hope Morell reached you safely with my jewellery. It would be really terrible if something had happened to it!

One can only say that the girl certainly did have her problems.

Stenographers *Dr* Haagen and Herrgesell stayed for one more day. On 22 April they recorded Hitler's decision to stay in Berlin and not to leave for the Obersalzberg as his entourage was suggesting he do. They then flew out during the night of 22 April. *Dr* Blaschke's dental assistant Käthe Heusermann[151] was also offered the chance to fly out. She declined—a decision she probably regretted many times during her stay of over ten years in Russian prisons:

> During the night of 20–21 April 1945 I was offered the chance to fly out to southern Germany. In Hitler's immediate circle the assumption was widely held that Hitler himself would also go to Berchtesgaden. I refused: I had no wish to go to Berchtesgaden with Hitler. At the time, I had an apartment in Berlin . . .

At 6.10 a.m. on 21 April the inhabitants of Berlin's northern suburbs were rudely awakened by Russian artillery fire. During the night Russian troops had crossed Highway 2 south of Bernau and now stood near Blumberg. Having been startled from his sleep by the gunfire, Linge woke Hitler up at 9.30 a.m., who then asked *General* Krebs where the fire was coming from. No one had expected the Soviets to advance so rapidly. During the morning the 3rd and 5th Soviet Attack Armies broke through the gap between CI Army and the LVI Panzer Corps of the 9th Army and advanced via Malchow-Niederschönhausen to Siegfriedstrasse in Lichtenberg and via Karow to Blankenburg and Blankenfelde. In the afternoon Buch was taken, and from the east Soviet troops advanced to Hoppegarten. At 1430 Keitel and Dönitz arrived for the briefing. Since 10.00 a.m. the Berlin city centre had been under heavy Soviet artillery fire. But it was the situation in the north of Berlin that occupied everyone's attention. Hitler and Krebs believed that the deep Russian penetration in the north offered a good chance for a counter-attack. The opinion was that this counter-attack could be carried out by the III Germanic SS Panzer Corps under *SS-Obergruppenführer* Felix Steiner. Steiner was also given command of everything remaining in Mecklenburg: *Panzerjäger* units, recruits, *Luftwaffe* auxiliaries, marines and a standby unit of the Reich Security Forces. At 1455 Chief of Staff Krebs informed the C-in-C of Army Group Vistula, Heinrici, of Hitler's strategic decision. In addition to Steiner's attack from the north, Busse's 9th Army was not only to establish a continuous front from Berlin through Königswusterhausen to Cottbus, but also to attack Marshal Konev's armoured forces that had broken through in its rear—a completely impossible assignment, but, as Jodl testified later, at the time Hitler was still determined to fight to the last:

> On 21 April Hitler said to me: 'I will continue to fight as long as I have a single soldier left. If the last soldier deserts me, I will shoot myself . . . I expected that the south would hold out longer than the north and therefore I sent the greater part of the staff to the south . . .'[152]

At 1650 on 21 April Hitler issued the order to *SS-Obergruppenführer* Steiner to attack for the relief of Berlin and also told him that he was making him responsible for the execution of his order at the price of his head. 'On the successful conclusion of your assignment,' Hitler wrote, 'depends the fate of the German capital.'[153]

Towards 2100 on 21 April fate also caught up with *Dr* Morell, who had been Hitler's physician since 1936. When Morell came to see Hitler together with *Dr* Stumpfegger, the *Führer* was sitting in his office in a tired, exhausted and depressed state. When Morell then suggested giving Hitler an injection of caffeine, Hitler shouted at him: 'Do you think I am crazy? You probably want to give me morphine!' Morell later testified: 'He knew that the Generals wanted to put him to sleep in order to cart him off to Berchtesgaden.' When Morell tried to reassure Hitler that he knew nothing about an intrigue, Hitler screamed: 'Do you take me for an imbecile?'[154] As Morell continues, Hitler then raved at him for some time and even threatened to have him shot. Finally he ordered Morell to go home, take off his uniform and 'act as if you had never known me'. Later on Morell allegedly 'cried like a baby': to his death in 1948 he never got over this farewell after he flew out of Berlin to Munich on 23 April.[155] Despite such clear evidence, O'Donnell and Bahnsen write on page 72 of their book *Die Katacombe*:

Hardly twenty-four hours had passed since personal physician *Dr* Theodor Morell had flown out to Bavaria, and one may assume that shortly before that he had injected Hitler with a further heavy sedative [!] . . .

On 22 April 1945 the increasingly heavy fire of the Soviet guns made Hitler get up at 9 a.m. The first briefing of the day took place at noon. It was the last that took place in a large group and also the shortest. Present were Keitel, Jodl, Krebs, Burgdorf and Bormann. The Chiefs of the Navy, *Luftwaffe* and SS, who had left Berlin in the meantime, were represented by their deputies, Dönitz by *Vizeadmiral* Hans-Erich Voss, Göring by *Generalmajor* Eckhard Christian[156] and Himmler by *SS-Gruppenführer* Hermann Fegelein. Foreign Minister von Ribbentrop was represented by Ambassador Walter Hewel.

The second briefing at 1550 on 22 April disclosed a hopeless picture. The Soviet forces in the north had advanced through Buchholz and Heinersdorf to Pankow. The front line was at Gesundbrunnen and in Bernauer Strasse. The Russian forces approaching from north and east had taken large parts of Lichtenberg and Friedrichsfelde, passed Mahlsdorf and Kaulsdorf and reached the northern border of Biesdorf. With this, the inner defensive ring around Berlin had been breached. In the south, Russian forces advancing from Luckenwalde and Zossen had reached Beelitz-Güterfelde and Stahnsdorf. The southern pincer of the Soviet encirclement was clearly discernible. A report by *General* Busse from the 9th Army stated:

The heavy fighting is characterised by the increasing exhaustion of the troops and irreplaceable losses of men and *matériel*.[157]

In the north, Soviet forces were now close to completing the encirclement of Berlin in Birkenwerder, Hohen Neudorf and Henningsdorf. When Hitler then asked about Steiner's Army Group he received conflicting answers, and when he demanded that the *Luftwaffe* check on

Steiner's whereabouts Krebs had to admit that no reports had been received and that Steiner had not yet launched his attack. As Steiner testified on 24 February 1948, he was unable to attack:

I didn't have anything to attack with. The three reserve divisions under my command in the Schorfheide had been ordered by OKW to support the desperate 2nd Army and had been swallowed up in a vain attempt to stop the Russian juggernaut rolling westwards. The two new divisions promised by Army Group Vistula never even arrived. I refused to employ the hastily assembled, inexperienced units. I did not want to lose soldiers in an operation that was doomed from the outset to fail decisively. The plan of attack was based on facts that no longer existed in reality but only in the fantasies of the Chancellery.[158]

Hitler, however, raved to the people attending the briefing about the failures and treachery of the Generals and then left the room as white as a sheet. Jodl later said:

On 22 April, shortly before the time set for flying out to the south, the *Führer* changed his mind and decided to stay in Berlin . . . When we reached the bunker on 22 April Hitler was in a highly excited state. He called me, Keitel and Bormann to him after Krebs had given his report and said he had decided to stay in Berlin. I replied that Berlin would fall within the next twenty-four hours. Hitler was very unhappy with the military operations for the defence of Berlin. He said that one could not give up the capital and that he would stay in order to inspire the soldiers . . .[159]

The fact that the SS had apparently betrayed him at the time of his greatest personal need was probably the final, decisive blow. According to the statement of *Luftwaffenoberleutnant* Volk, Hitler had screamed at those present at the briefing:

I regard the battle as lost and feel myself betrayed and deceived by those in whom I placed my trust, and I have decided to stay in the capital of the fight against Bolshevism and to take over the direction of the battle personally . . .[160]

Hitler then said that the others could go where they liked: he had no further orders for them.

This briefing was also described after the war by Hitler's adjutant Otto Günsche and by Julius Schaub. Günsche testified on 21 June 1956:

That Hitler intended to end his life if Berlin were to be lost I heard from his own mouth on 22 April 1945. On this day the report came in during the briefing at which I—as was always the case—was present that the northern Oder front south of Stettin had now also been broken. Upon hearing this, Hitler jumped up and left the room in great agitation, saying that under these circumstances there was nothing left to command and that he would stay in Berlin and shoot himself here.

There now followed urgent remonstrations by Keitel, Jodl, Dönitz [Dönitz was not in fact present], Bormann, Goebbels and Fegelein as well as Burgdorf, who went singly or in twos and threes into Hitler's private rooms, into which he had withdrawn after making the statements reported above. I was present during a part of these discussions. The gist of the remonstrations was that the situation was in no way hopeless. Recommendations for re-groupings to stabilise the front were made, the talk being mainly of the 12th Army (*General* Wenk), which was in the process of being formed, and also of Army Group Schörner and the formation of an Army Group Steiner.

Adolf Hitler declared his general agreement. The briefings then continued over the following days, with, however, far fewer and different participants, after the senior staffs had left Berlin. Shortly before 22 April preparations for moving headquarters to the Berchtesgaden–Reichenhall–Salzburg area had already begun. Between 22 and 25 April the bulk of headquarters was transferred to this region by truck and planes. Between 23 and 29 April Adolf Hitler received urgent requests from many sides, among others from Bormann, Goebbels, Speer, Ribbentrop, Axmann, *General* Weidling and even Göring (from him by radio) to leave Berlin. To all of these Hitler replied in the negative, in the sense that he would stay in Berlin and shoot himself here if the capital were to be lost . . .

On 22 March 1948 adjutant Julius Schaub said in Garmisch:

I was not in attendance during the briefing of 22 April 1945, but was in the antechamber [waiting room] when a great commotion broke out behind the locked door to the map room [briefing room]. Through the door I could hear a highly excited Hitler screaming in a cracking voice: 'The war is lost . . . I refuse to go on . . . My generals have deceived and betrayed me . . . It has all become senseless.' And, after a pause, he added: 'So that we understand each other, gentlemen, I no longer believe that Berlin can be relieved.'

Shortly thereafter the door was thrown open and Hitler, hunched and pale as a ghost, hurried across the hall into his living room without looking right or left. The participants in the briefing were left in the briefing room completely nonplussed and at their wits' end. Following this briefing a sort of feeling of disaster began to spread throughout all the bunkers in the Chancellery. Not that everybody ran around in despair, much less moaning and wailing, but everyone now knew that it was all over . . .[161]

The statements made by *Major* von Loringhoven on 13 March 1948 aptly describe the general sense of disaster in the Chancellery:

As far as I could see, most of the people spent the final days in their rooms. If they came out, they wandered about in the hallways, talked with each other and were avid to hear news from outside, particularly any news about a relief of Berlin. A major topic in all the conversations was when and how one was supposed to kill oneself.[162]

To the question 'Is that what people discussed?', von Loringhoven answered:

Yes, because most of the people had nothing left to do there. They all thought about this matter and considered suicide. They called the place 'the funeral parlour', i.e. in the bunker, and in the whole area they saw themselves as living corpses . . .[163]

All attempts by the people present, as well as those by Himmler and Dönitz, who had been informed by telephone, to get Hitler to change his mind were to no avail. Even Goebbels, who was also present, failed, while Ribbentrop, who had hurried to the bunker, was not even received by Hitler.

Luftwaffenoberleutnant Hans Volk, who had accompanied *Generaloberst* Christian to the briefing, testified after the war how

. . . they all seriously tried to get Hitler to change his mind and suggested moving troops from the west for deployment in the east. He answered that everything was falling apart anyway and that he could not do this: the *Reichsmarschall* [Göring] should do it later. To a remark by someone that not a single soldier would fight for the *Reichsmarschall*, Hitler replied: 'What do you mean, fight? There is not much left to fight, and when it becomes a matter of negotiations the *Reichsmarschall* is better at that than I am!' The most recent developments in the situation made a strong impression on him; he spoke about betrayal and failure everywhere, about corruption among the troops and in the leadership. Even the SS is now lying to him: Sepp Dietrich. Steiner did not attack, and that was the final straw . . .[164]

Jodl testified later:

> I was with Hitler until 23 April. That day the General Staff left Berlin. Hitler took the decision to stay in Berlin and send the rest of us way on 22 April. Up till then I had tried to get Hitler to go north or south because it was clear that southern Germany would be cut off from northern Germany. Hitler would not discuss it. We wanted to install independent commands in the south and north . . . That day Keitel and I had a discussion with the *Führer* lasting several hours, during which he said, among other things, 'I should not have left the "Wolfsschanze" after all . . .'[165]

And, finally, Keitel also testified later:

> On 22 April the *Führer* decided to stay in Berlin. He declared that he would not leave the city under any circumstances and would await the course of Fate while personally leading the troops. On this day the *Führer* made a very deep impression on me: up to then I had never had any doubts about his psychological stability. Despite the serious consequences of the assassination attempt on 20 July 1944, he was always in control of the situation. However, on 22 April it appeared to me that the *Führer*'s morale was deteriorating and that his inner resistance had been broken. He ordered me to go to Berchtesgaden immediately: the tone of the conversation was very harsh and matters ended with the *Führer* simply chasing me out of the room. On leaving I said to *Generaloberst* Jodl, 'This is the final collapse!'[166]

Later several people reported that Hitler collapsed after a fit of rage, others that he had done so because of the admission that the war was lost. If anything, it was most probably the latter.

Several witnesses have described Hitler's poor state of health during the final days and hours. He had turned grey, there were red spots on his cheeks, his stare was rigid and his eyes protruded and appeared to be lifeless. Even his manner of speaking had changed: he spoke in a very soft voice. His body was hunched over and he walked dragging his feet. The left hand, indeed the whole left side of the body, twitched. He had to hold his left hand with his right and cross his right leg over his left when seated in order to make the tremors less noticeable. When he wanted to sit down, a chair had to be pushed under him. On 10 September 1945 *Dr* von Hasselbach testified:

> During the final months his hair turned completely grey. Hitler's body bent over forwards (cyphosis of the spine), which was probably due to a

lack of any sort of physical activity. He refused to walk even short distances. A tremor of the head and the hands was clearly noticeable [films show only a tremor of the left hand], particularly when he lifted a cup of tea to his mouth or signed documents . . .[167]

Hitler's mind, however, stayed active. Despite the physical devastation, his energy and willpower remained unbroken to the end—something that must have astonished those who witnessed it from day to day. He fought against his physical decline with an incredible will and determination and rebelled against his fate to the very last, driven by the need to try to disguise his physical, psychological, political and military defeat.

After Hitler had realised that the war was lost and allowed members of his staff to depart as they pleased on 22 April, the High Command was suddenly gone and everyone expected chaos on the various fronts. Keitel, Krebs and Burgdorf tried to prop Hitler up and show him that the military situation was not completely hopeless. Jodl was also still present, and he probably had the clearest appreciation of the true situation. The others continued to discuss possible means of saving Hitler and Berlin. The suggestion was made to order the 12th Army, which was defending a 200km wide sector on the Elbe river against the Americans, to turn around and attack Konev's troops in the rear, break through the Russian lines and advance to Berlin. Hitler finally agreed and signed an order to Wenck, Commander of the 12th Army. Whether the 12th Army would be capable of saving the situation in Berlin was another matter entirely. It had only been formed at the beginning of April 1945, was poorly trained and had only very weak armoured forces. However, at 1720 Jodl issued the following order to *General* Busse:

> While covering its rear and flanks, the 9th Army is to attack westwards and establish a link with the 12th Army. It will depend on the performance of the 9th Army whether the enemy forces that have penetrated the defences of Berlin can be successfully cut off and cleared from the capital of the Reich, in which the *Führer* is residing with trust in his soldiers.[168]

Keitel and Jodl were then ordered by Hitler to leave the bunker and to lead the relief attack from outside Berlin. While Jodl was to gather all available forces outside Berlin and lead them into the battle, Keitel drove to 12th Army headquarters during the night of 23 April to try to bring about the link-up between the 12th and 9th Armies. Keitel said later, 'I tried to go back into the city on 24 April, was unable to land, however, and had to remain outside Berlin . . .' Actually Keitel probably did not want to go back into the 'mousetrap', as many at OKW now called Berlin, although landing on the East–West Axis between the Victory Column and the Brandenburg Gate was possible until 29 April.

According to the War Diary of Command Staff North, a radio message from Hitler to Dönitz was received in the evening of 23 April asking for help:

> 1915. Radio message to *Grossadmiral* Dönitz received in which the *Führer* describes the battle for Berlin as 'the battle which will decide Germany's fate'. Compared to this, all other assignments and fronts are secondary. Admiral is ordered to support this battle ahead of all other naval operations by flying troops into the city and bringing troops by water and land to the fronts around Berlin.[169]

Hitler next ordered that his personal papers and files were to be destroyed. He told his adjutant Julius Schaub to find petrol and burn the contents of his three safes. Otto Günsche stated on 20 June 1956:

> Petrol had been required once before and sent over on Kempka's request. On Hitler's orders, on 22 or 23 April, Schaub burned all of Hitler's personal papers in the garden about 20m from the garden exit. These consisted of a large quantity of personal notes, memoranda and the like, which Hitler had stored in his personal safes . . .

During his interrogation in Nuremberg on 24 March 1947 Schaub gave a detailed account. According to this, Hitler had given him the keys to his personal safes and had personally emptied the safe which stood at the foot of his bed in his bedroom in the bunker. Schaub said that this 'was stuffed with files, papers and letters'. Then the two safes in Hitler's still largely undamaged bedroom on the second floor of the Old Chancellery were emptied. The contents filled five large suitcases, which were carried into the garden by men from the bodyguard and there burned by Schaub with the help of petrol in a shell crater about 20 to 25m from the emergency exit of the bunker. According to Schaub's report, Hitler suddenly appeared at his side and stood silently looking at his burning papers and files that were going up in smoke and ashes like his collapsing *Reich*.

In the end there were only fifteen people left in the bunker: Hitler and Eva Braun, Goebbels with his wife and six children, Schwäger-mann, *Dr* Stumpfegger, Linge, Günsche and *Fräulein* Manziarly. In addition there were about ten men of the bodyguard. The others all lived in the bunker in Voss-strasse and came to the bunker when re-quired or when they wanted to. The confined conditions of living underground and the isolation from what was happening elsewhere in Berlin had made people apathetic. Night and day were the same in the bunker. The lights were on all the time. Apart from Eva Braun, the secretaries Christian and Junge and *Frau* Goebbels, no one went top-side anymore. People slept when and where they could find a place to sleep. Those in the *Führerbunker* were living in their own disinte-grating world, and, although they were still alive, they felt they had already been buried. But death, of which many of them had a premo-nition, was not mentioned in this indescribable atmosphere. Even though some of them later survived, in the final days no one believed that he would escape with his life. Years later Günsche said:

> I did not think I would survive either. But when the last moment came to quit this life one way or the other, somehow the step was not taken. Things start to look different then . . .

However, the oft-quoted '*Götterdämmerung*' in the bunker did not take place, according to the witnesses. Hitler was fully occupied with the immediate military defence of the Chancellery and the prepara-tions for this. On 21 June 1956 Günsche stated:

> In addition to my duties as Hitler's personal adjutant, I was Chancellery *Kampfkommandant* from the beginning of March to 22 April 1945, a po-sition that was then taken over by *SS-Gruppenführer* Mohnke . . .

On 22 April 1945 Hitler made Mohnke responsible for the defence of the Chancellery and appointed him *Kampfkommandant* of the 'Cita-del', the final innermost piece of ground over which Hitler still held power. On 26 April 1956 Mohnke made the following statement:

After a time spent in hospital due to being wounded—I was wounded seven times in all—I was then assigned to the *Führerreserve* in Berlin from 1 April 1945 onwards. During the night of 22–23 or 23–24 April 1945, following my own suggestion, which Hitler's personal adjutant *SS-Sturmbannführer* Günsche had made to Hitler on my behalf, I was ordered by Adolf Hitler to collect all available members of the *Waffen-SS* in Berlin, including the bodyguard, for the defence of the centre of the capital. I then carried out this order without delay and formed a total of 4,000 men of the *Waffen-SS* into '*Kampfgruppe Mohnke*'. I formed two regiments with battalions and companies which I then deployed immediately. Subsequently further small units or groups from the Army and the *Luftwaffe*, and finally also a company of 160 men from the Navy, were put under my command. In my command area there were also units of the Hitler Youth under Axmann. Of these, one company under an officer was engaged in fighting at Pichelsdorfer Bridge but the others were only used to bring up supplies and perform similar duties. I myself reported to the *Kampfkommandant* of Berlin. The *Kampfkommandant* was initially *Oberst* Bremer, and from about 27 April onwards *General der Artillerie* Weidling.

As well as to the *Kampfkommandant* of Berlin, I also had to report on all my activities and on the situation to *General* Krebs, who was responsible for the duties of Chief of Staff of the Army. From about 27 April I also had to take part in the regular briefings in the *Führerbunker*. My own command post was in the bunker under the New Chancellery . . .

On 23 April, at 15 minutes past midnight, a meeting between Jodl and the Chief of Staff of the *Luftwaffe*, Karl Koller, took place at OKW in Krampnitz near Potsdam. Koller had himself informed about the events in the bunker on 22 April and Jodl allegedly told him:

> We will turn the 12th Army around facing east for an attack against the left flank of the 3rd Armoured Guard Army, regardless of what the Americans on the Elbe will then do. Only by such an action may it be possible to prove to the others that we actually only want to fight the Soviets.[170]

General Koller felt that it was urgent that Göring be informed at the Obersalzberg about the events in the *Führerbunker*. Jodl agreed and at 0330 Koller took off from Gatow in a fighter plane to fly to Munich and from there drive to Göring by car.

After Hitler had agreed with Keitel and Krebs that the 9th and 12th Armies should mount a joint attack with the objective of relieving Berlin, Keitel personally drove to see Wenck. Keitel arrived at Wenck's command post in a hunting lodge in Wiesenburger Forest near Beelitz south-west of Berlin towards 1 p.m. On arriving, Keitel said, 'We must free the *Führer!*' He then explained the plan. The 12th and 9th Armies were to advance towards each other, unite south of Berlin and then fight their way clear from Potsdam into the capital. Despite not previously having received any orders, Wenck had already set such a plan in motion. Because of the relative quiet on the American side, he had pulled the Army back from the Elbe and started to deploy it against the advancing Russians. On 21 April the 12th Army had even beaten back a Soviet tank attack near Belzig. Keitel and Wenck agreed that the 12th Army should attack from the Treuenbrietzen–Belzig area and relieve Berlin.

Hitler's mood—after he had slowly begun to recover himself—had turned around over night. His imagination was particularly captured by the 12th Army, which stood only 60km from Berlin, and he sent telexes to Dönitz, Himmler and the *Luftwaffe* with orders to send reinforcements to Berlin. And on the morning of 23 April Krebs told Hitler that there were still several days before the Russian offensive against the inner city need be expected, because the major Soviet effort was concentrated on completing the encirclement of the city. On 23 April the front line in Berlin ran from Tegel through Humboldthain, from Wollankstrasse to the Friedrichshain underground station, along the elevated railway line from Landsberger Allee station to Frankfurter Allee and then to the Teltow Canal. Most of Pankow, as well as Köpenick, Adlershof and Karlshorst were already in Soviet hands. During the afternoon briefing at 1500, Hitler ordered that 'all available reserves must be put at Wenck's disposal, even if they are poorly armed, to fill the gaps. Nothing more need go to Steiner [who had not obeyed Hitler's orders].' Keitel answered, '*Jawohl*, my *Führer*. It shall be done.'[171]

On 23 April Armaments Minister Speer landed on the East–West Axis in a Fieseler Storch.[172] 'Hitler was particularly moved,' Schaub said later, 'that Speer had not only come in person to congratulate him on his birthday but that he came to him once again to say goodbye,' A flight into the centre of Berlin at this time was not without danger. In a very open exchange, Speer pleaded for Hitler to stay in

Berlin. A withdrawal to the Alps would now only look like a desperate, ridiculous attempt to flee. 'After a very emotional farewell,' said Schaub, Speer flew out of Berlin at 3.30 a.m. the following morning.

Hitler was himself very much aware that he could now no longer leave Berlin. Two days later he said during the briefing:

If fate were to decide otherwise, then I would disappear from the stage of world history as a dishonoured runaway. I would consider it to be a thousand times more cowardly to commit suicide on the Obersalzberg than to stand here and fall. No one shall be able to say, 'You, as the *Führer . . .*'

I am the *Führer*, as long as I can still lead. I cannot lead by going away and sitting on a mountain somewhere, but only if I have authority over armies who obey me. Let me win a victory here, and, be it hard and difficult, I will then again have the right to eliminate those sluggish elements that constantly do nothing but obstruct; then I will work with those Generals who have proved themselves. Only a heroic stance can enable us to survive these difficult times . . .[173]

While Hitler was talking to Speer, a telegram from Göring arrived. Göring had written this telegram with the help of Minister and Chief of the Chancellery Heinrich Lammers, and its purpose was to confirm his position as Hitler's successor and make it legally binding:

My *Führer*,
Are you in agreement after your decision to hold out in Fortress Berlin that, in accordance with the law of 29.6.41, I now take over the leadership of the Reich with all powers internally and externally? If I have received no reply by 2200 I will assume that you are no longer free to act and will therefore consider the conditions of your law as having been met and act on my own responsibility in the best interests of our country and our people. What I feel in this most difficult hour of my life cannot be expressed. May God protect you and I hope that you will still come here from Berlin.

Your loyal
Hermann Göring[174]

Even though Martin Bormann tried to convince Hitler that Göring had given him an ultimatum by setting 2200 as the deadline for an answer, Hitler is alleged to have reacted apathetically. This, however, suddenly changed when a telegram of 1759 from Göring to Ribbentrop was received:

I have requested the *Führer* to give me instructions by 2200 on 23.4. If by this time it becomes clear that the *Führer* no longer has the freedom to act as the Leader of the Reich, his edict of 29.6.1941 will come into effect, in which I as his deputy will succeed to all of his offices. If you do not receive any contrary order either directly from the *Führer* or from me by 2400 on 23.4.45, I ask that you come to me by air without delay.

Göring, *Reichsmarschall*[175]

It is worth noting here that on 19 March 1945—as was revealed after the war—Foreign Minister von Ribbentrop had already begun to explore the possibilities of a separate peace with the Western Allies through a secret agent in Stockholm. Hitler now signed the draft of a telegram to Göring that Bormann had put before him. In it, Hitler had Göring informed that his conduct constituted treason to National Socialism, which was punishable by death, but that the death penalty would not be carried out if he immediately resigned all of his offices and waived his right of succession. In Hitler's name, Bormann simultaneously ordered the Commander of the Obersalzberg, *SS-Obersturmbannführer Dr* Bernhard Frank, and *SS-Obersturmführer* Wilhelm von Bredow to arrest Göring and his staff. Göring was then taken to the SS camp in Salzburg and subsequently to his castle at Mauterndorf.

Towards 1800 the Commander of LVI Panzer Corps, *General der Artillerie* Helmuth Weidling, reported to the Chancellery to justify himself. Hitler had ordered him to be shot because he had allegedly moved the command post of the corps from the west of Berlin to Döberitz without permission. Weidling later gave the following description of his journey to Hitler's room in the bunker and the meeting with Hitler:

Another long walk through an underground passage to the *Führerbunker*, which lay about two storeys below the surface. Again, one check after the other. At one of the last guardposts my pistol and holster were taken from me. Through the kitchen we came into a sort of dining room in which many SS officers were having dinner. A further staircase downwards into the *Führer*'s waiting room. There were several men waiting there, among whom I recognised Foreign Minister von Ribbentrop.

Krebs and Burgdorf quickly led me into the *Führer*'s room. Behind a table with maps sat the *Führer* of the German Reich. When I came in he turned his head with the eyes of a person sick with fever towards me. The

Führer tried to get up. I noticed, to my horror, that his hand and one of his legs were twitching uncontrollably. With a great effort he managed to stand up. He gave me his hand with a distorted smile, his face like a grinning mask. After this the *Führer* sat down again in his armchair with great effort. Even when seated his left leg was in constant movement; the knee moved like the pendulum of a clock, only more rapidly . . .[176]

After the misunderstanding had been cleared up and a report on LVI Panzer Corps' situation had been given, Hitler put *General* Weidling in charge of the defence of the eastern and south-eastern sectors of Berlin:

I was allowed to leave. The *Führer* again tried to get up, but he did not succeed. He gave me his hand while seated. I left the room, deeply shattered about the physical condition of the *Führer* . . .[177]

On 24 April, towards noon, Weidling received a telephone call from *General* Krebs, who told him:

With your report yesterday you made a good impression on the *Führer*. He has appointed you *Kommandant* of the Defence of Berlin . . .[178]

Weidling replaced *Oberst* Ernst Kaether, whom Hitler had just appointed to this position on 22 April. He was supposed to beat back two and a half million Soviet soldiers with a hotchpotch of forces consisting of about 44,600 soldiers, 42,500 men of the *Volkssturm*, 3,500 Hitler Youth, some workers' battalions and members of the *Organisation Todt*—an impossible assignment. Weidling said later:

On 24 April I was already convinced that it was impossible to defend Berlin and that it was also senseless from the military point of view, because the German command did not have sufficient forces available . . .[179]

On 24 April Soviet soldiers of the 1st Belorussian Front linked up with those of the 1st Ukrainian Front in the south-eastern suburbs of Berlin. The 9th Army was now encircled by Russian troops. In the north of Berlin, the Soviets advanced via Kremmen and Velten to Nauen. The Tegel, Wittenau and Reinickendorf districts in the north and Rudow in the south-east were occupied. In Zehlendorf, Tempelhof and Neukölln heavy street fighting erupted and from their bridgehead at Schöneweide the Soviets advanced to Rummelsberg station. Vicious fighting was reported from Friedrichshain, in Frankfurter Allee, at Küstriner Platz and at the Silesian railway station. Towards noon a report was received in the bunker that Tempelhof airport was under Russian artillery fire and at 1700 Gatow airport reported that it, too, was receiving heavy shelling. During the night of 24–25 April the Chancellery came under heavy artillery fire. In the bunker, however, all sense of reality had disappeared, to such an extent that, during the evening briefing, Hitler was able to declare:

> In Berlin it looks worse than it is. The Berlin area must be fully utilised for people as far as this is at all possible. The divisions deployed in Berlin must be filled up from the population in any way possible. Collection units must be formed in order to gather everything in . . .[180]

And once again Hitler explained to those present why he had not gone to southern Germany:

> South-west Germany is fragile. It makes no sense at all to sit in the south because there I would have no influence, no armies. I would be there alone with my staff. Therefore the only possibility I see to recover the situation is to gain a victory at some point. And I can only gain a success here. And if I gain such a success, be it only a moral success, then at least that offers the possibility of saving face and gaining time . . .[181]

The Soviet forces of the 1st Belorussian and 1st Ukrainian Fronts linked up towards noon on 25 April near Ketzin. With this, the Soviet ring around the capital was complete. The Russians also took Alt-Glienicke, Tegel, Wittenau, Reinickendorf, Mariendorf and Lankwitz. They continued to advance towards Treptow and Britz, and towards 1300 near Strehla (Torgau), on the Elbe river, Soviet and US soldiers met. With this, the German Reich was split in two.

What was going on in Hitler's mind and what he was contemplating on 25 April 1945 can clearly be seen from his comments during the second briefing on that day:

> *Voss*: Wenck is coming, my *Führer*! The only question is, can he do it alone?

> *Hitler*: Just imagine. This will spread like wildfire throughout Berlin when it becomes known: a German army has broken in from the west and linked up with the fortress. The only thing the Russian can do is to keep throwing new things in, in order to try to hold his widely separated positions. This here will become a focal point of the first magnitude. The Russian

has used up a substantial part of his power in crossing the Oder, particularly the northern army group. Secondly, he is using up very many forces in the street fighting. If up to 50 T-34s or Stalins are destroyed every day, then this adds up to 500 to 600 tanks in ten days which are destroyed.

Tonight I am going to bed a little more at ease and wish only to be awakened if there is a Russian tank outside my sleeping cabin so that I have time to prepare myself.

With all this back and forth there is really no other way than this to inflict real damage on the enemy. We must hold Berlin, because here the Russian can be forced to bleed himself to death. What else would be able to stop the Russian if he were able to march through here smoothly? . . .[182]

After the evening briefing Hitler sent the following radio message to Jodl and Wenck:

The aggravation of the situation in Berlin and the encirclement of the capital which has meanwhile occurred require the most rapid execution of all relief attacks in the directions previously ordered. Only if the attack forces, concentrated with strength and determination, complete the breakthrough without regard for neighbouring forces and flanks will the 9th Army succeed in re-establishing the link to Berlin and destroying powerful enemy forces in the process.[183]

As can be seen from the War Diary of Command Staff North, a telex from Hitler arrived there shortly after midnight on 26 April:

0025: Received a telex by the *Führer* to *Generaloberst* Jodl and 12th Army. Most rapid execution of all relief attacks in the directions previously ordered urgently required. 12th Army is to deploy on the line Beelitz–Ferch and to continue attack in eastwardly direction without delay until link-up with 9th Army.

9th Army is to attack to the west by the shortest route and link up with 12th Army. After merging of the two armies, all will depend on destroying enemy forces in the southern part of Berlin by turning north and establishing a wide link with Berlin.[184]

On 26 April both sides engaged in the most vicious street fighting yet to occur. After Soviet forces had rapidly taken the suburbs in the north-east and east of the city, they ran into heavy resistance from German forces in the densely built-up sectors of the inner city. The Soviet soldiers fought their way along Frankfurter Allee metre by metre. On the morning of 26 April they occupied the area around

Andreas Square and by the evening they had reached the Schilling-strasse underground station and were close to Alexanderplatz. During 26 April the government sector and the Chancellery lay under such heavy Russian artillery fire that the ventilation in the bunker had to be shut down time and again because, despite the filters, smoke instead of fresh air kept being drawn into it. On the other hand, the news that two Ju 52 transport planes had landed on the East–West Axis led to outbursts of exuberance because they had brought reinforcements to Berlin. A drop in the ocean! Shortly thereafter fighter planes dropped supply canisters, which, however, could only partly be recovered by the troops. At 1800 Jodl had his last telephone conversation with Hitler. During this Hitler ordered him to make it clear to the 9th Army that 'it was to turn sharply north together with the 12th Army in order to relieve the fighting in Berlin'.[185]

The day before, on 25 April, Hitler had radioed an urgent order to *Generaloberst der Luftwaffe* Robert *Ritter* von Greim,[186] at the time C-in-C of the *Luftflotte 6* in Munich, to report to Berlin and the bunker, without giving him any further explanation. He intended to appoint von Greim as Göring's successor. Von Greim knew Hitler from the days of the so-called Kapp *Putsch* when he, as a young *Leutnant*, had flown Hitler to Berlin on 16 March 1920, Hitler's first trip by air, and had inexplicably become one of his most fanatical adherents. Greim took off from Munich during the night of 25–26 April 1945. He took along a friend of many years' standing, Hanna Reitsch, the famous test pilot and avid supporter of Hitler, as companion and co-pilot. They flew to Berlin in stages, first to Rechlin and from there to Gatow, where the runway was already pock-marked by Russian shells. Von Greim then changed to a Fieseler Storch to fly into the centre of Berlin. Immediately before the landing a shell tore open the belly of the plane and seriously injured von Greim's right foot. In the midst of the flying shrapnel, Hanna Reitsch took over the controls and landed the plane on the East–West Axis. There Reitsch commandeered an army vehicle which took her and the injured von Greim to the Chancellery. After his wound had been treated in the field hospital, Hitler promoted von Greim to become the last *Generalfeldmarschall* of the German *Wehrmacht* and appointed him C-in-C of the *Luftwaffe* in succession to Göring. Hanna Reitsch testified to this on 25 November 1954:

Coming from Gatow, I landed together with *Generaloberst Ritter* von Greim near the Brandenburg Gate in Berlin in a Storch on 26 April 1945 between 1800 and 1900. During the flight *Generaloberst* von Greim was wounded in the right foot by a tank shell. From the Brandenburg Gate we immediately went to the *Führerbunker* in the Chancellery in a truck. We remained there until 1.30 a.m. on 29 April 1945.

Upon our arrival, we were greeted by Adolf Hitler. *Generaloberst* von Greim received medical treatment in the field hospital of the Chancellery and was promoted to *Generalfeldmarschall* and C-in-C of the *Luftwaffe* by Hitler . . .[187]

At 2200 von Greim's promotion was announced on German radio. Von Greim was not angry that he had had to make this dangerous flight to Berlin for something Hitler could readily have told him by radio. Nor did his injury detract from his admiration for Hitler in any way. On the contrary, both von Greim and Hanna Reitsch asked for permission—which Hitler granted—to stay in the bunker and go down with him.

When General Weidling then drew attention to the catastrophic situation in the city during the afternoon briefing on 26 April—lack of ammunition, desertion by members of the *Volkssturm*—and recommended a break-out, Hitler immediately declined. He supposedly said to Weidling that he had no intention of being caught in the woods as a runaway.

At 2212 hours *Vizeadmiral* Voss sent the following message by naval radio link to *Grossadmiral* Dönitz:

In battle for Berlin encouraging successes. Army Wenck from SW and 9th Army from SE. Also Attack Group Steiner making progress from the north. In inner city aggravation of the situation, particularly government sector under continuous heavy artillery fire and bombs. *Führer* expects operations outside Berlin to alleviate situation in the city. All possible measures must be undertaken most urgently. In my opinion the next 48 hours will be decisive.[188]

On 27 April the Soviet forces advanced ever closer to the government sector. They took Tempelhof and Gatow airports as well as

Spandau and penetrated into Schöneberg and Kreuzberg. From Charlottenburg in the north-west and Tempelhof in the south, Russian troops continued to advance into the centre. The bloodiest fighting occurred at the Tiergarten bunker (AA shelter) and at Alexanderplatz between Neuer Königsstrasse and Dirsenstrasse and at the Halle Gate. For the second day now, the Chancellery lay under unremitting heavy fire by Russian guns. Hitler complained that he could not even sleep any more. 'If one really does fall asleep, then the shelling starts,' he is supposed to have said.

The relief attempts by the forces under Holste and Steiner were beaten off and these forces were then deployed by Jodl against the Soviet troops advancing via Prenzlau. With this, the battle for Berlin in the north was over for the OKW. Bormann wrote in his diary:

Friday 27 April
The divisions marching to our relief are being detained by Himmler and Jodl!
   We will stand and fall with the *Führer*, faithful unto death. Others believe they have to act 'from higher understanding': they sacrifice the *Führer* and their treachery—ugh, how disgusting!—is akin to their 'sense of honour'![189]

On 28 April Hitler and Krebs, in the bunker, realised that relief from the north by *Generalleutnant* Rudolf Holste's and *SS-Obergruppenführer* Felix Steiner's corps could no longer be expected. Krebs therefore sent the following message to Jodl at 2.17 a.m.:

It remains mandatory to bring comprehensive attack for the relief of the capital to a successful conclusion by all means and with greatest urgency by utilisation of all forces fighting between Elbe and Oder rivers. As compared to this decisive task, engagement of enemy breaking into Mecklenburg must wait.[190]

Then Krebs called Keitel towards 3.00 a.m. and asked him several questions. Keitel would still not admit that the attempts to relieve Berlin from the north had failed and only said that one had been forced to withdraw one division. The following exchange then took place:

Krebs: What concerns the *Führer* most is the attack to the west of Oranienburg. What is the situation there? Is the attack making progress? The *Führer* refuses to have Steiner in command there!!! Has Holste taken over command there? If we do not receive any help within the next 36 to 48 hours it will be too late!!!

Keitel: . . . We will push Wenck and Busse with utmost energy. There the possibility for relief exists by advancing north.

Krebs: The *Führer* expects most urgent help. There are only 48 hours left. If no help has arrived by then, it will be too late! The *Führer* asked me to repeat that again!!![191]

The 9th Army, however, was encircled and had been split in three by the Soviet forces. On the morning of 28 April it reported:

Break-through attempt failed. Only attack points with valuable units apparently broke out to the west against explicit orders. Other attacking units stopped, partially overthrown, with heavy losses.[192]

General Busse and a part of the 9th Army were able to break out to the west, but the rest of the 9th was destroyed a few days later with heavy loss of life in the Halbe area.

The depressed and increasingly more hopeless atmosphere in the bunker—there was no news from Wenck's 12th Army either—come through clearly in a telegram Martin Bormann sent to Munich:

Instead of driving on the troops that are to relieve us with orders and appeals, the key men remain silent. Loyalty seems to be giving way to treason. We will stay here. Chancellery already in ruins.[193]

And in his diary Bormann wrote:

Saturday 28 April
Our RK [Chancellery] is becoming a pile of ruins: 'The world now rests on the point of a sword'.
 High treason—unconditional surrender is announced abroad.
 Fegelein disgraced—attempted a cowardly flight from Berlin in civilian clothes.[194]

On top of all this, at 5 a.m. on 28 April the radio link between the bunker in Berlin and OKW in Rheinsberg (the Neu-Roofen camp) broke down. Until 1630, when short-wave radio contact was re-established, there was only haphazard contact with LVI Panzer Corps in Berlin.

At this point something needs to be said about the communications links between the Chancellery—Hitler's bunker—and the various military institutions. As already mentioned, when *Führer* headquarters was transferred from East Prussia to Berlin on 20 November 1944, Hitler did not move into the Zossen camp because he reportedly did not consider it to be adequately protected against bombs. Thus the leadership of the German armed forces command became fragmented. As Supreme Commander Armed Forces, Hitler—and therefore *Führer* headquarters—was in the Chancellery and later in the bunker. The Command Staff and the General Staff of the Army (the actual working staffs) were in the 'Zeppelin' camp in Zossen. The Chief of OKW (Keitel) and the Chief of the Command Staff (Jodl) lived in different villas in Berlin-Dahlem, each having a small staff. Generals and their staffs had to travel back and forth between Zossen and Berlin, frequently several times a day, and the whole communications system had to be reorganised. This was particularly the case after the Red Army broke through on the Oder and encircled Berlin.

Initially, communications between the various command groups was taken over by 'Section 500', the large armed forces telephone exchange at 'Zeppelin' in Zossen. Until it was captured by the Soviets on 20–21 April 1945, this functioned well and permitted telephone contact to army posts on all fronts. But as the war moved deeper into Germany, the links were no longer secure and there was a fear of conversations being tapped.

After Zossen was lost, the telephone links from Berlin to the staffs of the armed forces could no longer be used. At the same time (see below), on 22–23 April the Army's communications unit left the Chancellery. Total chaos in communications began to develop and during the final days things reached the point where the bunker was poorly informed and could only maintain contact to OKW with great difficulty. During the night briefing of 27 April an incensed Hitler remarked about this:

> It must be possible to contact the 9th Army. There is radio contact for half an hour a day. Tito communicates with his partisans throughout the whole of the Balkans by short-wave.[195]

Schaub testified during his interrogation at Nuremberg on 7 December 1946:

Radio contact from the bunker to the outside became worse and worse during the final days. There was only a naval radio team still operational in the cellar of the Propaganda Ministry on the other side of Wilhelmstrasse. Contact was only possible by courier. They had to make their way through debris and under fire to carry and fetch messages. There was no longer any contact with the offices and command posts throughout the city. No one knew who was still there or where they were . . .

Based on the evidence, the following reconstruction can be attempted. After Hitler's return from the Ardennes offensive, a Navy radio unit was added to the Army team in the Chancellery, which was to maintain contact with *Grossadmiral* Dönitz and later with Command Staff North (A). On 23 April a directional radio link to OKW and the Command Staff at Zossen was quickly installed, which permitted telephone calls to be made up to 29 April.

Between the middle and the end of April there were therefore the following communications installations in the Chancellery:

(a) The short wave directional radio link
From the Berlin radio tower only a few kilometres from the bunker—which was linked to the bunker by a cable running via the anti-aircraft bunker in the Tiergarten—a short-wave (10cm) directional beam was aimed at a balloon floating 100 to 200m high at Rheinsberg, about 60km away. Through this link only telephone conversations between the bunker and the Armed Forces and Army Staffs could be held. Krebs' adjutant von Loringhoven later described this link:

The OKW, Keitel and Jodl were able to talk directly with Army Group Vistula, with Wenck, with the forces fighting against the Americans and the British, with our forces in Italy etc. by radio. We in the bunker in Berlin, however, only received our news second-hand from Rheinsberg from OKW. And if we wanted to speak with someone we had to tell OKW, who then transmitted our message on. I could not talk to anyone else, only to OKW near the balloon, and that was often difficult. It was impossible to say much because reception was very weak. I often talked via this link. The radio tower was only a few kilometres from our bunker and the balloon was not far from OKW, but, as I said, reception was sometimes very, very poor . . .[196]

Until 29 April this link worked with difficulty. Around 1250 on that day the balloon was shot down during an air raid. From that point on there was no longer a direct link between Hitler's bunker and OKW. Both Keitel and Jodl later confirmed this:

> I was in contact with *Führer* headquarters by short-wave directional radio until 29 April. I did not talk directly to the *Führer*, but I received repeated orders and questions from Hitler through *General* Krebs, in which he demanded a speeding-up of the relief effort by the 12th and 9th Armies, an immediate counter-attack etc. After the equipment had been lost I received no further messages from Hitler's headquarters . . .[197]

Jodl testified later:

> Until 1230 on 29 April I was in telephone contact with Berlin. My last telephone conversation with Hitler took place on the evening of the 28th or the morning of the 29th. The last radio message with Hitler's signature was received during the night of 29–30 April . . .[198]

(b) The Army communications unit

This unit was part of *Führer* headquarters, had the required equipment and Army radio codes and was able to establish radio contact with OKW, all the various Armies and other armed forces installations. But when it was really needed, that is, after the cable link became non-operational, it was no longer there. Von Loringhoven testified in Nuremberg on 13 March 1948:

> I do not know why, during the night of 22–23 April, when Hitler's staff [secretaries, stenographers, bodyguards etc.] began to disperse, the Army communications unit, which was a part of Hitler's headquarters, suddenly disappeared. I do not know who gave them the order to leave Berlin [which was shortly to be encircled], but they were suddenly gone and we no longer had direct radio contact with OKW. It became very difficult to issue orders or to ask questions with regard to the military situation, because we no longer had an Army communications unit. Bormann's party transmitter was still there, which we then used. This was very difficult, however, because Party radio traffic used a different code from that of the Army.
>
> Until the encirclement of Berlin was complete there were of course still telephone links, but thereafter the cable links were gone because the Russians destroyed them, or else they were not secure, because we did not know whether the Russians had occupied the relay stations and could listen in on everything we said . . .

Q: How did it come about that no one anticipated the difficulties of communications as they then occurred towards the end of April in the bunker in Berlin? Why was a transmitter not installed there?

A: All these difficulties could not be anticipated because, as I have mentioned already, I too thought that the Army communications unit would stay in *Führer* headquarters. It belonged to Hitler's headquarters and suddenly this unit disappeared, just like Schaub and *Dr* Morell and all those other people.

Q: Would you have had radio contact if they had stayed?

A: Most certainly. They had a large transmitter and with it we were able to contact all the armed forces. We could transmit to OKW, to Dönitz, to Army Group Vistula, to Italy and Kesselring, wherever we wanted.

Q: Did Hitler know that the unit disappeared?

A: No, that was a matter that was never completely cleared up—who had actually given the order that the unit was to leave during the night.

Q: I am surprised that he did not have someone shot. After all, this was a very serious matter.

A: Yes, but the man who could have been held responsible was the special communications officer in Hitler's headquarters and he had gone too, and there were no other military people who could have been made responsible except Chief of Staff Krebs or Burgdorf. They told Hitler that they had never given an order that this gentleman and his unit could leave . . .[199]

(c) The Navy communications unit

The Navy communications unit was only stationed in the Propaganda Ministry in April 1945 and was the only one that worked dependably until the very end. It used new, previously unissued two-way codes that offered maximum security. On 24 April Bormann requested that Dönitz reinforce the unit with additional men and the Armed Forces Command Staff also requested the formation of further such mobile naval units. In the Chancellery it was under the command of *Vizeadmiral* Voss and the final messages from the bunker on 30 April and 1 May were all sent by him to Dönitz through the naval communications unit.[200]

(d) The Party communications unit

As Chief of the Central Party Office, Martin Bormann had his own communications unit (Party radio), with which he maintained contact to the *Gauleiter* throughout the Reich. The Party radio used its own code, which was different from those of either the Army or the Navy. When, for example, Hitler began to mistrust Keitel and Jodl on 29–30 April 1945, Bormann contacted Dönitz in Plön via his Party radio link to Hildebrandt, the *Gauleiter* in Mecklenburg, to inform him that Keitel was under suspicion and that Dönitz should take quick and ruthless action against all traitors.

Apart from these four communications systems, there was an indirect link to the communications unit of LVI Panzer Corps in Berlin, which was very difficult to use because it could only be activated by means of couriers and the communications equipment of the Press Officer.

A lot of nonsense has also been written about all this. One need only to read what O'Donnell and Bahnsen write on page 37 of *Die Katacombe*, where they claim that the Army communications unit was in the bunker long after it had gone, they make no mention at all of the Navy communications unit, they forget Bormann's Party radio and they even insist that Press Officer Heinz Lorenz regularly attended the military briefings, even though he is not listed once in the minutes as having been present.

The vicious street fighting in Berlin continued throughout 28 April and Soviet troops penetrated the final defensive ring in Berlin, the so-called 'Citadel'. They reached Königsplatz to the north of the Chancellery, crossed the Landwehr Canal and advanced to Potsdamer Platz, to the Halle Gate and to Belle-Alliance-Platz. In the south of Berlin, the Red Army took Grunewald, Ruhleben and Friedenau. Now the major part of the capital was in Soviet hands. On 28 April the *Wehrmacht* reported:

> The heroic fight of the city of Berlin once again demonstrates to the world the fateful battle of the German nation against Bolshevism. While the capital is being defended in a grandiose struggle that is unique in the annals of modern history, our troops on the Elbe have turned their backs

on the Americans in order to relieve the defenders of Berlin by an attack from outside.

The enemy has penetrated the inner defensive ring from the north in Charlottenburg and over the Tempelhof Field in the south. The battle for the city centre has begun at the Halle Gate, at the Silesian Station and at Alexanderplatz. The East–West Axis is under heavy fire . . .

In the bunker, 28 April was characterised by the lack of any news— owing partly to the break-down of over ten hours in the directional radio link—of the activities of the 9th and 12th Armies, on which, however, great hopes for the relief of Berlin were still pinned. In the rooms of the German Press Office (DNB) under its chief Heinz Lorenz, one of the latter's members of staff, Wolfgang Beigs, was monitoring foreign radio broadcasts. The 28 April morning news bulletin from Radio Stockholm reported that *Reichsführer der SS* Heinrich Himmler had proposed a surrender to the United States and Great Britain. However, the two Allies had rejected Himmler's offer, because only a general surrender including the Soviet Union was acceptable. At 1650 Hitler reacted to this information by asking Dönitz whether there was any truth in the matter. The *Grossadmiral* knew nothing and at 1720 telephoned Himmler, who is alleged to have said, 'this information is false', however, he 'did not want a denial broadcast over the radio but simply to have the message ignored'.[201]

But Himmler was lying: in fact he *had* tried to make contact to the Western Allies. On 12 February 1945 he had met the Swedish diplomat and President of the Swedish Red Cross, Count Folke Bernadotte, who he hoped would be willing to act as a go-between for himself and the Americans. After a further meeting on 2 April they met for the third time on 21 April in the sanatorium of *SS-Arzt Dr* Karl Gebhard. At this meeting Himmler promised to release prisoners held in concentration camps. After Hitler's briefing of 22 April, in which the *Führer* had thrown in the towel, Himmler again met Bernadotte on 23–24 April in the Swedish consulate in Lübeck. There he is alleged to have said that Hitler was as good as dead and made further promises. He asked Bernadotte to arrange separate negotiations with the Western Powers via the Swedish government. This time, without giving Himmler any great hopes, Bernadotte agreed to pass on his written request to his government for transmission to the Western Allies. On 26 April, however, the Allies turned Himmler's proposal down.

Shortly before 2100 on 28 April a report by Reuters, broadcast by the BBC, was received in the bunker which confirmed the news report from Stockholm and added that 'Himmler had informed the Western Allies that he could initiate an unconditional surrender and would guarantee this personally'. This news cut Hitler to the quick. His 'loyal Heinrich' had betrayed him and was already posturing as his successor! He regarded Himmler's action as treason and a personal betrayal. Hitler immediately charged *Generalfeldmarschall* von Greim, who had wanted to commit suicide in the bunker with Hitler and Hanna Reitsch, to fly to Dönitz in Plön without delay and to make sure that Himmler did not escape his just deserts. At the same time von Greim was to assure Dönitz that the remnants of the *Luftwaffe* supported the German counter-offensive. In the meantime, however, the Fieseler Storch in which both of them had flown in from Gatow had been destroyed by shellfire near the Victory Column. A new plane was summoned from Rechlin airfield. At midnight on 29 April a *Luftwaffe* pilot landed an Arado trainer on Charlottenburg Chaussee between the Brandenburg Gate and the Victory Column in what can only be termed a masterpiece of aeronautics and took von Greim and Hanna Reitsch back to Rechlin. Reitsch then flew von Greim to Plön, where, in accordance with Hitler's orders, he sent the *Luftwaffe*'s last remaining aircraft into the battle for Berlin. He also confronted Himmler, who testified later that von Greim had 'reproached' him.

Shortly after midnight—von Greim and Reitsch were still present—Hitler had *SS-Gruppenführer* Hermann Fegelein, the Waffen-SS liaison officer (and soon to be his own brother-in-law) shot for desertion and complicity in Himmler's treason by security troops under *SS-Obergruppenführer* Johann Rattenhuber.[202]

In this context one further point needs to be dealt with. In a White Paper published on 25 April 1956 by the Swedish government covering Himmler's attempts to conclude a peace deal with the Western Powers through mediation by the Swedes, one reads, among other things, that

In the autumn of 1944 Stockholm learned of plans by Himmler to depose
Hitler and initiate peace negotiations . . .

Going through Christine Schroeder's shorthand notes, I found the
following entry:

7.7.1947

I had to go a second time to have my teeth x-rayed in the city hospital in
Ludwigsburg. I had a short meeting with Stenger [?] and had him call
Erich Kempka, with whom I then again spoke at some length.

I asked him about Fegelein's death. F. allegedly left the Chancellery,
had himself driven to his apartment on the Kurfürstendamm and then
sent the car back. He was then looked for. Eva spoke with him on the
phone and pleaded with him to come back immediately in order to reha-
bilitate himself. When Fegelein could not be found, Martin Bormann is
supposed to have said, 'It is not enough to have loyalty stamped on one's
belt-buckle: one must also have it in one's heart!' Fegelein allegedly told
Kempka that there was a briefcase in the bunker [he probably meant the
bunker in the new Chancellery, where Fegelein had a room] with important documents. If Fegelein were not to return from his reconnaissance
trip in time and the Russians were approaching, Kempka was to destroy
the briefcase . . .

The briefcase contained papers about the *Reichsführer*'s (Himmler's)
negotiations with Switzerland (1944) and Sweden. The courts-martial then
assembled and handed down the death sentence, which was executed
immediately in the Tiergarten . . .

Even though I am very sceptical about some of Kempka's statements, I have the feeling that these events explain Hitler's order to
have Fegelein summarily shot. Kempka did not repeat his statements
about Himmler's 1944 negotiations in his book. As a member of the
SS, he apparently did not want to appear guilty of fouling his own
nest. Nevertheless, there can be no doubt that Himmler put out feelers
for peace negotiations from mid-1944 onwards, in order to try to save
his own skin and without regard for his oath of loyalty, adherence to
which until death he ruthlessly demanded from his subordinates to
the end. As late as March 1945, for example, Himmler issued the
following order to the *SS-Freiwillig* Panzer-Grenadier Division 'Nord-
land und Neederland':

You are engaged in the decisive battle in the East. There is no going back or evading. You have to hold to the last man or attack. The fate of Europe rests in your hands. Think of your dead comrades and of the millions of Germanic women and children. I expect you to fight ruthlessly and do your duty to the utmost.

[signed] H. Himmler[203]

Towards 4.45 a.m. on 29 April Martin Bormann sent identical telegrams to Dönitz, Keitel and *Generaloberst* Heinrici, saying:

Foreign press reports new treason. The *Führer* expects you to intervene like lightning and with an iron hand, without regard to persons.[204]

What had made Hitler so immeasurably furious about Himmler's betrayal can be seen from a letter to *General* Wenck of the 12th Army which is in Bormann's handwriting and was sent off that evening (but did not, in fact, reach Wenck):

As can be seen from the attached reports, *Reichsführer-SS* Himmler has proposed to the Anglo-Americans to deliver our nation unconditionally into the hands of the plutocrats. A turn-around can only be achieved by the *Führer*, and by no one else but him![205]

However, neither Dönitz nor Keitel, nor Heinrici, made any move against Himmler. For the German leadership slowly assembling in Flensburg, unity was more important for the moment, because otherwise they feared complete chaos.

From then on, Hitler only attended to his personal affairs. He decided to marry his companion of many years, Eva Braun. The marriage took place towards midnight on 28 April. The ceremony was performed in the bunker by Walter Wagner, a member of the city council and head of the *Gau* Office who had worked for Goebbels and who had been brought to the bunker in an armoured personnel carrier. Goebbels and Bormann acted as best men and Hitler's immediate circle, Goebbels and his wife, Hitler's secretaries Christian and Junge, *Generäle* Krebs and Burgdorf, *Oberst* von Below and Hitler's cook Constance Manziarly offered their congratulations around 1.30 a.m. It was not a large celebration, and in former times Eva Braun probably had other ideas about her wedding day.

Afterwards—towards 2 a.m.—Hitler dictated his personal and political wills to secretary Gertraud Junge. On 24 February 1954 she testified:

As his secretary, I worked for Hitler every day until the end and, like the other three personal secretaries, was also present at all meals. The other secretaries were *Frau* Christian, *Fräulein* Wolf and *Fräulein* Schroeder. *Fräulein* Wolf and *Fräulein* Schroeder left Berlin on 21 April 1945. In the final days Eva Braun also regularly took part in the meals, as did occasionally also the cook, *Fräulein* Manziarly.

The majority of Hitler's immediate staff left Berlin on 20 and 21 April. On 22 April a further group of Hitler's entourage were flown out or taken south in motor vehicles. That day Hitler urged me and *Frau* Christian as well as *Fräulein* Manziarly to leave Berlin as well and talked about a last aircraft. This disclosure was made directly after the briefing during which Hitler had declared that a relief of Berlin was now no longer to be thought of. This remark of his was immediately reported to me by one or more of the participants in this briefing. In connection with his suggestion that we now leave Berlin, Hitler told *Frau* Christian, *Fräulein* Manziarly and me —in the presence of Eva Braun—that he would depart this life. The suggestion to leave Berlin was, by the way, also explicitly directed at Eva Braun. Eva Braun, *Frau* Christian and I, as well as *Fräulein* Manziarly, rejected this suggestion without hesitation and declared that we would stay on to the end.

The immediate cause for Hitler selecting the time of his suicide had probably been the news about Himmler having entered into negotiations with Bernadotte. Hitler declared that this step by Himmler was treason and said that apparently Himmler wanted to hand him over to the enemy alive. He said as much on 28 April. It was during lunch or dinner.

The same day and during the night of 28–29 April 1945 respectively, the marriage with Eva Braun and the conclusion of the wills took place. I had learned of the intended marriage during the day [28 April 1945] through a hint dropped by Eva Braun.

Shortly after supper began, in which *Dr* Goebbels, *Frau* Goebbels and Bormann took part this evening, Hitler asked me to take some dictation. He immediately took me into the briefing room (also called the conference room). Here he first dictated his personal will and then his political testament. I took the dictation down in shorthand, which was completely against his usual practice, because he normally only dictated directly into the typewriter. The dictation began shortly before midnight. In the political testament the names of the future members of the government remained open. While I was transferring the shorthand into typewriting, Hitler came in several times to ask about the progress of the work—which, by the way, was also completely against his normal practice. While I was then typing the clean copies Goebbels or Bormann also came in alternately to give me the names of the ministers of the future government. Goebbels also dictated a personal statement to me that was to be attached to Hitler's will. My work was finished by 5 a.m. In the meantime the marriage had taken place.

There were three copies of each will. Hitler took the clean copies. His signature and those of the people acting as witnesses were added without my being present.

29 April 1945 then passed without any notable occurrences. Everyone was visibly at pains not to talk about Hitler's impending death. On this day I learned from Günsche that one was only waiting for confirmation that the wills, which had been taken out by couriers to three different recipients, had been received . . .

Hitler's last personal will was a simple document. He declared that he and his wife were committing suicide in order to 'avoid the shame of running away or surrendering'. He was leaving his personal property to the NSDAP, or if this no longer existed, to the German State. The will goes on: 'Should the State also be destroyed, no further decisions by me are required'. In his political testament, Hitler rejected any blame for the war and put it on those 'international statesmen who were either Jewish or who worked for Jewish interests'. He saw himself as the victim of disloyalty and treason. He named a successor government with *Grossadmiral* Dönitz at its head as Reich President. Goebbels was to succeed Hitler as Chancellor and Bormann was appointed Party Minister. The traitors Himmler and Göring were condemned and thrown out of the party, but Albert Speer was named in the cabinet. Hitler demanded of the new government that it continue the war by any and all means and also pursue Hitler's personal war against all his enemies. In order to underline the importance of this rejoinder, he again mentioned the principle to which he had dedicated his life: hatred of all things Jewish. This remarkable document closed with a declaration that, in Hitler's opinion, formed the guideline for any good government: 'Unrelenting opposition against the poisoner of all nations, international Jewery!'

Shortly after 5 a.m. Bormann, Goebbels and *General* Krebs signed the political testament and Bormann, Goebbels and *Oberst* von Below the private will. Prior to this Goebbels had had secretary Junge write a codicil to Hitler's private will. In it he renounced his appointment as Chancellor. He declared that he would not leave the bunker to head up the new government, even if this was to be the first time that he refused Hitler obedience: 'In the midst of the delirium of treason surrounding the *Führer*, there must be at least a few who stand by him unconditionally and unto death'. Goebbels' wife Magda, who believed fanatically in Hitler, was also prepared to share his fate. The decision by the couple to commit suicide was also the death sentence for their six children, who had moved into the bunker with their parents on 22 April 1945.

At 8 a.m. *General* Burgdorf ordered *Major* Willi Johannmeier to take a copy of Hitler's wills to *Generalfeldmarschall* Schörner, Bormann sent *SS-Standartenführer* Wilhelm Zander to Dönitz with a copy and Goebbels had Heinz Lorenz's adjutant take a copy to the Brown House in Munich.

In the early hours of 29 April the Soviets launched their all-out offensive against the centre of Berlin. Fighting was already in progress on Kurfürstendamm and on Bismarckstrasse and Kantstrasse. The front line was now only 400m from the Chancellery.

During the briefing at noon on 29 April Weidling, the *Kampfkommandant* of Berlin, reported to Hitler that the Soviet forces had begun an encircling attack on the remnants of the 'Citadel' from three sides—from Alexanderplatz, from the Tiergarten and from Potsdamer Platz. Resistance, he said, could not be maintained much longer.

After the briefing *Major* von Loringhoven (Krebs' adjutant), *Rittmeister* Gerhardt Boldt (Krebs' orderly officer) and *Oberstleutnant* Rudolf Weiss (*General* Burgdorf's adjutant) were ordered around 1330 to break through to *General* Wenck's 12th Army and ask for the immediate urgent relief of Berlin. They never reached Wenck. Von Loringhoven and Boldt managed to get through the Russian lines but Weiss was captured.

Hitler ate lunch at around 1400 as usual in the company of secretaries Christian and Junge. On 3 July 1954 *Frau* Christian recalled:

On 29 April I took part in the meals as usual. Nothing was spoken about Hitler's intention to quit this life nor about the manner in which this was to take place . . .

The *Wehrmacht* gave a report about the fighting in Berlin on 29 April 1945:

The fanatical house-to-house fighting in the city centre of Berlin is raging day and night. The brave garrison is defending itself in a bitter struggle against the unremittingly attacking Bolshevik masses. Despite this, a further penetration of individual city sectors by the enemy could not be prevented. Across Potsdamer Strasse and at Belle-Alliance-Platz heavy street fighting is going on. The enemy is pushing forward from Plötzensee to the Spree [river].

To the south of Berlin the Soviets are bringing in new forces against our attacking divisions, who are engaging them with varying results. Beelitz has been retaken and a link to the defensive perimeter of Potsdam established. Attacks against the eastern flank of this advance have been bloodily beaten back north-west and south-west of Treuenbrietzen.

Shortly before the afternoon briefing at 1600 Hitler gave *Dr* Werner Haase and the dog handler *Wehrmachtsfeldwebel* Fritz Tornow orders to poison his dog Blondi. After Himmler's betrayal, Hitler now mistrusted *SS-Arzt Dr* Stumpfegger and also the prussic acid ampoules he had brought with him from Himmler. The almost 2m tall SS man Stumpfegger was completely shattered by Hitler's mistrust and, according to several witnesses, withdrew from his presence. Hitler wanted to avoid at all costs the possibility that his dog should fall into Russian hands. The thought alone, he once said to his secretary Christine Schroeder, was enough to make him sick. Hitler loved the dog very much. Albert Speer probably hit upon the truth when he said:

The German shepherd dog probably played the most important role in Hitler's life: it was more important than even his closest associates.[206]

As *Frau* Schroeder reported later, during the final days in the bunker Hitler often said, 'Animals are more loyal than people', and when he looked at the picture of Frederick the Great while drinking tea in his living room he kept quoting Frederick's remark, 'Since I have learned to know man, I love dogs.' Even Eva Braun did not have the same importance for Hitler as the dog. She was angry that Hitler now only talked about dogs and she often did not appear at the nightly (morning) teas which Hitler took with his secretaries. *Frau* Schroeder told me that the two stays in Berlin at the beginning of 1945 were very disappointing for Eva Braun for several reasons. Hitler, who had been living as an even stricter vegetarian for over a year because of his stomach cramps, tried to convert Eva Braun as well. Schaub testified in Nuremberg in 1947 that 'Eva Braun shared his vegetarian fair'. However, Eva Braun is alleged to have told *Frau* Schroeder:

> We have the same argument every day and I simply can't eat that stuff. And besides, this time everything is so much different from before. I had looked forward very much to Berlin, but now he is so changed. The Boss only talks to me about the dogs and food. I'm often really fed up with Blondi. Sometimes I give the beast a good kick under the table and Adolf is then amazed at the crazy antics of the animal. That is my revenge.[207]

Speer also recalls the daily walks at *Führer* headquarters in the 'Wolfs-schanze':

> When taking a walk, Hitler was normally not interested in his companion but only in his dog Blondi . . .[208]

The dog often slept in Hitler's room. Even during the First World War, when Hitler had his first dog, the terrier Foxl, which had crossed over from the British lines, he had said, 'It is of key importance that a dog always sleeps with its master.'

Goebbels gave a detailed description of Hitler's relationship to his dog in an entry in his diary dated 30 May 1942:

> He [Hitler] has bought himself a young German shepherd dog called 'Blondi' which is the apple of his eye. It was touching listening to him say that he enjoyed walking with this dog so much, because only with it could he be sure that [his companion] would not start talking about the war or about politics. One notices time and again that the *Führer* is slowly but surely becoming lonely. It is very touching to see him play with this young German shepherd dog. The animal has grown so accustomed to him that it will hardly take a step without him. It is very nice to watch the *Führer* with his dog. At the moment the dog is the only living thing that is constantly with him. At night it sleeps at the foot of his bed, it is allowed into his sleeping compartment in the special train and enjoys a number of

privileges . . . that no human being would ever dare to claim. He bought the dog from a minor official in the post office in Ingolstadt . . .

The dog had whelped at the beginning of April and was now nursing five puppies. As Schaub and the secretaries reported later, Hitler was very attached to the puppies and personally fed them several times a day. The dog and her little ones had a run in the bathroom of the bunker and during the final days of his life Hitler spent much time with them. He often took up one of the puppies and then sat on the upholstered bench in the waiting room silently holding it without paying any attention to his surroundings. As already mentioned, Hitler talked a lot about dogs during these days. In the final hours of his life they were more important to him than people—who had only betrayed and deceived him.

Contrary to later claims, Hitler was not present when *Dr* Haase and Tornow forced open the dog's mouth and crushed one of Hitler's prussic acid ampoules in its throat with a pair of pliers. Günsche testified on 21 June 1956:

> On 29 April the effect of the poison was tried out on his dog Blondi on Hitler's orders. *Professor* Haase administered the poison by crushing a phial in its throat with a pair of pliers, while dog handler *Feldwebel* Tornow was holding it open. The dog then fell dead as if struck by lightning. I was personally present when this took place. Adolf Hitler was not present, but came to look for himself immediately afterwards and to take his leave of the dog. The same poison was probably also used for the Goebbels children: *Dr* Stumpfegger told me on 1 May 1945 that he had poisoned the children at the urging of their parents . . .

Fräulein Junge later said of Hitler, after he had seen his dead dog, 'His face was like his own death mask. He locked himself into his room without a word.'

Later on Hitler attended the routine briefing. When one considers it, the scene was unbelievable: there sat the Supreme Commander of the German Armed Forces at a briefing, having absolutely no idea about what was happening at the various fronts because he had no communications to his OKW. Towards 1625 *Vizeadmiral* Voss asked *Grossadmiral* Dönitz for a situation report at Hitler's request via the Navy communications unit, because all other links had been cut:

All external links with Army cut off. Urgently request information on battle outside Berlin by Navy radio.[209]

A short time later a radio message from *Generaloberst* Jodl was received, which in essence said:

The OKW knows nothing about the 9th Army. We believe Wenck's 12th Army to be near Potsdam and OKW can only report a hasty withdrawal westwards by Army Group Vistula.[210]

When Soviet forces then approached the Neu-Roofen camp in Rheinsberg towards 1900, the OKW withdrew to Dobbin, where a radio message from Berlin arrived:

1931: Radio message from *General* Krebs and *Reichsleiter* Bormann to *Feldmarschall* Keitel received. According to this, foreign press is spreading new treason. The *Führer* expects you to intervene lightning quick and with an iron hand without regard for persons. From Wenck, Schörner and others the *Führer* expects proof of their loyalty by most urgent relief of Berlin.[211]

During the evening briefing at 2200 all Hitler received was further messages of disaster. In Berlin the Soviet troops were moving ever closer to the Chancellery. Mounting confusion and increasing despair about the relief of Berlin prevailed. Towards 2230 Hitler received the news that Benito Mussolini and his mistress Clara Petacci had been shot by partisans and that their bodies had been hung upside down at a petrol station on the Piazzale Loreto in Milan, where the people had beaten and thrown rocks at them. This confirmed Hitler in his resolve to commit suicide so that his body could be burned before the Soviets got hold of it.

Since there was no longer any clear appreciation of the fronts and the two Armies (9th and 12th) in the bunker, Hitler had had a radio message sent to Jodl at 2010, which however was only received at OKW at 2300 because of the poor communications. Hitler now wanted to know 'immediately' and in as few words as possible:

Report to me immediately:
1. Where are Wenck's attack points?
2. When will they continue to attack?
3. Where is the 9th Army?

4. In which direction is the 9th Army breaking through?

5. Where are Holste's attack points?[212]

It appears that Hitler and Krebs still believed in the relief of Berlin. But this hope had to be buried after the most recent events and after a situation report from the 12th Army was received at 2330:

> The Army, and particularly XX Corps, which was able to establish a link with the Potsdam defences for a period of time, has now been forced into the defensive along its whole front to such an extent that a further advance towards Berlin is now no longer possible, especially since support by the forces of the 9th Army can no longer be counted upon.[213]

From midnight on 29 April the relief of the capital by *General* Wenck, Hitler's last hope, could no longer to be expected. Hitler's end had come. He had only sixteen hours left to live.

4. The Suicides

In the *Führerbunker* the morning of 30 April began with a shattering message from *Generalfeldmarschall* Keitel. At 2.57 a.m. he sent an answer from OKW headquarters in Dobbin to Hitler's questions of 29 April, 2300, which said, without mincing words:

1. Attack points Wenck stopped south of Lake Schwielow.
2. 12th Army can therefore not continue attack towards Berlin.
3. Mass of 9th Army encircled.
4. Corps Holste forced on to the defensive.[214]

Keitel summarised the completely hopeless military situation with the words 'Attacks towards Berlin not advanced anywhere'. With this, the OKW had to all intents and purposes given up the battle for Berlin. Hitler now knew for certain that a relief of the encircled capital could no longer be expected, and he prepared himself for his suicide.

By 1.30 a.m. Hitler had already said goodbye to some of his remaining staff. *SS-Unterscharführer* Maximilian Kölz of the bodyguard testified on 24 November 1954:

From the foot of the stairs I saw Hitler saying goodbye to his entourage during the night of 29–30 April 1945. The people present were: *Dr* Goebbels; *Frau* Goebbels; Bormann; *General* Burgdorf; *General* Krebs; Rattenhuber; Högl; *SS-Gruppenführer* Mohnke; *Vizeadmiral* Voss; *Dr* Stumpfegger; State Secretary Naumann;[215] Ambassador Hewel; *Flugkapitän* Baur; *Flugkapitän* Beetz [he meant Betz]; Manzialy, Hitler's cook [he meant Manziarly]; *SS-Obersturmbannführer* Schedle [he meant Schädle]; [and] *SS-Hauptsturmführer* Beermann.

I saw that Hitler shook each person's hand. If something was said, what this was I do not know. If something had been said, I could not have heard it because of the noises caused by the machines. The electric generator and the ventilation equipment were running simultaneously, both driven by diesel engines.

Immediately following this scene, one of the participants told me that Hitler would now shortly kill himself. This information did not surprise me in the least: in recent days we older officers had reached the conclusion that the relief [of Berlin] could no longer be counted upon . . .

SS-Gruppenführer Mohnke recalled this farewell on 26 April 1956:

During the night of 29–30 April I was present when Hitler took leave of a number of his closer associates in the central hallway of the *Führerbunker*. Adolf Hitler shook each person's hand and expressed his thanks . . .

A further participant in the leave-taking was *SS-Oberscharführer* Erwin Jakubeck, one of Hitler's servants. He recalled on 23 November 1954:

From March 1938 onwards I was constantly in the personal employ of Adolf Hitler as a waiter. In 1943 I was drafted. I received an eight-week basic training in the *Führer* bodyguard, which, however, did not affect my duties with Hitler. During the final period I had my quarters in the Voss-strasse bunker, where the secretaries also lived . . . During the night of 29–30 April 1945 I was present when Hitler said goodbye to his staff. There were about twenty people present. Hitler said that he did not want to fall into the hands of the Russians and had therefore decided to take his own life. He was releasing us from our oaths. It was his wish that we should reach the English or American lines. He thanked us all for our service. Hitler shook hands with each of us . . .

In Munich on 6 February 1948 Musmanno had already questioned Jakubeck about this occurrence and Jakubeck had said that Hitler had taken leave of about 20 to 25 people from his staff at around 2 a.m. on 30 April, mostly servants (four) and guards (bodyguards and security guards). This had taken place in the hallway of the upper bunker, and Hitler had said the following:

In view of Himmler's treason, I do not wish to be taken prisoner by the Russians and displayed like an exhibit in a museum, and I have therefore decided to take my own life and I now say goodbye to all of you. I herewith release each of you from his oath and it is my wish that you make an effort to reach either the English or the American lines, because I do not want any of you to fall into the hands of the Russians, just as I myself do not want to fall into their hands.

Then Hitler thanked them with the words:

> And I now also want to thank you all for the services you have rendered me.

Towards 2 a.m. Hitler then took his leave of *Dr* Werner Haase and *Dr* Günther Schenk and thanked them, and also said goodbye to several nurses who worked in the field hospital in the Voss-strasse bunker, apologising for having 'roused them at such a late hour'. *Dr* Blascke's dental assistant *Frau* Heusermann recalled this leave-taking on 27 April 1956:

> On the evening of 29 April 1945 [it was actually the morning of 30 April] I was present when Adolf Hitler took leave of a larger number of people in the upper part of the *Führerbunker*, especially members of the medical staff. He shook each person's hand . . .

Keitel's devastating reply to Hitler's questions about the military situation had caused a great feeling of depression in the bunker. Hitler now also began to mistrust Keitel and Jodl. During his trial in Nuremberg Jodl testified concerning his relationship with Hitler on 16 October 1946:

> I never held any affection for him, but I often admired him and more often did not understand him. I never had a personal relationship with him, only a working relationship. I was never included in his private circle. He hardly ever made a personal remark to me, except after the death of my first wife and during the final days in April 1945 in the bunker in Berlin, after he had already chosen death . . .
>
> He never admitted to having made a mistake; no one ever heard him say 'So you were right after all!' He probably never even admitted to himself that he had made a mistake! His belief in his talents and in his mission was too strong for that. He believed in himself and in his mission: if something went wrong, the reasons could only be someone else's failure. He came to the conclusion that the SS, the armed forces, especially the *Luftwaffe*, [and] many of the old fighters in who he had placed his trust—Göring, Sepp Dietrich, Himmler, etc.—had deceived or betrayed him . . .[216]

This explains Bormann's message to Dönitz in Plön via *Gauleiter* Hildebrandt in Mecklenburg, which on Hitler's orders he sent at 3.15 a.m. by the still functioning Party radio transmitter:

Dönitz! It is becoming ever clearer to us that the divisions in the combat sector of Berlin have been marking time for many days instead of blasting the *Führer* free. We only receive information that is being monitored, suppressed or coloured by Teilhaus [by Teilhaus he means Keitel]. In general we can only transmit via Teilhaus. The *Führer* orders you to take measures against all traitors immediately and ruthlessly.

[signed] Bormann[217]

A postscript contained the sentence, 'The Führer lives and leads the defence of Berlin.'

On the last day of his life Hitler only had about three hours of sleep. At 5 a.m. Soviet artillery again opened up on the government district. It had by now zeroed in on the Chancellery and took it under constant fire. According to several witnesses, the intensity of the fire varied. Sometimes there was interdictory fire with rounds coming in every three minutes, sometimes barrage fire with constant shelling lasting for about an hour.

Hitler next called the *Kommandant* of the Chancellery, Mohnke, to report to him in the bunker and asked him how much longer the Chancellery could hold out:

Towards 6 a.m. on 30 April I was called on the telephone to report to Adolf Hitler. Dressed in a bathrobe and slippers, he asked me in the ante-chamber to his office how much longer I could hold out. I spoke of one to two days. The Russians were at Potsdamer Platz, less than 400 metres from the Chancellery, they had reached Wilhelmstrasse and the greater part of the Tiergarten and they had penetrated the subway tunnels under Friedrichstrasse. Hitler listened to me without interrupting, then gave me his hand in parting and said, 'All the best. I thank you. It was not only for Germany!' The meeting was over towards 6.30 a.m. and I returned to my command post . . .

Towards 8 a.m. heavy aimed artillery fire against the Chancellery began and the fear of an impending Russian ground attack mounted. The guards in the Chancellery, at the entrances to the bunkers, at the air locks and in the corridors, were increased. The corridors in the bunkers were barricaded by SS men. Hand grenades and sub-machine guns were distributed to the members of the bodyguard and the security guards.

During the morning Bormann sent a further message to Dönitz, this time in Navy code via the naval communications unit of *Vizeadmiral* Voss:

New treason afoot. According to enemy radio *Reichsführer* has made surrender proposal via Sweden. *Führer* expects you to act against all traitors with lightning speed and as hard as steel.

[signed] Bormann[218]

Dönitz, however, had no intention whatsoever of having Himmler arrested. As he said later, for him

... the maintenance of order was the most important thing in view of my responsibility. And what was the sense of the order, that I should proceed 'lightning quick and hard as steel' against the *Reichsführer*, who still held command over his police and SS forces? I had no means whatsoever with which to do this ... I could therefore not proceed against Himmler by force. Nor did I want to, because the result would only have been chaos. My decision was therefore easily and quickly made. I asked Himmler for a meeting. I wanted to know what he was playing at. We agreed to meet in a police station in Lübeck ... In the police station in Lübeck all the senior SS officers who could be reached had apparently been assembled. Himmler kept me waiting. He seemed to feel that he was already the head of state. I asked him whether the information was true that he had tried to contact the Allies via Count Bernadotte. He declared that this was not true. Furthermore, he too was of the opinion that now, at the end of the war, no additional chaos should be created by disunity. We parted amicably ...[219]

In other words Dönitz and Himmler reached an agreement that 'unity was the primary need of the hour'.

Towards noon Hitler's last briefing began. *General der Artillerie* Weidling, the *Kampfkommandant* of Berlin, came over from his command post in the bunker in Bendlerstrasse, seat of the Supreme Command of the Armed Forces, and reported that Soviet troops were storming the *Reichstag*, that there was fighting in the Red City Hall, that the Friedrichstrasse station had been reached by Soviet stormtroopers and that the Russians had penetrated the tunnel in Vossstrasse. Later, Weidling testified at length:

I went to the briefing with a heavy heart. As usual, I first reported on the enemy's activities and then on the situation of our own forces. I spoke about the vicious fighting that had taken place during the preceding twenty-four hours, about the compression into a narrow space, the lack of ammunition, the lack of anti-tank rockets—an indispensable weapon in street fighting—about the declining supply by air and the sinking morale of the troops . . .

In my summary I clearly stressed that in all probability the battle for Berlin would be over by the evening of 30 April, because, based on the experiences during recent nights, a large-scale supply by air could no longer be counted upon.

A long silence then occurred, which this time none of those present felt the need to interrupt. In a tired voice the *Führer* then asked *Brigadeführer* Mohnke whether he had gathered the same evidence in his command area of the 'Citadel'. Mohnke answered in the affirmative . . .

I again mentioned the possibility of a break-out and drew attention to the general situation. Like a man who has completely resigned himself to his fate, the *Führer* answered me while pointing to his map, on which the situation had been entered.

First of all, the positions of our troops had been entered on to the map on the basis of reports by foreign radio broadcasts, because our own staffs were no longer reporting them; secondly, since his orders were no longer being obeyed anyway, it was senseless to expect anything, for example help from the 7th Panzer Division, which, according to its orders, was supposed to have attacked from the Nauen area.

With the intention of allowing me to depart, the completely broken man got up from his armchair with great effort. However, I urgently requested that a decision be taken in case our ammunition were to be completely exhausted, which would happen no later than tomorrow evening. After a short exchange with *General* Krebs the *Führer* replied that only then could a break-out in small groups be considered because he, as before, refused to surrender Berlin. I was now allowed to go . . .

While I was still considering how *General* Krebs and *Brigadeführer* Mohnke could be informed about such a decision [a break-out by small groups at 2200 in the evening], an *SS-Sturmführer* from Battle Group Mohnke arrived towards 1600 and brought me a letter from the *Führer* that he was to hand to me personally . . . The letter said that, if the ammunition ran out, small groups were to break out of the encirclement. Hitler still flatly refused a surrender, as he had always done before . . .[220]

Against all expectations, in the end Hitler approved a break-out by the remaining forces, if ammunition were to run out. Hitler now signed the last '*Führer* order' of his life, which he then sent to Weidling in his command post in Bendlerstrasse:

To the Commander of the Defence of Berlin,
Gen. d. Art. Weidling.
In the event of ammunition and supplies to the defenders of the capital being in danger of running out, I give my permission for a break-out. The break-out is to take place in small groups, which are to attempt a link-up with forces still fighting elsewhere. Where this is not successful, the fight is to continue in the forests.

[signed] Adolf Hitler[221]

Hitler sent an identical written order to the *Kampfkommandant* of the 'Citadel', *SS-Gruppenführer* Mohnke. Mohnke testified on 26 April 1956:

Shortly after 1500 on 30 April I received an order, signed by Hitler personally, that I should break out of Berlin either as a unit or in small groups if the development of the situation made further resistance appear to be impossible. The same order was also sent to General Weidling . . .

On 30 April 1945 the *Wehrmacht* reported on the military situation in Berlin:

The heroic struggle for the centre of the capital continues with unabated ferocity. Troops from all branches of the armed forces, Hitler Youth and *Volkssturm* are holding the inner city in bitter house and street fighting. A shining symbol of German heroism. The enemy, who had broken in at Anhalter station, along Potsdamer Strasse and in Schöneberg, was stopped in his tracks. Air force units again dropped ammunition over the city at great sacrifice to their crews.

South of Berlin our divisions deployed for the relief of the capital are engaged on their extended flanks with strong Bolshevik forces that have been beaten back with heavy, bloody losses . . .

After the noon briefing on the catastrophic military situation—the Russians were only a few hundred metres from the bunker—Hitler decided that the time had come to end his life and so informed Bormann. Otto Günsche testified to this on 20 June 1956:

On 30 April 1945 Bormann informed me, towards noon, that Hitler's decision was now final: he would shoot himself today. Eva Braun would also commit suicide. The bodies were to be burnt. Bormann told me this in the central hallway of the *Führerbunker*. He had just left Hitler's rooms. Bormann then told me that I was to make the preparations and carry them out.

Shortly after this I met Adolf Hitler in the antechamber to his office. He then also told me, himself, that he would now shoot himself and that *Fräulein* Braun would also depart this life. He did not want to fall into the hands of the Russians either alive or dead and then be put on display in a freak show, meaning in Moscow. The bodies were to be burnt. He was charging me with the necessary preparations. The way he expressed it, I was to be personally responsible to him for this! I then assured Adolf Hitler that I would carry out his orders. This conversation took place in great haste. Towards the end of the conversation Rattenhuber, Baur and Beetz [he meant Georg Betz, Hitler's second pilot] had also come in . . .

According to *SS-Gruppenführer* Johann Rattenhuber, Chief of the RSD (Reich Security Service), Hitler even gave Günsche a written order that his body was to be burnt. Rattenhuber testified on 26 November 1955:

On 30 April a further personal letter written by Hitler was given to me by Günsche to read. This letter was addressed to Günsche and also personally signed by Hitler. It said that Hitler's body was to be burnt. When giving me this letter, Günsche said that Hitler wanted to avoid at all costs his corpse being put on display . . .

I did not make any personal observations concerning the immediate circumstances of Hitler's death. Around 22 April 1945 it became known among Hitler's entourage that he had decided to stay in Berlin and to die here, if a relief were not to succeed. On one of the following days I was a witness to a conversation between Hitler and persons—I do not now recall who these were—of his immediate staff. During this Hitler said, where was he to go, now that Himmler had also betrayed him? He would rather die here than go under somewhere on the streets. I can still accurately recall the exact wording of this statement. The conversation took place in the central hallway in the *Führerbunker* in front of Hitler's private rooms.

Towards noon on 29 April Hitler personally said goodbye to me by giving me his hand. During this he said in effect that he would now depart this life and he wished to thank me for my services; he was releasing me from his service; I should try to get out with one of the combat units. Hitler said that he himself would 'stand eternal watch here'. I also recall the exact wording of this statement. This farewell took place in the central corridor of the *Führerbunker* in front of Hitler's private rooms . . .

In a conversation Günsche had on 20 March 1967 with David Irving—eleven years after the testimony cited above—he gave the same description of the events:

On this day, 30 April 1945, I met Bormann in the bunker and he said to me, 'Now look *Herr* Günsche'—he said '*Herr*' and not 'Party Comrade' or just the name—'I have just come from the *Führer* and he is going to depart this life today with his wife. He has ordered that his body is to be burnt. You will please take care that this burning is carried out and please make sure that there is petrol etc. available.' I said something like, 'Yes, I will do that.'

Then the *Führer* himself came out of his room and repeated practically the same thing to me and made me personally responsible for burning his corpse and [said] that he did not want 'his body to be displayed in a freak show'. His use of this expression was because of the shock of what had happened to Mussolini—about which he had been informed—who had been hung up by his feet. That must have been shortly beforehand. He did not want this to happen under any circumstances. Otherwise he would probably have fought—he was not a coward—but he was physically unable to do so and would not have had any assurance that, if he were to be hit, he would be killed. He preferred the sure, direct route. For him death came as a relief from this situation. He also wished that nothing should remain of himself, at least, that the Russians should not be allowed to desecrate his body or display it in any way . . . which I am quite sure would have happened. I am therefore happy that I carried out the cremation in such a way that this was not possible!

Hitler then said that he also wished to have his wife cremated with him. I assured him that I would do this. I do not recall my exact words . . . I probably said something like, '*Jawohl, mein Führer*, I will carry out the order . . .' In any case, I said something.

We were standing in front of his room, then *Gruppenführer* Baur and Rattenhuber came in—it was a terrible situation, because it was practically the final farewell. Hitler was very calm and unchanged. During the whole time in the bunker I never saw him let himself go in any way, unshaven or badly dressed. When he was outside he was always, as usual, calm, clean, shaven and not in any way in panic—perish the thought. He spoke very clearly and weighed his words.

I personally am of the opinion that he would have taken his life sooner, immediately after 22 or 23 April when the situation became completely hopeless, when the Russians had broken through the whole Eastern Front and encircled Berlin. It is probably mainly due to the encouragement offered by Dönitz, Keitel and particularly Bormann, but also Schörner, that he did not do so. (He was still receiving Schörner in the bunker at this time: he came to Berlin and was promoted to *Feldmarschall*.) Hitler was no longer optimistic; however, he still saw a chance that Berlin might still remain as a bastion. He did not want to give up Berlin; he wanted to build up a front out of the possibilities that had been suggested to him, with Berlin as a cornerstone. And there were other things too: Roosevelt died and he became optimistic when the news came over the radio . . . Hitler then went back into his room and came out later with Eva Braun . . .[222]

Following these orders, Günsche immediately began making the necessary preparations for Hitler's cremation, because, in view of the danger of a Russian attack on the Chancellery, there was a need for haste:

> I immediately ordered Kempka by phone to fetch some petrol. I did not tell him the reason. Kempka could only promise 200 litres. I also asked him to come to me. Kempka then brought the petrol without delay. I myself checked on this: as ordered, there were nine or ten cans of petrol in the garden exit . . .

Erich Kempka was questioned about Hitler's suicide on 2 December 1953, in other words roughly three years before Günsche, who was only questioned in the GDR on 2 May 1956 after his return from Russian captivity and Bautzen penitentiary. Regarding the events of the afternoon of 30 April, Kempka said:

> Early in the afternoon of 30 April 1945—it was probably about 1330— while in the bunker near the garages I mentioned earlier, I received a telephone call from the *Führerbunker* from Hitler's personal adjutant Otto Günsche, with whom I was on friendly terms. Günsche asked me to bring 200 litres of petrol to the *Führerbunker*, and there to the garden exit, as quickly as possible. To my question as to what this petrol was for, Günsche replied that he could not tell me over the phone.
>
> I then said that such an amount was no longer available here and that I would have to draw on the supply depot in the Tiergarten, but that I wanted to wait until the Russian shelling abated, mentioning 1700. [In the Tiergarten, about 100m from the garden of the Chancellery, there were garages for about fifteen vehicles and an underground petrol dump holding about 38,000 litres.] Günsche replied that there was not a second to waste. I should try to make up the requirement by draining the tanks. I promised to do this and then gave my deputy, *Hauptsturmführer* Schneider, the necessary orders . . .

When questioned about this, Günsche said later:

I did not order Kempka to provide 200 litres of petrol but to find as much petrol as possible. The whole matter was conducted in great haste, because the Russian troops were only a few hundred metres from the walls of the Chancellery and could storm the garden at any moment.

Since Kempka had been arrested in Hintersee near Berchtesgarden by the US Army on 20 June 1945, he was the first witness the Americans had who was able to confirm Hitler's death and who testified to it on 3 July 1946 before the International Military Tribunal in Nuremberg:

Cross-examination by Mr Dodd:

Q: You are the only person who was able to state that Hitler is dead, the only one able to state that Bormann is dead. Is this true according to the best of your knowledge?

A: I can testify that Hitler is dead and that he died on 30 April in the afternoon between 2 and 3 p.m.

Q: I know that, but you did not see him die, did you?

A: No, I did not see him die.

Q: You told the examining officers that you believe you had carried his body out of the bunker and set fire to it. You were the man who said that, weren't you?

A: I carried Adolf Hitler's wife outside and saw Adolf Hitler himself wrapped in a blanket.

Q: You actually saw Hitler?

A: Not actually him. The blanket in which he was wrapped was a bit short and only his legs hung out.

Mr Dodd: I have no further questions, Mr President.

Dr Bergold: I have no further questions either.

The Court: The witness may step down.[223]

On 2 December 1953 Kempka commented on his examination by the IMT in Nuremberg:

Initially my interrogation was only concerned with Bormann, about whose fate I was questioned at length. Towards the end the American prosecutor Dodd asked me some questions concerning Hitler. Dodd also asked me whether I had actually seen Hitler. I answered this question in the sense that the legs had been uncovered. Actually, however, both during the journey through the bunker as well as at the site of the cremation, besides the legs the upper part of the head and the upper face to the base of the nose as well as the left arm were uncovered. At Nuremberg I was not able to mention or add this, however, because I was immediately sent out of the witness stand and had no further opportunity of making a statement . . .

Kempka is responsible for a number of false claims and untrue statements which keep surfacing in published literature. One is that he was to provide '200 litres' of petrol (Günsche asked for 'as much petrol as possible') and that there was not enough petrol available. There was in fact more than enough to burn the corpses—see, for example, the testimonies by Hans Fritzsche from the Propaganda Ministry and by *SS-Untersturmführer* Kölz of the security guard and others. Interestingly, in his 1950 book Kempka wrote on page 117, in complete contradiction to his previous statements, 'Under the most difficult conditions I had had my men fetch several hundred [*sic*] litres of petrol during the afternoon . . .' Another is that Hitler shot himself in the mouth. Erich Kern, who published a new edition of Kempka's book in 1975 and expanded it with his own comments, obviously forgot what Kempka had written in 1950 (Kempka in 1950, p. 109: 'The Boss shot himself in the mouth with his pistol in his office . . .'; Kern in 1975, p. 94: 'The Boss shot himself with his pistol . . .').

Furthermore, Kempka (and unfortunately also Trevor-Roper in *Hitler's Last Days*) portrayed the role played by Rattenhuber in Hitler's suicide, the cremation of his body and the disposal of the remains completely falsely. On page 120 of his book, for example, Kempka recounts a story only he could have dreamt up:

When I came to the *Führerbunker* in the evening for my orders, I met General of Police Rattenhuber. From him I learned that he, some of his policemen and Hitler's personal orderly Linge had been present when the flames died out. The charred remains of Hitler's body and that of his wife were then scraped together. These were then buried in a small grave next to the wall of the apartment house where I lived . . .

And Trevor-Roper writes about Rattenhuber on page 188 of his book:

> Late that evening *Brigadeführer* Rattenhuber, the Chief of the Police Guard, entered the 'dog bunker' where the guards spent their free time and spoke to a sergeant of the SS bodyguard. He ordered him to report to his commanding officer Schedle [Schädle] and to select three dependable men, who were to bury the bodies. Shortly after this Rattenhuber returned to the 'dog bunker' and made a short speech to the men. He made them swear by all they held holy to keep the events of the day secret. Anybody who talked would be shot . . .

This is a story that Trevor-Roper plucked out of thin air or was based on a false account by 'some witness or other'.

Still later Kempka made other statements concerning Rattenhuber that were completely false. On 2 December 1953, for example, he said:

> When I returned to the bunker, however, I was asked by Rattenhuber . . . to provide further petrol in order to continue the cremation . . . Towards 1930 I again went to the site of the cremation with Rattenhuber, which Rattenhuber had asked me to do with the words 'We have to find out how far things have now progressed . . .' Rattenhuber then said that he had ordered that the remains were to be buried nearby . . . Rattenhuber then told me late on the evening of 30 April that the ashes had been buried . . .

Rattenhuber himself testified to this on 26 November 1955:

> I know nothing about the amount of petrol used in the cremation. I gave no orders having to do with this. The contradictory statement by Kempka is incorrect. His claim that I went to the site of the cremation with him is also untrue. The claim by Mansfeld that I assigned him to bury Hitler's and Eva Braun's remains is also incorrect. On this matter also—as I said before—I gave no orders. Furthermore, I had received no orders on this matter from Adolf Hitler!

It must also be mentioned that 30 April 1945 was the date of Rattenhuber's 48th birthday and he was probably not quite sober, particularly since the announcement of Hitler's suicide cut him to the quick. Secretary Junge wrote again and again in her various (mostly English-language) publications and statements that Rattenhuber celebrated his 60th (!) birthday on 22 or 26 April 1945! A glimpse of *Frau* Junge on 26 April 1945 is as follows:

> Chief of the *Reich* Security Service Rattenhuber celebrated his 60th birthday. Eva Braun and I are sitting with him in the dining room and drinking

a glass to his health. We all three stem from Munich and we are wallowing in reminiscences. The old man had tears in his eyes when he thought about never seeing his beloved Munich again . . .[224]

Other statements by secretary Junge must be treated with caution. The fact is that Rattenhuber died in Munich on 30 June 1957 at the age of 60.

In his testimony on 26 November 1955 Rattenhuber continued:

During the night of 29–30 April Hitler once again spoke to me. It was between 1 and 2 a.m. in the upper part of the *Führerbunker*, where Hitler had gone to say goodbye to the nurses and attendants of the Chancellery hospital. Before he went he came to me and said that today was my birthday. He congratulated me and wished me all the best and shook my hand. That was the last time I saw Hitler . . .

According to the statements of secretaries Junge and Christian, Hitler had lunch as usual towards 1300. *Frau* Junge testified on 24 February 1954:

On 30 April 1945 we—*Frau* Christian and I—came to lunch as usual. Eva Braun was not present. Hitler was in a cheerful, relaxed mood. There was no talk about suicide. I withdrew immediately following lunch and shortly afterwards was surprised by Günsche with the news that Hitler now wanted to say goodbye. I met him in the central corridor of the bunker. He shook my hand and said a few words, which, however, I did not understand. He said goodbye to *Frau* Christian and some of the others in the same way . . .

On 3 July 1954 Gerda Christian also recalled the event:

On 30 April lunch—which took place at the usual time towards 1300— passed without anything unusual. Eva Braun was not present. Hitler showed no sign of excitement. There was no talk of the end now being imminent.

About an hour to an hour and a half after lunch—it was now about 1500—I was informed that Adolf Hitler was now going to say goodbye. The farewell took place in the central hallway of the bunker. Hitler stepped out into the hall with Eva Braun and without a word shook each of us by the hand . . .

Linge, who on 30 April had brought the food—reportedly spaghetti with a light sauce—to the table as was customary, testified on 9 February 1956:

The meal on 30 April 1945 took place as usual. Besides Hitler, the two secretaries *Frau* Junge and *Frau* Christian took part, possibly also the cook, Manziarly. Lunch was over by 1400. A short while later I accompanied Hitler to *Dr* Goebbels, who was constantly present in the *Führerbunker* during the final days and used the room opposite the antechamber to Hitler's office as his office. *Dr* Goebbels once again made urgent representations to Hitler to the effect that he should leave Berlin. Hitler refused in a few brief words by saying, 'Doctor, you know my decision. It stands!'

Hitler then suggested to Goebbels that he himself leave Berlin with his family, which Goebbels declined. Following this, Hitler said goodbye to *Dr* Goebbels, then took his leave of *Frau* Goebbels in the adjoining room and then went back into his own office.

While I was then standing in the doorway between the office and the antechamber I asked to be released. Hitler told me that he had issued the order to break out in small groups. I should attach myself to one of these groups and break out to the west. I then asked, for whom I should break out. Hitler replied, 'For the coming man!' I then expressed my loyalty to Adolf Hitler after and beyond death. Adolf Hitler then gave me his hand, whereupon I withdrew after saluting.

I was shattered and rushed through the hall and staircase of the lower bunker to the upper bunker, where I stayed for a short time with the men of the *Führer* staff . . .

The time had now come! Everybody was waiting for Hitler to end his life. As the Supreme Commander of the Armed Forces who was not willing to surrender, he should actually have sought a soldier's death, as Hitler himself had often said in the past. For example, during the crisis besetting the Eastern armies at the gates of Moscow in December 1941, he had announced to the *Gauleiter*, 'If this war should ever really be lost, you will find me at the head of the last battalion of the army that is still fighting and I will then fight to the last breath.'[225] He said much the same thing to *Dr* Giesing on 13 February 1945: 'Should the war be lost, I will put myself at the head of my troops and fall.'[226] But in 1945 Hitler was no longer capable of doing this. *Frau* Schroeder once told me that once, during evening tea in his office in the bunker, Hitler had said something like, 'If a person is no more than a living ruin, why continue to live? One cannot prevent the decline of physical abilities anyway!' And secretary Johanna Wolf said on 25 February 1948:

His health declined from day to day during this time. He looked very bad and he complained that his health was getting worse and worse . . . He frequently said to us that he was getting old and 'It is terrible to realise that one is declining physically' . . .[227]

However that may be, no one can dispute that in his final days Hitler was a very sick man. He himself knew this. *Generaloberst* Jodl quoted a statement Hitler made shortly after midnight on 23 April 1945:

He was unable to fight for physical reasons; he would also not fight personally, because he did not want to risk the possibility of falling into enemy hands wounded.[228]

Towards 1515 Hitler took his leave of his immediate associates, in other words Goebbels (*Frau* Goebbels was not present; because of the impending death of her children, she did not leave her room all day), Bormann, *Generäle* Krebs and Burgdorf, *Frau* Christian, *Frau* Junge and *Fräulein* Manziarly and Police Director Högl, with a silent handshake, while Günsche was already making preparations to carry out Hitler's final order. As Günsche kept stressing later, there was a need for haste because a Russian ground attack on the Chancellery and the bunker might be imminent. In retrospect it appears odd that the Russians waited until the morning of 2 May before attacking the Chancellery, taking the bunker towards 9 a.m. in the process. The explanation is, however, quite simple: the Russians assumed that Hitler was no longer in Berlin! They believed he had withdrawn to the south, like a large part of the government and his staffs (which fact had not escaped the Russians' attention).

Günsche described his preparations:

Kempka had not yet come. I called Högl and Schädle as well as *Obersturmführer* Lindloff and Reisser and, after putting them in the picture, asked them to stand by to help, specifically mentioning carrying the bodies outside into the garden. I then cleared the lower part of the *Führerbunker* of all persons not belonging to the immediate circle and put a guard on the staircase leading to the upper part of the bunker with orders not to let anyone in any more. I gave the same order to Criminal Secretary Hofbeck, who was standing guard on the garden exit. During this time Adolf Hitler was still saying goodbye to several people in the central hallway, among others the secretaries, *Generäle* Burgdorf and Krebs and the Goebbels. Eva Braun was also present and also said goodbye. Adolf Hitler then retired into his office, and Eva Braun accompanied *Frau* Goebbels into her room. Immediately afterwards *Frau* Goebbels came to me again with the request that she wished to speak with Hitler once more . . . I therefore went to Hitler in his office. Hitler was very annoyed, but then went to see *Frau* Goebbels once again. I do not know from my own observations what was said between *Frau* Goebbels and Adolf Hitler. I later learned that *Frau* Goebbels had again asked Hitler to leave Berlin. She told me this herself, and added that Hitler had again refused. After this conversation Hitler again withdrew into his office. Shortly after this Eva Braun followed him.

Hitler had said goodbye to me before; Eva Braun now did so on her way from *Frau* Goebbels back to Hitler's office. About three hours had passed since I had received the last order from Hitler . . .

Between 1520 and 1525 Hitler withdrew into his office with Eva Braun-Hitler for the last time. The wait for his death now began, accompanied by the noise from the ventilators and the throbbing of the diesel engines in the machine room. Günsche had posted himself outside the door of Hitler's antechamber. There Linge joined him. Linge had briefly been upstairs in the upper bunker and, trying to cope with the horror of his leader's imminent demise, had had a few glasses of schnapps with the guards. Günsche then had quickly looked in on the men of the *Führer*'s staff. Goebbels, Axmann, Krebs, Burgdorf, Naumann, Hewel and *Dr* Stumpfegger had gathered in the briefing room. Högl, Schädle, Lindloff, Reisser and two further men from the *Führer* bodyguard were waiting in the telephone exchange, where Rochus Misch was on duty.

Witness accounts as to the time of death of Adolf Hitler and Eva Braun vary only slightly. Heinz Linge put the time of death at 1550. He allegedly noted it by the grandfather clock in the antechamber to Hitler's office, a clock he had always been at pains to keep running very accurately since Hitler himself took his time from this clock. Otto Günsche puts the time of death at 1530. He claims to have looked at his wristwatch. Günsche stated that

Hitler's suicide took place at 1530 on 30 April 1945. [He could] recall this time very accurately. After that only about ten minutes passed until the start of the cremation of the bodies; carrying the bodies out into the garden and the immediate preparations for the cremation had been done in great haste ...

The small time difference of twenty minutes between the two statements is probably of no importance, given the stresses of the situation at the time. Objectively, it will serve the truth if we put the time of death of Adolf Hitler at between 1530 and 1550 on 30 April 1945.

The time of death for Eva Braun needs to be set a fraction earlier. While it is only an assumption that Eva Braun died first, this assumption has a high degree of probability for psychological reasons. The decision to commit suicide together had been taken, and one can be sure that the actual execution had been decided upon in detail beforehand. In such a situation it is virtually inconceivable that Eva Braun would have looked on while Hitler shot himself. This would not only have been contrary to her emotional make-up but also to Hitler's. One may also assume—given Hitler's ever-active mistrust, even towards those in his closest circle—that he wanted to be sure of the death of his wife.

During their various interrogations Günsche and Linge both confirmed that they were now both physically and mentally prepared for what was inevitably going to take place in Hitler's rooms sooner or later, and that when then entering to living room-cum-office they registered the suicides unemotionally and immediately began mechanically to carry out Hitler's last orders.

On 9 February 1956 Linge described what then took place:

I then returned to the lower bunker. My instinct told me that now was the time. In the central corridor of the lower bunker I met Günsche, to whom I said it must now have happened. I then went into the antechamber to Hitler's room, where I found the door to his room closed and smelt powder smoke. In order to have a witness with me before going into the living room, I then returned to the corridor, where I found Bormann standing at a table. I addressed Bormann with the words '*Herr Reichsleiter*, it has happened!', whereupon we both immediately went into the living room.

Later, in prison, Günsche told me that, after we had met in the central corridor, he had immediately gone into the waiting room to the briefing room next to Hitler's living room and reported there that it had happened.

There he had found Goebbels, Bormann, Axmann, Burgdorf and Krebs. Günsche did not mention *Dr* Stumpfegger in this connection.

When we came into the living room Bormann and I saw the following. The bodies of Adolf Hitler and Eva Braun were in a seated position on the sofa standing against the wall opposite the door from the antechamber. Seen from this door, Adolf Hitler sat on the left side of the sofa. His head was canted to the left and slightly forwards. His lower right arm was between the armrest of the sofa and his right thigh, and his open hand lay on his right knee, palm upwards. His feet were on the floor. They were pointing forwards and were about 30 to 40cm apart. Hitler was dressed as usual in a uniform blouse, black trousers, black socks and black gloves.

On his right temple I noticed a dark circular spot about the size of a ten pfennig piece. From this spot, a streaked trail of blood ran down to about the middle of his cheek. Directly next to the sofa I saw a puddle of blood about the size of a medium-sized plate, from which drops had splattered on to the frame of the sofa and the wall. Hitler's eyes were open.

About 30cm away from Hitler was the body of Eva Braun-Hitler. She had drawn her legs up on to the sofa. The legs pointed to the left. Her upper body rested against the back of the sofa; the head was upright. Her eyes were open and her lips were compressed. The body was dressed in a blue dress with a white collar and stockings. The shoes stood side by side on the floor in front of the sofa. Her face appeared completely unchanged. There were no injuries. There were also no traces of blood.

Both of Hitler's pistols, with which I was very familiar, lay directly by the points of Hitler's feet, the 7.65mm pistol by the right and the 6.35mm pistol by the left foot . . .

Günsche, who entered Hitler's room immediately after Linge and Bormann, gave the following description on 20 June 1956:

After Hitler and Eva Braun had withdrawn I took up position in front of Hitler's rooms. After a while I briefly went to see Högl, Schädle, Kempka, Lindloff and Reisser in the telephone exchange in the lower bunker and the duty room in front of it. Bormann, Goebbels, Krebs, Burgdorf and Naumann were waiting in the briefing room. I do not recall whether Axmann was also there, but this is possible. I then saw—I did not hear a shot—Linge open the door to Hitler's office and Linge and Bormann go inside. I thereupon immediately went into the antechamber myself—things had to happen quickly now because the Russians were at the door—and entered Hitler's office behind Bormann and Linge. There I saw the following:

Eva Braun was lying on the sofa standing against the wall opposite the door from the antechamber. The head was on the left side of the sofa as seen from the door to the antechamber. She was lying on her back. Both lower legs were drawn up slightly. The body was completely still. The eyes were open. My immediate impression was that Eva Braun, as well as Hitler, was dead. The body was dressed as before in a blue dress with white facings and stockings. The shoes were lying on the sofa a short distance away from the feet.

Hitler himself sat in an armchair standing to the left and slightly forward—as seen from the antechamber—but very close to the sofa. His body was slightly sunk together and slanted slightly to the right over the armrest. The right arm hung down over the armrest. The head was canted slightly forward to the right. I noticed an injury to the head slightly above the outer end of the angle of the right eyelid. I saw blood and a dark discoloration. The whole thing was about the size of an old three mark piece. The mouth was slightly open. There was a small puddle of blood on the floor to the right of the armchair.

Linge then immediately returned to the antechamber and picked up the blanket that had been made ready there. At this point I left the antechamber in order to summon the people I had put on call (Högl, Schädle, Lindloff, Reisser) and to inform those waiting in the briefing room. The latter I did by reporting, 'The *Führer* is dead!' . . .

After Günsche had reported 'the *Führer* is dead' to those waiting in the briefing room, Goebbels, Axmann, Krebs and Burgdorf also immediately went into Hitler's office. Axmann testified on 1 December 1953:

After a short while Günsche came into the room and reported, 'The *Führer* is dead.' Shortly before that *Dr* Goebbels had said, in the form of a question, that there had been a shot. I myself did not hear a shot. After Günsche's report *Dr* Goebbels, Bormann and I immediately went through the antechamber into Hitler's living room-cum-office. This is what we saw:

Adolf Hitler was sitting on the sofa standing against the wall opposite the door from the antechamber, leaning against the armrest on the left side as seen from the door. His head was slanted to the right, his right arm hung down over the armrest. There were thin blood trails running down from both temples. Apart from that, neither the face nor the front part of the head showed any signs of injuries, but the lower jaw, however, was slightly pushed to the side. I do not know whether the back of the head showed signs of injuries. I did not make any observations on this . . .

Later, on 2 September 1955, Axmann elaborated on his testimony when questioned about his 'assumption' that Hitler had shot himself through the mouth:

Based on the signs I found, I had to assume that Adolf Hitler had shot himself in the mouth. For me the chin, which was pushed to the side, and the blood trails on the temples caused by an internal explosion in the head, all pointed to this. Later the same day *SS-Sturmbannführer* Günsche confirmed my assumption. [What Günsche—who was still a Russian prisoner-of-war at the time—is supposed to have said and what words have been put into his mouth by others is quite unbelievable.]

I assume that after hearing the shot, and before reporting to us, Günsche had gone into the room Adolf Hitler was in. Günsche had been standing in front of Adolf Hitler's rooms and had received orders not to let anyone in. As I have already stated during my initial interrogation, I wanted to say goodbye to Adolf Hitler but Günsche would not let me in. For me it is therefore a foregone conclusion that Günsche was the first person to go to Hitler after he had shot himself.

I did not fire a shot at Hitler. I stick to my statement based on the signs I saw, that Adolf Hitler shot himself in the mouth. I can also testify here with a clear conscience that I saw Adolf Hitler's body.

To the statement that Linge supposedly reported to Bormann with the words '*Herr Reichsleiter*, it has happened', I can only say that this could have taken place after Günsche reported to those of us in the briefing room, 'I report: the *Führer* is dead.' From Linge's own statements one can see that he had gone away for a time and cannot accurately state how long he was absent. This can be explained by the fact that he had drunk alcohol, that the sense of time in the bunker, which was artificially lit day and night, was in disorder, i.e. that one can make very big errors about elapsed time.

During my initial interrogation and during my interrogation today, I have made detailed statements about Hitler's injuries and I can only confirm that I stand by these. I have nothing to add about these injuries . . .

Regarding Eva Braun-Hitler's death, Axmann made a further statement on 1 December 1953:

Eva Hitler sat next to Adolf Hitler on the sofa with her head leaning on Hitler's left shoulder. She looked as if she were asleep. She bore no signs of injuries or blood. Together with Goebbels and Bormann, I remained with the bodies for several minutes in silence . . .

In these statements, Axmann makes no mention whatsoever that Hitler had taken poison. However, if one looks at the statements Axmann made in the court building in Nuremberg in 1947, one sees that he said something entirely different then. In both his interrogation on 10 October by Robert Kempner and that on 16 October by M. B. Urney, Axmann stated that 'he believed that Hitler had first taken poison'. According to Kempner,

> Axmann testified that he believed Hitler had first taken poison and then shot himself through the mouth, and that the explosion explained the blood on the *Führer*'s temples...[229]

And in his statements to Urney, questioning him on behalf of Judge Musmanno:

> *Q*: Yes. You have said that he first took poison and then shot himself. Since the effect of the poison is practically instantaneous, how could he have found the strength to pull the trigger of the pistol after he had taken the poison?

> *A*: I said what Günsche had told me, namely that Hitler had first taken poison and then shot himself through the mouth. He really wanted to commit suicide and carried this out according to what I said in my last interrogation, in that he did not only shoot himself but also took poison.

> *Q*: Oh, I did not know that. You claim that Hitler first took poison?

> *A*: He took poison and then he shot himself in the mouth. At least, that is what Günsche told me . . .[230]

Twice, therefore, Axmann claimed that Günsche told him that Hitler had poisoned himself. *Herr* Günsche never told him anything of the sort, as he confirmed to me, and one can only wonder how Axmann came to make such claims at the time. Later on, during the 1950s, he did not repeat these stories.

Of the people who came into Hitler's small living room-cum-office and saw Hitler and Eva Braun lying dead there, only Günsche, Linge and Axmann survived the end of the war. Kempka and all the other surviving witnesses only saw Hitler and Eva Braun in the antechamber, the hallway, the staircase or the garden, after they had died and their bodies were being carried out of the bunker to be cremated. However, the testimonies of these three key witnesses vary greatly as to the position of the bodies and other details. One could reasonably expect that their descriptions of what they found when entering the room one behind the other, in particular the position of the bodies, would be identical. In fact, however, there are substantial discrepancies concerning the location of Hitler's body and about the position of Eva Braun's.

There are several possible explanations for this. First of all, the initial impressions retained by the witnesses under the extreme urgency of the situation could have been mere flashes, so that later on they experienced difficulty precisely fixing the positions of the bodies. One may also assume that, because of the state of excitement brought on by these extraordinary happenings, Linge, Günsche and Axmann were unable to make precise observations or retain details, so that they were unable later to give accurate descriptions of these details.

It is highly probable that, at the time, the witnesses only registered the positions of the two bodies subconsciously. Only later, during their long captivity, did the rigorous interrogations by the Russians (or, in the case of Axmann, by the Americans), lasting many months, then bring the impressions retained to the surface of consciousness, creating more or less clear pictures which were then incorporated into their testimonies. Each such 'flash-back' picture was then described by the individual witness in the firm conviction that his was the 'true' observation.

Naturally, during the interrogations between 1952 and 1956 (in the court case in Berchtesgaden), there was a suspicion

> ... that those witnesses who were key to the events would be anxious to have the events appear in a certain light, because, for example, there was a secret agreement to this effect, and would therefore have agreed their testimonies. Particular attention was paid to such an eventuality during the interrogations. However, there was not a scrap of evidence discovered to support this. Moreover, the spontaneous answers given made it apparent that the witnesses were clearly and truthfully dissociating themselves from such a possibility ...

As the 83-page report presented on 31 July 1956 by the Bavarian Criminal Investigation Office goes on to say,

. . . the indications given above demonstrate the difficulties encountered by the experts in evaluating the testimonies of the witnesses. The experts were required to evaluate the substantial discrepancies in the testimonies from the point of view of scientific criminology, forensic medicine and criminal psychology by critically examining them as to their truthfulness and/or probability. Only the latter permits the formation of an expert opinion . . .

The criminological experts came to the conclusion that a discussion of the different versions of Hitler's gunshot wound offered the key to the examination of the situation as a whole. Based on the descriptions given by the various witnesses, the following situations were possible and were reconstructed and photographed in 1956:

(a) *Linge/Axmann:* Hitler, sitting on sofa and slightly leaning on right armrest. Head canted slightly forward/right. On the floor two pistols, a 7.65mm in front of right foot and a 6.35mm in front of left foot.
Eva Braun also on sofa, seated next to Hitler to his left.
Linge: Gunshot (entry) wound on Hitler's right temple.
Axmann: Blood on both temples. Plate-sized puddle of blood on floor to the right of sofa.
Both agree: No signs of injuries on Eva Braun.

(b) *Günsche:* Hitler seated on armchair located right and slightly forward of sofa but very close to it. Body slightly sunken and canted slightly to right over armrest. Right arm hanging down over armrest.
Eva Braun lying on sofa, head in direction of right end of sofa.
On floor in front of Hitler's armchair two pistols, a 7.65mm in front of right foot and a 6.35mm in front of left foot. Gunshot (entry) wound on Hitler's right temple. Small puddle of blood on rug to right of armchair.
No gunshot wounds or traces of blood on Eva Braun.

Apart from Günsche, Linge and Axmann, Schneider claims to have seen coagulated blood on both of Hitler's temples when he helped carry the body outside. Mengershausen stated that from his position outside the bunker exit he had seen that Hitler had an entry wound—

a small hole, clearly recognisable despite the discoloration—on his right temple.

Another important point is that Axmann assumed Hitler had shot himself through the mouth. Axmann made this assumption because of the blood on both of Hitler's temples. According to the statement of secretary *Frau* Junge, Hitler repeated several times during meals that 'he intended to shoot himself in the mouth'. (To me this does not seem credible, like much else that *Frau* Junge said.)

Because of these discrepancies in the statements as to whether Hitler had shot himself in the temple or in the mouth and whether the bullet had gone through or remained inside the head, the experts decided to conduct ballistic experiments and to determine from them which of the statements was likely to be correct.

Günsche recalled that, after having set fire to the bodies in the garden, he returned to Hitler's room:

> I subsequently went back into Hitler's office. Here I observed a puddle of blood on the floor, directly next to the right armrest of the armchair mentioned above, the size of a medium-sized plate. Next to it there were spots of blood on the wall. Directly in front of the armchair lay two pistols, one of 7.65mm calibre and one of 6.35mm. The 7.65mm pistol lay in front of the right armrest. The 6.35mm pistol lay in front of the left armrest. Both pistols were Walthers. I was very familiar with both pistols as being Hitler's personal weapons. I immediately unloaded both pistols and in the process discovered that one shot had been fired from the 7.65mm pistol. The smell of powder smoke could clearly be detected. The 6.35mm pistol was still fully loaded. There were no traces of blood on either of the pistols. Linge and I then tried to find the cartridge case from the shot fired from the 7.65mm pistol. We did not succeed, but on the other hand we did not look carefully enough . . .

One can conclude from further statements made by Günsche and Linge that the cartridge case was taken out into the garden with the rug, which was burned there, and lost. None of the witnesses stated that the bullet itself was found nor that a bullet hole in the wall—made after the bullet had gone through Hitler's head—was discovered. If one believes Linge's statements, the Russians searched in vain for bullet damage to the wall of the office in his presence in April 1946.

Günsche stated that both pistols were taken as keepsakes by Axmann's adjutant Gerhard Welzin (who was captured by the Russians and later died in Russian captivity). According to both Günsche and Linge, these were Hitler's personal weapons; according to Linge, they were a self-loading Walther Model PPK or PP (7.65mm) and a Model 8.

The statements made by Günsche and Linge are confirmed by *SS-Oberscharführer* Schwiedel of the bodyguard, who said on 15 October 1956:

Linge ordered me and my comrade Heinz Krüger to roll up the rug in Hitler's office and to burn it in the garden. It was about 1615. Krüger and I immediately went into Hitler's office. Here is what we saw. The sofa and the two armchairs were standing at their usual places, the sofa against the wall and the armchairs slightly to the side and forward of the sofa. The table had been pulled away from the sofa. Directly next to the right armrest of the sofa there was a puddle of blood about the size of a large dinner plate. We immediately went to work and pushed the table aside. In the process I saw a 7.65mm Walther pistol lying on the rug. It lay slightly forward of the right front corner of the sofa. I picked this pistol up and put it on the desk.

Krüger and I then carried the rug up the stairs of the garden exit into the garden and put it down directly next to the exit. For the moment it was not possible to set light to it because the garden lay under very heavy fire. When we were taking the rug outside we saw Hitler's and Eva Braun's bodies. They were lying somewhat to the left of the exit and were burning.

After carrying out this assignment I did not go back into Hitler's office. I do not know what became of the 7.65mm pistol.

While taking the rug outside I do not recall having seen Hitler's second pistol (6.35mm). I do distinctly remember, however, that when I found the 7.65mm pistol I also found a cartridge case of the same calibre. This case was also lying on the rug, about 1m distant from the pistol. Given the circumstances it was clear to me that the case came from Hitler's pistol. However, I did not check this. I showed the case to Krüger and then pocketed it. After I had spent two years as a POW it became lost.

Günsche went on to state:

It had been clear to me for a long time that Hitler intended to shoot himself. Between 22 and 25 April 1945 *Obergruppenführer* Schaub told me that Hitler had changed his pistol—the one which he always carried with him—after the briefing on 22 April. Up until then he always carried the 6.35mm pistol in his holster, whereas the 7.65mm pistol was kept in his office or bedroom. From that time on he carried the 7.65mm pistol in his holster. He then shot himself with it . . .

Walther self-loading pistols are virtually foolproof fully automatic weapons. Their technical performance meets the most stringent demands. The PPK and PP models are designed in such a way that both the setting and the releasing of the safety catch and the cocking of the hammer can be done with one hand. After a shot has been fired, the empty cartridge case is ejected to the right.

According to Günsche's credible testimony, Hitler supposedly used a 7.65mm PPK or PP to commit suicide. Günsche was able to ascertain this immediately after the deed by the smell of powder smoke from the muzzle of the barrel and by checking the cartridges when he unloaded the pistol. A shot fired from a 7.65 mm pistol will, according to the experts, penetrate a 100mm thick slab of pine wood at 50 metres. In order to determine the effects on the human body, the Institute of Forensic Medicine at Berlin University carried out experiments in the 1920s during which shots from pistols of various calibres were fired into human corpses.[231] The following average results were obtained with pistols of calibre 7.65mm. Shots into the head, chest and stomach always penetrated. Exceptions were noted, for example when the bullet became lodged when hitting the breastbone or the spine, but there were also cases noted when it penetrated these as well. *Dr* Berg, a pathologist, published an extensive paper on the penetrability of pistols on living bodies[232] and listed 47 cases in which pistols of 7.65mm calibre had been used. Of the 47 shots fired at living bodies, 26 had passed through and 21 had become lodged, including, respectively, eleven and seven shots (sagittal and transverse) to the head. Based on these results, the experts came to the conclusion that in cases of shots to the head with a pistol of 7.65mm calibre, the probability that the bullet will go through is not significantly higher than the probability that it will become lodged.

Turning to Axmann's 'assumption' that Hitler shot himself in the mouth, the following arguments can be raised. A projectile entering a living body first of all causes *direct* mechanical destruction, and the larger the projectile the greater this destruction. *Indirect* mechanical damage is primarily caused by a hydrodynamic effect, based on the fact that liquids cannot be compressed: if the projectile passes tissue or organs that contain liquid (blood), this liquid must be displaced in an unchanged condition and thereby rapidly driven forward or to the side, rupturing the tissue or the organ in the process.

> Applying this to Hitler's suicide [wrote the experts in Munich] forces one to reject the claim by Axmann that a shot in the mouth with explosive eruptions of the temples had taken place, because a projectile fired from a 7.65mm cartridge only has an initial velocity of 297 metres per second. The hydrodynamic effect (rupture of tissue and organs), however, only takes place where the velocity is above 300m/s.

To summarise. The 'shot in the mouth' version, which is to be found extensively in the literature, was propounded solely by Axmann and Kempka. Axmann 'assumed' that Hitler had killed himself with a shot through the mouth. When he wrote this in his book Kempka was lying, just as he was when he testified that Günsche had told him this, or had indicated as much with his fingers. Günsche confirmed to me that he never said or indicated any such thing to Kempka.

To the statements made by witnesses with regard to the 'entry wound' and the 'sound of the shot', the experts reached the following conclusions:

(a) Entry wound
According to Linge, Günsche and Mengershausen, there was a small injury about the size of a ten pfennig piece with a surrounding discoloration of the size of a three mark piece in the area of the right temple of Hitler's corpse.

Experience shows that even when using modern, smokeless powder, if the shot is fired from a very close distance or with the mouth of the weapon resting against the skin, then a discoloration of the surroundings of the entry wound can be observed. In addition to the powder stains deposited on the skin, there is also discoloration caused by powder particles being forced under the skin and causing destruction.

According to the symptoms described by the witnesses, the assumption of a shot fired from a very close distance or with the weapon touching the skin is justified. In addition, all the witnesses have declared that Hitler did not suffer from a tremor of the right hand—and this is confirmed in film of him—and that the hand was completely still. Being right-handed, he could have fired such a shot quite easily.

(b) Sound of the shot
Of all of the witnesses heard on the matter, only *Dr* Werner Naumann and secretary Gertraud Junge claim to have heard a shot a few minutes after 1500 (Junge). At this time *Frau* Junge was far away on the stairs leading from the lower into the upper bunker. This alleged 'observation' by the two witnesses is probably due to their having been deceived by the sounds of the running diesel engines and/or the heavy shelling of the Chancellery.

Kempka wrote on page 111 of his book *Ich habe Adolf Hitler verbrannt*, published in 1950: 'Bormann, Linge and I had heard the shot and rushed into the room. *Dr* Stumpfegger came in to make an examination . . .' Later on, Kempka expressly retracted this, as well as many other statements in his book!

Because of various statements made by *Frau* Junge, Günsche had to return to Munich on 21 June 1956 to give further evidence. On this occasion Günsche declared 'in all clarity' and conclusively,

. . .that he—contradicting to the statements made by several other witnesses, particularly *Frau* Junge—had only said on 30 April 1945 and in other statements made later that Adolf Hitler had shot himself, while Eva Braun had taken poison, and that the bodies had been burnt in the garden. He had never made any additional statements.

In order to complete the evaluations made by the Bavarian experts, let us briefly turn to the question of 'the smell of powder smoke', which Günsche testified to having detected. The experts said:

. . . according to general experience and observations with the use of handguns, after a shot the powder smoke can usually be clearly detected by smell, particularly in enclosed spaces. Under normal conditions, the powder smoke dissipates after several minutes. On the weapon itself, and depending on the circumstances, the smell of the burned powder gases can be detected at the mouth of the barrel up to several hours after the shot [has been fired].

If Linge, as he claimed, smelled powder smoke in the antechamber to Hitler's office, this is most likely due to the fact that, as Hentschel stated, the fresh air was pumped into the bunker through the living quarters and the stale air sucked out through the central corridor.

Therefore the powder gases caused by Hitler's shot were sucked out of his office into the antechamber through the slit under the door and then drawn out of the bunker via the corridor. In detail, mechanic Johannes Hentschel stated:

> There was a wooden door between Hitler's office and the antechamber, which opened into the office. To make allowances for the rug in the office, the door had a gap at the bottom. Therefore there was the possibility of air, and also gas, seeping under the door from the office into the antechamber, all the more so because the partitioning off of the antechamber from the office—the building of a dividing wall—had been done later, so the antechamber did not have its own ventilation. The draught from the office into the antechamber had to be all the greater if the door from the antechamber to the central corridor—i.e., to the ventilation system—were open . . .

Returning now to the manner in which Hitler committed suicide, we can say, in summary, that the version involving 'a shot in mouth' with secondary injuries to the temples must be rejected. This is not only highly unlikely in view of the fact that the overwhelming majority of witnesses saw an entry wound in the temple, but also because, in the case of a shot in the mouth, the projectile would most probably have exited through the back of the head. According to all the witnesses, however, there were allegedly no injuries to the back of Hitler's head. Finally, none of the witnesses report having seen any traces of blood on Hitler's face, particularly not in the region of the mouth. All the observations speak in favour of a shot in the temple. Whether the bullet went through or lodged could not be ascertained. The possibility did however exist that the projectile penetrated partially or completely through the skull and then lodged in the left temple directly under the skin, causing damage to the tissue and a haematoma, which would explain the error made by several witnesses who claimed to have seen an exit wound.

The assumption of a shot in the temple is also supported by psychological considerations. Hitler always saw himself as being a soldier. A soldier does not shoot himself in the mouth but in the temple. Anyone who knew Hitler well or who has taken the trouble to study him will appreciate that he would only shoot himself in the temple.

With this he wished to demonstrate, as already mentioned, that he was a soldier, and perhaps he also wanted to set his Generals and officers an example of the proper conduct of a German soldier.

During the very emotional briefing in the bunker on 22 April 1945, and faced with the hopelessness of the military situation, Hitler had, according to Günsche, made a statement about shooting himself:

Under these conditions the situation can no longer be recovered . . . I will not consider leaving Berlin . . . Under these conditions I can no longer lead: I will shoot myself . . . I will act as the commander of a fortress . . .

A pathological evaluation of the evidence also points to Hitler having died from a shot into the right temple. This can very well have been a shot where the projectile lodged in the head, so that there need not have been an exit wound. Given that no exit wound was observed, nothing at all can be deduced as to the path the projectile might have taken. General experience, however, shows that with shots in the temple vital brain centres can be hit. The result of the destruction of the substance of the brain is normally instant immobilisation and death. The witnesses found Hitler's body in a seated position. The armrest of the sofa (mentioned in Linge's and Axmann's testimonies) probably prevented the body from falling over. In any case, rigor mortis had not yet set in. This can be deduced from the loosely hanging arms, the open palms and also the observations made during the carrying of the body into the garden.

After the experts had reached the conclusion that Hitler's death had been caused by a gunshot, the claim of 'poisoning'—on which the Russians kept insisting for political and ideological reasons—was also investigated. Despite the fact that all of the witnesses detained in Moscow—with the exception of Rattenhuber and Mengershausen—spoke of Hitler having committed suicide with a pistol, the Russians officially continued to adhere to the idea of poisoning. Rattenhuber's completely inexplicable theory that Hitler had poisoned himself runs like a thread through all the books and periodicals. On 26 November 1955 Rattenhuber testified:

As far as the cause of Hitler's death is concerned, I have always assumed that he poisoned himself with cyanide. During the late afternoon and early evening of 30 April 1945 there was a strong smell of cyanide in the *Führerbunker*. During my interrogations as a prisoner I was confronted with the statement that Hitler had allegedly shot himself. I always maintained that he had poisoned himself with cyanide . . .

Rattenhuber was the only one of Hitler's inner circle who assumed poisoning, for whatever reasons. One of his deputies, *SS-Obersturmbannführer* Ludwig Forster, who was also Chief of RSD Section 15 (the Chancellery complex), made a statement on 6 February 1956 which contradicts Rattenhuber:

> My last posting was in Berlin. Section 15 was responsible for the whole complex of the Chancellery, with the exception of the *Führerbunker*, which was the sole responsibility of Section 1 under *Kriminaldirektor* Peter Högl.
>
> On 30 April 1945 it became known in the Chancellery that Hitler had shot himself and that Eva Braun was also dead. During the course of the afternoon this was confirmed to me by Rattenhuber, Högl and Kempka. As far as the method of the suicide is concerned, I always heard that Hitler shot himself. I never heard that he took poison. I did know, however, that he possessed poison. I do not recall who gave me this information . . .

SS-Unterscharführer Hans Hofbeck, who was on guard at the door of the garden exit from the bunker on the afternoon of 30 April 1945, testified on 25 November 1955:

> Concerning how Hitler died, on 30 April and on 1 May 1945 and later, I never heard anything other than that he had shot himself in the temple. That the cause of death could have been poison, or about poisoning in general, I never heard anything until my interrogation today . . .

The witnesses heard during the court case in the 1950s mainly agree that several days before his death (from about 24 April 1945 onwards) Hitler had distributed poison ampoules to the people of his immediate circle. These had been provided by Himmler and some of them had been brought into the bunker and handed out by *Dr* Stumpfegger. Rattenhuber testified to this on 26 November 1955:

> During the course of 30 April 1945 *Dr* Stumpfegger showed me a letter Hitler had sent him and signed personally, in which Hitler requested him to provide cyanide. *Dr* Stumpfegger asked me to read this letter so that I would be a witness to its contents, because he then intended to tear it up. The letter was typed and was on Hitler's letterhead. I do not recall when it was dated . . .

According to a directive of the Director of the Reich Criminal Police Department in the Reich Central Security Office, *SS-Gruppenführer* Arthur Nebe, between 3,000 and 4,000 so-called 'self-destructors' were developed in the department's laboratories in the Criminological-Technological Institute. The chemists used dehydrated prussic acid (HCN) with an additive of 2 per cent oxylic acid. The ampoules were produced in the department's laboratories in the Sachsenhausen concentration camp near Oranienburg north-west of Berlin. Linge has stated that Hitler had about twelve of these ampoules, whereas *Frau* Junge spoke of ten. This, however, is irrelevant to the question of their having been used. On 10 February 1956 Linge elaborated on his testimony:

> It is correct that poison ampoules were provided for Adolf Hitler, which he then distributed to people in his entourage. They were provided by *Dr* Stumpfegger, who had had Hitler confirm this order to him in writing. I do not know whether Adolf Hitler retained one of these ampoules for his own use . . .

In any case, there were large quantities of poison ampoules available, which were given to the inhabitants of the bunker, partly at their request but mostly without having been specifically asked for. The ampoules were mainly given to the women who had remained in the bunker. It is worth noting that the witness accounts speak of cyanide, whereas in fact the poison was prussic acid. Secretary Gertraud Junge testified to this on 24 February 1954:

> During the final days, conversations at meals were mostly about whether Hitler could or would still leave Berlin. All suggestions in this direction, which were mainly voiced by *Frau* Christian and myself, were categorically rejected by Hitler. I then also raised the question whether it would not be better if he sought death in battle. [I have my doubts whether secretary Junge would dare to ask Hitler such a question.] Hitler rejected this, saying that he could not under any circumstances fall into enemy hands alive, referring to the Russians. In this context he also mentioned that he could be wounded and that no one would then dare to shoot him, even if he gave the order to do so.
>
> After the irrevocability of Hitler's decision to commit suicide was accepted, the conversations repeatedly turned to the question about how the suicide was to take place. In this context Hitler declared that he would

shoot himself in the mouth [this statement by *Frau* Junge must also be sharply questioned: *Frau* Christian, for example, who also took part in the lunches, did not recall ever having heard Hitler make such a statement) and was only considering whether to swallow a cyanide ampoule immediately before shooting himself. He regarded a shot in the mouth to be the safest means, particularly bearing in mind the tremors in both his hands. [How *Frau* Junge came to make such a statement is completely inexplicable: as many other witnesses credibly testified, and as is proved by film footage, Hitler had a tremor only in his left hand.] Eva Braun said that she would take poison.

In the context of such conversations, Adolf Hitler also repeatedly said that he must not fall into enemy hands as a corpse. His body was to be cremated and lost for all time. In this context he mentioned the desecration of Mussolini's body. During this time—it was probably on 25 April 1945—Hitler also gave *Frau* Christian and me a cyanide ampoule at our request. Other members of his entourage also requested cyanide ampoules and received them. In total he had ten ampoules available, with which Himmler had provided him . . .

Secretary Gerda Christian made similar statements about the distribution of the poison ampoules. On 23 July 1954 she said:

During the final days in Berlin, but also earlier, Hitler repeatedly said that he could not fall into enemy hands alive under any circumstances. In this context he said that he would shoot himself and wished to be cremated without a trace. During the very last days he also said that he would shoot himself but for safety reasons also bite a cyanide ampoule simultaneously with the shot. In my presence he never said that he would shoot himself through the mouth. I also know nothing about statements that Himmler wanted to hand him over alive. In these conversations Eva Braun said that she would take poison. At one of these conversations Hitler offered me a cyanide ampoule. I had already provided myself with one from another source . . .

When they left the bunker, secretaries Wolf and Schroeder were given poison ampoules by Hitler. *Frau* Schroeder had hers with her for a longer period of time, while she was held captive by the Americans.

Dental assistant Käthe Heusermann testified on 27 April 1956:

On 24 April 1945 I was asked by Eva Braun in the *Führerbunker* if I had anything with which to take my life if the Russians came. After I had answered in the negative, Hitler joined us. He then had a glass ampoule in a yellow brass casing brought, with the remark that one only needed to bite down on it: swallowing was not necessary . . .

Hanna Reitsch also reported on 25 November 1954 that she and *Ritter* von Greim had received poison ampoules from Hitler (von Greim used his to commit suicide in American captivity in Salzburg on 24 May 1945):

> On 28 April 1945—I do not recall the exact time—Hitler had me called to him. During a longer conversation he then told me that he would voluntarily depart this life together with Eva Braun, if the hope of a relief of Berlin by *General* Wenck were dashed. He did not want to fall into Russian hands alive, nor should anything recognisable of his body fall into enemy hands. In this context he handed me two small phials containing poison, one for me and one for *Generaloberst* von Greim, so that—as he said—*Herr* von Greim and I would always have the freedom of choice . . .

In general, the witnesses describe the ampoules as containing about 1cc of transparent liquid. The descriptions of the shape of the ampoules vary considerably and refer to having been made of glass or plastic and being handed out with or without yellow brass casings. A detailed description of the ampoules and how they were distributed was given by *SS-Sturmbannführer* Josef Kiermaier, who was the head of Section 4 of the RSD. This post was responsible for the personal protection of *Reichsführer der SS* Heinrich Himmler and towards the end had a complement of 45 men (!). Kiermaier said on 23 April 1956:

> Some months before the collapse—it was probably in early April 1945—I was supplied with a poison ampoule in Berlin by *SS-Brigadeführer Professor Dr* Karl Gebhardt. *Professor* Gebhardt also gave such ampoules to other members of Himmler's immediate entourage. *Professor* Gebhardt said that the contents would cause instant death if one bit on it.
> The ampoule I was given by Gebhardt consisted of thin glass. It was inside a yellow brass casing. The casing was about 5cm long and had a diameter of about 1.5cm. I recall that the casing had an inner lining of felt or some such material, but my memory on this point is not exact. I can also not recall the exact shape of the ampoule, particularly not whether it had a capillary extension on only one or on both ends. The content of the ampoule was a transparent, colourless liquid without any sediment. The

case had a screw-on cap. Both case and ampoule appeared to have been mass-produced. The ampoule was filled nearly to the top.

Himmler had a similar case with an ampoule. He showed it to me, opening the case and pulling out the ampoule . . .

I do not know whether Gebhardt distributed these ampoules to me and others on Himmler's orders. I also do not know whether the ampoules distributed to Hitler's immediate circle originated with *Professor* Gebhardt, but in view of the overall circumstances I assume this to be probable. To my question about the content of the ampoules, *Professor* Gebhardt spoke of prussic acid . . .

Käthe Heusermann also gave a detailed description of the poison ampoule she had received from Hitler. She said on 27 April 1956:

I kept the ampoule Hitler gave me on 24 April 1945 until 1953. It was a glass ampoule with a volume content of about 1 to 1.5cc, which had a capillary extension. The glass of the capillary extension was blue; the glass of the body was colourless. The contents were initially completely colourless but turned slightly yellow over the years. The ampoule was contained in a yellow brass case somewhat like a lipstick case. The case was not lined with cloth or any similar material . . .

Poison ampoules in many shapes have been used by espionage agents for a long time. Their contents have always been prussic acid and not cyanide, because only pure prussic acid has the optimum effect. The transparent liquid in the ampoules Hitler distributed also points to prussic acid. While the extremely high internal pressure of prussic acid, and therefore its tendency to evaporate rapidly, prevents water-soluble concentrations of more than about 20 per cent, such a concentration is quite lethal for a human being.

According to the literature, the lethal dose for prussic acid is 1mg per kg of body weight. Assuming a 20 per cent concentration, an average body weighing 70kg would receive 200mg of prussic acid, far more than the lethal dose. While, as with all poisons, individual reactions may vary, this high a dose will always cause instant paralysis of all vital functions.

Prussic acid has a characteristic smell of burnt almonds, which is retained in clothing for a long time and is even detectable in very low concentrations. The corpse, particularly its body cavities when opened, also exudes this smell and it can almost always be detected in rooms in which the poison has been administered. Cyanide, on the other hand, is not always lethal when taken orally. When ingested it only acts by means of the prussic acid released in the stomach by the hydrochloric acid contained in the digestive juices. With people who suffer from antacidity of the stomach, cyanide need not be lethal, even when a high dose is administered.

From all this we can safely conclude that the contents of the poison ampoules distributed to the members of Hitler's entourage—and to other personnel in the Nazi power structure—contained prussic acid and not cyanide. In common usage, however, and without a clear understanding of the active components which make the poisons lethal, cyanide is normally equated with prussic acid: one usually speaks of 'cyanide poisoning' regardless of whether the poison in question was actually cyanide or prussic acid.

The fact that Hitler had his dog poisoned with one of the ampoules provided by Himmler—which has been construed as his test that they were reliable—does not permit any conclusions as to whether Hitler himself considered committing suicide with one of them. It is far more likely that, because of the decision that Eva Braun would take poison, Hitler—who did not want his dog to fall into the hands of the Russians either—had the poison tried out on the animal.

Mohnke, Rattenhuber and Günsche all confirm that on the afternoon of 30 April 1945 there was a smell of burnt almonds in the bunker. The smell, according to Günsche, was still present after several days. Günsche, who carried Eva Braun's body outside, detected an intensive odour of burnt almonds on the corpse, whereas Hitler's body had 'absolutely no odour', let alone one of burnt almonds. He testified on 20 June 1956 that, after having deposited Eva Braun's body on the ground, he again bent over Hitler and detected no such odour:

> In contrast to Eva Braun's body, there was no odour detectable on Hitler's corpse. But, apart from that, I am unshakeably convinced that Adolf Hitler did not take poison. A number of people in Hitler's entourage were supplied with prussic acid ampoules, among others the secretaries as well as Bormann and Burgdorf. Bormann showed me his on 1 May 1945 with the remark that he would make use of it if necessary . . .

Furthermore, none of the others present ever testified to having detected a noticeable odour on Hitler's body.

The Russians, however, wanted the world to believe otherwise. We turn to the report on Hitler's autopsy which Bezemensky published in 1968. On page 70 of his report, under the heading '13 Corpses' (by November 1945 the Russians had exhumed between 100 and 160 bodies in their search for Hitler's), he writes:

> The remains of a crushed glass ampoule in the oral cavity and similar ampoules in the oral cavities of other corpses, the strong smell of burnt almonds emanating from the bodies and the pathological examination of the inner organs, during which cyanide compounds were discovered, permitted the commission to draw the conclusion that [Hitler's] death in this case had been caused by a cyanide compound . . .[233]

And later:

> Furthermore, the remains of a crushed ampoule was found in the [Hitler's] oral cavity. With regard to the fact that similar ampoules exist in other bodies, that during the autopsies of the corpses a strong smell of bitter almonds occurs, and the pathological examination of the inner organs of those bodies that contained cyanide compounds, the commission comes to the conclusion that, despite the heavy wound in the breast, the immediate cause of [Hitler's] death was poisoning by a cyanide compound . . .[234]

Any pathologist will tell you that extreme heat, such as that generated when Hitler's body was burnt, in combination with the high volatility of prussic acid, will cause an accelerated evaporation of the acid. Nevertheless, Bezemensky wants us to believe that the body—if there ever was a body—still smelled of burnt almonds after four days.

Let us hear what the Bavarian experts had to say about this in 1956:

> The formation of compounds, together with the high volatility of prussic acid, can lead to prussic acid not being detectable in the body at all. For this reason, and given the extreme heat that develops when a body is burnt, which must lead to an accelerated evaporation of prussic acid, the testimony by *Flugkapitän* Hans Baur during his interrogation in Moscow—that he had been informed that the same poison had been found in Hitler's body as in Eva Braun's—does not appear credible . . .

Even if we assume that Hitler possessed a prussic acid ampoule and that there was a 'poisoning psychosis' prevalent in the bunker, there is no evidence whatsoever that Hitler's death was brought about by prussic acid. On the other hand, there can be no doubt that Eva Braun's death *was* caused by poisoning with prussic acid.

To round off this topic finally, toxicological considerations did not lead to any indication that Hitler could have died from taking one of his numerous medicines. As Linge explained in detail, these medicines consisted of sleeping pills (barbiturates) such as Tempidorm, Luminal and Evipan, belladonna against stomach cramps and laxatives administered in massive doses during cures to prevent corpulence, together with opium to calm the digestive tract and, in addition to glucose and vitamin injections, the 'anti-gas' pills containing strychnine administered by *Dr* Morell against flatulence which Linge occasionally had to taste.

Linge testified that, after the bodies had been removed, he had cleared out all the medicines in Hitler's rooms and destroyed them:

After returning to the bunker, I then immediately carried out my further assignments. I removed Hitler's clothing, his personal effects and his medicines. I had the rug in the office, on which the pool of blood next to the sofa had collected, removed by two orderlies (Schwiedel and Krüger) and burned in the garden . . .

When I returned to the office, the two pistols were no longer there. I believe I recall that I had previously picked them up from the floor and put them on the desk. I did not see a cartridge case, nor did I look for one. Maybe the case was taken into the garden with the rug. I did not detect damage to the wall caused by a bullet, nor did I particularly look for it. There were no champagne glasses on the table nor anywhere else . . .

After having set fire to the corpses, Kempka also returned to the bunker and went into Hitler's office one more time:

After I had ordered Schneider by phone to send over more petrol, I returned to Hitler's living and working room together with Günsche and an HJ [Hitler Youth] leader who was unknown to me. The room was furnished as I have shown in the drawing in my book (page 110). There was a vase on the table which had fallen over.

There was a circular bloodstain with a diameter of about 20 to 25cm on the rug in front of about the middle of the small sofa. In front of the sofa lay two pistols, 7.65mm and 6.35mm calibre. I do not know what became of these pistols . . .

The bloodstain on the floor of Hitler's office, caused by the gunshot wound on the right temple, has naturally drawn much attention. The size of this stain has been described by the witnesses as that of a medium-sized plate, which would equate to a diameter of about 15cm. The Bavarian experts calculated that a stain of this size would require between 30 and 50cc of blood. This is a fairly substantial amount.

Secretary Gerda Christian also looked into the office after the bodies had been removed. She said on 3 July 1954:

After the farewells I went to the rooms in the bunker under the New Chancellery which served as quarters for us secretaries. About two hours later— it was then probably about 1500—I again returned to the *Führerbunker*. Here I learned from Linge that he, together with Bormann and Kempka, had carried the bodies into the garden, where the cremation was still in progress. I then once again went into Hitler's living room-cum-office. There I saw a bloodstain about the size of a hand on the rug directly next to the sofa, on the left as seen from the door. I myself did not see the bodies . . .

Several witnesses therefore saw and confirmed a bloodstain on the floor of Hitler's office. But one witness—Günsche—saw it in a different place from all the others! For a long time after having become involved in this subject, I was inclined to believe Günsche in preference to the others. The Bavarian specialists also inclined towards Günsche's version. However, it is wrong. When I received the photographs showing the sofa, on which bloodstains can clearly be seen, it became clear to me that Linge's and Axmann's version had to be correct and that Günsche's statement (Hitler sitting in the armchair) had to be wrong. The words of the various witnesses with regard to the bloodstain on the rug are as follows:

Linge (9 February 1956): . . . directly next to the sofa, I detected a puddle of blood the size of a medium-sized plate . . .

Kempka (2 December 1953): . . . there was a circular bloodstain of about 20 to 25cm diameter on the rug in front of about the middle of the small sofa . . .

Christian (3 July 1954): . . . there I saw a bloodstain about the size of a hand . . . on the rug directly next to the sofa . . .

Schwiedel (15 October 1956): . . . directly next to the left armrest of the sofa there was a puddle of blood about the size of a dinner plate. There were also bloodstains on the right outer side of the sofa . . .

Günsche (19 June1956): . . . a small puddle of blood on the rug to the right of the armchair . . .

Hitler shot himself in the right temple. Photographs show bloodstains on the right outer side of the sofa. Hitler therefore cannot have been seated in the armchair as Günsche claimed because this stood apart from the sofa slightly forward and to its right: he must have been seated on the sofa itself, as the other witnesses claim.

A further confusion of the issue was caused by authors in the GDR, who uncritically accepted statements by Russian authors without conducting any research of their own. Olaf Groehler, for example, writes on page 33 of his booklet *Das Ende der Reichskanzlei* (1978):

He [Hitler] did not die in combat, as his successor Dönitz lied later. He did not kill himself with a revolver, but had himself shot like a dog by his adjutant, after he and Eva Braun had first swallowed cyanide . . .

Bezemensky had written earlier:

. . . it therefore turns out that someone shot Hitler down after he had taken poison, as a sort of insurance measure . . . The question is, who was this?

The real question is not who but why someone should shoot Hitler when he was already dead. Let us briefly examine whether a shot— for whatever reasons—was fired at Hitler posthumously, in other words, after an assumed poisoning had taken effect.

Wilhelm Mohnke, *Kampfkommandant* of the Chancellery, made a rather odd statement on 26 April 1956 in which this subject is mentioned:

From my personal observations I know nothing about the circumstances surrounding Hitler's or Eva Hitler's deaths, apart from the fact that when I entered the *Führerbunker* on the afternoon of 30 April I detected an intense smell of prussic acid. During the course of the afternoon of 30 April there was talk in the *Führerbunker* of whether Adolf Hitler had poisoned or shot himself. One of the secretaries, *Frau* Junge or *Frau* Christian, expressed the opinion that, in view of a bloodstain that was discovered, one had to assume that Adolf Hitler had shot himself. Günsche then spoke of a statement made by Hitler that, after poisoning, he should be shot in the head to make sure. In this context he mentioned Linge, in the sense that Linge was the one who should do this. It is possible that Günsche also said that Hitler had made the same request to him. This, however, I do not recall accurately. I cannot recall either whether Günsche said that this request had actually been carried out or if it was understood as Hitler's merely having considered having this done, without it actually having been carried out. I never heard anywhere else that someone actually did fire a shot at Adolf Hitler. After his death, I did not again enter Adolf Hitler's office . . .

In reply to my question to him about this, *Herr* Günsche declared that he had never made any such statements.

Besides Mohnke's unsupported statement—there is not a single statement or hint in support of it in the testimony of any other witness—and the completely undocumented claims by certain Russian authors and others who simply copied from them, not a shred of evidence has been uncovered that someone shot Hitler posthumously. Furthermore, the sequence of events surrounding the suicide and the positions of the witnesses during these events all speak against such an occurrence.

Finally, there is the evidence of the copious bloodstains on the rug on the floor, which stem from the injury in the temple and which indicate a lethal wound. Following death in a seated position, gravity causes the blood to drain down into the lower parts of the body very rapidly. A free flow of blood from a posthumous wound in the head is therefore highly unlikely, even if the shot were administered fairly shortly after death had taken place.

Another theory that has appeared in literature and has been repeated, with variations, time and time again is the suicide by simultaneous poisoning and shooting. A classic example of this can be found in O'Donnell and Bahnsen's book *Die Katacombe*, in which, on page 211, the authors write:

Hitler took both of his pistols and put the larger one, 7.65mm calibre, which he had carried in his jacket pocket since 22 April, in his right hand. The other one (6.35mm), which for many years he had carried in a special leather pocket in his trousers, he placed on the living room table in case of a misfire. He then sat down in the left corner (as seen from the door to the living room) of the small sofa and pushed a prussic acid ampoule into his mouth; a second one he put on the table in reserve [*sic*]. His wife took off her black suede shoes and sat down with legs drawn up in the other corner, about 30cm distant from her husband. She took a poison ampoule out of a detachable plastic casing and also placed her small pistol on the table in front of her next to a raspberry-coloured silk shawl. Hitler put the mouth of the 7.65mm pistol horizontally directly against his right temple at about eye level, pulled the trigger and at this instant simultaneously bit down on the poison ampoule in a final unified act of willpower. Eva Hitler also bit down on the ampoule at this instant. Obviously her willpower was insufficient for her to shoot herself as her husband had done. The pistol slid from Hitler's hand and dropped on to the carpeting. Eva Hitler remained in the squatting position she had assumed during the final minute of her life. Her eyes were closed, the lips discoloured blue and slightly pressed together. She had not used her pistol. Death probably occurred within seconds for both . . .

Other authors have also kept repeating versions of this story without ever attempting to refer to eyewitnesses as their source. Where a reference to a 'source' is made, the authors refer to some vague statements by *Dr* Günther Schenck, who in his turn refers to something allegedly said by *Dr* Werner Haase, who died in Russian captivity in 1946.

If one examines the probability of suicide by simultaneous poisoning and shooting, the key question obviously is, is it physically possible? The poison Hitler would have taken—as discussed above—was prussic acid. All the experts agree that when prussic acid is administered to the body death is instantaneous, that is, all bodily functions are arrested within such a brief fraction of a second that the body can perform no further act of will or voluntary muscular action. Holding a pistol firmly to the head and pulling the trigger would be such an act requiring will and voluntary muscular action. If, therefore, Hitler had first bitten down on the poison ampoule, it would have been virtually impossible for him to shoot. The other possibility is that he shot first, before biting the ampoule. This is, very theoretically, physically possible, and would depend on the length of time, again measured in fractions of a second, that remained to him before brain damage caused by the bullet arrested all bodily functions. If we were to assume that he was still able to bite the ampoule, or that a muscular reflex in the jaw led to the ampoule being crushed, we are then faced with another problem. Prussic acid causes a short muscular spasm in the body in the instant before death. As the experts who also considered this method of 'simultaneous suicide' wrote:

> Therefore one would have had to expect that blood from the wound in the temple would have splattered on the shoulder or elsewhere on the immediate surroundings. None of the statements by the witnesses give even the slightest indication that such was the case. Death caused by such a method must therefore be ruled out.

Finally, it must be noted that all the witnesses agree that Hitler had prepared two pistols. He obviously did this in case the first pistol were to misfire. Such a precaution would have been totally unnecessary if he had even considered using poison as well.

Let us now turn to the question of a double. Over the last fifty years the story has surfaced time and again that a double was shot and cremated in place of Hitler, the real Hitler escaping from Berlin in the meantime. Again it was the Soviets—who did not find a corpse—who insisted on this untenable story. As discussed earlier, they even went so far as to present 'Hitler's body' to the world on 4 May 1945, all decoratively laid out and photographed in the Chancellery. When the story came unstuck (or perhaps when new directives from Moscow were received), this body was converted into 'Hitler's double'. Later on, when resurrecting 'Hitler's body' in his publications in 1992, Bezemensky simply referred to these pictures as 'the well-known fraud'. He wrote that '. . . the pictures were taken by a Soviet camera team on 4 May 1945 and exposed as a fraud the same day. . .'[235]

Yet despite all the witnesses from Hitler's immediate entourage (Günsche, Linge, Baur, Rattenhuber etc.) whom they held and continued to interrogate for many months until 1946, the suspicious Soviets did not believe the testimonies and continued to assume that Hitler had escaped, while a double had been shot and cremated instead. This unwittingly proves, of course, that the Russians never found a body, otherwise all this nonsense would not have been necessary. But, even more strangely, since 1945 even American authors have continued to repeat the story of a double, right up to 1994, as can be seen, for example, in publications by Gregory Douglas.

Many contemporary witnesses have testified that Hitler never had a double at all. Secretary Johanna Wolf, for example, was questioned about this double in Nuremberg on 25 February 1948,[236] whom Herbert Moore and James W. Barrett had described in detail in July 1947 in their book *Who Killed Hitler?* She considered this to be 'ridiculous'—as did all the others who were questioned about it at the time. She said it would have been impossible for someone to have been in the bunker who pretended to be the *Führer*; furthermore, 'the *Führer* would never have tolerated this'.

Even if a double for Hitler had existed, given the number of people who were in the confined space of the bunker, this could never have been kept secret and after the war something would have been bound to come out. No one anywhere, however, ever mentioned a double or even made an assumption as to the possibility of a double.

Let us turn finally to Eva Braun-Hitler. It can safely be assumed that she died of poisoning by the ingestion of prussic acid. It is also safe to assume that the dose in the poison ampoule was calculated to cause instant death. In these circumstances we must assume that she collapsed instantaneously or after a short spasm. An upright, seated position of the body, as Linge described it, is hardly likely, particularly since rigor mortis had not had time to set in, as Günsche credibly testified. The most likely probability is as Axmann described it—that Eva Braun-Hitler, seated as she was on the narrow sofa, collapsed sideways on to Hitler after having taken the poison. Shortly after this Hitler must have shot himself. Being right-handed, he could readily do so, despite Eva Braun leaning against his left side.

We can now summarise. After evaluating all the testimony and photographs, and after considering all the known circumstances *in situ*, Hitler (on the right) and Eva Braun (on the left) were sitting on the narrow, 1.70m long sofa in Hitler's living room-cum-office before the suicide. Eva Braun-Hitler then bit down on the prussic acid ampoule and probably fell over on to Hitler sideways. Subsequently

Hitler lifted the pistol to his temple and pulled the trigger. After the shot his body then remained seated between Eva Braun and the armrest of the sofa, with the head canted slightly forward to the right. The drooping right arm let go of the pistol, which fell to the floor. With the shot into the temple, blood dripped on to the armrest of the sofa and then flowed in a copious amount on to the rug in front of the armrest of the sofa.

There can be no reasonable doubt that the bodies were those of Adolf Hitler and Eva Braun-Hitler, given the witness accounts which agree on all major points. The bodies were seen in the office by Linge, Günsche and Axmann. Kempka, Hofbeck, Schneider and Mansfeld credibly testified that the bodies carried out of the office into the garden for cremation were those of Adolf Hitler and Eva Braun-Hitler. Unmistakable identification was possible because Hitler's head was partially uncovered and his lower limbs with the black trousers, black socks and shoes were visible. Eva Braun-Hitler's corpse was uncovered.

Hitler was dead. He had died by his own hand and had thwarted any attempt to bring him to account. He had turned the battle for Berlin into a gigantic, bloody and completely senseless mass slaughter. Half a million human beings were to die in it. In the souls of the German people, Hitler left an unspeakable disillusionment and shame, and in Europe a monstrous landscape of ruin and death, with millions upon millions of crippled, murdered and slain.

Field Marshal Keitel knew nothing of Hitler's suicide in the bunker. Towards 1600, when Hitler's body was already burning in the garden, Keitel sent *Generalleutnant* August Winter, Chief of Staff of Command Staff B in Berchtesgaden, the following message from OKW in Dobbin:

> Relief attempts for Berlin failed. City centre closely invested in final battle . . . Battle to gain political time must be continued; any signs of political or military dissolution must be ruthlessly suppressed . . . OKW in close contact with Himmler, Greim. Chancellery can still be contacted by radio . . .[237]

With or without Hitler, the OKW was unwilling, or possibly not yet able, to end the war immediately. 'The main objective,' as Keitel explained in his message, was 'to save as much territory from Bolshevism as possible in the east' and to enable as many soldiers and German civilians as possible to retreat to the west. In actual fact, however, this was of very little use, because the partitioning of Germany had long been decided upon at the Yalta conference between 4 and 11 February 1945.

Mohnke reported on 26 April 1956 that, after the bodies of Hitler and Eva Braun had been set ablaze in the garden, a meeting took place in the bunker about what was now to be done:

Following these events [the carrying out and firing of the bodies], I then took part in a meeting held in the briefing room at which Goebbels, Bormann, Krebs, Burgdorf and Hewel were present. Krebs stated that, shortly before his last birthday, Hitler had said to him that one must try to reach an understanding with the Russians. Adolf Hitler had said that Russia had eliminated capitalism and Judaism, whereas America was fostering these forces to the detriment of her people. He (Krebs) believed that, by his suicide, Hitler had intended to open the way for such a development and he therefore recommended trying to contact the Russians in this sense, particularly since Himmler had tried to contact the Western Powers. I do not know whether such a conversation actually did take place between Adolf Hitler and *General* Krebs. Goebbels, Bormann and Krebs then quickly agreed that negotiations should be opened immediately and that *General* Krebs should try to speak to Marshal Zhukov personally.

Oberstleutnant Seiffert was now sent through the front line near the Hotel Excelsior. He returned towards 2130 with the message that *General* Krebs was expected at the Excelsior at 2200. Accompanied by *Oberst* Düffing [he meant von Dufring], *General* Krebs then went to see Zhukov in the spirit of the agreement. I accompanied *General* Krebs and *Oberst* Düffing to the front line and saw that they were received by a Russian officer. Krebs returned on 1 May 1945 towards 6 a.m. He reported that the Russian side insisted on unconditional surrender and that a declaration to this effect was demanded by 1600.

On 1 May the break-out from the Chancellery then took place under my direction. I myself was taken prisoner by the Russians during the night of 2–3 May 1945, from which I returned on 11 October 1955.

I do not know from my own observations what became of Hitler's body. From statements made by other people in Hitler's entourage—as early as 30 April 1945—I learned that both bodies were actually soaked in petrol and cremated in the garden. I do not know from my own observations what became of the remains, nor did I learn anything about this from others . . .

After the meeting described above, and after Hitler's body had almost completely burnt, at 1807 Goebbels, Bormann and *Vizeadmiral* Voss sent a deliberately vague message to Dönitz via the Navy radio unit informing him that Hitler had appointed Dönitz as his successor instead of Göring. Voss testified to this on 29 May 1955:

> On 30 April and 1 May 1945 I sent the three final messages from the Chancellery to *Grossadmiral* Dönitz via our Navy radio team. This was the only radio link that was still functioning to the end . . . These final messages were drafted by me together with Bormann and Goebbels . . .

The message to Dönitz read:

> FRR to *Grossadmiral* Dönitz.
> Instead of former *Reichsmarschall* 'Göring', the *Führer* has appointed you, *Herr Grossadmiral*, as his successor. Written authority on the way. As of now you are to take whatever measures the present situation may require.
>
> Bormann[238]

Jodl and Keitel in the OKW in Dobbin were also advised about the new situation at 2215 hours in a phone call from *Korvettenkapitän* Lüdde-Neurath, Dönitz's adjutant. *Oberstleutnant* Brudermüller, Jodl's adjutant, took down the message:

> *Generalfeldmarschall* Keitel and *Generaloberst* Jodl are requested to come to the *Grossadmiral* as quickly as possible, bringing all the documents of the military command with them. The *Grossadmiral* has been named as his successor by the *Führer*. The message was transmitted by radio. Advise time when *Generalfeldmarschall* Keitel and *Generaloberst* Jodl can arrive.[239]

Dönitz said that he 'wanted to have himself briefed as quickly as possible on the military situation'. He went on:

> This appointment took me completely by surprise. Never had he [Hitler] given me the slightest indication that he was considering me as his successor.[240]

However, at 1.22 a.m. on 1 May Dönitz sent the following reply to the *Führer* (who was, to the best of his knowledge, still alive):

FRR *Führer* Headquarters.
My *Führer*, my loyalty to you will remain unchangeable. I will therefore undertake whatever is possible to relieve you in Berlin. If, however, fate forces me to lead the Third Reich as your appointed successor, I will conduct this war to the end in the manner demanded by the heroic struggle of the German nation.

Grossadmiral Dönitz[241]

Towards 2000 the Berlin *Kampfkommandant*, *General* Weidling, returned to the bunker for the last time. Weidling, who was to die in Russian captivity in November 1955, said later:

The telephone line to the Chancellery had still not been re-established so I decided to go there myself, report my decision [to break out in small groups] personally and at the same time say goodbye.

I was still waiting for the guards who were to accompany me when an SS messenger arrived from the Chancellery. The content of the letter was as follows: '*General* Weidling is to report to *General* Krebs in the Chancellery immediately. All measures intended for 30 April are to be stopped immediately.' The letter was signed by *Brigadeführer* Mohnke's adjutant . . . It was clear to me that . . . the battle for Berlin would [thus] be extended for a further twenty-four hours and that after the day's fighting and the continued advances by the enemy a break-out could now hardly be achieved. It was only a matter of hours before the two enemy spearheads pushing forwards from the north and south towards the station in the zoo would unite. The enemy had pushed forward deep wedges in the area of Potsdamer Platz and the Anhalter station. From Belle-Alliance-Platz the enemy had driven a wedge along Wilhelmstrasse almost to the Air Ministry . . .

What could be the reason behind this order? Had the *Führer* changed his mind? Maybe he had let himself be talked into surrendering, based on a correct evaluation of the enemy's forces? In this case it would have been a mistake not to issue counter-orders immediately.

I decided to countermand the orders [to break out] I had previously given and to go to the Chancellery. It took me almost an hour to make my way from the Bendler Block to the Chancellery (about 1,200m). One could only move through the debris of ruined buildings and partially caved-in cellars.

In the Chancellery I was immediately taken into the *Führer*'s room.
Here I found *Reichsminister Dr* Goebbels, *Reichsleiter* Bormann and
General Krebs.

General Krebs then informed me:

1. Today, on 30 April, during the second half of the day towards 1515, the
   Führer committed suicide.
2. His body had already been cremated in a shell crater in the garden of
   the Chancellery.
3. The *Führer*'s suicide had to remain strictly secret. I was personally made
   to swear not to divulge the secret pending further developments.
4. The only person outside who was being informed about the *Führer*'s
   suicide by radio was Marshal Stalin [?].
5. *Brigadeführer* Mohnke's subordinate sector commander *Oberstleutnant*
   Seiffert had already been ordered to contact the local Russian command authorities and to request that they conduct *General* Krebs to the
   Russian Supreme Command.
6. *General* Krebs intended to tell the Russian Supreme Command:
   (a) of the *Führer*'s suicide;
   (b) the content of his testament, according to which a new German
       Reich Government had been appointed, consisting of:
       Reich President: *Grossadmiral* Dönitz,
       Reich Chancellor: *Dr* Goebbels,
       Foreign Minister: *Reichsleiter* Bormann,
       Minister of the Interior: Seyss-Inquart,
       War Minister: *Generalfeldmarschall* Schörner
       (I was not informed who the other ministers were to be);
   (c) of a request for a cease-fire until the new government could assem-
       ble in Berlin;
   (d) of the wish of the government to enter into negotiations with Russia
       for Germany's surrender;
7. In order to hold the possibilities for such negotiations open, all measures intended for the evening of 30 April had to be cancelled.
   I was deeply shattered. This, then, was the end . . .[242]

On the morning of 1 May 1945 a further radio message was sent to
Dönitz which was received at his headquarters in Plön at 1053:

FRR *Grossadmiral* Dönitz (Chief only)
Testament in force. I will come to you as quickly as possible. Until then,
in my opinion, no announcement.

Bormann[243]

The German *Wehrmacht* and the German people still did not know that Hitler was dead. Dönitz stated later that he had gathered from this message that Hitler was no longer alive:

> I only learned later that, when the first message with my appointment was sent from Berlin at 1815 on 30 April, Hitler was no longer alive. Why his death was kept secret from me I do not know . . .[244]

The *Wehrmacht* reported on 1 May concerning the military situation in Berlin:

> In the city centre of Berlin the brave garrison is grouped around our *Führer* and defending itself in a confined space against the Bolshevik superiority. The heroic struggle continues under very heavy enemy artillery fire and waves of bombing attacks.
>
> South of the capital the forces of our 9th Army have managed to link up with the main forces and together with these are engaged in a ferocious battle of defence against the constantly attacking Soviets on a line Nie-megk–Beelitz–Werder. Our troops are also holding fast against strong enemy attacks between Rathenow and Fehrbellin . . .

At 1446 on 1 May 1945—almost exactly twenty-four hours after Hitler's suicide—Goebbels and Bormann finally decided to announce that Hitler was dead, but without divulging any details. In a further radio message to Dönitz—the last that was sent from the Chancellery—he was informed:

> FRR *Grossadmiral* Dönitz (Chief only! Via officer only!)
> *Führer* deceased yesterday 1530. Testament of 29.4 appoints you to office of Reich President, *Reichsminister Dr* Goebbels to office of Reich Chancellor, *Reichsleiter* Bormann to office of Party Minister, *Reichsminister* Seyss-Inquart to office of Reich Foreign Minister. On the *Führer*'s orders, the testament was sent from Berlin to you, to *Feldmarschall* Schörner and to preserve it for the public. *Reichsleiter* Bormann will try to come to you today in order to brief you on the situation. Manner and time of announcement to the forces and the public is up to you. Confirm receipt.
>
> Goebbels[245]

It finally took another seven hours before the German *Wehrmacht* and the German nation were informed by Radio Hamburg, at 2226 on 1 May 1945, that Hitler was dead:

Führer headquarters reports that our *Führer* Adolf Hitler fell this afternoon in his command post in the Chancellery while fighting against Bolshevism to his last breath. On 30 April the *Führer* appointed *Grossadmiral*
Dönitz as his successor.

Dönitz' adjutant, *Korvettenkapitän* Walter Lüdde-Neurath, later
tried to explain the untruthful phrase 'fighting against Bolshevism
to his last breath' by saying that the second message, 'testament in
force',

> . . . was the first news we received of Hitler's death. It said nothing about
> the time and manner of his death. We believed Hitler had sought and found
> it in combat. The words 'the *Führer* has fallen', which Dönitz chose in the
> afternoon of the same day and which were broadcast by North German
> Radio that evening, were based on this mistaken assumption . . .[246]

Dönitz himself stated later:

> The only thing I was able to gather from the second message, 'testament
> in force', was that Hitler was no longer alive. I knew nothing about a
> suicide. Given my appreciation of his personality, I did not believe a sui-
> cide to be possible but rather assumed that he had sought and found death
> in the fighting for Berlin. It therefore seemed appropriate to me to formu-
> late the announcement of his death in an honourable manner . . . At the
> time my sense of decency told me to formulate the announcement in the
> way I did . . .[247]

Following the announcement of Hitler's death on North German
Radio, Dönitz then addressed the German nation. He glorified Hitler over and beyond death without mentioning suicide by so much as
a single word. His message to the German *Wehrmacht* and the German people was to continue fighting and hold out:

> German men and women, soldiers of the German *Wehrmacht*. Our *Führer*
> Adolf Hitler has fallen. The German nation bows its head in deepest sor-
> row and reverence. He recognised the dangers of Bolshevism early on and
> dedicated his existence to this struggle. The end of his fight and his unwa-
> veringly straight road through life is marked by a hero's death in the capi-
> tal of the Reich. His whole life was but to serve Germany. Above and
> beyond that, his dedication to the struggle against the Bolshevist tidal wave
> was meant to serve all of Europe and the whole civilised world . . .

After *General* Weidling had come to recognise that a successful break-out through the Russian encirclement was now no longer possible and that any further resistance would be senseless, he saw surrender as the only alternative. By now Soviet forces had taken the station in the Tiergarten, the East–West Axis (Charlottenburger Chaussee) up to the Brandenburg Gate, the Weidendamm Bridge, the Spittel Market, Leipzigstrasse, Potsdamer Platz, Potsdam Bridge and Bendler Bridge. Despite the fact that only a few short hours beforehand Goebbels had said to *General* Krebs and Weidling that 'the last will of the *Führer* must be sacrosanct for them as well and that one could therefore only consider a cease-fire but not a capitulation', *General* Weidling decided towards midnight on 1–2 May to approach the Russian command with a view to initiating surrender negotiations. At 6 a.m. on 2 May Weidling and two of his Generals arrived at General Chuikov's staff headquarters and informed him that he had given the order to surrender. He also told the Russians that Adolf Hitler had committed suicide on 30 April and that his body had been cremated. At Chuikov's headquarters he wrote the following order to surrender to the forces defending Berlin:

Order
Berlin, 2.5.45
On 30.4.45 the *Führer* killed himself and left us, who had sworn loyalty to him, in the lurch.

Because of the *Führer*'s orders you still believe you must continue to fight for Berlin, even though the lack of heavy weapons, ammunition and the overall situation make the fight appear to be senseless. Every hour you continue fighting only prolongs the terrible sufferings of the civilian inhabitants of Berlin and our own wounded. Anybody who now falls in the defence of Berlin is sacrificing himself in vain.

In agreement with the Supreme Command of the Soviet forces, I hereby request you to lay down your arms immediately.

Weidling
General of Artillery
and Commander Defences Berlin[248]

Weidling's surrender of Berlin on the morning of 2 May 1945 was not announced to the German *Wehrmacht* or to the German people. The *Wehrmacht*'s report of 2 May only spoke of continuing fighting in Berlin and only now—40 to 45 hours after the fact—announced Hitler's death:

> The *Führer* has fallen at the head of the heroic defenders of the capital. Inspired by the will to save his nation and Europe from destruction by Bolshevism, he has sacrificed his life. This example of 'loyalty unto death' is binding for each and every soldier.
> The remnants of the brave Berlin garrison are continuing to fight in small groups in the government district . . .

On 3 May the *Wehrmacht* was still reporting fighting in the government district, despite the fact that the Chancellery had already been taken on the morning of 2 May by the 248th and 301st Rifle Divisions of the Russian 5th Attack Army:

> In the capital, remnants of the brave defenders are continuing their heroic defence against the Bolshevists in individual blocks and in the government district . . .

It was not until 4 May 1945 that the *Wehrmacht* admitted to the German people that the battle for Berlin was over:

> The battle for the capital of the Reich is over. True to their oath to the flag, forces from all branches of the *Wehrmacht* and units of the *Volkssturm* have set an example of the best of German soldiery by their unprecedented heroic resistance to the last breath . . .

In his bunker 7.6m underground—where he could not hear the curses of the people he had deceived and disappointed, nor the screams of the wounded, the displaced, the homeless, the starving, the captured, the tortured and the dying—Hitler had committed suicide on 30 April 1945. But the German *Wehrmacht*, facing destruction, and the suffering German nation, which was experiencing the most catastrophic defeat in its history, knew nothing of this. Hitler left them all in the lurch. He left the German people to their fate: what would become of them no longer interested him. They alone had failed, not he. The Germans had proved unworthy of him.

'Germans, give us four years and then judge and decide,' Hitler had shouted to the people on 10 February 1933 in the Berlin Sportpalast. Adolf Hitler's Reich had lasted twelve years, three months and ten days and in Germany had left a legacy of ruin and death.

Cato had said, in the days of the Roman Empire, 'Quidquid agis, prudenter agas et respice finem' (Whatever you do, do prudently and consider the ending).

But, then, Hitler had probably never heard of Cato.

5. The Disposal of the Bodies

Linge immediately began the preparations for the disposal of Hitler's and Eva Braun's bodies, which, he claims, Hitler had personally charged him with doing.

I fetched a blanket from the antechamber of the office and Bormann returned to the corridor to call other people to lend a hand; I recall a remark by Bormann to this effect although I do not remember the exact words. I immediately spread the blanket in front of the sofa and, aided by a second man, placed Hitler's body on it. I myself took the body by the feet, the other man by the head. The other man and I then folded the blanket over the body, whereupon we picked it up and immediately moved off through the central corridor in the direction of the garden exit.

At the time the body was taken from the sofa and while it was being carried out, there were other people present in the office. I do not recall who they were, because I was concentrating carefully on my assignment and not paying attention to anything else. I also do not recall who the second man was who helped me lift the body off the sofa and carry it out.

When we arrived upstairs in the garden I noticed that two SS officers had helped carry the other end of the body. Who these two SS officers were I do not recall. I do remember, however, that I was surprised to see them at the other end [head] of the body. Up to then I had been under the impression that it was Bormann who was helping me with the body. As I left the office I had called to one of the others present that the blanket for Eva Hitler was in Adolf Hitler's bedroom. The person I addressed in this manner was already occupied with Eva Hitler's body. Who this was I do not recall. I also do not recall that *Dr* Stumpfegger was present in the office, nor do I recall having seen *Dr* Stumpfegger during the remainder of the proceedings . . .

. . . We placed Hitler's body a short distance from the garden exit of the bunker. Immediately after this Günsche appeared with Eva Hitler's body, which was placed next to that of Adolf Hitler. The bodies lay directly next to each other with the feet pointing towards the bunker exit . . .

Günsche, who had returned to the office after having made his report in the briefing room, saw that Hitler's body was already being carried out:

When, after reporting, I stepped out of the briefing room into the corridor, Adolf Hitler's body was already being carried past in the direction of the garden exit. The porters were Linge at the front end and Högl, Lindloff and Reisser at the back end. Schädle, who had an injury to his leg, probably also helped. The only thing that could be seen of Hitler, who was wrapped in a blanket, were his lower legs with the well-known black trousers, black silk socks and black leather shoes.

Krebs, Burgdorf and Goebbels, who had come out of the briefing room into the central corridor behind me, followed Hitler's body. Bormann came out of the antechamber with Eva Braun's body. At this moment Kempka arrived in the central corridor and took over the body from Bormann. At the stairs I then took over Eva Braun's body from Kempka without saying a word. The body was still supple: rigor mortis had not yet set in. I immediately noticed an intense smell of almonds emanating from the body. The body showed no signs of injury, nor was there foam from the mouth.

I then went up the stairs to the garden directly behind the people accompanying Adolf Hitler's body. Hofbeck was standing at the door. The door was open. Hitler's body was already lying outside the door, about 3–4m away. It was completely wrapped in a blanket. I then placed Eva Braun's body directly next to Hitler's, to Hitler's right. The rest of the garden looked like a field full of shell craters, but the spot were the bodies had been laid down was still level. At the moment I was putting Eva Braun's body down, Bormann again stepped up to Hitler's body and freed the head from the blanket. While I was still bent over, having put Eva Braun's body down, I again saw Hitler's head for a short moment. In the meantime the bloodstains from the temple had spread further over the face. The face, however, was still clearly recognisable. As far as the position of the bodies during the cremation is concerned, I want to make it clear that the heads were pointing in the direction of the bunker exit, and that—seen from the bunker exit—Eva Braun was lying to Hitler's right . . .

According to the testimony of *Obersturmführer* Reisser of the bodyguard, Hitler's corpse was carried up the stairs with Linge at the front and Lindloff, Högl and Reisser himself at the back. On 31 July 1956 Reisser said:

I was called . . . by Otto Günsche. He informed me that Hitler was dead and that I should lend a hand. Immediately afterwards Hitler's body, which was wrapped in a blanket, was carried out of the antechamber of his office. I then took hold at the back end on the right side. The corpse was then carried up the stairs into the garden. Besides myself, Linge, Högl and a third man were involved. On the stairs some blood from the corpse dripped on to my trousers. We deposited Adolf Hitler's body a few metres from the garden exit of the bunker. Immediately after this Eva Hitler's body was placed next to that of Adolf Hitler. I then immediately returned downstairs. A short time later Günsche also came back from above . . .

Besides these three witnesses, who personally helped carry the bodies out of the bunker and into the garden, several other witnesses saw the 'funeral procession' and later testified to their observations. Axmann, *Reichsleiter* of the Hitler Youth, testified:

We then returned to the briefing room, where presently Adolf Hitler's and Eva Hitler's corpses were carried past the open door. I do not recall exactly who was carrying Adolf Hitler. I seem to remember, however, that Günsche and the valet Linge were involved. Adolf Hitler was wrapped in a blanket. He was covered down to the lower legs. The lower legs hung down. They were dressed in black trousers and black shoes such as Hitler habitually wore. Eva Hitler was carried by Bormann alone. *Dr* Goebbels followed the two bodies towards the garden exit. I stayed in the briefing room. A short while later *Dr* Goebbels returned there alone and remarked that he had not been able to stand the sight any longer.

I myself did not witness the cremation, did not make any other observations concerning it, nor did I visit the site later.

Dr Werner Naumann, State Secretary in the Propaganda Ministry:

As far as I recall, Bormann, Linge and Kempka went into the room and shortly afterwards came back out with two bodies wrapped in blankets, which were then carried into the garden of the Chancellery and burnt . . .

SS-Untersturmführer Maximilian Kölz of the Reich Security Service, on guard duty in the bunker:

On the afternoon of 30 April 1945—I was standing at the top of the stairs from the upper bunker—Rattenhuber told me that Hitler and Eva Braun were dead. I thereupon went down the stairs and from the bottom saw Hitler being carried out of the antechamber to his rooms in the direction of the garden exit. He was wrapped in a blanket. One lower arm and one of the lower legs were hanging out. Otherwise the body was completely covered by the blanket. I clearly recognised the familiar black shoe on the foot and the black trousers that Hitler habitually wore. The trousers had slipped up so that his socks and underpants were visible. Hitler was obviously dead. He was being carried by several people from his immediate entourage, one of whom was Linge. I do not recall who the others were. I observed this scene only for a brief moment and then turned away, deeply shattered, and went back upstairs . . .

Besides these witnesses, *SS-Obersturmführer* Johann Bergmüller of the RSD and *SS-Hauptsturmführer* Günther Schwägermann, Goebbels' personal adjutant, also saw the bodies being carried out, and they described the event in similar terms to the witnesses quoted above.

After Hitler had retired with Eva Braun, Günsche had called the *Kommandant der Reichskanzlei*, Mohnke, to inform him about the most recent developments. Mohnke later stated:

At 15 or 16 minutes past 3 p.m. on 30 April—I remember the exact time— I was called to the *Führerbunker* by telephone. The call came from Günsche. He spoke about a briefing. Coming from the upper bunker, I then arrived in the lower part of the *Führerbunker* about ten minutes later. Here, standing directly beside the door from the antechamber to Hitler's office, the first thing I saw was Adolf Hitler being carried out of this room towards the garden exit by several people, one of whom was Linge. Adolf Hitler was obviously dead. The lower legs and feet hung out of the wrapping around the corpse. I clearly recognised the familiar black trousers, black silk socks and black shoes. The lower legs were hanging down loosely. There was nothing to be seen of the head and the rest of the body. While the porters were moving away with the body in the direction of the garden exit, I saw *Dr* Goebbels, Bormann, Krebs and Günsche standing in the central corridor. It is possible that Axmann and *Dr* Stumpfegger—whom I knew from a stay in the Hohenlychen Hospital—were also there. Krebs told me that the *Führer* was dead; he had shot himself. Immediately after this Eva Braun's body was carried out in the same manner; it was, however, uncovered, but completely dressed except for the shoes. Günsche was carrying it. I learned from one of those present—I do not recall who this was—that the bodies were now going to be cremated in the garden. I did not go upstairs . . .

Despite the fact that there are some minor discrepancies between the statements of the various witnesses as to who was actually carrying the bodies at any given time and whether Hitler was completely or only partially covered by the blanket, we can now summarise. Towards 1540—the bodies had lain in the living room-cum-office for about ten minutes—Hitler's corpse was carried out first, wrapped in a blanket so that only the lower extremities, clad in black trousers, black silk socks and black leather shoes such as Hitler habitually wore, were visible and clearly recognisable. There were several people involved in the process, with Linge at the front carrying the legs and Reisser and at least two others behind carrying the head and shoulders. The body was taken through the central corridor of the bunker and up the stairs leading to the emergency exit into the garden. It was followed by some of Hitler's closest associates, among them Goebbels and *Generäle* Krebs and Burgdorf. None of the witnesses, not even those who were not directly involved in the transport, had any doubt that the body was that of Hitler. Eva Braun-Hitler's body was carried out next. Her corpse was not covered and she was clearly recognisable to all who saw her. She was brought out of the office by Bormann, taken over by Kempka and then carried upstairs into the garden by Günsche.

The only witness to tell a markedly different story in some of the important details was Kempka. We have already seen that Kempka, both in statements during several interrogations as a witness and in his book, tends to be at variance with almost all the other witnesses, particularly Linge and Günsche. When describing the events of 30 April, Kempka said:

I then immediately went into the *Führerbunker*, where I met Günsche in the central corridor . . . as he was coming out of Hitler's rooms. Günsche informed me that Hitler was dead, making a gesture towards his mouth with his right hand which was obviously intended to indicate that Hitler had shot himself in the mouth. [Günsche flatly denies having made such a gesture; if anything, he made a gesture towards the temple.]

I then asked about Eva. Günsche replied that she was with him [Hitler] and then also said that Bormann, Linge and he had heard the shot and immediately rushed into the room. [Again, Günsche flatly denies having said this.]

. . . Shortly after this Linge and *Dr* Stumpfegger came out of Hitler's antechamber . . . carrying Hitler between them on a blanket. Hitler was lying with his face turned upwards and wrapped in the blanket so that only the upper part of his head and his face down to the bridge of the nose was visible, as were his left arm and his legs up to the knees. I recognised Hitler's head beyond any doubt. On the legs, which were hanging out from the blanket, I saw the familiar black trousers and black shoes . . . *Dr* Stumpfegger and Linge, followed by Günsche, moved rapidly towards the staircase leading to the garden exit. Directly behind them came Bormann, who was carrying Eva Hitler in his arms. I took her from him without saying a word and followed Stumpfegger and Linge. Eva Hitler was dead beyond any question. She was wearing a black dress [according to most of the other witnesses, Eva Braun-Hitler was wearing a blue dress with white facings on the collar and on the sleeves. This dress can be seen in several photographs, for example in those of Hitler's 55th birthday celebrations at the Berghof] that was damp on the left side. She bore no signs of injuries or blood. When I had reached the middle landing of the staircase with Eva Hitler's body, Günsche came down the steps towards me and then helped me carry it up . . .

As discussed before, after the war Erich Kempka developed a tendency to exaggerate his own role in the events and to make himself appear more important in the scheme of things than he actually was. In the course of time, when other witnesses held captive in Russia became available to tell their stories, Kempka changed his statements and in some cases completely retracted them.

Once the bodies had been brought up into the garden, Linge, Günsche and Kempka began the cremation. Linge stated on 10 February 1956:

The petrol which had been provided was then immediately poured over the bodies. Besides myself, Günsche and Kempka took part in this. I emptied two cans. I do not know how many cans Günsche and Kempka emptied. Because of the heavy shelling, it was not possible to ignite the petrol directly. The surrounding buildings were burning and shells were coming in thick and fast. Standing in the exit from the bunker, I therefore twisted a piece of paper into a spill which Bormann lit with a match and which I then threw. I do not recall whether others also attempted to ignite the petrol. In any case, I did not see a piece of cloth. When the petrol caught fire, a gigantic flame shot upwards. We then observed the cremation through a slit in the closed bunker door. One thing that has stuck in my mind is that within a very short while one of Eva Hitler's knees was lifted up. One could see that the flesh of the knee was already being roasted. About eight minutes after the cremation began I went back downstairs. Before that, all of those present in the exit from the bunker had given Adolf Hitler a final salute. Besides myself, Günsche, Kempka, Goebbels and Bormann were present in the exit and several people, including *Generäle* Krebs and Burgdorf, were standing at the top of the stairs. I did not make any observations about the further progress of the fire. I did not return to the site of the fire, nor did I learn anything from other sources . . .

On 2 December 1953 Kempka recalled:

There were several cans of petrol standing inside the exit from the bunker. I immediately picked up one of these cans, went back outside and poured the contents over Adolf Hitler, after I had moved his left arm, which was extended sideways, closer to the body. I then jumped back into the exit and then emptied two further cans over Adolf Hitler and Eva Hitler, while Günsche and Linge were similarly engaged. While this was going on, the garden was still under very heavy fire. In the bunker exit we then discussed how to light the petrol. Günsche suggested throwing a hand-grenade, which I rejected. We then found a large rag lying next to the fire hoses in the exit. Günsche picked this rag up. I opened a can still standing in the exit and wet this rag with petrol. *Dr* Goebbels handed me a box of matches. I lit the rag. Günsche threw the burning rag on to Adolf and Eva Hitler. They immediately caught fire, which burst up in a mighty flame.

After we had saluted, we followed Goebbels back into the bunker. Here Goebbels told me that I was to continue to perform my duties under him as before. I was not personally involved in the continuation of the cremation nor did I make any personal observations with regard to this . . .

Günsche, the third person involved in setting fire to the bodies, stated on 21 June 1956:

When I turned back towards the bunker exit after I had put the body of Eva Braun down, Kempka and Linge had already stepped out with open cans of petrol in their hands. We three then poured petrol on to the bodies; it is possible that some of the others present also took part. In the course of this, probably all of the nine or ten cans that had been provided—these were Army cans holding 20 litres and they were filled to the top—were emptied. Lighting the petrol presented a problem because of the heavy shelling. Attempts with matches failed. I then considered using a stick grenade which was available. While I was unscrewing the cap I saw that Linge had already made a paper spill which Bormann was in the process of lighting. Bormann then immediately threw this spill outside, whereupon the bunker door was closed. While the door was closing, a bright flare of fire could just be seen. I then remained in the exit for a short while, and I again ordered Hofbeck not to let anyone in or out. Subsequently I, like all the others, went back down into the bunker. Before leaving, each of us saluted, some from outside the exit from the bunker, others from inside . . .

The burning of the bodies was of course also witnessed by several men of the RSD who were on guard duty on the garden side of the bunker, namely Hofbeck,[249] Karnau and Mansfeld. Hofbeck, who was on guard at the door of the garden exit, testified on 25 November 1955:

Linge, Günsche and Kempka immediately poured petrol over the bodies. I had previously seen some of the cans they used standing on the topmost turn of the staircase. I do not know how much petrol was used, but it was probably at least five, but no more than ten, cans full. While this was being done, I was the one who let Kempka, Günsche and Linge in and out of the exit by opening and shutting the door for an instant each time. At the time there was again heavy firing going on. After the cans had been emptied, *Dr* Goebbels, Bormann, *General* Krebs, *General* Burgdorf and Schädle as well as Kempka each stepped outside the bunker door for a short moment and saluted the dead by raising their right arms. Everybody involved then quickly returned to the bunker, whereupon I again shut the door. Immediately after this Bormann handed up a box of matches from the top turning of the staircase, which Günsche, Linge or Kempka took. Kempka then wet a rag with petrol. Either he or Günsche lit this rag and Günsche threw it on to the bodies, for which purpose I again opened the door. At this moment, the artillery fire had slackened. Through the partially opened door of the bunker we then saw a huge flame rising up, followed immediately by heavy smoke.

After the bodies had been set alight, all the people mentioned above returned to the interior of the bunker. I remained on guard and again opened the door a short time later, which however was only possible for a brief moment because heavy petrol fumes and smoke blew towards me. There was a wind blowing towards the exit. On opening the door I could see that the bodies were still burning. I had the impression that they had shrunk together. On both bodies the knees were drawn up somewhat.

Being very much moved by this experience, I gave over my post to one of my subordinates. At 2200 I again had a look out of the door of the bunker. However, there was nothing left to be seen of the bodies . . .

Karnau described the burning on 13 November 1953:

During the early afternoon of 30 April 1945—it was shortly after 1400—Hitler's valet Heinz Linge told me to leave this room, without giving me a reason [Karnau is referring to the room next to the staircase leading from the bunker up to the emergency exit into the garden, which served as the duty and day room for the guards]. At first I refused but then finally gave in to Linge's urgings and went through the central corridor of the bunker to the main entrance [Karnau is here referring to the staircase leading down into the bunker from the banqueting hall of the Old Chancellery], where my comrade Poppen was on guard duty. I exchanged a few words with Poppen and then went outside through the main door, intending to return to our duty room via the garden exit. The main door was about 40m from the garden exit. When I came near the garden exit, I chanced upon two bodies lying next to each other in the open about 2 to 2.5m from the exit. I immediately recognised one of these bodies as Adolf Hitler. It was lying on its back wrapped in a blanket. The blanket was folded open on both sides of the upper body, so that the head and chest were uncovered. The skull was partially caved in and the face encrusted with blood. The face, however, could still be clearly recognised. The second corpse was lying with its back upwards. It was completely covered by the blanket except for the lower legs. The lower legs were uncovered up to the knees. On the feet I recognised Eva Hitler's shoes, which were familiar to me from frequent encounters in the bunker. These were black suede shoes.

While I was still standing near the bodies, a burning rag came flying out of the garden exit (steel door) and landed in the region of the feet of the corpses, where it caused a huge burst of flame. I do not know who threw the rag. From where I stood, the interior of the exit was not visible. There was no one apart from myself outside the bunker. With the upward rush of flame, the upper body and both legs of Hitler's corpse rose upwards. There was also movement on *Frau* Hitler's corpse. These movements were obviously caused by the flames, or rather the heat. While this was taking place, the whole complex of the Chancellery lay under heavy fire.

I then made my way back to the main door by the same route, mostly crawling. On the way I looked back towards the bodies several times and saw that both were still burning. At the main door I again met Poppen and told him about my observations and then returned inside . . . to the day room . . . At the foot of the stairs to the garden exit I met *SS-Sturmbannführer* Schädle. Schädle told me that Hitler was dead and was lying in the garden and burning . . .

Hilko Poppen confirmed on 30 June 1954 that he had learned of Hitler's death from Karnau:

In the afternoon of 30 April 1945 I was on guard duty in the *Führerbunker* (main entrance). Here Karnau appeared and told me that Adolf Hitler and Eva Braun were dead and lying in the garden and burning . . .

Erich Mansfeld was questioned in Bremen on 1 July 1954 about what he had seen of the events of 30 April 1945:

Mengershausen and I were normally on duty in the observation tower which had been erected very near the garden exit of the bunker but was not yet finished. The tower was about 5–6m high. At a height of about 3.5m it had three small observation windows measuring about 60 by 60cm and covered by steel shutters. The internal entrance from the bunker into the tower was not yet finished. Because of this, the tower could only be entered from outside via the scaffolding which was still there. Of the three windows, one looked out in the direction of Unter den Linden, the second in the direction of Wilhelmsplatz and the third in the direction of the garden exit of the bunker . . . Mengershausen and I shared the duty between us in that we relieved each other every three hours . . .

On 30 April 1945 I relieved Mengershausen at 1400. As in the preceding days, the garden lay under heavy artillery and mortar fire from time to time . . .

Mansfeld goes on to say that he had to leave his post in order to fetch his equipment from the guard's day room in the bunker and describes how he saw two bodies being carried up the stairs and laid on the ground near the bunker exit. He clearly recognised Eva Braun but did not recognise Hitler, owing to the body being wrapped in a blanket. After having climbed back up into the tower, Mansfeld made further observations:

Through the window looking towards the bunker exit I saw several men of the *Leibstandarte*—I believe I recall that one of them was Jansen—running towards the garden exit from the Old Chancellery. The men were carrying petrol cans. I immediately closed the shutter of the window looking towards the bunker exit and opened the one on the window looking towards Unter den Linden in order to continue my observations. When I opened the shutter, however, heavy clouds of smoke blew towards me, so I quickly closed it again without having seen anything. Shortly after that I again opened the shutter of the window looking towards the garden exit and now saw that the bodies were burning brightly. I also saw several cans of petrol being thrown out of the bunker exit to land near the bodies. There were no people to be seen.

I was then in the tower until about 1800. During this time the bodies continued to burn. I repeatedly saw cans of petrol being thrown out of the garden exit towards the bodies. I do not remember having heard explosions. During this time the garden and the surrounding buildings were under intermittent shellfire . . .

All of the others who were still in the Chancellery and the bunker on 30 April 1945 and who survived and were questioned later confirmed that Hitler's and Eva Braun's bodies were actually cremated.

However, a question that has been asked in literature since 1945 is whether Adolf and Eva Hitler's corpses were completely burned or whether they were only partially burned—as was the case with the Goebbels' corpses—so that there were remains that could have been identifiable. As we have seen before, the Russians at various times and for various reasons made claims that such remains had been found, identified, spirited away, buried somewhere and re-discovered later. Bezemensky even went so far as to publish a report about an autopsy that had allegedly been carried out on Hitler's corpse!

These stories are all based on two fundamental assumptions, namely that the bodies were laid in a hollow, a trench, a shell crater or some such depression in the ground, which prevented the circulation of air and thus hindered the burning, and that there was not enough petrol available to do the job thoroughly.

The claim has been made repeatedly that the corpses were laid in a shell crater, a pit or a hollow. Russian photographs also show a pit or a shell crater. In 1965 Kuby, for example, wrote on page 194 of his book[250] that 'the bodies were deposited in what is commonly known as a slit trench, an elongated trench, in the midst of the construction debris and the ruins'. And on page 195 Kuby continues: 'Petrol from several cans was then actually poured on the wrapped bodies in this elongated depression, which then hindered the circulation of air.' The same erroneous statements can also be found in O'Donnell and Bahnsen's *Die Katacombe* (see page 214). All the witnesses directly involved in the cremation—Linge, Günsche and Kempka—and most of those who saw it take place from various positions at which they were on duty or simply happened to be, have stated that the bodies were placed next to each other on a flat stretch of sandy ground only a short distance away from the bunker exit. As all the witnesses go on to confirm that at the time the Chancellery lay under heavy Soviet artillery and mortar fire, so that it was extremely dangerous for anybody to stay in the open for any length of time. We may safely assume that none of the men involved had any inclination to venture far out into the garden with the bodies and the petrol cans, particularly when they could minimise personal risk by placing and burning the bodies conveniently close to the bunker exit. There would be no reason to question these statements, were it not for the stories told by *SS-Rottenführer* Harry Mengershausen,[251] one of the bodyguards, who was on duty in the Chancellery on the garden side of the bunker.

Mengershausen is a very peculiar sort of witness. On the one hand he made statements that are compatible with those of other witnesses and would therefore appear to be true; on the other he made statements that are so fundamentally different from anything all the others said that we must doubt their veracity. However, since Mengershausen was apparently, at least initially, regarded as the 'key witness' by the Russians[252]—which did not spare him almost eleven years of captivity in various prisons and labour camps—we must deal with his testimony.

Whether Mengershausen voluntarily gave himself up to the Russians as a witness, as Lieutenant-Colonel Ivan Klimenko 'supposedly' said,[253] or whether he only confessed to having been on duty in the Chancellery after he was apprehended during the Russians' somewhat belated search between 3/4 and 12 May 1945 for people from Hitler's immediate entourage, is a question that we can safely leave unanswered. In any case, he lied to the Russians. And Bezemensky—who at the time of his writings in 1968 and 1982 had not had access to the so-called Moscow 'Stalin File', which contained all the testimonies of the other witnesses and all the other information gathered on Hitler's death—believed these lies and published them. To give but one example. On pages 168 and 169 of his book *The Death of Adolf Hitler* (1982 edition), Bezemensky writes:

> The witness, Mengershausen, Harry, declared that, as a member of the SS Combat Group Mundtke [Mohnke], he was assigned to the defence of the

Chancellery and the personal protection of Adolf Hitler from 20 to 30 April 1945. Around noon on 30 April 1945 he was on guard duty in the building of the New Chancellery, where he had to patrol the corridor from Hitler's office to the blue dining room [he probably means the mosaic room].

While patrolling through the corridor mentioned above, Mengershausen stopped before the furthermost window of the blue dining room, which was the one closest to the garden exit, and observed what was going on in the garden of the Chancellery . . .

During the visit to the places which Mengershausen pointed out, his statements proved to be true [?]. During his patrol on 30 April 1945, Mengershausen was able to observe clearly what was taking place near the emergency exit of the *Führerbunker* from the window in the blue dining room. The testimony of the witness Mengershausen is all the more credible since in May 1945 we pulled the charred bodies of a man and a woman, as well as two dogs which had been poisoned, out of the crater he indicated, which other witnesses recognised as belonging to Hitler and his private secretary Ifa Braun [*sic*].

A rough sketch of the spot where the corpses of Hitler and his wife were discovered, as well as photographs of the places the witness Mengershausen showed, are attached . . .

After being taken in, Mengershausen was immediately handed over to a special NKVD group of the Soviet Peoples' Commissariat for Internal Affairs, which continued to interrogate him. On 25 April 1956, Mengershausen described his experiences:

. . . after having been captured on 2 May 1945, I first presented a forged document of identification. However, I was then identified as being Harry Mengershausen. At first I then claimed that I had only observed the process of Hitler's burial at a distance from the New Chancellery, which was initially believed. I was then subsequently interrogated repeatedly, particularly after chief cook Lange had told the Russians that my initial testimony was false . . .

With this, the story of *Herr* Mengershausen begins. Besides many other tall tales, Mengershausen told the Russians two fundamental lies, first that *Dr* Stumpfegger had killed Hitler by giving him an intravenous cyanide injection, and secondly that he himself had buried Hitler's and Eva Braun-Hitler's bodies in a crater, just by the way and without having received any orders or instructions to do so.

As regards the burning of the bodies, Mengershausen said that some time later he was again on duty at the garden exit (he probably replaced Hofbeck, who, as we have already seen, had himself relieved because of his emotional state after seeing Hitler dead):

> When I opened it [the door of the garden exit], the two burning bodies were lying immediately outside the door and two or three empty petrol cans were lying to the right directly in front of the door. The bodies were about 2–2.5m from the exit and parallel to the door, with the heads pointing in the direction of the New Chancellery and the feet in the direction of the tea house. Eva Braun was lying in the direction of the exit. The blanket and parts of Hitler's uniform were already burnt out, with only ashes remaining. Eva Braun's clothing was completely burnt off . . . The fire had almost died out completely; there were only a few very small flames, because most of the petrol had been absorbed by the sandy ground. The bodies were still in one piece and had not shrunk noticeably; the faces were still clearly recognisable, the hair on both singed off. There were no bones to be seen. Eva Braun appeared as a naked corpse. A part of Hitler's skin was charred black. Eva Braun had more of a brown colour.
>
> What I now noticed was that Hitler had an entry wound on his right temple. I could see this from the exit. The entry wound was a small hole and was clearly visible despite the charring to the head. I cannot say whether this was from a shot; in any case, it was a small hole . . .

'Later on' he stepped up to the bodies and again saw the entry wound or small hole in Hitler's right temple. There were no other wounds. Hitler's head was 'slightly pulled up' and 'resting on the ground on the narrow part of the head'. A 'sort of hollow' had formed. The back of the skull was not crushed. If this had been the case, it would have been visible. Eva Braun had no gunshot wounds—at least, he had seen none. There had been no other external injuries visible either.

It was only now that Hofbeck had come up from below to join him. At that moment he had still been standing next to the corpses. 'Then other people came as well. One of them was Mansfeld.' Hofbeck had then gone back downstairs into the bunker with the others, while he had stayed on duty at the exit together with an *SS-Unterscharführer* from the bodyguard called Glanzer. Together they had then emptied two petrol cans which were still standing on the landing over the bodies. By this time the fire had been completely 'extinguished'. He had then taken a piece of paper, lit it and again set fire to the corpses. At the moment of ignition, there had been a 'slight explosion', then initially a large flame, which then died down. Then there was heavy black smoke. The whole thing had only lasted for a few minutes. The bodies had not been lying in a 'crater': the spot had rather 'still been flat'.

Mengershausen concludes this part of his statement:

> In the further course of events, I was then relieved and again went on duty at the garden exit towards 1900 together with Glanzer . . .

In the light of all the other evidence, it can safely be assumed that Mengershausen—even though he is the only available witness for this time period—is not telling the truth. Just how far he went in inventing stories can be seen from a report in *The Times* of 13 January 1956 (page 7):

> 285 prisoners, mostly civilians, arrived today at the East–West border in Herleshausen after having been repatriated by the Soviet Union . . . Among the men released was a former SS officer called Harry Mengershausen, who claims that he cremated Adolf Hitler's and Eva Braun's bodies on 30 April 1945. Even though he had poured several cans of petrol over the corpses, afterwards they were still in a good condition, he relates. He then buried them in a shell crater. The Russians asked him to identify the bodies towards the end of June 1945. He was taken to a thicket near Berlin, where he was shown two corpses in wooden crates.

I believe no further comments are necessary! Let us therefore turn to the question of the petrol.

We have already seen from the testimony of several witnesses, including Günsche, Linge, Kempka and the guard Hofbeck, that when the bodies were carried out of the bunker and laid in the garden there were between five (Hofbeck's minimum number) and ten cans—more likely between eight and ten cans, according to the other witnesses—of petrol standing at the top of the staircase. According to several other witnesses, it appears that on 29 April 1945 more petrol had been brought to the machine room of the *Führerbunker*. Kempka's deputy, *SS-Hauptsturmführer* Karl Schneider, stated on 7 February 1956 that

... on 28 April 1945 a request for petrol came to my office by telephone from the *Führerbunker*. I was asked how much petrol was available. Kempka, who happened to be with me, was the one who took the call. I was only able to provide eight cans. That was all there was. I then immediately sent four men with these eight cans to the *Führerbunker*. I also sent some flares, which had also been asked for. I do not know who the person was who called from the *Führerbunker*. I gave no thought as to what the petrol might be needed for. I assumed the petrol was required as fuel for a machine ...

Schneider's testimony is borne out by Fritz Echtmann,[254] *Dr Blaschke's* dental technician, who stated on 15 October 1954:

I was in the same cell with Schneider in the Leforto prison in Moscow from August 1945 to January 1948. I frequently talked with him about our experiences in the Chancellery. Schneider repeatedly told me that, two to three days before Hitler's death, Günsche had ordered petrol from him. He had delivered 120 litres in six cans. He had not had any more. Günsche had asked for a larger amount but had then been satisfied with the 120 litres. He [Schneider] had assumed at the time that the petrol was needed as fuel for a machine. He had learned later that it had been used to burn the bodies. ...

Vizeadmiral Hans-Erich Voss said on 29 March 1955 that

... garage supervisor Schneider told me in prison in Moscow that he had supplied the petrol. On 29 April 1945 I myself had seen about twelve cans standing in the upper part of the *Führerbunker* which were no longer there on 30 April 1945 ...

On 22 November 1955, former machine operator Johannes Hentschel made the following statement about the petrol situation:

... from 21 April 1945 on I was constantly in the machine room of the *Führerbunker*. On 29 April Linge, Günsche and Kempka brought eight to ten cans full of petrol into the machine room, where they were then deposited. A statement about the purpose of this petrol ... was not made, nor did I ask. It was of no use in the machine room because all of the machines ran only on diesel oil, of which there was an adequate supply (ten to twelve barrels of 150 to 200 litres each).

I was astonished that these eight to ten cans of petrol were brought into the machine room. It occurred to me that they must have something to do with the imminently expected break-out ...

During the afternoon of 30 April 1945—it was probably between 1500 and 1600—Günsche and Linge came and took six to eight cans away again. Nothing was said then either . . .

From this testimony we can see that, before the cremation of the bodies began on the afternoon of 30 April 1945, there were between eight to ten cans of petrol of 20 litres each in the machine room of the bunker, in addition to the cans standing in the garden exit of the bunker. But that was not all there was.

In his statement on 24 November 1954 (already quoted from above), guard Maximilian Kölz said:

Shortly after this [after he had seen Hitler's and Eva Braun-Hitler's bodies being carried out of the bunker on 30 April 1945], when I was again standing at the top of the staircase [at the main entrance to the *Führerbunker*], petrol cans were repeatedly carried downstairs from the upper bunker to the central corridor. Who was carrying the cans I do not recall; Günsche and Linge were not involved in any case. It was clear to me, that this petrol would be used to burn Hitler's corpse . . .

Another member of the bodyguard, *SS-Obersturmführer* Johann Bergmüller, confirmed on 30 April 1954 in Munich that after Hitler's death several cans of petrol were brought from the upper bunker to the central corridor of the *Führerbunker*:

. . . soon after this [i.e. after the bodies of Hitler and Eva Braun-Hitler had been carried upstairs] several men came from the upper bunker, each carrying two cans of petrol—these were normal petrol cans—through the central corridor of the lower bunker in the direction of the garden exit. I knew these people by sight as being drivers from the vehicle park of the Chancellery . . .

While there are some discrepancies in this whole mass of testimony, we can still summarise that, at the time when the cremation of the bodies began, there was apparently much more petrol available than has previously generally been assumed. And, as Kempka also stated, during the course of the late afternoon of 30 April 1945 'further petrol' to continue the cremation was demanded and provided. Kempka said:

When I returned to the bunker from burning the bodies in the garden, Rattenhuber . . .asked me to provide further petrol with which to continue the cremation, which I agreed to do. From the *Führerbunker* I immediately gave the appropriate order to *SS-Hauptsturmführer* Schneider by telephone. When in the course of the afternoon I returned to the bunker near the garages, Schneider reported to me that he had carried out my orders. I do not know how much petrol was involved . . .

This would tie in with Mansfeld's statement, quoted above, that while he was on guard duty in the observation tower during the afternoon of 30 April he observed 'several men of the *Leibstandarte* . . . running towards the garden exit from the Old Chancellery' with cans of petrol.

It is interesting to note at this point that in 1950 Kempka, who previously had always talked about a lack of petrol, wrote in his book *Ich habe Adolf Hitler verbrannt* (page 117):

The cremation lasted from about 1400 to approximately 1930 in the evening. Under the most difficult conditions, I had had my men fetch several hundred [!] additional litres of petrol during the afternoon . . .

We have previously heard *SS-Hauptsturmführer* Schneider, the supervisor of the garages, state that, when Günsche originally ordered him to provide petrol, he had only been able to supply eight cans, because that was all he had available. However, that was not all the petrol there was in the vicinity of the Chancellery and the *Führerbunker*. Hans Fritzsche, Director and Head of the Radio Department in Goebbels' Propaganda Ministry, made the following statement on 5 February 1948 in Nuremberg:

A: May I add something at this point? I know that many people have debated the question whether it was possible to cremate Hitler's and Eva Braun's corpses with only 180 litres of petrol. I do not understand this objection at all, because during the final weeks in Berlin I had more petrol available to me than during the whole of the war. It had been brought over from the airports that had had to be evacuated. And I had 20 to 30 or even more barrels filled with petrol in the garden of the Propaganda Ministry. On 27 or 28 April I called the Chancellery and asked if they needed petrol because I had so much and actually thought it could be a bit dangerous. Those in the Chancellery told me, 'We have too much ourselves.' I then had the barrels taken to the Tiergarten through Voss-strasse in order to get rid of them. When the Russians later brought me to the garden near the *Führerbunker*, I saw with my own eyes many cans standing about.

Q: Petrol cans?

A: Yes. I kicked them, the cans, with my foot and they were all full. That is why I can hardly understand the debate about the 180 litres. I do not understand the problem. Naturally, it arose from the statements made by Kempka, Hitler's driver.

Q: What would you say—is it possible that he himself provided the 180 litres to keep the fire burning, but that later on the fire was then kept alight by the large amounts of petrol that were available?

A: In my opinion there can be no doubt that there was enough petrol available . . .[255]

The conclusion from all this is that not only were there eight to ten cans of petrol available, which Kempka's men had deposited in the emergency exit of the bunker before 29 April, but also another eight to ten cans that had been ordered previously for whatever purpose and were then fetched from Hentschel's machine room by Günsche and Linge and also used in the cremation. Furthermore, as Kempka, Voss, Kölz, Mansfeld and Schneider have stated, additional petrol was also brought over from the Old Chancellery during the afternoon after the cremation had begun, so that there were at least 300 litres available to burn Hitler's and Eva Braun-Hitler's bodies. And, if we believe Fritzsche, when it was all over there were still several cans of petrol left.

It can easily be understood why the Russians did not make any clear and credible statements about this, since according to their doctrine they found a 'corpse', i.e. a complete human body. Naturally, therefore, there could not have been that much petrol available! As a final piece of evidence on this topic, Schneider stated that, when he was taken into the garden by the Russians on 2 May 1945, 'there were as many as twelve empty petrol cans lying near the bunker exit . . .' Since an Army petrol can holds 20 litres and the cans were probably full, this alone would amount to 240 litres.

What now actually became of Hitler's body? How far was it burned? Did the Russians find anything like a corpse? The burning of a corpse in the open is not of course comparable to a cremation in a crematorium, and not even to the burning of a body or parts of a body in a stove such as occurs from time to time in criminal cases. During a cremation, the enveloping heat reflected from the walls of the oven leads to the intensive destruction of organic matter. If a corpse is burned in the open, as was the case with Hitler and Eva Braun-Hitler, the distribution of heat varies and consequently so does the depth of destruction, besides which much heat is lost by radiation into the atmosphere. When a human body is burned in the open by means of petrol, the first thing that burns off is the extraneous petrol, which causes a strong heating up of the corpse. Then, because they act like a wick, the fire spreads to the clothes, which burn away more or less quickly depending on the nature and structure of the fabric. When the open flames then act directly on the body surface for a longer period of time—according to the witnesses, the corpses burned at least from 1600 to 1830—the final result is carbonisation. During the process, steam forms in the subcutaneous tissue and in the course of the burning the pressure can rise dramatically, so that the body surface bursts open in many places. The skull can also burst from the same effect. The heat causes the protein in the cells of the muscles to congeal, which then contract. This leads to contortions (arms) or the lifting up and contracting of the upper body and legs, which stay in this position because of posthumous heat rigor (so called 'fencer's stance'). The heat causes the body fat to melt and the fatty acids released hydrolytically run out of the gashes in the skin, are absorbed by any fabrics still remaining and, because they are flammable just like the fat tissue itself, support the further burning process. Because of the major loss of substance (water and fat), the carbonated corpse or torso shrinks to a substantial degree. If the burning continues for an extended period of time, the soft tissue is almost completely consumed. The only thing that remains is fragile, calcified bones that can easily disintegrate even without external force being applied.

If we now turn to the statements made by the various witnesses to the start of the cremation, we can assume that, from the supply provided in the exit from the bunker, somewhere between 150 and 200 litres of petrol were initially poured over the corpses, occupying an estimated area of about 2.5m^2. Even if we deduct a certain amount of petrol which ran off and was absorbed by the sandy ground, we can safely assume that at least half of the amount of petrol used was absorbed by the clothing or collected on the skin and on the blanket in hollows between the bodies.

The corpses were then set on fire without any delay, so we need not assume that much of the petrol had time to evaporate. This assumption is supported by the observations that when the fire caught there was no 'explosion' but that a huge flame shot up into the air. Linge, who claims to have watched the fire for about ten minutes, every time the door was opened for a brief moment, reported that there was a strong upward draught which caused the flames to rise.

All this indicates both the conditions for and the fact of an intense fire at the outset. The observations reported by the witnesses to this phase of the process tend to confirm this. 'When the flame first rose, the upper part of Hitler's body and his legs rose. There was also movement to be seen by *Frau* Hitler's corpse.' (Karnau); 'One of Eva Hitler's knees was quickly forced upwards during the burning. The flesh on this knee was already roasted.' (Linge); 'When I opened the door, I had the impression that both corpses had shrunk together. On both corpses the knees were slightly pulled up at an angle.' (Hofbeck). These are all phenomena that are characteristic of the primary phase of an intense fire and we need not assume that the witnesses were experts on such matters and therefore knew how to slant their testimony.

However, what is then important is how long the burning of the corpses continued. Mengershausen stated that he, together with Glanzer, poured further petrol from two remaining cans standing at the top of the bunker stairs over the corpses. Kempka, Kölz and Voss testified that further petrol was brought over with which to continue the cremation. *SS-Hauptsturmführer* Ewald Lindloff, who was requested by Günsche after only (!) 30 minutes to go and see how far the cremation had progressed, reported that the bodies were already charred and torn open, partially due to posthumous injuries caused by shrapnel. This statement by Lindloff is not in contradiction to the testimony of Karnau and Mansfeld, according to which, on the one hand, the destruction of the major parts of the corpses had already occurred between 1600 and 1700 while, on the other hand, the corpses continued to burn until at least 1830.

If, therefore, after only 30 minutes the corpses were 'already heavily charred and the burning far advanced', what did the corpses—or rather the remains, because we can no longer speak of 'corpses'—look like after two and a half hours of cremation? If we take the remains of Goebbels and his wife as a comparison—they were seen by several witnesses during their identification by the Russians on 1 May 1945—then we must assume that all that remained of Hitler was some charred bones with burnt particles of tissue attached. The corpses of Goebbels and his wife were set on fire with only a relatively small amount of petrol (not even four cans, i.e. less than 80 litres; the remainder was used to set fire to the waiting room in the bunker) and only burned for a relatively short period of time. Despite this, the destruction was so heavy that on Goebbels, for example, a lower arm was completely burnt off and his wife Magda was burnt to such a degree as to be 'completely unrecognisable'.

The only statements we have as to the actual condition of Hitler's and Eva Braun-Hitler's remains after the burning are those of the guards, Karnau, Mansfeld and Mengershausen. Karnau testified on 13 November 1953:

> During the latter part of the afternoon on 30 April 1945 I again left the bunker via the main exit [through the banqueting hall of the New Chancellery]. In the interim I had been completely alone. I then saw—it was probably around 1700—that both corpses had meanwhile burned down to skeletons. There were no more flames to be seen, but there were still flakes of white ash blowing upwards. With the intention of consigning the remains to the earth in a half-meter deep crater that was about 1m away, I tried to shove the remains into this crater with my foot. At the first touch both skeletons crumbled. I was then not able to carry out my intentions because very heavy artillery fire again set in . . .

Karnau was questioned again about the condition of the remains on 30 June 1954, and he elaborated on his earlier testimony:

> Concerning the term 'skeletons' which I used during my interrogation on 13 November 1953, I would like to make a correction and add that I did not see any bones. What I found was a pile of ashes which disintegrated when touched by my foot.

I still do not know what then became of the remains. I believe that the remains were scattered by the continuing heavy fire and bombing . . . I did not again visit the remains in the garden . . .

Before this, however, in an interview on North-West German Radio (in 'Echo of the Day' in 1951), Karnau had told a different story as to the timing:

Q: And what happened then to the burning corpses, or rather to the remains, in other words to the ashes?

A: Towards 1800 I went to this spot again. I had to collect something from my duty room in the bunker. I saw that Hitler and Eva Braun had now burnt so far that the distinctive skeleton could still be seen. Towards 2000— I cannot say whether petrol had again been poured on these remains during the time between 1800 and 2000—but when I was there again at 2000 the flakes were blowing in the wind.

In 1954 Karnau said that he had not visited the remains in the garden again, but in 1951 he had said that he had been at the site of the fire again around 2000. A poor memory? It will probably never be possible to clear this up. In any case, on both occasions Karnau unequivocally stated that the only thing left of Hitler was crumbling bones.

Mansfeld testified on 1 July 1954:

Karnau then appeared at the tower towards 1800. He called to me that I should come down; it was all over now anyway. We then went to the site of the fire. There we saw two charred and shrunken corpses that were no longer identifiable . . .

Mansfeld goes on to relate that everyone now prepared themselves for the break-out. Among other things, he was told by his superior, Högl, that he should burn his identification papers:

I thereupon immediately burnt my identification card outside the garden exit. At this time [in other words after 1800] the corpses were still burning.

Mansfeld was questioned again on 7 September 1955 and said that 'the last time I saw the corpses they lay on the site of the fire in a completely charred condition'.

Of the three surviving witnesses who made statements about the condition of the corpses after the fire, two claim that there was nothing left except 'a pile of ashes' (Karnau) or 'completely charred corpses' (Mansfeld). The third witness, Harry Mengershausen, again tells a completely different story, with which we must deal at greater length below. Included in his statement which he made on 25 April 1956 is the following description of the remains:

> Hitler was burned to the degree that his feet could no longer be seen. The feet were completely burned off up to the middle of the calves—there was nothing left to be seen of them—and the upper body, the head . . . the shape of the head, that part, could still be recognised as being Hitler . . .

Mengershausen goes on to say that the surface of the body was encrusted and that the face, although charred black, was still completely preserved!

If we believe Karnau and Mansfeld, then by about 1830 on 30 April 1945 there was nothing left of Hitler's and Eva Braun-Hitler's bodies except some ashes and calcified bones, and certainly nothing that could be identified later on. It is therefore not surprising that no one in the bunker was concerned with 'burying the remains', since there were no remains to bury.

In actual fact, most of the people remaining in the bunker were no longer concerned with Hitler at all. The war was lost, the *Führer* was dead, the Russians were only a few hundred metres from the Chancellery and the German defences were crumbling. What now concerned everyone was his or her own personal fate—to commit suicide? to fight on to the end? to try and break out to the west? to stay and be captured by the Russians?

That this was actually so can be deduced from the testimony of the survivors. As we have seen, the only survivors who were able to make any statements at all about the burning of the corpses and their condition between about 1600 when the fire was lit and about 1830 when the last credible witnesses claim to have seen them are the SS guards Karnau, Mansfeld and Mengershausen. Not a single member of the higher echelon—Rattenhuber, Günsche, Linge, Kempka, Mohnke, Axmann or Baur—later stated that they had gone back outside to see what had become of the bodies and whether or not Hitler's last orders, to ensure that his and Eva Braun-Hitler's corpses were completely burnt, had been carried out. One can understand that some wanted to spare themselves the horrible sight of the slowly burning and roasting bodies and that others, as Goebbels is supposed to have said, simply could not stand seeing their former leader and idol burning away before their eyes. Be that as it may, it is still surprising that Günsche and Linge, for example, who had each been personally charged by Hitler to carry this order out, did not go back upstairs again.

Linge was questioned about this on 9 February 1956. He said:

> I personally was not active in the continuation of the cremation, nor did I make any personal observations about it. Furthermore, I did not make any observations about what became of the remains. During our captivity Günsche told me that he had ordered an SS officer called Hans Reisser to take some men of the *Leibstandarte* and bury the remains. Günsche did not say anything about whether this order had been carried out . . .

This leaves Hitler's personal adjutant Otto Günsche, whom Hitler had ordered 'to burn his corpse', for which he would 'hold him personally responsible'. But if one believes his testimony in 1956, Günsche, too, seems not to have given much thought to the condition of the corpses and the state of the remains. If one considers his otherwise strong personality, this is barely comprehensible, being completely contrary to his normal behaviour. Despite what Günsche intimated to me when I talked to him, it appears that Trevor-Roper was correct when he concluded from testimony in 1946:

> From this moment on no one seems to have given a damn any more about the past or the two bodies that were still sizzling in the garden . . . As the upset guard stated, it was sad to see how indifferent everyone had become to the body of the *Führer* . . .[256]

Trevor-Roper is referring to the statement Hermann Karnau made when he was questioned by the former at British headquarters in Bad Oeynhausen on 20 June 1945: 'It is sad that none of the officers appeared to be concerned with the body of the *Führer* . . .'[257]

On 20 June 1956 Günsche had the following to say about the disposal of the remains:

I did not go back to the site of the fire and therefore I cannot say from personal observation how far the corpses had been destroyed by the fire. I took care of the disposal of the remains by ordering *SS-Hauptsturmführer* Lindloff to bury them in the garden in an appropriate place. I gave this order to Lindloff about half an hour after I had returned from the site of the fire. During the course of the day Lindloff reported to me that he had carried out my orders together with another member of the bodyguard. He also told me the name of this comrade. I believe I recall that it was *SS-Obersturmführer* Hans Reisser.

When Lindloff reported to me about his having disposed of the remains of Adolf Hitler and Eva Braun on 30 April, he told me that after 30 minutes the corpses had already been charred and torn open. The remains, which were in a 'horrible condition', had also shown gaping wounds. In my opinion it is possible that such wounds were caused by the detonation of shells or bombs. During 30 April and 1 May—as in the previous days— the garden lay under heavy shellfire and bombing, including napalm.

From about 25 April onwards, many corpses were buried in the garden, which was mostly sandy ground. These were mainly people who had died in the field hospital which had been installed in the Chancellery . . .

Günsche claims that Lindloff and Reisser were the ones who had taken care of the disposal of the remains. Hans Reisser was questioned about this on 31 July 1956 and said:

Günsche then gave me the order to dispose of the remains of the two corpses after everything was over. I was to do this with Ewald Lindloff. About an hour and a half later Günsche then said that this was no longer necessary; Lindloff had already taken care of it. Therefore I did not go back to the site of the fire again. Lindloff did not say anything to me about the carrying out of our orders, nor did I learn anything about what happened to Adolf Hitler's remains from others . . .

We can no longer question Ewald Lindloff about this, nor about whether he used some other means to destroy Hitler's remains. He was killed at Weidendamm Bridge during the break-out on 2 May 1945. However, from the evidence available, we can assume that *SS-Hauptsturmführer* Ewald Lindloff—if anyone—was Hitler's undertaker.

I never could and still cannot understand Linge's and Günsche's conduct at the time. Neither of them personally took care of the burning corpses nor of the disposal of the remains. When I interviewed him, *Herr* Günsche was unable to give me a satisfactory explanation for this. However, one must take into consideration the fact that both Linge and Günsche had spent a long time in daily contact with Hitler and had developed close ties to him. Since both of them liked and respected Hitler, it is understandable that they did not want to see their boss roasting, burning and crumbling to pieces. As secretaries Else Krüger and Gertraud Junge both stated later, Günsche allegedly said that the cremation of Hitler's body had been the most terrible experience of his life.

Let us now try to envisage the picture that the evidence compiled and discussed so far presents of Hitler's departure from the world stage. The Chancellery is in ruins, the buildings burning from bombing attacks and shellfire. The Russians are firing heavy guns, mortars and the dreaded 'Stalin organs'. High explosives and napalm shells are detonating in the garden, fountains of earth are rising and falling, craters form and are covered over again. In all this devastation and ruin lie two burning corpses, torn by shrapnel and slowly disintegrating. A truly infernal scene! And this bombardment continued not only during the whole of 30 April but well on into 1 May— in other words for one and a half days.

Even if no one actually did attempt to bury what little could have remained of Adolf Hitler, it is small wonder that the Russians never found his corpse. Yet from the very beginning, they claimed that they had! In order to try to understand this, we must return again to the statements made by Harry Mengershausen, who was the Russians' 'key witness' in 1945. After his return home from Russian captivity, Mengershausen told a quite incredible story when interviewed on 25 April 1956:

> And since Hitler had expressed the wish that he not be permitted to fall into the hands of his enemies either alive or dead, we [Mengershausen and Glanzer] now decided to bury the two bodies. I knew of this wish and we therefore first looked for a shovel . . .

Mengershausen goes on to describe that Glanzer brought the shovel and also fetched two boards. He, Mengershausen, then levelled in the bottom of a two-metre deep (*sic*) crater and 'dug a small cavity in the lower side wall of the crater'. The boards were then laid in the bottom of the crater. The work had to be interrupted several times because of the shelling. The whole job took about one and a half hours.

Mengershausen claims that the surface of the body had been 'crusted over'; the face, however, was still completely preserved, although black in colour. Then about a metre of earth was shovelled over the corpses. While doing this, he, Mengershausen, had uncovered the dog Blondi and had then covered it over again.

At dusk—it was about 2030—Bormann had come up and asked about the location of the corpses. He had not asked to be shown the exact spot. Bormann had then soon gone back downstairs again. About ten minutes later Rattenhuber had also appeared. He had cried. 'I have served the *Führer* for ten years, and now he lies here.' Those were Rattenhuber's last words. The burial of the corpses had been carried out by him, Mengershausen, and Glanzer on their own initiative and without any instructions . . .

This is a story that is completely at odds with what the other witnesses said. Mengershausen wants us to believe that he and Glanzer worked for one and a half hours under heavy enemy fire in order to bury the corpses in a 2m deep crater a few metres to the right of the bunker exit. Mengershausen describes this in great detail: Glanzer brings a shovel; Mengershausen levels in the bottom of the crater and digs a small hollow; two boards, which Glanzer brings, are laid in the crater; the bodies are pulled into the crater and laid out side by side; they are covered with a metre of earth; the dog is found and buried again with its master.

It is the standing and personality of Harry Mengershausen which makes the whole thing so incredible. He claims that he buried the corpses on his own initiative, without having received any instructions to do so. Given the circumstances at the time, this is simply unbelievable. Mengershausen was only a junior subaltern in the RSD. That he risked his life to bury Hitler and Eva Braun-Hitler out of sheer affection and admiration for the *Führer*—without having received any direct orders to do so—just cannot be so.

It is far more probable that one of the senior people on Hitler's staff—if anybody—took care of the burial, if burial there was. And it was Günsche, ahead of everybody else, who had received Hitler's direct order in this matter. While we have already seen that Günsche, for whatever reason, did not attend to the matter personally, he did order Ewald Lindloff to take care of it. And according to Günsche's unequivocal statement, Lindloff reported to him towards 1830 that what little had remained of Adolf Hitler after several hours of burning and shellfire had been disposed of. No doubt this version is much closer to the truth.

Mengershausen claims that after he had been captured he showed the Russians the spot where the bodies were buried on 8 or 9 May 1945 (according to Russian statements, it was on 4 May 1945). In 1948, for example, he made a statement about this to Fritz Echtmann while they were in prison together in Moscow. Echtmann recalled on 15 October 1954:

> From January 1948 to August 1951 I was in the same cell with Mengershausen, first in Leforto prison and later in Butyr prison . . . We often talked about our experiences in the Chancellery. Mengershausen told me that he had witnessed the burning of Hitler's and Eva Braun's corpses . . . The bodies had been put into a bomb crater. Later on, after the fire had gone out, he had taken a closer look at the corpses. Hitler had still been recognisable to those who had known him while alive . . . Later on he had been ordered by Rattenhuber . . . to bury the remains of both corpses in the garden. The remains were buried against a wall. Mengershausen did not describe the spot exactly, except to say that it had been in the part of the garden close to Hermann-Göring-Strasse. Mengershausen also said that he had shown the Russians the spot . . .

Besides Mengershausen, with his fantastic story, other people also 'testified' to the Russians about the spot where 'the corpses had been buried'. Mechanic Johannes Hentschel, for example, 'had heard' that Hitler's remains had been buried near the pergola between the garden exit and the tea house. His source of information had allegedly been the orderly officers Wauer and Arndt. Arndt, however, had gone down on 22 April 1945 in the plane that crashed near Börnersdorf and Wauer was killed during the break-out from the Chancellery on 2 May 1945.

Guard Maximilian Kölz also made a statement based on hearsay, in which he said that, while he had not made any personal observations, he had heard that Hitler's and Eva Braun's remains had been thrown into the pool in the garden of the New Chancellery:

> . . . the pool in the garden in front of Hitler's office . . . The pool was a decorative piece of work measuring about 20 by 30m and always filled with water. Whether it was Hofbeck or Henschel who told me this I do not recall. Nor do I know whether Hofbeck or Henschel had this information from their own observations. It was while we were assembling for the break-out in the late night hours of 1 May 1945 . . .

And Kempka in his turn stated on 2 December 1953 that the remains had been buried near the ruined wall of his and Linge's house some distance from the exit from the bunker:

> Towards 1930 Rattenhuber and I again went to the site of the fire, which Rattenhuber had asked me to do, remarking that we should go and see how far things had now progressed. All we found was ashes. The fire was out. Rattenhuber then said that he had ordered that the remains should be buried near the ruins of the house that I had formerly lived in, which was about 25m away from the bunker exit. I myself made no observations whether this intention was carried out or by whom. However, Rattenhuber told me during late evening of 30 April that the ashes had been buried . . .

As we have already seen, Rattenhuber testified on 26 November 1955 that he had not been to the spot where the bodies were burnt, nor given any orders about the disposal of the remains. The claim that he had visited the site with Kempka was not true.

Interestingly enough, after his arrest by the CIC in Hintersee near Berchtesgaden, Kempka had made a totally different statement on 20 June 1945:

> To the best of my knowledge, nothing was later done to remove any traces of the corpses from the site of the fire. This was also unnecessary, because the traces were readily destroyed by the unceasing artillery fire on the government sector . . .

SS-Hauptsturmführer Karl Schneider also contributed hearsay evidence when he stated on 7 February 1945:

> Towards midnight on 30 April 1945 I again went back into the *Führerbunker* and then to the garden exit. Here I was told that the remains had been buried near the house Kempka and Linge had lived in. I do not recall who told me this. I did not visit the place indicated to me . . .

If we analyse all this, we come up with several different 'graves' containing anything from 'still identifiable corpses' to 'only ashes'.

Let us now turn to the Russians. They—after some weeks of hesitation—claimed that they had found Hitler's body. They did in fact find many corpses in the garden of the Chancellery, in the ruins of the buildings and in the bunkers. The suspicious Russians took photographs of all the other corpses, of Goebbels, Magda Goebbels, the Goebbels children, *General* Krebs etc., and to make absolutely sure had them identified by all the available witnesses—Hans Fritzsche, Wilhelm Exhold, Karl Schneider and Käthe Heusermann to name but a few. Surprisingly, however, in the case of Hitler's body, the Russians failed to do this! To this day the Russians have not presented a single piece of evidence that they found Hitler's corpse. In this context we can forget Bezemensky's dilettantish 'autopsy report'. Where are the authentic photographs? Where is the picture of Hitler's skull with an upper and a lower jaw? Where is the allegedly lead-lined box with Hitler's identifiable corpse? Why was this not shown to the witnesses the Russians had captured? Even though in 1945—and during their reconstruction of the events in 1946—the Russians kept telling Linge, Günsche, Baur, Hofbeck, Henschel and the others that they would be 'confronted with Hitler's body', they never showed it to any of these people.

We will return to this topic later, but let us now hear what Linge and Baur said about it. On 9 February 1956 Heinz Linge testified:

> In Berlin [at the end of April 1946] I asked the interrogator if they had Hitler's corpse in their possession. I was then told that many bodies had been found but that it was not known whether one of them was Hitler's. I had this conversation with the Lieutenant-Colonel Klaus [Klausen] mentioned before . . .

And *Flugkapitän* Hans Baur said on 24 November 1955:

> . . . after we arrived in Berlin I was interrogated by a Commissar I already knew called Krause [Klausen], who had come with us from Moscow. This Commissar held the rank of Lieutenant-Colonel. He told me that it was now high time to decide what to do with the corpses. We would be shown the bodies and should say whether we recognised any features which could indicate the identity of Hitler or Eva Braun. Up to now the bodies had

been preserved. It was now time to decide if this should remain so or whether they should be destroyed. A confrontation with the corpses did not take place, however . . .

The only person who claimed to have seen Hitler's corpse is again our friend Harry Mengershausen. He recounts that, in early June 1945, an inspection of 'the place' where Hitler's corpse had allegedly been buried took place. The crater had been dug up! We must remember that the garden of the Chancellery and the area around the bunker was a huge field of craters. That Mengershausen spoke of a specific crater is already an indication that he was lying. Mengershausen goes on to say that in early July he was taken from the prison in Friedrichshagen to an open pit in woods nearby in order to identify three corpses. Each of the corpses was by itself in a 'small wooden casket'. The corpses had been those of Hitler and *Herr* and *Frau* Goebbels. Mengershausen claims to have 'clearly recognised' Hitler by the shape of the head, the distinctive shape of the nose and the missing feet. 'From the distance' he had not been able to see if Hitler's jaw had still been there. The whole 'viewing of the bodies' had lasted for less than two minutes!

Once again, Mengershausen is telling a story—in great detail as usual—that simply does not fit the circumstances. It is impossible that Mengershausen was able to detect the 'distinctive shape of Hitler's nose'. The nose, like all the other soft tissues of the face, the torso and the extremities, must surely have burned away during the relatively long cremation process. A skull that is exposed to strong heat can preserve its bony shape for quite some time, but not its distinctive features, which it takes from the soft tissue of the face.

There was another witness available in 1945, who had been as closely involved in the final phase of the destruction of Adolf Hitler's and Eva Braun's bodies as Harry Mengershausen, if not more closely. This witness was Hermann Karnau, who was a prisoner of the British. On 13 November 1953 Karnau said:

In November 1945 I was taken from Esterwegen to Berlin. Here I was told by an officer of the Secret Service that I was to lend a hand in the local search for Hitler's remains. However, this did not take place because of the refusal of the Russians . . .

In 1946 Trevor-Roper wrote of this: 'They [the Russians] ignored Hermann Karnau and his testimony . . .'[258] Why did the Russians refuse to hear Karnau at the end of 1945 or to use his help in identifying Hitler's body? There is really only one possible answer to this: they had no corpse!

Various witnesses later testified completely independently of one another that 13 to 15 corpses, or parts of corpses, had been found in the vicinity of the bunker exit, of which some were no longer identifiable. To give but one example, Artur Axmann, during his interrogation by Musmanno, testified on 16 October 1947:

> During the final days many people died in the area of the Chancellery. Some were killed during bombing attacks and others by shellfire, and they were burned all around the Chancellery. The rest were simply thrown into bomb or shell craters in the garden. Hitler did not want to see corpses lying about when he went into the garden for his half-hour walks . . .

Russian General Boltin, co-editor of the Soviet history of the war, is supposed to have told Erich Kuby in the 1960s that during the early days in May 1945 'two new "*Führers*" were found every day'. 'As far as he [General Boltin] was concerned,' wrote Kuby in 1965, 'Hitler's body had still not been found.'[259]

Let me close this topic by repeating what Otto Günsche told me in several telephone conversations and wrote in several letters:

> That Adolf Hitler was not completely burnt up with the help of the petrol is correct. The remains were scattered and shellfire did the rest . . . The heavy artillery and napalm fire went on until 2 May. Nothing was left that could point to Hitler . . . Often I can only shake my head about the claims of so-called witnesses, some of whom were not even there and are only repeating hearsay from others as their own observations. Maybe such claims, which were made immediately after the end of the war and have been repeated in various versions, are the answer to the fact that no one was in a position to prove what was left of the *Führer*'s corpse and where this could be seen. None of the reports about this can be proved: they are falsifications and, as is well known, have often been retracted . . .
>
> I can only repeat what I have already told you on the phone. The destruction of the *Führer*'s corpse and that of his wife was complete through various causes. I carried out my orders under the circumstances existing at the time and this gives me satisfaction. Who knows what will be dished up again in May of the coming year. Let us wait and see . . .

By 'several causes' Günsche meant the long duration of the fire and the destruction of the remains by the heavy bombardment lasting almost a day and a half. In the previously mentioned book *Voices from the Bunker*, Günsche was quoted as saying:

> The place where the corpses were placed lay under heavy artillery fire, with napalm and all kinds of calibres, so that it is not surprising that nothing of Hitler was ever found.
>
> The Russians were never in a position to display the remains of Hitler's body, which they certainly would have done if they had found it. But they did find Goebbels' corpse, shrunk together and hardly recognisable, which they did display. Photographs of this were published. If the Russians had found Hitler's corpse, I would not have been questioned for such a long time—not only I but the others as well . . .
>
> The interrogations lasted for a very long time—about one or one and a half years. They kept repeating the same questions time and again and finally the realisation that they had obviously not found the corpse gave me a sort of satisfaction. Later I asked some of my companions in misery, including Linge, about this: they were never shown any remains of Hitler's corpse for identification . . .[260]

Trevor-Roper was probably correct when he wrote, forty years ago, that later on no one concerned himself with the bodies. It was simply chance, an quirk of fate, that the only thing to remain of Hitler was a gold bridge with porcelain facets from his upper jaw and the lower jawbone with some teeth and two bridges.

In his book *The Death of Adolf Hitler*, Bezemensky shows a photograph with the caption 'The box with Adolf Hitler's corpse'. Even with the best intentions, one cannot recognise 'Adolf Hitler's corpse' but only in indefinable blackness something which could be anything (but certainly not Hitler's corpse!). Bezemensky would have been much better advised to show the cigar box in which resided the only things that can conclusively be attributed to Hitler. There can no longer be any doubt that all that was left of Hitler easily fitted into a cigar box.

And in 1950, after having heard some 200 witnesses, Judge Musmanno had already come to the conclusion that 'it is no secret that Hitler's corpse was never found. . .'[261]

6. Odontological Identification

As with any criminological and forensic investigation to identify an unknown or partially destroyed body, odontological identification plays a very important role. However, this requires that the dentist who treated the person to be identified is available. In the case of Adolf Hitler and Eva Braun-Hitler, this was relatively easy because Hitler's dentist, *Professor* Hugo Blaschke, was known and had been arrested by the CIC in Dorfgastein on 20 May 1945. His employees, dental assistant Käthe Heusermann and dental technician Fritz Echtmann, were arrested in Berlin by the Soviets between 8 and 9 May 1945. The experts who could make a positive odontological identification of Hitler were therefore available; what was missing was Hitler's and Eva Braun-Hitler's skulls.

As was reported in the New York *BMA News Review* (November 1981 issue, p. 13), after Stalin had informed Truman, Byrnes and Leahy over lunch in Potsdam on 17 July 1945 that 'Hitler had escaped', an American team was formed for the purpose of reconstructing Hitler's skull and head from the photographs, x-rays and other anthropological data available. One of the experts involved in this project was Professor Wilton Marion Krogman, an American anthropologist who had developed a means of reconstructing physiognomical details by combining x-ray pictures of the front, back and side of the head.

Using this method, a picture of Hitler's head and teeth could be made. This picture would have made it possible to identify the remains of Hitler's skull, if such remains had been found. Even if a part of the cranium had been missing—as Bezemensky claims in his alleged autopsy report—Hitler's skull could have been reconstructed from the remains. This method, for example, was used to identify

Martin Bormann's skull, which was found on 8 December 1972 in Berlin at 63–68 Invalidenstrasse, and the identification was absolutely positive.

The Russians, however, never presented a skull that would have permitted such an identification: therefore they never had one, nor did they ever examine one! On the other hand—still according to Bezemensky—on 8 May 1945 the Russian Secret Service (SMERSH) 'took a bridge made of yellow metal consisting of nine teeth out of Hitler's upper jaw and a singed lower jaw consisting of 15 teeth out of Hitler's skull'. Did they break the upper jaw out of the skull? Why? Where is there a photograph of this skull, either with or without the upper jaw? And why was something 'taken out' of the skull? Would it not have been easier, as with any normal criminological investigation, to show the skull complete with upper and lower jaw and have it anthropologically and forensically examined? None of these questions have been answered by the Russians.

As an aside, some comments on the identification of the alleged corpse of Eva Braun-Hitler are in order. How was it possible that Eva Braun-Hitler had several shrapnel wounds in her chest which caused extensive bleeding—as Bezemensky's autopsy report claims—when Hitler, who was lying directly next to her, had none? Even though Eva Braun-Hitler's body had been cremated, it is supposed to have shown fresh blood from shrapnel wounds ('clearly recognisable haematomae')? Can she have bled when she was already dead? Blood can only flow from a wound as long as it is still in liquid form and has not yet congealed. If one follows Bezemensky, the discovery of Eva Braun-Hitler's plastic bridge is also a mystery. According to the supposed autopsy report, her skull and jaws were completely burnt, while the bridge with the teeth, 'which were still white', was not. Would not the plastic in the bridge have melted in the heat or at least been carbonated? The questions never end!

As noted, there were three people who knew Hitler's and Eva Braun's dental status. These were Hitler's dentist *Dr* Blaschke, dental assistant Käthe Heusermann and dental technician Fritz Echtmann. In his book *The Last Battle*, Cornelius Ryan wrote about Blaschke:

Dr Blaschke, who had treated Hitler and his closest associates since 1934 [actually since 1933], had been elevated to the rank of *SS-Brigadeführer* [this had to do with how he was paid] and made head of the dental department of the Berlin SS clinic. He was an avid Nazi and owed his dental practice, which was the largest and most lucrative in Berlin, to his connections with Hitler . . .[262]

While this is not true—*Dr* Blaschke did not have a large and lucrative practice in Berlin, neither was he head of the dental department of the SS clinic—Blaschke *had* become Hitler's personal dentist. In 1930 one of his patients, *Prinz* Viktor zu Wied, had recommended him to Hermann Göring, who became his patient and passed him on to other Nazi leaders. *Dr* Blaschke then joined the NSDAP on 1 February 1931. On Göring's recommendation Blaschke was called to the Chancellery to treat Hitler for the first time towards the end of 1933. After a correct diagnosis and a successful treatment, Blaschke remained Hitler's personal dentist until 22 April 1945 and treated him whenever required in Berlin, on the Obersalzberg or at *Führer* headquarters, where complete dental treatment stations had been installed. Apart from Hitler, *Dr* Blaschke also treated Himmler, Goebbels, Bormann, Eva Braun and other prominent people.

Dr Blaschke's 'SS career' began when Himmler asked him to join the SS on 2 May 1935 and made him an officer on his staff on 1 April 1936. On 20 April 1941 Blaschke was promoted to *Oberführer der SS* and appointed director of the dental department under the *Reichsarzt der SS*. From 1 January 1942 on he was paid an additional 500 marks a month on top of his Army pay for work he performed on the side. On 25 June 1943 Hitler rewarded him for his dental services by making him a professor and on 31 August 1943 he was appointed chief dentist of the SS and promoted to *Generalmajor der Waffen-SS*.

As already mentioned, in mid-October 1944 Hitler was suddenly seized by a very bad toothache. From the daily notes taken by Heinz Linge, we know that *Dr* Blaschke came to *Führer* headquarters in the 'Wolfsschanze' on 14 October 1944, where he treated Hitler at 1815. He found that tooth No 6 in the left upper jaw was heavily infected, as was the surrounding tissue, and, as an x-ray showed, it had a deep fistula. (During his interrogation in 1954 *Dr* Blaschke spoke of tooth No 7, left. However, the three x-rays taken on 19 September and the two taken on 21 October 1944 in the Karlshof field hospital near Rastenburg, which were only discovered in the National Archives in Washington DC in 1972, show that tooth 7 was no longer there.)

On 7 November 1944 *Dr* Blaschke returned to Führer headquarters and decided to recommend extracting tooth 6, because Hitler would not put up with lengthy treatment and was also suffering from a sinus infection. *Dr* Blaschke also felt that this was necessary to prevent the infected tooth from further infecting the sinuses. After his capture on 20 May 1945 Dr Blaschke made three important statements on three separate occasions. The first, which was taken down in December 1945, was filed under the heading 'Final Interrogation Report OI FIR 31' and is signed by Malcolm S. Hilty, Chief of Department OI of the Military Intelligence Service, Headquarters US Forces Europe. It contains several sketches of Hitler's teeth and has *Dr* Blaschke's description of Hitler's dental history as well as additional information on Eva Braun's and Martin Bormann's teeth attached. The second statement was made when Judge Musmanno interrogated *Dr* Blaschke in the labour camp in Nuremberg-Langwasser on 19 and 21 April 1948, and the third was made by *Dr* Blaschke on 24 June 1954. The gist of these statements is as follows:

From 1933 onwards I was Hitler's regular and only dentist . . . In the final months before the collapse—after Hitler had returned to Berlin—I had a dental treatment station in the Chancellery which I attended in addition to my own practice. The last time I saw Hitler was on 20 April 1945 . . .

From 1938 onwards I employed Fritz Echtmann as a dental technician, and *Frau* Käthe Heusermann was in my employ as a dental assistant from about the same time.

In 1933 I made and installed a large bridge in Hitler's upper jaw. It extended from No 7, left, to No 6, right. The bridge was anchored on several—probably five—existing teeth. The bridge was made of gold. There were several smaller bridges in the lower jaw.

In the autumn of 1944 [it was actually on 10 November] the left rear part of the bridge from No 7 to No 5 had to be cut off because of an infection of the gums, and No 7, upper left, had to be removed [it was actually No 6 which had to be extracted]. During the operation and the pre- and post-operative treatment *Frau* Heusermann assisted me.

I have not seen Echtmann nor *Frau* Heusermann since 21 April 1945. I have been held under arrest since 20 May 1945.

Because of *Frau* Heusermann's involvement during the removal of the left upper part of Hitler's bridge in 1944—*Frau* Heusermann was constantly standing next to the treatment chair—one can assume that the bone shown to *Frau* Heusermann actually is Hitler's upper jawbone. In this context it should be noted that the removal of a part of a bridge is exceptional practice. There were many x-rays of Hitler's upper jaw in the dental station in the Chancellery. I do not know whether *Frau* Heusermann had x-rays available when she was shown the bone.

During my imprisonment in Langwasser Musmanno questioned me repeatedly—I believe it was three or four times. At his request I told him about my work for Hitler and drew his attention to an article in a dental paper—I do not recall the details—about a jawbone of Hitler's having been discovered and identified by *Frau* Heusermann. In this context I mentioned that in the circumstances the article was probably based on the truth . . .

Dr Blaschke does not appear to have had a very good memory after the war, because several details of his statement are incorrect and do not agree with the statements by *Frau* Heusermann and *Herr* Echtmann.

After *Dr* Blaschke had cut off a part of the bridge with teeth Nos 6 and 5, upper left, and again treated Hitler on 11 and 13 November 1944, he returned to Berlin. There he once more treated Hitler on 23 November and subsequently also on 16 and 17 December in the 'Adlerhorst' headquarters. *Dr* Blaschke saw Hitler for the last time on 20 April 1945, and when Hitler 'reduced' his staff on 21 April Blaschke, like many others, was ordered to leave Berlin by air. As transpired during his interrogation by the US Army, all the files on Hitler's dental treatments as well as several x-rays were kept in the dental station in the Voss-strasse air raid shelter of the Chancellery. As he later testified, *Dr* Blaschke had only one hour during the night of 21–22 April 1945 to pack his things. *Frau* Heusermann and *Dr* Rohkamm helped him do this. He took a small portable treatment set, files, notes and all the x-rays, which were then loaded in *Major* Gundelfinger's Ju 352. As already mentioned, this aircraft crashed and caught fire near Börnersdorf. Thus there were no known documents left detailing Hitler's and Eva Braun's dental status until the x-rays taken on 19 September and 21 October 1944 were discovered in the US National Archives in Washington in 1972. The only thing available until then were statements by *Dr* Blaschke, *Frau* Heusermann and *Herr* Echtmann, which, however, were to prove to have been correct.

In December 1972 Professor Reidar F. Sognnaes of UCLA and Professor Ferdinand Stroem of Oslo University published a paper in which they scientifically traced and documented Hitler's and Eva Braun's dental status.[263] Long before then, but kept secret by the Russians on Stalin's orders, *Dr* Blaschke's dental assistant Käthe Heusermann and dental technician Fritz Echtmann had identified bridges the Russians had found among the remains of about 13 to 15 corpses scattered near the bunker exit during their intensive search for Hitler's body between 4 and 8 May 1945. On 27 April 1956 *Frau* Heusermann testified to this in detail:

> I assisted *Dr* Blaschke when he shortened the bridge in Hitler's upper jaw, which he carried out in Rastenburg in the autumn of 1944. This treatment was carried out in Hitler's mouth, i.e. the bridge was not taken out. The operation lasted for about one and a half hours. I was present the whole time and can recall the event in detail. It was a gold bridge of eleven segments that reached from No 5 right to No 6 left and was shortened by two segments, namely Nos 5 and 6 left. Before this, the condition was as follows: 5 right—crown; 4 and 3 right—pontics; 2 right—pin post; 1 right—fenestrated crown; 1 left—pin post; 2 left—pontic; 3 left—pin post; 4 and 5 left—pontics; 6 left—gold crown. Nos 5 right, 2 right, 1 right, 1 left, 3 left and 6 left served as abutments. The operation had become necessary because the terminal abutment No 6 left was badly infected.
>
> . . . I left the Chancellery in the evening of 1 May 1945 together with a large group and stayed with this group until we reached the Schultheiss-Patzenhofer brewery in Schönhauser Allee. From there I made my way to my apartment in Paris Strasse on 2 May and arrived there on 3 May.
>
> On 9 May 1945 I had a visit from a dentist who had taken over *Dr* Blaschke's practice and who asked me to come to the surgery where they were searching for Hitler's files and x-rays. I followed this summons. At the surgery I met a Russian colonel and a female interpreter. The Colonel had a foreign-looking man with him who was introduced as an expert.

When nothing was found at the practice, I was taken to the Chancellery, where a search was also conducted. The search was senseless to begin with, because all of the files had been put on the plane to Berchtesgaden. I told the Colonel this.

The Colonel then took me to Schwanebeck, where on 9 May 1945 I was shown:

1. A gold bridge with porcelain facets from an upper jaw;
2. A complete lower jawbone with teeth and bridges;
3. A small gold filling;
4. A bridge from a lower jaw made of synthetic resin with a gold crown.

I was immediately able to identify the bridge from the upper jaw as well as the lower jawbone as belonging to Adolf Hitler. The lower jawbone contained a larger and a smaller gold bridge with which I was exactly familiar, both from the shortening of the bridge in the upper jaw in Rastenburg described above as well as from numerous treatments of the gums. An unmistakable sign of recognition for the bridge from the upper jaw was the surface where it had been cut. I also recognised the gold filling and the synthetic resin bridge as belonging to Eva Braun. I clearly and unequivocally stated this to the Colonel. I was kept in Schwanebeck until 11 May and then driven to my apartment.

On 13 May 1945, however, I was again picked up and taken to Finow together with Echtmann. Towards the end of May I was driven from Finow to Friedrichshagen. During very many interrogations in Finow and Friedrichshagen, I kept repeating what I knew, much as I have described it today. No one expressed to my face any doubts about my statements. My requests and pleas to be released were answered to the effect that I was a very important witness who still had to be questioned by higher officers.

In May 1945—it was probably towards the end of the month—I was taken from Finow to a wood very close to Finow. Here, in the presence of a General and many officers, I was shown seven crates with human corpses and one crate with the corpses of two dogs. All of these crates were in a hole that was about one metre deep. I was made to climb down into the hole and inspect the corpses. I clearly recognised the corpse of *Dr* Goebbels, and the other six corpses were those of his children. *Dr* Goebbels' corpse was hardly burned. The head was easily recognisable, as was the crippled leg. The children lay in the crates with their mouths open. They were dressed in pyjamas which were open at the front. All the bodies, including that of *Dr* Geobbels, showed autopsy cuts that had been sewn up . . .

I unequivocally told the Russians my convictions as to the identity of the corpses. I also asked about the body of *Frau* Goebbels. I was then told that she had been so badly burned that she was no longer recognisable.

In July 1945 in Finow I was again shown a cigar box containing what the Colonel had shown me on 9 May 1945 in Schwanebeck. I again stated that it was Hitler's bridge from his upper jaw and his lower jawbone, recognisable by the two bridges and a gold filling, and the bridge from Eva Braun's lower jaw. With these things there was now an Iron Cross 1st Class, a gold party badge, a large gold watch and a few small pieces of cloth. I was asked whether I recognised these things. I answered this question in the negative. I was then told that they also had belonged to Adolf Hitler . . .

Frau Heusermann, who was 36 years old when she made these statements, was not to know at the time that she would spend almost ten years in prisons and labour camps as a captive of the Russians.

Dr Blaschke's dental technician, Fritz Echtmann, had a similar experience with the Russians in Berlin. On 10 July 1954 he testified:

I was employed as a dental technician by *Professor* Blaschke . . . from 1 July 1938 onwards. In the autumn of 1944 *Professor* Blaschke and his assistant *Frau* Heusermann travelled to *Führer* headquarters in Rastenburg to carry out some technical work on Hitler. He had to remove a crown and a heavy gold bridge segment from the left side of the upper gold bridge because the natural tooth was damaged. When he returned from Rastenburg *Professor* Blaschke gave me a crown with a massive attachment which he had removed from the bridge and told me that this was from Hitler. *Frau* Heusermann, who had assisted during the operation in Rastenburg, confirmed this that same day. I was to use the gold from the segment of the bridge that had been removed to make the framework for a synthetic resin bridge for Eva Braun, which I subsequently did.

Some time later *Professor* Blaschke intended to make a skeletal denture for Hitler. In order to prepare the work for this I studied Hitler's x-ray status in detail at the end of 1944 or in January 1945, because I had to gain the most accurate picture possible of the foundations.

The x-rays were kept at Blaschke's practice in the Chancellery, and since 1938 I had carefully studied them on several occasions. When I studied the x-rays at the end of 1944 I found one on which the shortening of the bridge, which *Professor* Blaschke had carried out shortly before in the autumn of 1944, could be clearly seen. Based on this x-ray I was able to ascertain beyond any doubt that the cut-off bridge segment which I had received from *Professor* Blaschke in the autumn of 1944 had actually belonged to Hitler . . .

In the afternoon of 9 May 1945 several Russians appeared in *Dr* Blaschke's practice on Kurfürstendamm, where I was at the time, and demanded all the x-rays of former members of the government. These x-rays, however, were not at the practice.

At the instigation of a *Dr* Bruk or Brukmann, who at the time was just taking over Blaschke's practice, the Russians went to *Frau* Heusermann in order to question her. On 11 May *Frau* Heusermann returned from her interrogation and told me to prepare myself because she had told the Russians that I knew more about the whole matter. I was then arrested on 11 May 1945 and taken to Schwanebeck near Berlin. There I first had to describe Hitler's upper bridge and Eva Braun's synthetic resin bridge in detail and prepare drawings. The Russians were so exacting that they even wanted me to describe the gold framework in Braun's synthetic resin bridge and then x-rayed it themselves by way of comparison. As the Russians confirmed to me later, my description of the framework was in complete agreement with the model picture taken subsequently. Despite this, they again became suspicious as to Eva Braun in 1946 and demanded further details from me.

I then told the Russians that Eva Braun had had four jacket crowns made out of porcelain on her upper front teeth—from No 2 to No 2—which had also been made at Blaschke's practice. This information was also probably checked by the Russians, because about two months later I was told that my description had been completely accurate and that there was now no more doubt about Eva Braun's death.

After I had made the statements described above during my first interrogation in Schwanebeck the Russians showed me a cigar box containing the following objects: Hitler's lower jaw and upper bridge, Eva Braun's lower synthetic resin bridge, an Iron Cross 1st Class and a gold party brooch. In answer to my question I was told that the Iron Cross and the party badge had been taken from the corpse.

When I examined the upper gold bridge more closely I was able to ascertain that it had been shortened. On the upper left side of the bridge there was a cut, the surface of which had only been lightly polished. From this one could conclude that the surface had been lightly buffed inside the mouth by means of a rubber polisher. A polish without a prior cut would have looked very different. Besides that, the surface of the cut on the gold bridge was precisely identical to the one on the massive segment that I had been given by *Professor* Blaschke in the autumn of 1944 with the remark that 'it came from Hitler'. In the lower jaw there were two larger gold bridges, one on the right and one on the left. The frontal sector consisted of natural teeth.

Since during my studies of Hitler's x-ray status I had also briefly looked at the x-rays of the lower jaw, I knew that there had in fact been two larger gold bridges there. During my interrogation I finally also carried out the so-called articulation test, which showed that the upper gold bridge and the lower jaw fitted together. After these examinations I had no doubts whatsoever that the dental segments shown me originated from Hitler's and Eva Braun's bodies . . .

In this context, it is worth noting that in his book *Adolf Hitler— Legend, Myth, Reality*, *Dr* Werner Maser wrote:

Echtmann explicitly told the author on 20 October 1971 that he had not been able to determine from the dentures shown to him whether the teeth had belonged to Hitler. He believed, however, that 'another factor' which he was 'unwilling', i.e. not able, to describe had pointed to Hitler, which is impossible since the Russians did not find Hitler's head . . .[264]

This is very surprising if one has read Fritz Echtmann's testimony on 10 July 1954!

Echtmann continues:

During this initial interrogation there was an expert present, who—he claimed—had allegedly removed the dental fragments from the corpses himself. After my interrogation was over and my statements had been checked by the expert, he also told me that there could be no doubt that the three dental fragments originated with Hitler and Eva Braun.

During my second interrogation on 24 or 25 May 1945 in Finow, virtually the same sequence was enacted as in Schwanebeck, except that there was no expert present. My signing of the second transcript took place in the presence of two Generals . . .

On 5 October 1954 Fritz Echtmann was again questioned on several of his statements. He added the following comments:

The lower jaw shown to me by the Russians in May 1945 in Schwanebeck near Berlin and again in Finow still showed minor remnants of singed and carbonated tissue. In other words, it had not yet been preserved. The upper bridge shown me at the same time consisted of nine segments, from No 4 left to No 6 right. I am still completely convinced that the jawbone and the bridge were Hitler's jaw and the bridge he wore. On top of that I was able to determine in the presence of a Russian or Polish dentist by means of an articulation test that the upper bridge on the one hand and the lower jawbone on the other, or rather the teeth, fitted together . . .

The question now is how resistant the bridges were against the heat of the fire, particularly since both *Frau* Heusermann and Echtmann stated that the lower jawbone still showed small pieces of 'singed and charred tissue'. As I had explained to me, the important thing is that fillings made out of a gold/platinum amalgam—as with fillings made out of copper amalgam such as were commonly used at the time—have proved to be much more heat resistant than fillings made out of plain amalgam. The latter can only withstand low temperatures and are melted out. The melting point for gold is 1063° Centigrade. Since gold is very soft, for practical purposes in dentistry one uses alloys of the precious metal. Hitler's gold bridge probably consisted of a mouth-resistant gold alloy containing no less than 18 carat gold. The melting point will therefore have been slightly under 1000° Centigrade. Given the actual circumstances of the largely dissipating heat of the open fire in the garden and the fact that Hitler's bridge was protected from direct heat by the charred facial muscles and the jawbone, one can assume that the gold bridge in the upper jaw would have survived without problems. The same can be said for Eva Braun-Hitler's dentures.

In summary one can therefore say that the testimony of *Herr* Fritz Echtmann and *Frau* Käthe Heusermann—respectively, *Dr* Hugo Blaschke's former dental technician and his dental assistant—round off the trail of evidence pointing to Adolf Hitler's and Eva Braun-Hitler's deaths. Both were shown Hitler's charred lower jawbone and upper bridge and Eva Braun-Hitler's lower synthetic resin bridge by Russian officers, repeatedly and in different places. Both identified the bridges as belonging to Adolf Hitler and Eva Braun-Hitler beyond any doubt. Both could accurately recall Adolf Hitler's dental status. *Frau* Heusermann was present when Hitler's upper bridge was shortened in the autumn of 1944. The operation was carried out by *Dr* Blaschke, who later confirmed *Frau* Heusermann's and Echtmann's testimony.

In the final analysis, by presenting the evidence coming from Adolf Hitler (upper bridge and complete lower jawbone with teeth and bridges) and from Eva Braun-Hitler (a small gold filling and a synthetic resin bridge with a gold crown), the Russians themselves—

and this must be emphasised—proved conclusively that Adolf Hitler and Eva Braun-Hitler were dead. However, this was not admitted to the world at large. On the contrary, as witnesses to Hitler's death in Berlin, Heusermann and Echtmann had to disappear—just like other witnesses from the Chancellery group. One must ask oneself what crime dental assistant Käthe Heusermann had committed that justified imprisoning her in inhumane conditions in Moscow prisons and labour camps for over ten years from 8 May 1945 to 2 June 1955. The justification was Paragraph 58/4, 'Regulation for rendering support to a bourgeois government'! What crime had dental technician Fritz Echtmann committed that justified imprisoning him in inhumane conditions for over nine years in Moscow prisons and labour camps? When Echtmann demanded to know, he was told that while everything had been cleared up, Beria had objected to his release on the grounds of state security.

It is not surprising that Mr Bezemensky did not write anything about all this. He also did not write that Linge, Günsche, Baur, Hofbeck, Henschel and others were beaten and tortured in Moscow prisons. Quite the opposite. On page 80 of his book he even writes:

As I learned from the former investigating judge, no pressure at all was put on either of them [Günsche and Linge] . . .

I doubt whether Bezemensky even knows who conducted those investigations. In any case, *Herr* Günsche wrote to me on this subject:

During my captivity in the Soviet Union I was interrogated for years under such circumstances. Today one would call these circumstances 'torture' . . .

On 27 April 1956 *Frau* Heusermann went on to say:

On 13 May 1945 I was again fetched by the Russians and taken to Finow together with Echtmann. Towards the end of May I was taken from Finow to Friedrichshagen and from there flown to Moscow on 29 July 1945. In the plane with me were *Professor Dr* Haase, Echtmann, chief cook Lange, *Admiral* Voss, garage superintendent Schneider, Mengershausen, *Dr* Kunz and Eckholt . . .

When Professor Reidar F. Sognnaes of UCLA questioned *Frau* Heusermann on several points in 1981, she told him that the cigar box with Eva Braun's bridge and two of Hitler's bridges had also been on the plane. Russian soldiers had gleefully shown the cigar box around and laughed 'Here is the *Führer*'.[265]

Frau Heusermann continued:

I spent six and a half years in various prisons in Moscow, always in a single cell, in which another German woman was occasionally also housed. In the autumn of 1951 I was again interrogated in Moscow about the former subject. Shortly after this interrogation I was informed that Paragraphs 7 and 35 applied to me. Upon my request to explain to me what this meant, I was told that the meaning was that I would now be employed for free labour within the Soviet Union.

On 27 November 1951 I was then informed that I had been sentenced to ten years' labour for the state, including the six and a half years for which I had already been imprisoned. This time Paragraph 58/4 was mentioned, and I was told that this paragraph contained the regulations for having rendered support to a 'bourgeois government'. From December 1951 on I was then in Tachet near Lake Baikal, where I had to undertake forced labour. Only during the last year were things a bit easier. I was allowed to receive my first package in July 1954 and my first postcard in October or November 1954. From this time on I was also allowed to write, which had been forbidden up to that time. After ten years I then arrived at the Friedland reception camp on 2 June 1955 . . .

Dental technician Fritz Echtmann's fate was very similar to that of *Frau* Heusermann. On 27 April 1953 he reported:

After having been arrested on 11 May 1945 I was kept in Berlin-Friedrichshagen until 29 July 1945. I was in the same cell as Fritzsche. Here I told Fritzsche about my two interrogations in Schwanebeck and Finow. I mentioned that the lower jaw and the bridge had been shown to *Frau* Heusermann before my own first interrogation and that *Frau* Heusermann had also clearly recognised them.

At the time *Frau* Heusermann was also being held in the prison in Berlin-Friedrichshagen. We frequently met in the prison yard and exchanged our observations and statements with respect to the jawbone and bridges. We were in complete agreement that there was no possible mistake. Among other things, *Frau* Heusermann had told me on 8 May 1945—before we were both arrested—that she had been raped by Russians on 2 May 1945.

Frau Heusermann was also still in Berlin on 29 July 1945. She was taken to Moscow on that day in the same plane as myself. There she was also initially held in Lubianka prison. Later on I no longer saw her. Between the autumn of 1945 and well into 1948 I communicated with her several times by means of tapped messages. At the time she was also being held at Leforto prison, in a cell very near to mine.

I was taken to Moscow by plane on 29 July 1945. Here I spent two days in Lubianka prison, was held in Leforto prison until March 1949 and subsequently in Butyr prison until November 1951. With the exception of the interrogation about Eva Braun in 1946 which I have already mentioned, I was then no longer questioned about Hitler's fate.

In the summer of 1947 I was once again called to a Russian colonel, the one who had headed the whole investigation into Hitler's and Eva Braun's deaths. This colonel told me that there was no longer any doubt about Hitler's death; everything had been cleared up. I was to be released. However, this did not come about. The colonel I have mentioned told me that everything was clear but that Beria had objected to my release for reasons of state security. From November 1951—after having been sentenced to ten years' hard labour in early 1951—I was then in the Workuta labour camp. On 5 December 1953 I was put on board a transport home.

Musmanno's claim in his book *Ten Days to Die* [see page 373] that I was offered 'a house and a job' in Russia is without any foundation . . .

Let us close this topic by again pointing to page 3 of *The Times* of 9 July 1945, where one can read *Frau* Heusermann's and *Herr* Echtmann's testimony. However, at the time no one appeared to believe it.

7. Confusing the Issue

The Russians had been apprised, at least no later than 23 April 1945, that Hitler was in Berlin. However, they considered this to be one of Goebbels' cheap propaganda tricks and did not believe a word of it. After the dramatic afternoon briefing session in the bunker on 22 April—during which Hitler had decided to stay in Berlin—Goebbels had had it announced over Greater German Radio that Hitler was personally leading the defence of Berlin. After a discussion with Hitler, he hoped that this would lead to a stronger motivation for and more determined resistance by the German soldiers. On 23 April 1945 the German people were informed by the *Wehrmacht* report that:

> The *Führer*, according to a statement made by *Gauleiter* and Commissar for the Defence of the Reich *Dr* Goebbels, has assumed command of all of the forces deployed for the defence of Berlin. The *Führer* is present in Berlin . . .

The next person to inform the Russians about Hitler's fate was Chief of Staff *General* Krebs. At 0355 on 1 May 1945 Krebs, without any preamble, told an astonished Russian General Chuikov:

> I have to inform you about something that is strictly confidential. You are the first foreigner to whom I announce that Hitler departed this life on 30 April. He committed suicide.[266]

General Chuikov immediately called Marshal Zhukov, who, as he reported later, contacted Stalin without delay:

> Immediately after this Stalin came on the line. I reported about the announcement of Hitler's suicide, *General* Krebs' appearance and my decision to delegate the negotiations with Krebs to General Sokolovsky. I then asked for further instructions. Stalin replied:

'So the bastard has thrown in his hand! A shame that we could not take him alive. Where is Hitler's body?'

'According to Krebs' report, Hitler's body has been burnt . . .'[267]

At 2226 on 1 May 1945 the Russians received further confirmation of Hitler's death. Via Greater German Radio the station in Hamburg informed the German people that Hitler had fallen in his command post 'while fighting against Bolshevism to his last breath'. The Russian leadership also took this news report to be nothing more than a cover-up of Hitler's escape.

The next person to provide information was the Berlin *Kampfkommandant*, *General* Helmuth Weidling. Weidling arrived at General Chuikov's staff headquarters towards 6 a.m. on 2 May 1945 and offered the surrender of the forces defending Berlin. After some discussion about the possibilities of capitulation, he was questioned by Generals Chuikov and Sokolovsky:

'Where have Hitler and Goebbels got to?'

'As far as I know, Goebbels and his family have committed suicide, the *Führer* already on 30 April . . . his wife poisoned herself.'

'Have you only heard about this or were you an eyewitness?'

'I was in the Chancellery towards evening on 30 April. Krebs, Bormann and Goebbels told me . . . Many still do not know that the *Führer* is dead because *Dr* Goebbels has forbidden any mention of it . . .'[268]

After Weidling, the next person to come to General Chuikov with further news was Hans Fritzsche, Head of the Radio Department in the Reich Propaganda Ministry. He reported to Chuikov at about 1130 on 2 May and suggested calling upon the German troops over the radio to give up all resistance in Berlin as quickly as possible. After a check with Zhukov he was given permission to do this. Naturally Fritzsche was also immediately asked about Hitler and Goebbels. 'And then,' as Fritzsche stated later, 'began the first of many interrogations that took place in Berlin, in Lubianka prison in Moscow and in Nuremberg.' He could only give a report on Hitler's fate—the suicide in the bunker and the cremation of the bodies in the garden—based on hearsay. On 3 May he was taken to the garden of the Chancellery, where he saw numerous petrol cans, one of which was still full, and about fifteen more or less obliterated corpses strewn about. On 4 May he was required to identify the body of his chief, *Dr* Goebbels.

Contrary to this, Zhukov—who had spoken to Fritzsche as late as 2 May—reported:

> To my question about Hitler's final plans, Fritzsche replied that he did not know exactly but had heard that different people from the leadership had retreated to Berchtesgaden and South Tyrol after our offensive on the Oder had begun. They had taken crates and baggage with them. The Supreme Command with Hitler at its head had also been supposed to fly out in that direction. At the final moment, when Soviet forces were already outside Berlin, there had been talk about an evacuation to Schleswig-Holstein. There had been aircraft ready for take-off near the Chancellery, which, however, had soon been destroyed by Soviet planes . . .[269]

Naturally the exodus from Berlin by German military and government officials on 21 and 22 April 1945, and the air traffic from Staaken and Gatow airports, as well as that later on from the East–West Axis, had not escaped the attention of the Soviet leadership. The Russians were firmly convinced that Hitler and his team had fled Berlin and that all statements to the contrary were only intended to cover up and disguise Hitler's escape. This was a mistake on the part of the suspicious Russians but they clung to it rigidly until mid-1946, as can be seen from statements made later by the so-called Chancellery Group. For example, Hitler's pilot Hans Baur testified on 24 November 1955:

> During the winter of 1945/46 and in the spring of 1946 I was interrogated (in Lubianka prison) time and time again, mainly by Commissar Dr Savelly [Savieliev]. During these interrogations I was accused time and again of flying Hitler out of Berlin. During this [time] I was handled very roughly. An officer whom Dr Savelly called in frequently hit me with heavy blows to the head with his fists . . .

Further confirmation that the Russians assumed that Hitler or his staff fled from Berlin is contained in the following statement by Marshal Zhukov:

> I do not recall the exact time, but it was already growing dark [on 1 May 1945] when the Commander of the 3rd Attack Army, General V. I. Kusnezov, called me and reported with great excitement:

'Just now a group of German Panzers, about 20 tanks, broke through in the sector of the 52nd Guard Division. They advanced to the north-western city limits at high speed.'

It was clear that someone was trying to escape from Berlin. The most frightful rumours began to circulate. One even supposed that the escaping Panzer group was taking Hitler, Goebbels and Bormann to safety. The alarm was sounded immediately, so that no one could leave the Berlin area . . .

At dawn on 2 May we discovered the Panzer group 15 kilometres north-west of Berlin and quickly annihilated it. The tanks were burnt out or shot to pieces. None of the crews that had been killed could be identified as one of the Nazi leaders. What was left in the burnt-out tanks was completely unidentifiable . . .[270]

On 2 May 1945 *Pravda* published an article that reflected the Kremlin's official doubt that Hitler was dead. In his historic order of the day, Stalin proclaimed 'Victory over Germany' and said that the Red Army was in possession of the ruins of Hitler's Chancellery. Soviet commentators welcomed this announcement and intimated that it would only be a matter of hours before Russian specialists in Berlin would be able to announce the true circumstances surrounding Hitler's fate. A communiqué issued in Moscow during the night of 2–3 May announced that Hitler and Goebbels had committed suicide. This statement was attributed to Goebbels' former employee Hans Fritzsche, who was being held in Berlin.

As Marshal Zhukov reported later, he visited Hitler's Chancellery on 3 May 1945:

After the Chancellery had been taken I drove to this building together with Colonel-General Bersarin, Member of the Army War Council, Lieutenant-General Bokov and others who took part in the attack, because we wanted to apprise ourselves on the spot of Hitler's, Goebbels' and other prominent Nazis' suicides.

This was difficult, however. We were told that the Fascists had buried all the corpses; no one knew exactly at which places and who had been involved. The statements contradicted each other.

Prisoners, mostly the wounded, were unable to say anything about Hitler and his entourage. In the Chancellery itself we had only taken a few dozen prisoners. Obviously members of the SS, officers and surviving Nazi leaders had made use of secret passages at the last moment and gone under cover in the city. We searched in vain for the pyres on which Hitler's and Goebbels' bodies had been burned. We did see traces of fires, but they were too small and probably had only served soldiers to boil water.

Just as we were ending our inspection of the Chancellery, a report came in that the bodies of the six Goebbels children had been discovered in a bunker. To be quite frank, I had qualms about going into the bunker to see children who had been murdered by their own parents. Soon after this the bodies of Goebbels and his wife were discovered not far from the bunker. We called in Fritzsche to make the identification and he confirmed our find.

The way the matter stood, I initially had my doubts that Hitler had actually committed suicide, all the more so since Bormann could not be found either. At the time I assumed that Hitler had escaped at the last moment, when there was no longer any hope of relief from outside.

I conveyed this view to Soviet and foreign correspondents at a press conference [on 9 June 1945] in Berlin . . .[271]

On 4 May 1945 Russian newspapers stressed the possibility that Hitler's remains had been destroyed in the fire that had raged in his bunker. On 6 May the official Soviet news agency sent a wireless communiqué to all communist newspapers published outside the Soviet Union:

Each day more and more bodies of prominent Nazis and *Gestapo* officials who have committed suicide are being discovered. In the meantime Soviet authorities are conducting a very thorough investigation into the matter of Hitler's fate and the world will soon know the true facts. Up to now Nazi deviousness and Machiavellian finesse have succeeded in shrouding this in mystery.

In an official Russian communiqué issued on 6 May the names of the witnesses Rattenhuber and Baur, whom the Russians had captured, were announced for the first time. However, the Russians refused point blank to allow these people to be questioned by Allied officers. On 7 May *Pravda* promised that the mystery surrounding Hitler's whereabouts would soon be cleared up and went on to say that 'an exhaustive search for Hitler's and Goebbels' corpses' was still in progress. Also on 7 May the Soviet Army newspaper *Red Star* drew attention to the fact that mass suicides by German General Staff officers, prominent leaders of the SA and other war criminals in the garden of the Chancellery were further proof that Hitler and Goebbels had not died heroes' deaths.

On 8 May the first report by Russian Intelligence containing a brief summary of the results of the investigations over the past weeks of Hitler's fate was allegedly presented to the Kremlin by the City Commander of Berlin, Colonel-General Nikolai E. Bersarin. According to unofficial Russian information, the following facts were supposedly reported. Hitler's body had been discovered in the ruins of the bunker; the corpse was riddled with bullets and had been beaten as if before and after death; photographs had been taken of the body and were on the way to Moscow by courier; several people from Hitler's staff who were in Russian captivity had seen the body, and all of them except a driver and a female servant had agreed that it was that of Hitler; the driver was insisting that it was the body of one of Hitler's cooks; he was saying that he had known the cook well and believed that the cook had been killed because of his remarkable resemblance to Hitler; the driver was also claiming that Hitler himself had escaped during the night of 1 May; investigations of this theory were being continued; and this body, as well as others that had been found in the underground area of the Chancellery, were still being investigated.[272] On 10 May dispatches reported the discovery of Goebbels' body to Moscow, as well as the discovery of four more bodies that 'had some resemblance to Hitler'. These four corpses had allegedly been found in the *Führerbunker*. With these discoveries the Soviet authorities were supposedly of the opinion that the mystery of Hitler's death and Goebbels' suicide had been solved, except for a few minor details. US and British military authorities had allegedly also come to this provisional conclusion.

But then the activities of the Russian Intelligence Services involved in this matter suddenly appeared to be moving in a different direction. While there was no public announcement, a chemical analysis of the corpse that had theoretically been taken to be Hitler's—or so it was claimed—gave no proof of death by means of a pistol shot.[273]

During an informal exchange on 13 May 1945 Allied counter-intelligence officers were told by Russian officers that Soviet specialists had found new proof that Hitler, mentally unbalanced and partially paralysed, had been killed in his bunker on 1 May by an injection of poison administered to him by his personal physician *Dr* Stumpfegger—something which was probably based on the statements made by Harry Mengershausen.[274]

At the beginning of May General Dwight D. Eisenhower was informed by Russian officers that a cremated corpse which had been dug up outside the bunker and examined by Russian doctors after the fall of Berlin had been identified as almost certainly belonging to Hitler. But only four weeks later, on 9 June, Marshal Zhukov made a new statement to the international press, according to which the Russians had not been able to identify Hitler and nothing definite could yet be stated about Hitler's fate.[275]

The second report by Russian Intelligence on Hitler's fate is alleged to have contained a summary of the results of the second and third weeks' investigations. It is supposed to have been brought to Stalin on 23 May 1945 by a courier from Marshal Zhukov and to have contained new findings and chemical analyses by doctors of the Red Army. Attached were excerpts from testimonies by prisoners from Hitler's entourage. These supposedly contained statements about how Hitler died from a poison injection administered by *Dr* Stumpfegger on 1 May. One of Hitler's personal servants described this death as a 'mercy killing'; others were of the opinion that it had been murder. They did not believe that the *Führer* had gone mad or that the tremors in his left arm and leg had been more acute on 1 May than during the preceding days in the bunker. With regard to this new information, their statements were all in agreement. Otto Günsche, Hitler's adjutant, had buried the corpse in a secret place.

In the evening of 25 May 1945 Harry L. Hopkins, President Truman's representative, arrived in Moscow for a preparatory meeting with Stalin. The meeting took place at 8 a.m. the next day. Present were Stalin, Molotov and Pavlov and, on the American side, Hopkins, Harriman and Bohlen. In the course of the conversation Stalin said that, in his opinion,

> ... Hitler was not dead but was hiding somewhere. He said that the Soviet doctors believed that they had identified the bodies of Goebbels and Hitler's driver, but that he himself doubted that Goebbels was dead and went

on to say that the whole matter was curious and that various remarks about burials had given him a very doubtful impression. He said he believed that Bormann, Goebbels, Hitler and probably Krebs had escaped and were hiding somewhere . . .[276]

Even though General Katukov, for example, had seen *General* Hans Krebs' body during his visit to the Chancellery on 2 May 1945, and there was no doubt that the Russians had identified Goebbels' body as early as 3 May 1945, Stalin was lying in the most convincing manner. Above all, after the initial interrogations of witnesses from the Chancellery Group, the Russians were already openly admitting that Hitler was dead, as, for example, Trevor-Roper reports:

> . . . there is no doubt that the Russians in Berlin admitted Hitler's death in the first weeks in June. When the Supreme Allied Commanders met on 5 June 1945 in order to organise the establishment of the Four-Power Government, 'responsible Russian officers' told officers from General Eisenhower's staff that Hitler's body had been discovered and 'identified with almost complete certainty'. As they said, the body was found in the bunker together with three others. It had been badly charred—a fact that the Russians falsely (as we now know) attributed to the flame-throwers with which their troops had advanced. [*Maschinenmeister* Hentschel, who was captured in the *Führerbunker* by the Russians towards 9 a.m. on 2 May 1945, made no mention of flame-throwers.] According to them, the bodies were examined by Russian doctors and this led to an 'almost certain identification'. If the Russians were not officially announcing Hitler's death, so the Russian officers said, this was only due to their reluctance to commit themselves as long as there was the 'slightest room for doubt'. However, they openly admitted that all the evidence available pointed to the conclusion that Hitler was dead . . .
>
> And when on 6 June 1945 Zhukov's staff officers assured Eisenhower's staff officers that Hitler's body had been discovered, exhumed and scientifically identified, Stalin in Moscow not only repeated to Hopkins that there was no proof of Hitler's death but also that he was 'convinced' that Hitler was still alive . . .[277]

On 6 June 1945 the Russians held an unofficial press conference in Berlin at which war correspondents from the United States, Great Britain and France were present. An officer from Marshal Zhukov's staff disclosed details of the search for Hitler's corpse and authorised the correspondents to report—without naming him as the source—that it had been found and identified with a high degree of probability. The *Führer*'s smoke-blackened and charred corpse was one of four that had been discovered in the bunker on 3 and 4 May. They had been burnt in the corridor by a flame-thrower, but despite this it had still been possible to identify Hitler. After examinations by chemists from the Red Army, there were indications that 'Hitler most probably died of poisoning'. The Soviet military spokesman added that there was no sure way of determining whether Hitler had poisoned himself or whether someone else had.

This was probably the last unauthorised statement Stalin was prepared to accept from Marshal Zhukov. He now sent Vyshinsky to Zhukov with appropriate instructions, and Vyshinsky never again left his side. When Zhukov said on 9 June 1945 that Hitler could well still be alive, Vyshinsky was standing directly next to him. Vyshinsky also accompanied Zhukov on his visit to Frankfurt and during his conversation with General Eisenhower.

A few months later Zhukov disappeared from the world stage. Stalin recalled him from Germany and for all practical purposes sent him into exile, first as CinC of the Russian home defence forces and then to Odessa as Military Governor. Colonel-General Nikolai E. Bersarin, Military Commander of Berlin, was killed in a motorcycle accident on 17 June 1945 in mysterious circumstances. Details of this never came to light. Thus were both Zhukov and Bersarin eliminated.

There is only one possible explanation for the strange conduct of the Russians from then on—Stalin. I was enlightened about this by an inconspicuous footnote on page 129 of the book *Khrushchev Remembers*: 'Stalin naturally insisted for a long time that Hitler was not dead at all . . .'[278] If we assume that Khrushchev's memory is correct, then this is the proof that the subsequent Russian manipulation of world opinion about Hitler's death was attributable to Josef Stalin alone.

What Stalin's objective was in all this is still not completely clear. Was the suppression of the announcement of the facts about Hitler's end intended to keep Hitler's disappearance from the world stage an open question in order to prevent the rebirth of a 'Hitler myth'? Or did Stalin want to put pressure on the Western Allies to get them to act against his arch-enemy Franco, with whom Hitler could have found refuge? In any case, Marshal Zhukov was immediately given orders to follow Stalin's new line and to announce no further details about Hitler. As far as can be assumed from the facts that have come to light in the meantime, this order was given on 7 or 8 June 1945. Zhukov lost no time in bringing the new propaganda line into the channels of the international press. He used the opportunity on 9 June 1945 in Berlin when he held a press conference for a group of American, British, French and Russian correspondents who had just arrived in Berlin and were the first foreign reporters to spend more than twenty-four hours in the captured German capital. Among other things, Marshal Zhukov declared that the Red Army had proof that Hitler had married Eva Braun two days before the Soviet forces had taken Berlin. Zhukov said: 'We found information about this marriage in the diary of Hitler's personal adjutant' (he meant the daily notes taken by Hitler's valet Linge). Hitler married! What a story for the journalists! Zhukov continued:

Adolf Hitler's present whereabouts are a mystery. We have not found a corpse which could be Hitler's and I am not able to make a positive statement about his fate or where he could at the moment be.

Zhukov did not say anything about the continuing Russian searches with the help of the witnesses who confirmed Hitler's suicide and the subsequent cremation, nor did he mention the dental bridges that had been discovered in the meantime and which proved Hitler's death:

We have not identified Hitler's corpse. I cannot say anything definite about his fate. He may have flown out of Berlin at the last moment. The condition of the landing strip [the East–West Axis] would have permitted this. Based on personal and official information, we can say that Hitler had the chance to get away with his bride. Hitler could have flown out at the very last moment.

When he was asked for his opinion on where Hitler could be hiding, Marshal Zhukov stated his personal view that Hitler was in Spain and added, 'It is up to the American and British forces to find him.' One may assume that this remark was made by Zhukov on Stalin's orders, since in 1945 Stalin repeatedly called for the overthrow of his old enemy General Franco in order to complete the victory over Fascism.

This astonishing news was wired all around the world—the complete text can be found in the 10 June 1945 edition of *Pravda*—and had the desired effect on world opinion. The door was opened wide for speculation, and the legends, lies and stories surrounding Hitler's end in subsequent years are legion.

When Zhukov was asked about the death of Martin Bormann, the discovery of whose body the Russians had announced on 10 May, he answered, 'We have no idea of the whereabouts of the *Führer*'s personal adjutant Mr Bormann.'

At the time Zhukov was launching Stalin's latest psychological campaign about Hitler's end, his colleague Colonel-General Bersarin, Commander of Berlin, was telling the same story to some foreign correspondents who were there on a visit. He said:

> We have found several bodies, one of which could possibly be Hitler's, but we cannot say whether he is dead. In my opinion Hitler went underground and is hiding somewhere in Europe, possibly with General Franco.

With this the subject was closed. From that time on it was never mentioned again by Russian Military Headquarters in Berlin. Nothing was again said about the circumstances of Hitler's death. The obviously insoluble mystery was clothed in impenetrable silence for decades.

On 17 July 1945 the Potsdam Conference began, in which Truman, Stalin and Churchill were to decide the future fate of Germany. US Foreign Minister James F. Byrnes reported later:

> Shortly after his arrival on July 17 Stalin called on the President . . . In speaking of our visit to Berlin, I asked the Generalissimo [Stalin] his views of how Hitler had died. To my surprise, he said he believed that Hitler was alive and that it was possible he was in either Spain or Argentina. Some ten days later I asked him if he had changed his views and he said he had not.[279]

The American Admiral William D. Leahy noted in his book *I Was There*:

Prime Minister Stalin reached Potsdam and had lunch with the President. It was their first meeting. Present were Molotov, Byrnes and I. With regard to Hitler, Stalin repeated what he had already told Hopkins in Moscow: he believed that the *Führer* had escaped and was hiding somewhere. He went on to say that the painstaking Soviet search had failed to discover any traces of Hitler's remains or positive proof of his death.[280]

This was piling lie upon lie, since no later than 8/9 May 1945 the Russians knew through the odontological identification of the bridges that Hitler was dead.

As the date for the Nuremberg War Crimes Trials approached, Russian newspapers again wrote, on 10 September 1945, of the probability that Hitler was still alive. The idea was even put forward that Hitler was in hiding in Germany. When the official report of British Intelligence, prepared by Major H. R. Trevor-Roper, was published in November 1945, commentators from Moscow disagreed: 'The Russians are still sceptical and cannot accept the suicide and cremation theory'. By this time many people in Europe and around the world shared the Russians' 'doubts': the Soviets had whisked away the witnesses and the proof, so Hitler's story would go on and continue to inspire journalists. Whether dead or alive, Stalin obviously still needed Hitler.

According to *The Times* of 8 and 13 October 1945, for example, General Eisenhower said to foreign journalists during a visit to Holland, 'Even though I initially believed that Hitler was dead, there are now reasons to assume that he is still alive.' After his return to Frankfurt, however, Eisenhower modified his statement by saying that he himself 'could hardly believe that Hitler was still alive' but that his Russian friends had assured him that 'they had not been able to come up with any proof of his death'. And as late as 3 November 1945 *Stars and Stripes* reported:

The Russians are still 'somewhat skeptical' about the death of Hitler and his mistress Eva Braun, since after having dug up at least 100 corpses in the garden of the Chancellery in Berlin they have found no conclusive proof, according to what a British Intelligence officer reported today.

The statement by the British officer was followed by the release of a report by British Headquarters, according to which all the available evidence indicates that Hitler and Eva Braun committed suicide and that their bodies were burnt in the Chancellery garden on 30 April of this year.[281]

I have only recorded a part of the almost unreadable and, with hindsight, absolutely incredible story of the official Russian portrayal of Hitler's end. From start to finish it appears to be nothing but personal prejudice on the part of Stalin, who clung to it because that, and nothing else, was what he wanted to believe; or because he wanted to demonstrate to the powerful military clique in Berlin who the political boss was; or out of anger, because he had not been able to lay his hands on a presentable Hitler corpse and did not believe the testimony of the witnesses from the Chancellery Group. He simply rejected the 'almost certain' and at least legitimate conclusion that Hitler had to be dead with a categorical claim that he was still alive. For many years he enveloped in silence and oblivion the more or less effective investigations by Russian officers in Berlin, the interrogations they conducted and the attempts at identification they made. He refused to accept the evidence of the Allies that could have been helpful in clarifying the events surrounding Hitler's death. Whatever his reasons may have been, he apparently regarded the question of Hitler's death as a political matter, which he decided accordingly.

That Hitler had died in Berlin and not escaped was at least indirectly admitted in 1968 by Lew Bezemensky in his book *The Death of Adolf Hitler*. The basis of Bezemensky's book is the 'alleged' autopsy report on a corpse purporting to be that of Hitler and two very poor photographs showing parts of two dental bridges which are attributed to Hitler. From the evidence I have compiled in the foregoing chapters, it is clear that there was no corpse as such. The extent of the cremation was so great that only remnants of calcified bones with charred particles of skin and tissue could possibly have been left, which were then more or less completely destroyed by explosions and shellfire. I do not know to which of the many bodies that lay around at the time the autopsy report refers. However, it cannot refer to Hitler's non-existent corpse.

Regarding the autopsy report itself, it should be noted that the German pathologist *Professor Dr* Otto Prokop, who claims to have conducted at least 45,000 autopsies in the course of his career, said:

Bezemensky's report is ridiculous . . . Any one of my assistants would have done better . . . the whole thing is a farce . . . it is intolerably bad work . . . the transcript of the post-mortem section of 8 April 1945 describes anything but Hitler . . .

Bezemensky called upon many people in order to prove that the bridges he shows belonged to Hitler. That, however, has not been in dispute since 9 July 1945.[282] As far as I am concerned it is also beyond dispute that Hitler's two bridges are in Moscow—as both *Frau* Heusermann and *Herr* Echtmann testified in 1956—and they will probably remain there for ever.

What I cannot understand, however, is that in 1992 Bezemensky published an article entitled 'How the Russians Disposed of Hitler'.[283] In this Bezemensky resurrects Hitler's corpse! After Bezemensky had written in his book in 1968 that after the post-mortem in 1945 Hitler's body had been burnt and 'the ashes scattered to the four winds', in 1992 he suddenly writes that the 'alleged' corpse had not been cremated then but rather buried and reburied several times in different places and then 'finally' burnt in April 1978.[284] As *Der Spiegel* said in 1992 in its article about Bezemensky's 'findings',

> He is now practising remorse. He runs the risk of ruining his academic reputation, [holding it] to be less important than belated honesty. Is he telling the truth now?

On the other hand, the solution of the 'Hitler case' could have been so easy. All that would have been required was the skill and knowledge of the average policeman, in order to compile the evidence and reconstruct the actual events with the help of the witnesses. It should have been possible to clarify the circumstances of how and when Hitler died and what became of his body without any undue delay. From the beginning the Russians were in possession of all the witnesses and all the evidence. From 2 May 1945 they had taken the Chancellery with the bunker and the garden and on the evening of the same day they were able to capture most of the members of Hitler's immediate staff in the Schultheiss-Patzenhofer brewery in Schönhauser Allee. And yet, because of their over-exaggerated suspicions, it took more than a year before they closed the file on the 'Hitler case'.

The manner in which the Russians proceeded in the Hitler investigation, and above all the brutal methods they employed, have been described by the former prisoners of the Chancellery Group. On 8 February 1956 Heinz Linge testified:

After I was captured on the evening of 2 May 1945 I was questioned by various Russian officers in Berlin and then taken to Moscow in December 1945. For the first two and a half months I was held in Lubianka prison and then transferred to the Butyrka prison. Here I was frequently interrogated for about two and a half weeks, always at night. The subject of these interrogations was mainly the question whether Hitler was dead or alive. The talk was always about whether he had not been flown out after all. There was also constant talk about whether a double had not been substituted in his place. I was always required to describe my experiences in connection with Hitler's suicide in detail. During these interrogations I was always maltreated. The people who took part in the interrogations were Colonel [Commissar] Stern, Professor Dr Saveliev [Savieliev], and two Commissars named Schweitzer and Klaus [Colonel Klausen] . . .

Towards the end of April 1946 I was taken to Berlin together with Günsche, Baur, Henschel, Hofbeck, Misch . . . During the journey to Berlin we were kept strictly apart . . . In Berlin I was required to draw exact plans of the rooms in the bunker and to describe their furnishings in detail. I was then also interrogated during a visit to the scene in the bunker . . . I had to describe the events during the suicide. The walls were inspected for signs of damage . . . I was also led into the garden, where I had to point out the site of the cremation. I was also asked about the place of burial of the remains . . . There were several important Russian functionaries present. Based on pictures I have seen in the meantime, I believe I recognise one of these functionaries, who was treated as a special authority by the others, to have been Marshal Sokolovsky. During the interrogations in Berlin I was asked about Hitler's measurements . . .

During these interrogations I was not mistreated . . .

After returning to Moscow I shared the same cell for seven months until January 1947 with Erich Ackermann. As far as his statements differ from mine, they are false . . . The version of the suicide contained in Ackermann's statements (poison, posthumous shooting) was frequently discussed between us only on Ackermann's insistence, but merely as a theory. It is not true that I 'came to the conclusion' that not only Eva Hitler but also Adolf Hitler had taken poison and that someone else had fired a shot at the dead Hitler. How Ackermann comes to make such a statement is beyond me . . .

It should be noted here that Ackermann, about whom I will not comment further, was most probably a spy working for the Russians and had been deliberately placed in Linge's cell. Ackermann later wrote:

These elaborations were the subject of lengthy discussions with Commissar Stern and also Dr Savieliev, allegedly a criminal psychologist at the Moscow University. During the final discussion General Kabulov, Beria's deputy, was also present. Stern told me later that my portrayal was in complete agreement, whether with his own opinion or with the official Russian opinion I no longer recall. In any case, since then I have never again heard anything and I also believe that Linge was then no longer questioned, because I learned that after his long period of suffering in Moscow Linge surfaced in the officers' camp in Volkovo shortly after my own release from the Lubianka, where he was seen as late as 1950 . . .

Linge continues:

. . . further interrogations then took place from the summer of 1948 to the end of 1949, together with Günsche with whom I shared a cell in Butyrka prison at the time. The reason for these interrogations was that we were supposed jointly to write a book about our experiences in Hitler's entourage. This suggestion was made both by Colonel Stern, whom I have mentioned before, as well as by General Kabulov. We were promised an improvement in our situation, which actually came about in that we were given better rations and also housed in a cell in the hospital which General Kabulov had selected. During the course of events we were even housed in private quarters with the widow of a General Melnikov who had been killed in the war. General Kabulov visited us there several times. Initially we had a captured German journalist assigned to us to help us in our work. His job was then taken over by Colonel Paparov. Paparov used the cover name 'Georgadze'. We were subsequently moved from our quarters with Mrs Melnikov to a country house near Moscow, where Paparov was constantly present during the final stages of the work. During this time Paparov compiled a manuscript that was about 300 pages long. I do not know what became of this manuscript [it will probably appear one day in exchange for hard currency].

From January 1950 on I was in the Volkovo officers' camp together with Günsche. There were no further interrogations.

In May 1950 I was sentenced in Ivanovo to 25 years' 'labour improvement camp'. The reasons given for this sentence were that I had helped Hitler to seize power, that I had aided and abetted the suppression of the democratic parties, that I had been a party to his criminal plans and that I had been present in the Vinniza-Shitomir area from 1942 to 1944, where 40,000 Russians had been shot at that time. Later I was also accused of having intended to flee from the East to the West Zone, this being based on the testimony of another German prisoner to whom I was alleged to have given addresses of friends of Adolf Hitler with the request that he inform them about my fate. From 2 May 1945 to 29 September 1955 I spent more than ten and a half years in Russian captivity.

On 25 November 1955 former SS guard Hans Hofbeck made the following statement:

I was captured by the Russians on 2 May 1945 in Schwartzkopfstrasse . . .

From February 1946 on I was in Butyrka prison in Moscow. Here I was questioned very frequently, since from the very beginning I was considered to be a key witness. The interrogations were mainly carried out by Commissar Colonel Stern and Dr Savelly [Savieliev]. During these I was often badly mistreated. On the other hand I was promised an early return home. At the time I was completely run down, both mentally and physically. I reached the point where I attempted to commit suicide: I wanted to hang myself with a strip of cloth, which however became torn. During this time I shared a cell with Josef Henschel. He persuaded me to give up the idea of suicide . . .

The interrogations in Moscow kept harping on the same questions. What were your assignments? Who was Hitler's double? Who shot the double? Who brought Hitler out? What did chief pilot Baur tell you? What were Baur's instruction to you about how to act? What instructions did Rattenhuber give you? Where did Högl go?

I answered the question about the double by saying that there had been a porter in the Chancellery who had borne a resemblance to Hitler. There actually was a man like that who was a porter. This man had facial features that resembled Hitler's and also a similar moustache and a similar hair style. However, he was a little shorter. Otherwise I kept insisting that Hitler was dead and that a double had not been shot and burned in his place.

At the beginning of May 1946 I was taken from Moscow to Berlin with Günsche, Linge, Baur, Josef Henschel and Rochus Misch . . . We were kept strictly apart. In Berlin we were housed in the Lichtenberg prison. There I was questioned by a Commissar with the rank of Lieutenant-Colonel [Klausen]. I already knew this Commissar from Moscow. The questions were again mainly the same ones. My answers were also the same. During the interrogations in Berlin I was once questioned in the company of Baur and Günsche. The talk was again about the double. During this interrogation Baur mentioned that a long time ago a man from Breslau had been presented who looked very much like Hitler. This man had been a baker. However, Hitler had strictly refused . . .

In Berlin I was asked about any distinguishing features Hitler had. I drew attention to a stiffening of the right hand, which had been a legacy of the assassination attempt of 20 July 1944. I was also asked who Hitler's dentist had been and whether, and to what extent, Hitler had worn dentures. I named *Dr* Blaschke and *Dr* Rohkamm as dentists. I had no knowledge concerning dentures.

Before the journey back to Moscow I underwent a very detailed physical examination in the presence of about fifteen Russian functionaries. I was not informed about the reason for this examination.

During the time we were held in Moscow and Lichtenberg I was able to exchange tapped signals with Günsche and Linge a few times, which however were nothing more than signals showing that we were still alive. In Moscow I was able to exchange a few brief words with Linge on one single occasion during a walk in the prison yard, when he whispered to me that we would soon be transferred from the prison to a camp. Apart from this I have not talked with Linge since 1 May 1945. With Günsche I was also able to exchange a few words on one single occasion. This was during our arrival in Berlin on the way to the Lichtenberg prison. Otherwise I have not spoken to Günsche either since 1 May 1945 . . .

On 15 October 1955 I returned to Germany after over ten and a half years in Russian captivity.

On 25 November 1955 Chief Pilot Hans Baur reported on his captivity in Russia:

During the break-out on 2 May 1945 I was wounded near the Charité and captured by the Russians . . . From 23 November 1945 onwards I was in Moscow, initially in Butyrka and later on in Lubianka prison. During the winter of 1945/46 and in the spring of 1946 I was questioned countless times, mainly by Commissar Dr Savelly [Savieliev]. During these interrogations I was accused again and again of flying Hitler out of Berlin. During this I was badly mistreated. An officer called in by Dr Savelly beat me heavily about the head with his fists several times. On the other hand I was offered jobs in Russia or somewhere else abroad. I was also promised that my wife and daughter would be brought to Moscow. On one occasion they even went so far as to claim that my wife and daughter were already waiting in the next room . . .

I was repeatedly asked about distinguishing features of Hitler and Eva Braun and about dentures. I knew of no distinguishing features. As far as dentures are concerned, I only knew that Hitler wore a bridge. This I stated truthfully.

All these interrogations hinged on the question of whether a double had been cremated in Hitler's place. I knew nothing about this. In the course of the interrogations I was also accused of having shot Beetz [Betz] in order to get rid of an uncomfortable witness . . .

On 3 May 1946 I arrived in Berlin together with Günsche, Linge, . . . Hofbeck, Henschel and . . . Misch . . . In Berlin we were housed in Lichtenberg prison . . . About a month after our arrival in Berlin I was questioned by Commissar Krause [Klausen] . . . He told me we would be confronted with the bodies and should then say whether we recognised any features that would indicate Hitler or Eva Braun . . . A confrontation with corpses never took place . . . I was then again questioned by a Russian colonel, when Hofbeck was also present. I was told that Hofbeck had claimed that I had been present during the cremation. I said that this was not true. Hofbeck then said that he had never made such a statement. I was then again asked if I had not flown Hitler out after all. Here the Colonel again voiced the suspicion that a double had been cremated instead . . . A transcript was then prepared which I signed. During the interrogations in Berlin force was no longer used.

Subsequently I was no longer questioned. From then on, however, I was questioned once a year by Beria's deputy, Lieutenant-General Kabulov, who asked me if I now wished to testify. He always told me that if I had nothing to say I would remain in prison and he would call me again in a year's time. On 8 October 1955 I was released from Russian captivity and returned to Germany.

Otto Günsche spoke very little about his imprisonment in Russia:

On 2 May 1945 I was captured in Berlin by the Russians . . . While I was in an officers' camp near Berlin, where I had passed myself off as Mohnke's adjutant, my true identity was disclosed through an indiscretion on the part of Weidling's adjutant and the Russian officers immediately began questioning me. One of the Russian officers asked me in German who I was. I replied that I was *General* Mohnke's adjutant. 'You are a liar,' he screamed at me. I answered that it was not a lie because at the time I actually was Mohnke's orderly. But this did not interest the Russians.

I was immediately separated from the other prisoners and after a few days—I do not recall the date—we were collected in a small group—*Generäle* Mohnke, Weidling and Rattenhuber and a few others—and packed into a plane. No one told us where we were going but we were able to figure it out for ourselves. The plane took off in an easterly direction and it was a long flight to Moscow. After we had landed we were taken to a prison where they continued to interrogate us. Next day we were taken to the infamous Lubianka. From that day on they never stopped questioning me about the same subject: what happened to the *Führer*? No matter how often I repeated that he had killed himself and that, in accordance with the orders he had given me, his body had been cremated, it was impossible to convince them. At one point they even said that I had deliberately let myself be captured in order to lead them up a false trail . . .

This lasted for a very long time—possibly a year to a year and a half. They kept repeating the same questions over and over again . . .

I was held in Russia for eleven years almost to the day—up to 28 April 1956—in a so-called 'reform camp' . . . Conditions there were very bad. Today one would call much of it torture . . .

On 2 May 1956 I was released from Bautzen Penitentiary and returned to West Germany.

Finally, let us hear what happened to Josef Henschel, one of the SS guards. Henschel said on 7 February 1956:

I was captured by the Russians in Schönhauser Allee on 2 May 1945 together with many others . . . In late February or early March 1946 I was then transferred from a POW camp to the Butyrka prison in Moscow together with my comrade Hans Hofbeck. In Butyrka I was frequently interrogated between 10 and 20 March 1946. The interrogations mainly took place at night. During these I was badly mistreated several times. During the beatings my right eardrum was ruptured . . . I was told that Hitler was still alive . . . The claim was made that someone else had been cremated instead: one had only been able to see the legs. In particular the claim was made that Hitler had been flown out by Baur or Hanna Reitsch . . .

On 25 April 1946 I was then put on a transport to Berlin together with Hofbeck. There we were housed in the Lichtenberg prison, where Linge, Günsche, Baur and Misch were also being held. We were kept strictly apart. In Berlin I was only questioned once by Lieutenant-Colonel Krause [Klausen]. This interrogation was very brief. I was not mistreated. I was not shown any bodies . . .

On Christmas Eve 1946 I was questioned for the last time in Butyrka prison by a Colonel or General Stern, whom I had not met before. This interrogation was also very short and dealt mainly with my membership in the Reich Security Service. I was not mistreated during this interrogation either . . .

In summary we can say that the 'Hitler case' does not do much credit to the Russians. Besides whatever objectives Stalin might have been pursuing, what comes out clearly in the conduct of the Russians is the fact that confirmation of Hitler's corpse was lacking. If there had been an identifiable corpse belonging to Hitler, the Russians would not have had to exert pressure for a whole year in order to extract a confession—even if only from one witness—concerning when, by what means and where to Hitler had supposedly disappeared from Berlin.

8. Eva Braun and Hermann Fegelein

The observant reader will have noticed that up to now I have only mentioned Eva Braun briefly in connection with the marriage on 29 April 1945 and her and Hitler's suicide on 30 April 1945. I now intend to provide some additional information that may contribute to the clarification of a number of interesting circumstances.

Basically, Eva Braun was a very unexciting person and not a figure that played any role in contemporary history. She displayed no interest whatsoever in politics and neither attempted to gain, nor actually had, any political influence on Hitler. And it was just this assumed or real disinterest on the part of Eva Braun that enabled Hitler to accept and tolerate her as his companion. Any attempt to gain influence, any disposition to act independently, any lack of discretion or any blatant familiarity would never have been tolerated by Hitler and would have made an intimate friendship with him impossible. Eva Braun had learned this very early on and she had seen how her arch-enemy, Hitler's resolute half-sister Angelika Raubal,[285] had been kicked out of the house by him.

Eva Braun was pretty rather than beautiful, had an attractive figure and loved all sorts of sport—track and field, swimming, skiing and cycling to name but a few. She was not very tall, which is why she preferred wearing high-soled cork shoes—which were in vogue at the time—and bought her clothing at one of Berlin's top fashion stores. Eva Braun took very good personal care of herself, practised extreme cleanliness and changed her clothes several times a day. She employed a personal hairdresser and a maid and had a car with a chauffeur at her disposal. She kept an exact record of her extensive and carefully selected wardrobe in a folder, which contained drawings with samples of the fabrics attached. She had a modest talent as a photographer—both 8mm film and still—and photography became one of her major occupations. She liked to listen to records, enjoyed reading magazines and crime stories and was always keen on the newest films, particularly those from America. She knew German and international film stars from the magazines and periodicals and admired them very much. Eva Braun was also full of curiosity and had a 'penchant for exciting things and sensations', as secretary Christine Schroeder reported. Although she appeared to be delicate, she also possessed energy and toughness as well as tenacity.

Even though Eva Braun was not very intelligent, from the start she was able to entertain Hitler and provide relaxation from his political life by her zestful, natural 'Bavarian' manner which, despite the fact that it may well have only been assumed, did not overstep the mark. Otto Wagener, for example, Hitler's economic expert at the time, recorded in his notes in 1932 that, during election campaigns in 1932, Hitler's photographer Heinrich Hoffmann[286] often 'took his little lab assistant Eva Braun along, whom Hitler liked to have at his table in the evening as a distraction'[287] but who, in his opinion, did not play any important role at that time.

Wagener had clearly recognised what was going on: Heinrich Hoffmann had paired Eva Braun off with Hitler. On the other hand, Eva Braun was able to distract Hitler from the cares of daily politics by her merry, natural, artless, intellectually unassuming chatter, and she was of no real importance! And that is how it remained through all the years until Eva Braun's death on 30 April 1945 in Berlin.

In Eva Braun's company Hitler was distracted and could relax. By and large she never betrayed his confidence and never attempted to influence him in his personal or political affairs. At the Berghof, Eva Braun's friendship even provided Hitler with a sort of homely atmosphere, although she deliberately never was, nor tried to play at being, a 'housekeeper'. In all these years she was Hitler's guest and had the right to invite guests in her turn, mainly her sisters and her girlfriends.

Eva Braun never exaggerated anything and chose a middle course in her demands and life style. Despite all the temptations and opportunities that came her way, she probably always weighed her situation as Hitler's companion against a possible love affair with someone else. She liked to flirt and loved to dance, something for which Hitler, who was 23 years older than her and from 1943 onwards was visibly declining and ageing, had little understanding. A typical example is the celebration of her 33rd birthday in Berlin on 6 February 1945. After the official part, which Hitler attended, there was dancing in her rooms upstairs while on the Oder and Neisse the Soviet armies were deploying for their assault on Berlin. On 7 February Bormann wrote to his wife:

> Yesterday evening I was invited to E.B.'s birthday party . . . E. was in a good mood but she complained about not having a good dancing partner; furthermore, she criticised various people with a sharpness that is new for her . . .[288]

Even though Eva Braun's girlish dreams and Hollywood fantasies had come true at Hitler's side, she was essentially still a very unhappy woman. She had no socially defined position in the hierarchy of the Third Reich and no official status in Hitler's entourage. She was, and remained, the '*Fräulein* Braun' who had to disappear at all official functions and was never allowed to accompany Hitler in public. Eva Braun's existence was one of the best-kept secrets of the Third Reich and it is interesting to note that after the end of the war in 1945 the German nation knew nothing about the friendship of almost sixteen years' duration between her and the *Führer*.

Keeping quiet, staying in the background and being discreet was what marked Eva Braun's life, and only Hitler's most intimate circle knew of her existence. That was one aspect of the burden she bore and it often made her act nastily and emotionally towards others. The other aspect was that there was no sexual relationship between Hitler and Eva Braun—she was a woman in the best years of her life, without sex and the tenderness she probably longed for. Photographer Walter Frentz, who was at Hitler's side daily from 1939 to April 1945, told me that Eva Braun had said to him in 1942 or 1943 that she 'lived like a bird in a gilded cage'.

For Hitler, the value of the relationship to Eva Braun lay in what he believed to be her idealism and loyalty. Whether this was actually so is another matter entirely. 'Many years of loyal friendship' is how, at the end of his life, Hitler described the relationship in his will on 29 April 1945.

If one examines the relationship between Hitler and Eva Braun, the frequently discussed question of Hitler's sex life naturally arises again. His unpleasant experiences with women as a young man, his syphilis, his impotency, that fact that he had only one testicle, the injury to his penis as a boy, his homosexuality and much more have been cited again and again. Was Hitler really the lonely, shy young man who had problems with the opposite sex and therefore later chose politics as a compensation for his passions? After evaluating all the available facts and documents, the many statements by con-temporary witnesses and Hitler's proven conduct, one must come to the conclusion that Hitler actually did live without women, in other words without a normal sex life. This 'abstinence' in all probability is also the reason, or rather the explanation, for Hitler's particularly marked aggressiveness, which any psychologist will confirm. Apart from his first love as a very young man in Vienna (as Hitler's secre-tary Christine Schroeder reported) and his undeniably real feelings for his step-niece Angela (Geli) Raubal,[289] who was nineteen years his junior, there is not a single indication, document or serious piece of testimony that Hitler had sexual relations with a woman, not even with Eva Braun. Hitler liked to surround himself with women and he approached them with a somewhat distant, but none the less seri-ously intended, veneration which he was able to project effectively by means of his 'Austrian charm'. In other words, Hitler was look-ing for female companionship, for conversation, even for eroticism—but not sex.

There is no evidence that Hitler was homosexually inclined, even though he spent his whole life in the company of men. There could have been a latent tendency, which is suggested among other things by his preference for very tall, slim, ideally blond adjutants, order-lies and servants and by his penchant for having 'Nordic' looking people in his entourage.

From about 1920 onwards Hitler was under close observation, particularly by his political enemies. If he had had a long-lasting sexual relationship with a woman, this would have been noticed. But none of his enemies nor any of his friends were able to make such a claim. And the women who knew Hitler most intimately— Maria Reiter, Eugenie Haug, Ada Klein, Sigrid von Laffert, Unity Mitford and Margarete Slezak to name but a few—all confirmed that Hitler was not after sex.

Hitler wanted people and so-called friends about him, but only as long as the relationship did not require any particular commitments on his part. During his whole life Hitler therefore avoided close friendships and intimacies. Eva Braun recognised this very early on and acted accordingly, even though this meant that she had to give up much of her life as a woman and a person. But apparently the advantages of a life of luxury, which she enjoyed through Hitler's friendship, were worth more to her than a fulfilled and happy life as a woman. She kept her distance and never presumed upon Hitler. This is what allowed her to keep his friendship through all the years. Basically, Hitler had no friends. He always broke off friendships when they threatened to become too intimate, regardless of whether the friends were men or women. He did, however, often remain grateful to them to an astonishing degree.

His bodyguard Graf, drivers Maurice, Schreck and Kempka, adjutant Schaub, photographer Hoffmann, housekeeper Winter,[290] servants, orderlies, secretaries and many others at different times and for different periods were with Hitler practically day and night right up to the end of his life in 1945. If one analyses the statements made by these people, then it actually does appear that Hitler—for whatever reasons—kept his relationships with women strictly platonic. His satisfactions were apparently triggered by the ecstasies of the masses, by the belief that he had been selected by Fate to be the *Führer* of the Greater German Reich.

Eva Braun confided to her hairdresser that Hitler was not having sex with her. As *Frau* Schroeder had learned from Henriette von Schirach, a report to that effect supposedly existed at the practice of Munich lawyer Claus von Schirach. The same statement was made by Nelly Scholten—the wife of gynaecologist *Dr* Gustav Scholten, who treated Martin Bormann's wife—to *Frau* Ada Schultze, *née*

Klein, who had been a friend of Hitler's in the 1920s and had married *Professor Dr* Walter Schultze in 1936. There had never been any sex between Hitler and the attractive, dark-haired Ada Klein, even though she had tried her best to seduce him. Hitler observed the same abstinence towards the actress and singer Gretl Slezak, although she too tried to get closer to Hitler.

There were three people who knew Hitler better than anybody else and were close to him for a long time. They were probably the only ones who were really familiar with Hitler's private life. These were Julius Schaub, Hitler's factotum since 1925, Heinrich Hoffmann, who knew him since 1920, and Anni Winter, since 1929 his housekeeper in his Prinzregentenplatz apartment in Munich. All three unequivocally stated that Hitler did not love Eva Braun as a lover, as this has always been portrayed in the literature, but only as a good friend.

According to the transcripts of their testimony in Nuremberg in 1945, Julius Schaub, for example, was asked:

Q: Did Hitler love Eva Braun?

A: He liked her.

Q: What does that mean? I do not know what it means when one says in Munich 'He liked her.' Did he love her?

A: He had affection for her.

And Heinrich Hoffmann testified:

From 1930 on Hitler was frequently in my store and on such occasions got to know the Braun girl and often met her . . . I believe Hitler's relationship to Eva Braun was strictly platonic . . .

On 6 March 1948 Anni Winter stated:

Eva Braun was not very intelligent . . . She entertained Hitler with her merry, shallow chatter and that was all he needed as a distraction . . . Even though Eva did not see the *Führer* often, he nonetheless spoiled her. She could have anything and she made the best of it. In his presence she was very talkative and childish, sometimes even a little too devoted. When Hitler was not there and she was in Munich or at the Berghof she had one party after another. All her young friends came and she flirted with them recklessly. She did everything Hitler did not like: she danced, drank and smoked. She had no compunctions at all and often did things that were out of keeping with Hitler's position. But naturally this was only known to the people around her and they never said anything to Hitler out of fear of her. I heard a lot of things from her girls at the Berghof . . . I am sure that if the war had not broken out Hitler would have ended his relationship with her. She loved a luxurious life and he would have paid her off and enabled her to live comfortably . . .[291]

But, as we know, the outcome was totally different. On 10 March 1944 Heinrich Himmler visited Hitler at the Berghof where Hitler had been staying since 23 February 1944. On this occasion Himmler introduced his new 'liaison officer of the *Waffen-SS* to the *Führer*', the 38-year-old *SS-Gruppenführer* Hermann Fegelein.

Fegelein was one of the most evil and disgusting careerists within the Nazi élite, the SS. He had studied at Munich University for two terms, then joined the Bavarian state police as an officer cadet in 1927, resigned in 1929 and gone to work at his father's riding school. In 1933 he joined the SS and, through the offices of Christian Weber, became the commander of the Central SS Riding Academy in Munich-Riem in 1937. From 5 August 1941 on he commanded an SS cavalry brigade, where he brutally sacrificed his men and was detested to an incredible degree. 'His orders,' according to subsequent reports by some of his former subordinates, 'bore the stamp of arrogance and his military actions where those of a dilettante.' For his inhumane leadership in combat he was rewarded with medals and promotions. From Fegelein's SS personnel file we gain the impression of a corrupt careerist who was servile towards his superiors and a womaniser to boot. He was only spared an SS court-martial, for example, after he and his regiment had had stolen money and luxury goods transported to Munich from Warsaw in trucks by members of the SS Riding Academy, by a direct order from Himmler on 23 April 1941. During this affair Fegelein wrote to Himmler:

> For the future as well as the past I give you my word of honour as an SS man and soldier that my actions were not governed by any base thoughts. Given your sense of judgement and justice, *Reichsführer*, one does not need to lie or to plunder . . .[292]

On top of that, Fegelein—who had been engaged several times to various German girls—stood accused in an SS court action on 16 May 1941:

> . . . that *SS-Staf.* Fegelein is suspected if not already proved to have maintained sexual relations with a Polish woman in Krakau, made her pregnant and then induced her to have an abortion . . .[293]

This case was also quashed through a 'special order' by Himmler, who had the following message sent to Fegelein on 30 June 1941:

> . . . in your case, dear Fegelein, the external circumstances are so favourable that the question of issue can only be touched upon in the context of a marriage. The only thing you are apparently lacking is the ultimate clarity and the necessary power of decision which, however, as an old National Socialist, should be part of your birthright.
>
> It is surprising in itself that you disregarded the deadline set for the announcement of your marriage and did not even apply for an extension. You may rest assured that I do not misunderstand the difficulties which work against such matters. In the final analysis, however, you have had time enough by now to find yourself a wife, and the war is no excuse in this context but a factor that makes the resolution of this question appear to be even more urgent.
>
> The *Reichsführer-SS* does not wish that you marry in erstwhile Poland of all places. He expects you to utilise the pleasant spring that is bound to follow upon the harsh winter, in order seriously to make an effort to find a wife and to report to him by the end of May that you are engaged.
>
> Note: Letter was not sent. *SS-Staf.* Fegelein met with *Reichsführer-SS* and *SS-Gruppenführer* Wolff and was apprised of this letter. He stated that he would shortly be engaged . . .[294]

On 16 November 1941 a grateful Fegelein wrote to his protector Himmler:

> In some cases in the past, the fact that I was repeatedly attacked from all sides might have been due to a certain ineptitude on my part, a lack of experience and too rigid a stance. I pass all these thoughts on to you today, *Reichsführer*, because every human being, and above all every soldier, needs a person somewhere with whom he can talk openly without holding anything back.
>
> Up to now there has been no opportunity to tell you all that one feels and thinks. I turned 35 this year and I fancy that I have the same number of years still left to live.

My desire is to spend these years, which may be numbered among my best years, for the good of yourself and the SS and to work along a very clear, great concept so that you may experience nothing but joy and I gain the feeling of having laid the foundations of a worthwhile life's work.

In all the years of my work and under your command, it has never been necessary for me to lie to you. That makes me feel very good . . .

I am honest enough to admit that it is my healthy ambition to become one of your best leaders. But I also know that I must therefore accept the highest responsibility and complete attention to duty in every phase of this struggle for life.

I beg you, most revered *Reichsführer*, to take all these thoughts and memories as expressions of my gratitude towards yourself as my superior and elder comrade. I have presumed to write this letter in recognition of the fact that ever since I have known you, you have always been well disposed towards me and my family . . .[295]

On the occasion of Himmler's 42nd birthday Fegelein wrote to him in a most sycophantic and disgusting manner:

In all of my life you were always my great protector, my strict superior and my ever-helpful comrade. You, together with *Obergruppenführer* Jüttner, have made me what I am today. For this, by way of being the most perfect birthday present, may I be permitted to say that I value a special characteristic of the Germanic soldier as my highest commandment, my gratitude towards you . . . My energy was given me by Nature, but my conscientiousness and my sense of responsibility together with my most stringent obedience to duty I was taught by you, and I believe that today I can tell you that I have always proved just how holy your orders have been for me.

Recently I would so much have liked to tell the *Führer*—had the other gentlemen not been present—just how much his soldiers venerate him and with how much affection they cling to him. Even if his orders sometimes appear to be unrelenting and are felt to be cruel when he says 'Hold on to the last man', one feeling is always still uppermost among the men who defend their Fatherland with weapon in hand, and that is that there is someone above them who comes directly after God . . .

Maybe you, *Reichsführer*, can inform the *Führer* of this on some occasion . . . For your new year of life, *Reichsführer*, I wish you the most pleasant and joyful thoughts and successes that a human being may wish for. With this I join the wish that I may continue to serve you and your life's work for many years to come in a position of responsibility . . .[296]

This is perhaps enough to characterise the 'new face' at the Berghof, that of Hermann Fegelein. Immediately after having been introduced, he began to sound out the situation and talked with one of Hitler's old acquaintances, *Frau* Marion Schönmann,[297] who had become a friend of Eva Braun's. 'He asked her,' Christine Schroeder learned after the war from *Frau* Schönmann, 'what he would have to do to be invited to stay for lunch.' *Frau* Schönmann introduced Fegelein to Eva Braun, and with this came not only an invitation to attend lunch at Hitler's table at the Berghof but the beginning of an affair between Eva Braun and Hermann Fegelein which was always kept covered by the cloak of 'brother-in-law', even though not only the secretaries must have noticed the special kind of affection the two of them felt for each other.

That Fegelein appealed to Eva Braun as a man was later confirmed by *Frau* Schönmann. Eva Braun allegedly confessed to her that Fegelein had made a strong impression on her and confided that 'Some years ago the boss said to me, if you should fall in love with some other man one day, then just tell me and I will let you go.' And, according to *Frau* Schönmann, Eva Braun continued: 'If I had met Fegelein ten years earlier, I would have asked the boss to let me go.'[298]

A letter was discovered among *Frau* Schroeder's papers in which *Frau* Schönmann had written to her on 21 May 1963:

> To your question about when Fegelein met E.B., I recall that this must have been in early March 1944 when I had been invited to spend a few days at the Berg. Fegelein, who had come with H.H., asked me what was to be done so that he could stay for lunch. If I had only suspected what I was to cause when I referred him to E.B! I could not have guessed that those two would develop such an affection for each other! But this must remain just between the two of us . . .

The female element at Hitler's court was very keen on the gentleman rider, womaniser and highly decorated *SS-General* Fegelein, as secretary Gertraud Junge described in detail in the book *Voices from the Bunker*:

> In the meantime a new face had appeared in Hitler's entourage. *SS-Gruppenführer* Fegelein was the liaison officer between Hitler and

Himmler. At the beginning he only came for the briefings, but after he had quickly made friends with Martin Bormann and others he soon became the focus of attention—the life and soul—of Berghof society. Fegelein never missed a single one of Bormann's nightly drinking bouts and he drank *Bruderschaft* with all the important people . . . As soon as he felt secure in his position, he regarded anybody who was not his friend as his enemy . . . He was devious and devoid of any scruples . . .

Fegelein was the archetypal romantic hero. He was incredibly cheeky and wore the Knight's Cross with Oak Leaves and Swords, and it was therefore not surprising that he was accustomed to have women throw themselves at him. He was also entertaining and habitually told funny and risqué stories without the slightest sign of embarrassment. He had the reputation of being a natural force and believed this of himself. He had advanced his career very rapidly and quite unexpectedly. He was even honest enough to admit that he was basically a coward and that he owed his decorations to fortunate circumstances that had only made him appear to be heroic. He also admitted quite openly that the only things that were important to him were his career and a life full of fun . . .[299]

Frau Schroeder wrote that

Eva Braun was attracted to Hermann Fegelein as a man, and that he liked the pretty girl very much—who was much better suited to him than to the sick old man [Hitler]—could not have escaped the attention of any observer who was present at the small, intimate parties that Eva Braun arranged in her room in the [upper floor of the] Chancellery in Berlin before or after air raids during the final weeks of her life.[300]

Secretary Junge also reported that

. . . the handsome Hermann had succeeded in gaining Eva Braun's favour so astonishingly quickly; on the other hand it was not really astonishing if one took into account how fresh, funny and amusing Fegelein could be when he wanted to . . .[301]

In any event, as *Frau* Junge reported, after Fegelein's arrival 'certain frictions and intrigues' developed between the Braun sisters. Gretl Braun, who lived with Eva, was dependent on her—officially she was employed by Heinrich Hoffmann from 1932 to 1943 and from 1 September 1943 onwards she was a student at the State Academy for Photography—and was sometimes treated as a servant,[302] offered herself as a solution to the problem. 'Gretl Braun was a good-natured person,' said *Dr* Brandt, 'easily manipulated and lacking a strong will.'

According to *Frau* Junge, Hermann Fegelein

> . . . had called Gretl Braun a silly goose before he learned that she was Eva Braun's sister, but as soon as he had been told he changed his mind immediately.[303]

Frau Schroeder stated:

> After several attempts to marry Eva Braun's younger sister off to men from Hitler's entourage—Ambassador Hewel, Adjutant Darges, Minister Wagner—had failed, Eva Braun now pursued a specific objective: Fegelein was to marry her sister Gretl.

And, as Secretary Junge reports,

> Within a short period of time we were in for a big surprise: in April 1944 Hermann Fegelein and Gretl Braun announced their engagement and, with this, Fegelein's excellent position was doubly secure . . .[304]

Eva and Gretl's mother, Franziska Braun, told Musmanno the following on 4 September 1948:

> I want to tell you something, and I have never spoken about this with anybody else. I am glad that Fegelein is dead. He was a bad man. We hardly knew him. Gretl came to me one day and asked whether she should marry Fegelein and I said we do not know him. Gretl laughed and said 'Mummy, I introduced him to you at the Berghof.' Then Fegelein came and asked my husband for her hand and eight days later they were married. I then only saw him once more when he took us to Zell am See. I did not like him . . .[305]

Frau Schroeder writes:

> . . . and so, under Eva Braun's direction, the marriage came about and was celebrated with great pomp in the Salzburg City Hall, on the Obersalzberg and in the tea house on the Kehlstein on 3 June 1944. Eva Braun had said, 'I want this marriage to be as beautiful as if it were my own!' And that is the way it was . . .[306]

Eva Braun blossomed after the event. Her inferiority complex with regard to her social position in Hitler's entourage, from which she had suffered for years, was gone overnight. 'The marriage of her sister gave her a certain security,' *Frau* Schroeder maintains. 'Now

I am somebody; now I am Fegelein's sister-in-law'. And *Frau* Junge wrote:

> And young, zestful Eva, who had to live such a withdrawn and demure life, was overjoyed that she finally had a brother-in-law (or boyfriend) with whom she could dance and flirt to her heart's content without running the risk of gossip . . .

One must ask oneself whether that was the only worry Eva Braun had while the Allied and Soviet armies were slowly advancing towards Germany's borders.

Eva Braun—who had previously seldom come to Berlin because she was completely ignored there—now came immediately after Hitler, with Fegelein, returned to the capital from the 'Wolfsschanze' headquarters on 20 November 1944. She then stayed until 10 December 1944, when Hitler and his staff, including Fegelein, left to go to the 'Adlerhorst' headquarters.

Fegelein amused himself at the 'Adlerhorst', as Martin Bormann wrote to his wife on 30 December 1944:

> After dinner excited discussions in small groups—then back home—about twenty minutes' drive—to our quarters. Then continuation of the happy party in my office. Master of ceremonies—Fegelein! Also present: Jodl, Burgdorf, Lorenz and the young girls Lechner and Unterholzner. Music, dancing and amusement.
>
> When Jeschke woke me up all the guests had gone. According to Fegelein they had continued to 'have fun with the girls' (Fegelein's own words), but that is not as bad as it sounds because the girls sleep two to a room in bunk beds . . .[307]

But how Fegelein was treating his wife in the meantime is also reported by Bormann in a letter of 27 December 1944:

> One thing is quite certain—in Fegelein Gretl has a rather difficult husband. He called her today from my office and I was able to listen in on the conversation. He gave her a real 'to-do list', to use his own expression. He ordered her to get up early in the morning and do some sort of work—e.g. to work in the kitchen during the time at the Berghof—instead of lolling around in bed and lazing away the day. He told her the same thing again today. He really does call a spade a spade![308]

When Hitler was back in Berlin with his staff on 19 January, Eva Braun immediately appeared again, this time in company with her pregnant sister Gretl. On 6 February Eva celebrated her 33rd birthday. After Hitler had retired, there was amusement on the upper floor of the Old Chancellery with dancing and champagne, during which she complained about the lack of dancing partners.

On 8 February there was a farewell party for Eva and her sister, who were intending to return to Munich on 9 February. Bormann writes:

> We had dinner with Fegelein and then talked until Evi [Eva Braun] appeared. She stayed with us for an hour and a half and then Heinrich [Himmler] had to leave to meet Kaltenbrunner and I went to take care of the mail that had arrived from Munich in the meantime . . .[309]

On 7 March Eva Braun came back to Berlin again by train, even though Hitler had instructed her to stay in Munich, as Bormann reports:

> The *Führer* told me that E.B. wanted to come back as soon as possible. She was told, however, to stay in Munich until further notice.[310]

Eva Braun was not drawn to the visibly deteriorating, badly ageing and shaking Hitler, burdened by cares: she wanted to see Hermann Fegelein, to be near him and to amuse herself with him. The zestful Eva would certainly not have travelled so dangerously close to the front had not her feelings for Fegelein impelled her to do so. *Major* Freytag von Loringhoven, who had frequently seen Eva Braun in the bunker, recalls:

> She was attractive, not beautiful but pretty, not all that young any more but well made up with all of Arden's skill, even in the bunker still well dressed, elegant dresses and shoes, in the winter fantastic furs. However, I found her—I hardly ever spoke with her—lower class, a *demi-monde* type, the kind a man likes to tumble occasionally . . .[311]

As secretaries Schroeder and Junge have reported, Eva Braun held small, intimate parties with dancing and champagne in her room in the Old Chancellery during the final weeks of her life, either before or after air raids. *Frau* Junge describes these parties:

She wanted to party, dance, drink . . . Whomever she met, whoever crossed her path, Eva Braun took upstairs to her former living room on the first floor . . . Eva Braun wanted to dance. It did not matter with whom, and she dragged everyone with her into a desperate frenzy . . . Champagne was drunk and there was shrill laughter . . .[312]

And, *Frau* Schroeder claims,

It could not escape anyone's attention that she was attracted to Hermann Fegelein as a man and that he also liked Eva Braun. While Hitler was conducting his briefings, in her room records were played, a glass of champagne was drunk and normally there was dancing with the officers who were off-duty. Hermann Fegelein was also present and often danced with Eva Braun. I have a picture etched in my mind: at the end of a dance Fegelein lifted Eva Braun up with both arms level with his chest. And as she lay in his arms, they gazed into each other's eyes with tenderness and longing. It was obvious that Eva Braun liked Hermann Fegelein very much and felt herself strongly attracted to him . . . From their looks, from their age and from their character they were made for each other. And the fact that Fegelein, after he had disappeared from the Chancellery on 25 April 1945, called Eva Braun and pleaded with her to leave the Chancellery and come to him, only confirms my observations . . .[313]

Furthermore *Frau* Schroeder—who was only four years older than Eva Braun—said to me during a conversation, her face inadvertently showing something akin to disgust, 'I would never have wanted to kiss Hitler. He had very yellow teeth and his breath smelt . . .'[314]

That is what a 37-year-old secretary recounts. And the 33-year-old Eva Braun is supposed to have 'loved' Hitler? If she had been his mistress, or merely a 'loving woman' at his side (as has always been portrayed), her conduct during the final weeks in Berlin would have had to be very much different. She never gave a fig about Hitler, the state of his health or his cares. She for the most part no longer even joined in the nightly teas and preferred to amuse herself instead. She even criticised Hitler's conduct in front of the secretaries. She preferred to dance while in the bunker, as Hitler had to digest one disaster after another.

That Eva Braun had no intention of going under with Hitler in the bunker can be seen from a letter she wrote to her friend Herta Schneider on 19 April 1945:

But if the worst comes to the worst, a way will certainly be found so that we can all see you again.[315]

On 25 April 1945 Fegelein left the Chancellery with the intention of deserting. Fegelein knew about Himmler's negotiations with the Allies. In all probability he even had written files about them and wanted to escape from the predictable end in Hitler's immediate vicinity. He did not ask for permission to leave, but simply drove off to Fürstenberg with his bodyguard, *SS-Obersturmführer* Hermann Bornhold of the FBK, to visit his friend and protector *SS-Obergruppenführer* Hans Jüttner, who had been Chief of the SS Central Command Staff since 1943. As Jüttner testified later, Fegelein supposedly told him, 'I definitely have no intention of dying in Berlin'.[316] And this from the man who had put Hitler 'directly after God' and who had wanted to display 'the highest responsibility and complete attention to duty in every phase of this struggle for life'!

As *SS-Obersturmführer* Bornhold later testified, the advance by the Soviet forces made a return to Berlin by car no longer possible. Fegelein, for reasons about which one can only speculate, then flew back to Berlin by plane, leaving Bornhold behind in Fürstenberg. In the meantime, as *Frau* Junge reports, Eva Braun was looking for Fegelein:

> Eva Braun was put out that Hermann Fegelein was not paying the slightest attention to her. She had not seen him for two days. And even before that she felt that he had been avoiding her. She asked me whether I had seen him. Fegelein had not appeared at all in the bunker that day. Even the officers with whom he shared a room in the cellar of the New Chancellery knew nothing . . .[317]

But then, on 26 April, occasional phone calls from Fegelein were received in which he asked about the latest news. These at least proved that he was still in Berlin and no further questions were asked, as both von Loringhoven and Boldt confirmed on 13 March 1948:

> Yes, Fegelein called from the city and asked about the military situation. He called either Boldt or me, and we informed him about the situation at the front . . .[318]

And, as *Frau* Junge stated, Fegelein supposedly called Eva Braun during the night of 26 April 1945:

> Eva Braun told me, full of disappointment and deeply shattered, that Hermann Fegelein had called her the night before from his apartment: 'Eva, you must leave the *Führer* . . . don't be so stupid, it is now a question of life and death . . .'[319]

It will never be possible to establish whether Eva Braun could not leave because Hitler had learned of Fegelein's phone call or whether she did not want to go because she still hoped for a break-out. Other witnesses have stated that she kept the telephone call secret from Hitler. It is questionable whether—as *Frau* Junge claims—Eva Braun said: 'Hermann, where are you? Come back immediately, the *Führer* is already asking after you. He wants to talk to you! But he had already put down the receiver', because Hitler only began looking for Fegelein on the afternoon of 27 April.

As he told me in a personal interview, Otto Günsche knew the telephone number of Fegelein's apartment at 4 Bleibtreustrasse. Rattenhuber, whom Hitler had ordered to look for Fegelein, called him there and told him to come back to the Chancellery immediately. Fegelein, who was under the influence of alcohol, declined. When a group of the bodyguard under *SS-Obersturmführer* Helmuth Frick was then sent to fetch Fegelein, the drunken *SS-Gruppenführer* refused to come.

Rattenhuber thereupon sent his deputy Peter Högl with several men from the Reich Security Service to arrest Fegelein. When Högl arrived, Fegelein was in the company of a young red-headed lady who managed to escape from the apartment under a pretext. As Günsche relates, Högl then brought Fegelein—still drunk—back to the Chancellery on the evening of 27 April.

Fegelein was immediately demoted for desertion, and, according to Günsche's testimony on 4 April 1971, Hitler initially

> . . . ordered that Fegelein was to be handed over to the Commander of the Chancellery, *SS-Gruppenführer* Mohnke, who was to employ him in the defence of Berlin. Bormann brought me this order but drew attention to the fact that Fegelein would also just run away from Mohnke's command.

Bormann and I presented this to Hitler, who agreed and ordered that Fegelein should be court-martialled. Mohnke was to be one of the officers of the court. The court-martial was a typical example of Hitler's insistence on the observance of the formalities . . .[320]

Other witnesses—Axmann, Kempka and *Frau* Junge—claim that Heinrich Müller, Head of the *Gestapo*, was the one to interrogate Fegelein.

However, when in addition to a small suitcase with jewels and foreign currency, which Högl had brought with him from Fegelein's apartment, a search of his room in the cellar of the New Chancellery most probably revealed a briefcase containing documents with proof of Himmler's long-standing negotiations with Count Bernadotte, or when Fegelein admitted that he knew about Himmler's negotiations, Hitler ordered his immediate execution. During the denazification proceedings against Fegelein, Erich Kempka testified that

. . . he [Kempka] had heard the next day [29 April] from Högl that the contents of the briefcase had constituted high treason.[321]

Where Fegelein was shot can no longer be ascertained. All possible places in and around the Chancellery have been mentioned, while telephone operator Misch spoke of a shooting in a cellar by two members of the Reich Security Service. According to general opinion, Fegelein was shot on 28 April 1945 shortly before midnight.

One can imagine what went on in Eva Braun's mind when she learned about the circumstances of Fegelein's arrest and, above all, that he had had a woman with him in his apartment. Statements differ as to whether Eva Braun pleaded with Hitler for Fegelein's life:

In any case [wrote *Frau* Schroeder], one must assume that this disappointment was an important factor in ending her life, or rather it made this decision easy for her.[322]

Shortly after Fegelein's execution, Hitler married Eva Braun. On 20 March 1967 Otto Günsche testified to this:

. . . it has been portrayed that a big party [at Hitler's marriage on 29 April 1945] took place. That was not the case, because I did not know, nor did I even notice, that the marriage had taken place. That happened by the way;

it was a matter of only a few minutes, at a time when I was absent from the bunker . . .

Hitler's marriage was just a 'gesture' towards his long-time—I would say—companion, because we always regarded her as a 'companion', we who belonged to the inner circle . . . One must look at the role Eva Braun played: she was always in the background, nobody was allowed to know that she existed; only very few knew that. She was just '*Fräulein* Braun', and any other woman, no matter where she came from, who was married to a party functionary or just married, had a social position that derived from the position of the husband. *Fräulein* Braun always had to disappear. I can imagine that inside she suffered terribly from this, but she bore it very, very bravely . . .

Actually, except on a very few occasions, she was only ever at the Obersalzberg. She was never at one of the headquarters and only very rarely in Berlin . . .

Normally he [Hitler] would never have married. And she knew that—not even later on. He told others that he could not be married: he had dedicated himself completely to his work, to his task, and he could not found a family which would certainly have distracted him from his task.[323]

What the marriage meant to Hitler can be seen from a further statement made by Günsche on 21 June 1956:

If in my previous testimony I have referred to 'Eva Braun' even for the period after the marriage, the reason is that Adolf Hitler himself called her '*Fräulein* Braun' or '*Fräulein* Eva' when he spoke to me and others about her during this time.

One can hardly credit it, but Günsche's testimony is quite clear: after the marriage Hitler did not refer to Eva Braun as 'my wife' or '*Frau* Hitler' on even a single occasion but continued to speak of '*Fräulein* Braun' or '*Fräulein* Eva'. Hitler also gave orders that, after his death, everything that could point to Eva Braun, particularly at the Berghof, was to be destroyed—quite inconceivable and barely comprehensible conduct on the part of Hitler, for which we will never be able to find an explanation.

Eva Braun's life was a struggle for success and recognition according to the glitter of her imaginary Hollywood world. She was an 'actress', and her life was but one big play. Through Fegelein she had found a role at Hitler's court and she continued to play this role even after she discovered that Fegelein had cruelly disappointed her. When Fegelein died, she was also dead. And a broken Eva Braun realised that only one more role remained to her: the end at Hitler's side. When Eva Braun bit the prussic acid ampoule, she was an unhappy woman whom life had disappointed.

Notes

1   Otto Günsche, born 24 September 1917 in Jena (Saxon-Anhalt). Secondary school. Joined *SS-Leibstandarte 'Adolf Hitler'* on 1 July 1934. From 1936 *Leutnant* in *Führerbegleitkommando* (see below). Training at SS officers' academy 1 January 1941 to 30 April 1942, promotion to *SS-Sturmführer* on 21 June 1942. Active service as commander of Panzer Grenadier company with motorised infantry regiment of *Leibstandarte 'Adolf Hitler'*. From 12 January to August 1943 Hitler's personal adjutant in 'Wolfsschanze' headquarters as replacement for *SS-Hauptsturmführer* Richard Schulze, who was ill. Active service August 1943 to 5 February 1944. Hitler's personal adjutant 6 February 1944 to 30 April 1945. Promoted to *SS-Sturmbannführer* 21 December 1944. Captured by Soviets 2 May 1945; various prisons and labour camps in the USSR and GDR. Released from Bautzen Penitentiary 2 May 1956. Now lives in northern Germany.

2   Albert Speer, born 19 March 1905 in Mannheim. Studied architecture. Assistant to *Professor* Tessenow in Berlin 1927–32. Joined NSDAP in 1931. Participated in reconstruction of the *Gauhaus* in Voss-strasse and refurbishment of Goebbels' Propaganda Ministry. Responsible for planning and execution of the May Day celebrations 1 May 1933, for which he used new methods of mass presentation creating a spectacle of previously unknown dimensions. After death of *Professor* Troost, became Hitler's favourite architect and member of his inner circle until 1945. In 1936 Hitler charged him with the plans for the rebuilding of Berlin. In 1937 he was named Chargé for Building on the Staff of the *Führer* and General Inspector of Building in Berlin. Reconstruction of Chancellery 1938–39. Succeeded *Dr* Todt as Reich Minister for Armament and Munitions 8 February 1942, at age 36. Arrested in Flensburg 23 May 1945 as member of Dönitz government. In Nuremberg, sentenced to 20 years' imprisonment as a war criminal 1 October 1946. Released from Spandau prison in Berlin 30 September 1966. Died of stroke in London 1 September 1981 aged 76.

3   Christine Schroeder, born 19 March 1908 in Hannoversch-Münden (Lower Saxony). Commercial apprenticeship and work as a clerk until 1929, then secretary in a law firm in Nagold and from March 1930 secretary in central office of NSDAP in Munich. From 4 March 1933 in Berlin; Hitler's personal secretary from June 1933 to the end. Arrested 28 May 1945 in Hintersee near Berchtesgaden; held by Americans until 12 May 1948. Subsequently worked as a secretary in Schwäbisch Gmünd and from September 1959 for construction company in Munich. Died in Munich on 28 June 1984 aged 76.

4   Hermann Giesler, born 2 August 1898 in Siegen (Westphalia). Worked as a mason, later as a carpenter. Studied architecture at Academy of Arts and Crafts in Munich and then worked for architectural firm in Augsburg and from 1926 in Berlin. Went into business for himself as a potter in 1928. Joined NSDAP 1 October 1931. District Con-

struction Officer in Sonthofen 1933; built Sonthofen 'Ordensburg'. Appointed professor by Hitler in 1938; drafted the plans for various major Nazi building projects, including NSDAP Leadership Academy on the Chiemsee. Appointed 'General Superintendent for the Reconstruction of Munich' 2 December 1938 and from 1941 worked as assistant to *Professor* Fick for reconstruction of Linz. Succeeded Speer as Hitler's favourite architect when Speer became Minister for Armaments. As senior official of OT, was held captive by Americans from May 1945 to October 1951. After release worked as architect. Died in Düsseldorf 20 January 1987 aged 89.

5   Walter Frentz, born 21 August 1907 in Heilbronn (Württemberg). Studied electrotechnology at Technical Universities of Munich and Berlin but then went into the film industry as cameraman with UFA; was later government cameraman with film director and Hitler *protégé* Leni Riefenstahl. When at the outset of the war against Poland a cameraman was required to film Hitler and his staff during the campaign, Frentz was appointed to this position at Führer headquarters. *Leutnant* in *Luftwaffe* from 1 February 1942. Accompanied Hitler on all of his trips. Took many colour pictures and portrait photos of Hitler's inner circle and guests at the 'Wolfsschanze'; also assigned by Hitler to photograph objects Hitler did not have the time to visit personally. Hitler placed great trust in Frentz's reports. Flown out of Berlin 24 April 1945; arrested by SS at Obersalzberg in connection with the Göring affair. Subsequently taken prisoner by Americans and held captive until late 1946. Now lives in southern Germany.

6   Adolf Dirr, born 14 February 1907 in Munich. Learned the trade of smith, was an avid boxer and won many regional championships (e.g. Munich lightweight champion 1929–36). Joined NSDAP and SA 1 May 1929 in order to be able to participate in SA boxing championships; after having been recommended to Hitler by Himmler as boxing trainer and bodyguard, became member of the Führer bodyguard 1 March 1932. Accompanied Hitler on election campaigns and later to all his various headquarters. Appointed *SS-Untersturmführer* 1 July 1934 and promoted to *SS-Hauptsturmführer* 20 April 1944. Flown out of Berlin 22 April 1945; continued to work at Berghof. When leaving Berghof, was arrested by Americans on 22 May 1945 and held until 27 April 1948. Now lives in southern Germany.

7   Michael A. Musmanno, judge and Captain in US Navy, conducted 'semi-official' interrogation of former employees and military staff members from Hitler's immediate entourage, whom he located and questioned in various prisons, POW camps and in their homes between mid 1945 and September 1948. Over 200 witnesses testified to their duties with Hitler and their observations during his final days in the bunker in Berlin. These accounts together form a document that is unique in its completeness and content. The testimony was written down in English and, since Musmanno's death on 14 October 1968, the documents have been preserved in the Duquesne University Library in Pittsburgh, Pennsylvania.

8   Erich Kempka, born 16 September 1910 in Oberhausen (Rheinland). Learned trade of electro-technician and worked as mechanic for motor manufacturer DKW. Joined NSDAP and SS 1 April 1930; worked as driver in Essen district party administration. On 29 February 1932 was transferred to Hitler's SS bodyguard in Munich as second driver. After first driver Schreck died in 1936, became Hitler's personal chauffeur and chief of the car fleet which by 1945 comprised about 40 vehicles and 60 drivers and mechanics. Was a witness to Hitler's cremation on 30 April 1945 in Berlin. On 1 May 1945 was successful in breaking out from the Chancellery and reaching Berchtesgaden.

Arrested by Americans 20 June 1945 and held until 9 October 1947. Later lived in Munich and other places in West Germany. Died in Freiburg 24 January 1975 aged 64.

9   Artur Axmann, born 18 February 1913 in Hagen (Westphalia). Studied law and founded the first Hitler Youth Group in Westphalia in 1928. Member of the Reich Leadership of the NSDAP from 1932, and from 1933 Chief of the Social Office in Reich Youth Leadership. Active service from 1940, and appointed Reich Youth Leader 1 August 1940. Wounded on Eastern Front 1941, then dedicated himself to leadership of the Hitler Youth and was in Berlin in 1945 with anti-tank unit of Hitler Youth. Towards end of April 1945 took part in Hitler's military briefings in the bunker and was witness to Hitler's suicide. Succeeded in breaking out to the West; arrested by CIC 15 December 1945 in Allgäu; was detained until 12 May 1949. Now lives in northern Germany.

10   Paula Hitler, born 26 January 1896 in Hafeld (Austria). Hitler's only full sister. Received commercial training and in 1920s worked as clerk with Austrian State Insurance Company in Vienna. Allegedly dismissed 2 August 1930 because of her brother. Hitler then supported her with a monthly payment of 250 schillings. During latter years of the war was clerk in field hospital in Vienna. Was brought to Berchtesgaden by two SS men 14 April 1945 under pseudonym of Paula Wolf (Wolf being a pseudonym Hitler had used in the 1920s), where Schaub paid her and her step-sister Angelika Raubal 100,000 marks on Hitler's orders. Arrested 26 May 1945 by CIC and interrogated, then released and returned to Vienna where she worked in an arts and crafts shop. Returned to Berchtesgaden on 1 December 1952 and took up permanent residence there in order to pursue her claims arising from Hitler's personal will, still under the name of Wolf, and continued to pursue these until her death in Schönau near Berchtesgaden on 1 June 1960 aged 64. Five months later Federal Court in Berchtesgaden issued a certificate of inheritance under which two-thirds of Hitler's estate was awarded to her.

11   Heinz Linge, born 23 March 1913 in Bremen. Learned masons' trade and subsequently attended technical high school. Joined SS-Leibstandarte 'Adolf Hitler' 17 March 1933. On 24 January 1935 was personally selected by Hitler to become one of his valets (he stood over 6ft tall) and took up his duties after attending hotel training school in Munich-Pasing. After Hitler had dismissed his previous valet Krause, became Krause's successor; from then was constantly in attendance upon Hitler. Promoted to SS-Untersturmführer 20 April 1939, Obersturmführer in 1941, Hauptsturmführer in 1943 and SS-Sturmbannführer in February 1945. Witnessed Hitler's suicide and cremation 30 April 1945. Was captured during break-out attempt 2 May 1945 and taken to Russia; sentenced to 25 years' hard labour in 1950. Released by Russians 29 September 1955. Died in Bremen 24 June 1980 aged 67.

12   Robert Payne, Stalin: Aufstieg und Fall, Hans E. Günther Verlag, Stuttgart 1967, p. 568.

13   Ibid., p. 569.

14   Ibid.

15   Eva Braun, born 6 February 1912 in Munich. Girls school and from 1928 convent school (commercial school) in Simbach/Inn. In 1929 worked for five months for gynaecologist Dr Gunther Hoffmann. Through advertisement found job with photographer Heinrich Hoffmann (accounting, general office work, selling films), who introduced her to Hitler in October 1929 when she was 17. By the end of 1930 the 41-year-old Hitler occasionally went out with the 18-year-old girl, something which Hoffmann

cleverly abetted. This led to a casual friendship. After Geli Raubal's suicide (see below) on 18 September 1931, she very cleverly succeeded in capturing Hitler's attention by staging a suicide attempt on 1 November 1932. After a second suicide attempt in 1935, with which she blackmailed Hitler, she moved into 'her own' first floor apartment (on the salary of a junior employee in Hoffmann's photographic shop!) at 42 Wiedenmeyerstrasse. After Hitler dismissed his step-sister and housekeeper Angelika Raubal (q.v.) on 18 February 1936, she continued to strengthen her position with Hitler. Towards the end of 1935 Hoffmann, acting as proxy for Hitler, bought a small villa for 35,000 marks in the Munich suburb of Bogenhausen, into which Eva Braun moved on 30 March 1936. In mid-1936 she first appeared at the Berghof and, with her sisters and girlfriends, became a fixture in Hitler's inner circle. She was not employed at the Berghof as a housekeeper but always classed as a guest. She had to stay out of sight during official occasions and suffered from the fact that she was not allowed to appear in public with Hitler. Her status only became 'official' as Fegelein's sister-in-law after Fegelein had married her sister Margarete (Gretl) Braun on 3 June 1944. She made out her will on 26 October 1944 and went to Berlin on 21 November 1944, where Hitler had returned from his 'Wolfsschanze' headquarters for the last time on 20 November, only to be sent back to Munich on 10 December 1944. She then returned to Berlin with her sister on 19 January 1945 and celebrated her 33rd birthday there. After having returned to Munich on 9 February 1945 she came back to Berlin for the last time on 7 March 1945. At a few minutes past midnight on 29 April 1945, Hitler married Eva Braun. She committed suicide on 30 April 1945 towards 1530, aged 33.

16 Payne, op. cit., p. 571.

17 Ibid., pp. 571–2.

18 Constanze Manziarly, born 14 April 1920 in Innsbruck. After secondary school and training as dietician, worked in the Zabel rehabilitation clinic in Bischofswiesen (Bavaria) from 13 September 1943. After Hitler dismissed his cook Helene Maria von Exner on 8 May 1944 she became his cook in the 'Wolfsschanze' headquarters from September 1944. During March and April 1945 she had a small kitchen in the upper bunker in Berlin where she prepared Hitler's meals. She also regularly took part in the nightly teas with Hitler. After the break-out from the Chancellery on 2 May 1945 she allegedly committed suicide by taking prussic acid, aged 25.

19 Hanna Reitsch, born 29 March 1912 in Hirschberg (Westphalia). Studied medicine but quit in order to devote herself to glider flying. 1932 world record for women's endurance flying (5$\frac{1}{2}$ hours); in 1933 flew 11$\frac{1}{2}$ hours. In 1934 set women's world altitude record at 2,800m and won German glider championship. In 1937 took pilot's licence and became test pilot during the war. In 1942 was decorated with the Iron Cross 2nd Class. From 1943 on had friendship with *Luftwaffe* officer *Ritter* von Greim, 20 years her senior. Flew to Berlin with von Greim 26 April 1945 and on 29 April from Berlin to Dönitz in Plön. Arrested with von Greim by Americans in Kitzbühel and taken to interrogation centre in Oberursel near Frankfurt, where she was held until October 1946. Underwent intensive questioning because it was assumed she had flown Hitler out of Berlin. Died in Frankfurt 28 August 1979 aged 67.

20 Michael A. Musmanno, *In zehn Tagen kommt der Tod. Augenzeugen berichten über das Ende Hitlers*, Droemersche Verlagsanstalt, Munich 1950, p. 187.

21 Colonel William F. Heimlich in the May issue of *Police Gazette* and also *Darmstädter Tageblatt* of 27 May 1952.

22 Martin Bormann, born 17 June 1900 in Halberstadt (Saxon-Anhalt). Secondary school. Drafted 5 June 1918 to Field Artillery Regiment No 55, discharged 1919 as gunner. Worked on farm in Mecklenburg, later in Herzenberg, where he received agricultural training and then worked as foreman. Section leader in paramilitary Rossbach organisation 1922–23. Implicated in lynching of fellow trainee, sentenced to one year in prison on 15 March 1924. Joined NSDAP 10 February 1927, became *Gau* Trustee in Thuringia 31 March 1928 and *Gau* General Manager in Jena from 1 April to 15 November 1928. Transferred to Central Staff of SA in Munich 16 November 1928. From 25 August 1930 was Chief of the Aid Fund of NSDAP until he became Chief of Staff to Deputy *Führer* (Rudolf Hess) on 4 July 1933. Shortly thereafter Hitler made him responsible for managing his private fortune and charged him with building up the *Organisation Obersalzberg*. After Rudolf Hess flew to England on 10 May 1941, the Staff of the Deputy *Führer* was renamed 'Party Chancellery' and Bormann became its chief with the powers of a Reich Minister. At this point, Hitler again took over personal leadership of the party. On 12 April 1943 Bormann was appointed Secretary to the *Führer* and remained at his side like a shadow until Hitler's death. During the break-out from the Chancellery, the 44-year-old Bormann committed suicide by taking prussic acid. Because his body was not found, the Federal Court in Berchtesgaden declared him legally dead on 10 March 1954. On 7–8 December 1972 a skeleton was found during excavations in Berlin and positively identified as belonging to Bormann.

23 Heinrich Müller, born 28 April 1900 in Munich. Aircraft mechanic. Joined Bavarian police in 1919 (Department IV, Political Police); investigator of Communist movements. Promoted to Inspector in 1933; made Police Chief with the rank of *SS-Obersturmbannführer in 1937* (even though he only joined the NSDAP in 1939). Promoted to *SS-Standartenführer* 1937 and became intimate associate of Reinhard Heydrich. From 1939 Head of Department IV (*Gestapo*) in the Reich Central Security Office in Berlin. Promoted to *SS-Gruppenführer* on 9 November 1941. Last seen in *Führerbunker* 29 April 1945 and listed as missing since then.

24 Hermann Fegelein, born 30 October 1906 in Ansbach (Franconia). Studied at Munich University for two terms. On 20 April 1927 joined State Police in Munich as officer cadet, from which he then resigned 16 August 1929 to work in his father's riding school. Joined SS 10 April 1933 and became leader of an SS equestrian group. Joined the Central SS Riding Academy in Munich in 1935, became its commander in 1937. Promoted to *SS-Sturmbannführer* 30 January 1936 and on 1 March 1940 to *SS-Obersturmbannführer* and Commander of *SS-Totenkopf-Reiterstandarte*. On 5 August 1941 Commander of *SS Kav. Brigade* and *Kampfbrigade Fegelein* with rank of *Brigadeführer*. Became liaison officer of *Waffen-SS* to Hitler from 1 January 1944. Married Eva Braun's sister Margarete in Salzburg in 1944. Promoted by Hitler to Lieutenant-General of the *Waffen-SS* on 21 June 1944. On 25 April 1945 he left the bunker and was arrested in his apartment at 4 Bleibtreustrasse in Berlin by *SS-Obersturmbannführer* Peter Högl on 27 April, after he had telephoned Eva Braun on 26 April and asked her to leave Berlin with him. Hitler demoted him and, after his complicity in Himmler's secret negotiations with Count Bernadotte became known, had him sentenced to death. Shot some time after 2300 during night of 28 April, aged 38.

25 Johann Rattenhuber, born 30 April 1897 in Oberhaching (Bavaria). Drafted into the 16th Bavarian Infantry Regiment in 1916 and promoted to *Leutnant* in October 1918. Garrison duty in Ingolstadt until discharged. From September 1919 two terms at Munich University until joining the police in Bayreuth on 5 September 1920. Transferred

to State Police in Munich 10 February 1922 and promoted to *Leutnant* 1 August 1925. On 10 March 1933 adjutant of Chief of Police Himmler and in April 1933 given task of forming a 'Command for Special Duties' for Hitler in Berlin. Promoted to police *Hauptmann* 1 June 1933 and on 4 July 1934 admitted to SS with rank of *SS-Obersturmbannführer.* Permanently transferred to Berlin, where from April 1935 he commanded the now independent Reich Security Service (RSD). Promoted to police *Major* on 20 April 1934 and to *SS-Standartenführer* on 15 September 1935. Promoted to *Generalmajor* on 30 January 1944 and to *SS-Gruppenführer* on 24 February 1945. Badly wounded in leg during break-out from Chancellery. Captured by Soviet troops on 2 May 1945; taken to Russia and only released 10 October 1955. Died 30 June 1957 in Munich aged 60.

26 Joseph Goebbels, born 29 November 1897 in Rheyt (Rhineland). Studied German language and literature. Doctor's degree 1921. Worked for Dresdner Bank in Cologne from 1923 to mid-1924, then editor with *Völkische Freiheit* magazine. Joined NSDAP in 1924 and worked for *Gauleiter* Kaufmann. Appointed *Gauleiter* of Berlin 1926 and elected to *Reichstag* May 1928. In November 1928 replaced Georg Strasser as head of the Nazi propaganda department. On 19 December 1931 married Magdalena Quandt, divorced wife of industrialist Günther Quandt. Appointed 'Reich Minister for Public Enlightenment and Propaganda' on 14 March 1933. Responsible for control and *Gleichschaltung* of all media in Germany. Announced 'total war' in speech in the Berlin *Sportspalast* 13 February 1943. Appointed 'Plenipotentiary for the Total War Effort' 1944. In bunker with Hitler from 20 April 1945. After having his six children poisoned by *Dr* Stumpfegger, Goebbels shot himself on 1 May 1945, aged 47.

27 Walter Hewel, born 25 March 1904 in Cologne. From 1923 on in Munich, where he was enrolled at the Technical University. Joined *'Stosstrupp Hitler'* (formation of the SA) 20 October 1923, took part in *putsch* attempt and served sentence in Landsberg prison until 30 December 1924. Commercial apprenticeship in Hamburg in 1926 and then one year in England. From 1927 gentleman planter in Dutch East Indies, where he joined NSDAP in June 1933. Returned to Germany in March 1936 and appointed Chief of East Asia Desk in Foreign Section of the NSDAP. From August 1937 Chief of the English Desk in office of Ambassador von Ribbentrop. Promoted to *SS-Sturmbannführer* 12 July 1937. From 1940 Ambassador and representative of Foreign Ministry to Hitler at Führer headquarters. Promoted to *Brigadeführer* 9 November 1942. In bunker with Hitler until the end and, after breaking out from Chancellery on 2 May 1945, shot himself in Berlin-Wedding, aged 41.

28 Wilhelm Burgdorf, born 15 February 1895. 1914 Officer cadet 1914, *Leutnant* in Grenadier Regiment No 12 1915. *Hauptmann* 1930, *Major* and instructor for tactics at the military academy in Dresden 1935. Adjutant on staff of IX Corps 1937. *Oberstleutnant* 1938. From May 1940 Commander of 529th Infantry Regiment; promoted *Oberst* September 1940. From May 1942 Chief of Department 2 of the Army Personnel Office; became Deputy Chief in October 1942 and was promoted to *Generalmajor*. Promoted to *Generalleutnant* on 12 October 1944; became Chief of the Army Personnel Office and Chief Adjutant of the Armed Forces to Hitler. In bunker with Hitler April 1945 and listed as missing since 2 May 1945.

29 Georg Betz, born 15 June 1903 in Kolbermoor near Rosenheim (Bavaria). Technical college for electro-technology and mechanical engineering in Munich. Trained as pilot with Lufthansa and from 1932; Captain on European routes. Taken on to staff of *Reichsführer-SS* with the rank of *SS-Untersturmführer* and appointed pilot of the re-

serve aircraft of *Führerstaffel* (Hitler's second pilot). Promoted *SS-Obersturmbann-führer* 30 January 1944. In Chancellery until 1 May 1945 and killed at Weidendamm Bridge 2 May by shot in head, aged 42.

30 *Münchner Merkur*, 2 December 1983, No 277, p. 11.

31 Paul Ludwig Troost, born 17 August 1878 in Elberfeld (Rhineland). Studied architecture at the Technical University, Darmstadt. Worked with *Professor* Dülfer in Munich from 1920; then qualified as a university lecturer and had own architectural company. Trip to USA 1922. On return joined Norddeutsche Lloyd as interior designer where until 1929 he was responsible for interior finishing of all the company's large passenger ships (e.g. *Berlin, Europa, München, Ohio, Homeric*). Met Hitler in 1929 in the offices of publisher Bruckmann and impressed him with his artistic talents. Hitler engaged him to reconstruct the Barlow Palais when it became the 'Brown House'. In 1932 commissioned to design 'Haus der Deutschen Kunst' museum and plan new design of Königsplatz in Munich (to include party buildings and a 'Temple of Honour'). Died 21 January 1934 aged 55.

32 'Reichskanzlei Berlin', Federal Archives Koblenz, R 431/1533.

33 Julius Gregor Schaub, born 20 August 1898 in Munich. Primary school and training as a pharmacist in Munich, then with the Trade Association of German Chemists. Drafted 31 January 1917 as medic. Injury to both legs caused by a fall. 1918 as contract worker with Munich Central Supply Office. Joined NSDAP 10 October 1920 and took part in 1923 *putsch* attempt. Fled to Kärnten (Austria), arrested and sentenced to 1½ years in prison in Landsberg. Early release 31 December 1924. Hired 1 January 1925 as personal employee by Hitler, for whom he worked as general factotum until 1945. Member of *Reichstag* and *SS-Obergruppenführer*. Flew to Munich from Berlin 26 April 1945 where, on Hitler's orders, he cleared out Hitler's private safes in Munich and the Berghof and destroyed the contents. On 27 April 1945 went to Zell am See and Mallnitz (Austria), blew up Hitler's private train and subsequently fled to Kitzbühel (Tyrol) with forged papers under name of Josef Huber. Arrested there on 8 May 1945 by Americans and held until 17 February 1949. Died Munich 27 December 1967 aged 69.

34 Johannes Hentschel, born 10 May 1908 in Berlin. Hired on 4 July 1934 as master electro-mechanic for Hitler's apartments in the Old Chancellery. From mid-April 1945 was responsible for machine room in the *Führerbunker*. On 2 May 1945 was last person in bunker, where he was captured by Soviets and held in Russian captivity until 4 April 1949.

35 Magdalena (Magda) Goebbels, née Ritschel, born 11 November 1901 in Berlin. Secondary school, graduation in 1919. On 4 January 1921 the 20-year-old Magda married millionaire industrialist Günther Quandt who was twenty years her senior. After joining the NSDAP in 1930 she worked as a voluntary (unpaid) secretary in the *Gau* office in Berlin, where she met Goebbels. They married on 19 December 1931 and she had six children by him. On 20 April 1945 she moved into the bunker with her husband and children. After having had her children poisoned by *Dr* Stumpfegger, she committed suicide in the Chancellery garden by taking prussic acid, aged 43.

36 RSD. Hitler's personal protection was the responsibility of the *Begleitkommando des Führers* (FBK) and the *Reichssicherheitsdienst* (RSD). The *Führerbegleitkommando*, as it was commonly called, was responsible for guarding Hitler's person. Formed on 29 February 1932, by 1944 the FBK consisted of thirteen SS officers, fourteen SS NCOs and 116 SS soldiers, totalling 143 men. In March 1933 a 'Command for Special

Duties' consisting of eight officers from the Bavarian State Police was formed under police *Leutnant* Rattenhuber. This unit was responsible for Hitler's protection, general security measures for Hitler and other members of the government and the preventative investigation and prosecution of assassination attempts against Hitler and other members of the government. From April 1935 this command was renamed *Reichssicherheitsdienst* (RSD, or Reich Security Service). By 1944 the RSD had 250 men, of whom 220 were police officers, organised into thirteen departments each under a department head.

37 Hans Krebs, born 4 March 1898. First World War volunteer in 1914, *Leutnant* in 78th Infantry Regiment in 1915, then company commander and adjutant. *Oberleutnant* 1925; company commander 17th Infantry Regiment 1928. *Hauptmann* in Defence Ministry 1931. Assistant to Military Attaché in Moscow 1933. General Staff of 24th Division 1935. *Major* 1936. General Staff of the Army (Department 11) 1937. *Oberstleutnant* 1939 and from December 1939 Chief of Staff VII Corps. *Oberst* 1940. Deputy Military Attaché in Moscow March 1941. Chief of Staff 9th Army January 1942, promoted to *Generalmajor* February 1942. Chief of Staff Army Group Centre March 1943, promoted *Generalleutnant* April 1943. General of Infantry August 1944, and from September 1944 Chief of Staff of Army Group B. Succeeded *Generaloberst* Guderian as Deputy Chief Army Command Staff 14 February 1945 and Army Chief of Staff 1 April 1945. With Hitler in the bunker from then on. Shot himself there on 1 May 1945, aged 47.

38 Bernd *Freiherr* Freytag von Loringhoven, born 6 February 1914. Joined Army in 1934, promoted to *Leutnant* in 1937. *Oberleutnant* on staff of 1st Panzer Division 1939, on staff of XIX Army Corps 1940. *Hauptmann* and Commander 2nd Panzer Regiment 1942. Transferred to staff of 111th Infantry Division 2 March 1943. War Academy October 1943 and promotion to *Major* November. Operations Department Army General Staff April 1944 and from 25 July 1944 adjutant to Chief of Army General Staff (initially Guderian, then Krebs). In bunker until 29 April 1945, where he received the order to break out with Boldt and Weiss, to try to reach General Wenck's 12th Army and to request immediate relief of Berlin. Did not reach Wenck and was captured by Americans on 3 May 1945. After the war, service in *Bundeswehr* from 1956 until retirement.

39 Musmanno papers.

40 Ibid.

41 Hans Fritzsche, born 21 April 1900 in Bochum (Rhineland). Studied history, modern languages and philosophy (no degree). Joined *Deutschnationale Volkspartei* (German National People's Party) 1923 and in 1924 became editor at *Telegraphen-Union*. Head of wireless news service at Radio Germany 1932. From 1 May 1933 head of news service in press department of Reich Propaganda Ministry under Goebbels. From 1938 chief of German Press Department. Appointed Undersecretary October 1942 and from November head of Radio Department. From 2 May 1945 prisoner of Soviets and interrogated in Moscow. Tried in Nuremberg in 1946, acquitted on 1 October 1946 and released on 29 September 1950. Died in Cologne 27 September 1953 aged 53.

42 Hans Heinrich Lammers, born 27 May 1879 in Lublinitz (Upper Silesia). Studied law. Judge in Beuthen 1912. Military service 1914–18. Doctor's degree and appointment as District President 1921. Director in Ministry of the Interior 1922. Joined NSDAP in 1932 and appointed State Secretary 30 January 1933. From 1933 Chief of Reich Chan-

cellery. Reich Minister without portfolio 1937. In 1939, member of Ministers' Council for the Defence of the Reich under its chairman Göring. Promoted to *SS-Obergruppenführer* 1940. During war gained great influence as part-time Chairman at cabinet meetings. From 1943 all documents for Hitler's signature had to be vetted by Lammers, Keitel and Bormann. Left Berlin April 1945 and went to 'branch office' of the Chancellery in Berchtesgaden where he, Keitel, Jodl etc. had their offices when Hitler was staying at the Berghof. Captured in Austria by Americans and tried in the so-called 'Wilhelmstrasse Trials', sentenced to 20 years on 14 April 1949 but released on 16 December 1951. Died in Düsseldorf 4 January 1962 aged 83.

43 Arthur Kannenberg, born 23 February 1896 in Berlin. Trained as cook, waiter, wine waiter and accountant in father's restaurant chain, which he took over in 1924. Bankrupt 1930. Subsequently General Manager of Pfuhl's Wine and Beer Rooms' in Königgrätzer Strasse, which right-wing and Nazi members of the Prussian Diet and the *Reichstag* (including Göring and Goebbels) frequented. Hitler met Kannenberg there and offered him managership of 'Brown House' canteen in Munich, which he took over on 1 December 1931. When Hitler became Chancellor, he called Kannenberg to Berlin on 23 March 1933, where he became Hitler's supply manager in the Chancellery, a position he held until the end. Left Berlin on 10 April 1945 and went to Karlstein near Bad Reichenhall (Bavaria). Interned from 27 May 1945 to 25 July 1946. In postwar Germany, Kannenberg had several jobs in different places; from September 1957 was manager of Schneider-Wibbel-Rooms restaurant in Düsseldorf, where he died on 26 January 1963 aged 68.

44 Alwin-Broder Albrecht, born 18 September 1903 in St Peter (Friesia). Joined Navy on 30 March 1922. *Fähnrich zur See* 1 March 1924; *Leutnant zur See* 1 October 1926; *Oberleutnant zur See* 1 July 1928; *Kapitänleutnant* 1 June 1934. When Karl-Jesko von Puttkamer, Hitler's liaison officer to the Navy, was transferred to active service on 19 June 1938 his stand-in from 27 June 1938 to 30 June 1939 was Albrecht, who was promoted to *Korvettenkapitän* on 1 November 1937. When in early 1939 Albrecht married a woman 'with a past', and the CinC of the Navy, *Grossadmiral* Raeder wanted to transfer him to Tokyo as a military attaché, Hitler simply appointed him as his one of his personal adjutants (1 July 1939). This led to a lasting quarrel between Hitler and Raeder. Under *Reichsleiter* Bouhler, Albrecht remained on Hitler's staff in the Chancellery, where he was responsible for drafting letters, overseeing numerous building activities and handling organisational matters. Listed as missing, but probably committed suicide on 1 May 1945, aged 41.

45 Hans-Erich Voss, born 30 October 1897 in Angermünde (Brandenburg). Naval cadet 1915, *Leutnant zur See* 1917, *Kapitänleutnant* 1928, *Korvettenkapitän* 1934, *Fregattenkapitän* 1937. Chief of Navy Petty Officers' School 1938. Staff officer in Navy Group East August 1939. *Kapitän zur See* and Chief of Navy Fleet and Training Department November 1939, subsequently Department Commander in the Navy Quartermaster Department. Took over command of heavy cruiser *Prinz Eugen* October 1942. Promoted to *Konteradmiral* 1 March 1943 and permanent representative of the Navy at *Führer* headquarters. Promoted to *Vizeadmiral* 1 August 1944. Was in the bunker and the Chancellery until 1 May 1945. Captured by Russians during break-out on 2 May, held captive until 21 January 1955.

46 *Rittmeister* Gerhardt Boldt was *General* Krebs' orderly officer and *Oberstleutnant* Rudolf Weiss was adjutant to *General* Burgdorf, Chief of the Army Personnel Department.

47 Werner Haase, born 2 August 1900 in Köthen (Saxon-Anhalt). After graduation from secondary school in 1918 and active service (66th Infantry Regiment), studied medicine. Doctor's degree in 1924, then surgeon. Ship's doctor 1927. From 1934 on staff of surgical clinic of Berlin University under *Professor* Magnus. Joined SS 1 April 1934. On *Dr* Brandt's recommendation, transferred to the *Führer* Staff as doctor in residence. Promoted to *SS-Sturmführer* 15 September 1935. Qualified as a university lecturer in Berlin 25 June 1936. Promoted to *SS-Obersturmführer* 20 April 1938 and to *SS-Obersturmbannführer* 16 June 1943. Senior doctor at Charité clinic in Berlin. In April 1945 Chief of Field Hospital in the bunker in Voss-strasse. Captured there by Soviets on 2 May 1945. Died in Russian captivity towards end of 1945 aged 45.

48 Ernst Günther Schenck, born 3 August 1904 in Marburg (Hessia). Degrees as PhD in 1927 and as MD in 1929. Joined NSDAP on 1 May 1937 and *Waffen-SS* as Medical Inspector with rank of *SS-Untersturmführer* on 20 April 1940. From 10 October 1940 with SS medical service in Berlin. From 1 April 1941 to 10 February 1942 active service with *Leibstandarte 'Adolf Hitler'*. Promoted to *SS-Sturmbannführer* 30 January 1942. From mid-1944 Inspector of the Armed Forces for 'troop supply and nourishment'. Promoted to *SS-Obersturmbannführer* 9 November 1944. During final days was in Chancellery, where he worked in the field hospital. Captured by Russians during break-out on 1 May 1945 and held until 1953. Since then, doctor in Munich and Aachen.

49 Ludwig Stumpfegger, born 11 July 1910 in Munich. Studied medicine from 1 May 1930 on, doctor's degree 11 August 1937. Joined SS 2 June 1933 and NSDAP 1 May 1935. From 30 January 1938 in the Hohenlychen SS clinic with the rank of *SS-Untersturmführer*. Promoted to *SS-Obersturmführer* on 1 November 1939 and transferred to the surgical department of the SS hospital in Berlin. Promoted *SS-Hauptsturmführer* 24 November 1939 and transferred back to Hohenlychen as adjutant to *SS-Oberführer Professor Dr* Gebhardt 19 March 1940. Promoted to *SS-Sturmbannführer* 3 September 1941 and to *SS-Obersturmbannführer* 20 April 1943. On Himmler's recommendation was transferred to 'Wolfsschanze' *Führer* headquarters as resident doctor on 9 October 1944. In Chancellery until 1 May 1945. During break-out on 2 May, committed suicide in Berlin-Wedding by taking prussic acid, aged 34.

50 Willi A. Boelke, *Deutschlands Rüstung im Zweiten Weltkrieg. Hitlers Konferenzen mit Albert Speer 1942–45*, Akademische Verlagsanstalt Athenaion, Frankfurt/Main 1969, p. 380 *et seq.*

51 Helmut Heiber, *Hitlers Lagebesprechungen. Protokollfragmente seiner militärischen Konferenzen 1942–1945*, Deutsche Verlagsanstalt, Stuttgart 1962, p. 936.

52 Musmanno papers.

53 Christine Schroeder, *Er war mein Chef. Aus dem Nachlass der Sekretärin von Adolf Hitler*, Langen Müller Verlag, Munich 1985, p. 199.

54 Albert Speer, *Erinnerungen*, Propyläen Verlag, Berlin 1969, p. 476.

55 Boelke, op. cit., p. 225.

56 Statement by Speer to the author.

57 Boelke, ibid.

58 Getraud Junge, née Humps, born 16 March 1920 in Munich. Secondary school and commercial school and then stenographer with United German Metal Company. From

October 1938 to January 1939 secretary in law firm; from February 1939 secretary on the editorial staff of *Rundschau-Verlag* in Munich. Drafted into Chancellery (Office of the *Führer*) in Berlin 1 September 1942. Ordered to 'Wolfsschanze' *Führer* headquarters 20 November 1942; employed by Hitler as secretary 30 January 1943. Married one of Hitler's orderlies, Hans Hermann Junge, 19 June 1943, who was killed in action on 13 August 1944. In Chancellery and bunker until 30 April 1945. Managed to make her way to West after break-out on 2 May 1945, but after returning to Berlin on 9 June 1945 was arrested by Soviets and held until 6 April 1946. Now lives in southern Germany.

59 Else Krüger, married James, born 9 February 1915 in Hamburg-Altona. Martin Bormann's secretary since end of 1942 and in bunker and Chancellery with him. Broke out of Chancellery on 1 May 1945 and fled to West. Arrested and held by British. Mrs James now lives in England.

60 Johanna Wolf, born 1 June 1900 in Munich. Primary and commercial school, then office work. From 1922 to 1928 worked for *Dr* Alexander Glaser, member of Bavarian Diet, and in 1923 temporarily for Dietrich Eckart. Recommended to Gregor Strasser; worked in the *Gau* headquarters of Lower Bavaria-Upper Palatinate. When Hitler's personal office was looking for a secretary in the autumn of 1929, she transferred to the *Reichsleitung* of the NSDAP on 1 November 1929 and joined the Party. Worked for Rudolf Hess and from 1930 on also for Hitler's adjutant Wilhelm Brückner. From 1933 spent time in Berlin, where she worked in Hitler's office and later on the personal adjutant's staff as Hitler's secretary. During the war she also worked in the various *Führer* headquarters. During the night of 21–22 April 1945 was released by Hitler together with *Frau* Schroeder, flew to Salzburg and went to the Berghof. Remained there until 2 May and then went to mother in Bad Tölz, where she was arrested by CIC on 23 May 1945 and held by Americans until 14 January 1948. She then lived in southern Germany, where she died on 5 June 1985 aged 85.

61 Theodor Morell, born 22 June 1886 in Trais-Münzenberg (Hesse). From 1906 on studied medicine in Giessen (1907), Heidelberg (1909), Grenoble (1910), Paris (1910) and Munich. Doctor's degree 23 May 1913. Worked as ship's doctor until 1914. Volunteered for active service and served as doctor of battalion until 1917. From 1918 practice in Berlin. Joined NSDAP 1933. Met Hitler 1936 in Munich through Heinrich Hoffmann and, after having treated him successfully, was his personal physician until 21 April 1945. Flown out of Berlin on 23 April 1945 to the Berghof, Morell was interrogated by the CIC in the City Clinic of Bad Reichenhall on 18 May and arrested on 17 July 1945. Taken gravely ill and died 26 May 1948 in Tegernsee hospital, aged 62.

62 See Musmanno papers.

63 Wilhelm Mohnke, born 15 March 1911 in Lübeck. Secondary school and trade school until 1929, then warehouse clerk, sales clerk and travelling salesman. Joined SS 1 November 1931 and from 17 March 1933 was with SS Special Command in Berlin which then became the *Leibstandarte 'Adolf Hitler'*. Promoted to *SS-Sturmführer* 28 June 1933. From then on permanently with *Leibstandarte* except for special assignments to SS Special Forces and *Waffen-SS*. Took part in various campaigns and was promoted to *SS-Sturmbannführer* 1 September 1940, *SS-Obersturmführer* 21 June 1943 and *SS-Standartenführer* 21 June 1944, when he was given command of an SS Panzer Grenadier Regiment. From 30 January 1945 *SS-Brigadeführer*; transferred to the

Führerreserve in Berlin on 10 February 1945. On 23 April 1945 Hitler put him in charge of the defence of the 'Citadel' (the Chancellery and its surroundings). Captured by Soviets during break-out on 2 May 1945 and held until 11 October 1955. Now lives in northern Germany.

64 Günther Schwägermann, born on 24 July 1915 in Uelzen (Lower Saxony). Secondary school and commercial training. Joined *Leibstandarte 'Adolf Hitler'* 8 April 1937. SS officers' school in Bad Tölz 4 October 1938 to September 1939, then with Security Police in Berlin and from there to SS Police Division and active service in France and Russia. After being wounded, transferred as adjutant to Goebbels with rank of *SS-Obersturmführer*. Promoted to *SS-Hauptsturmführer* 29 November 1944. After bodies of Goebbels and his wife had been cremated, break-out from Chancellery on 1 May 1945 and escape to West. Held by Americans from 25 June 1945 to 24 April 1947. Later lived in northern Germany.

65 See Musmanno papers.

66 Karl Schneider, born 20 February 1899 in Berlin. Apprenticeship as fitter. From 1 August 1937 garage superintendent in Hitler's car fleet and deputy to Erich Kempka. Transferred to *Leibstandarte 'Adolf Hitler'* in September 1939 with rank of *Hauptscharführer*. Promoted to *SS-Obersturmführer* in 1942 and to *SS-Hauptsturmführer* 9 November 1944. Taken prisoner by Soviets in Chancellery 2 May 1945 and held until 20 October 1955.

67 See Musmanno papers.

68 Hermann Karnau, born 30 October 1912 in Oldenburg (Westphalia). From 1928 to 1931 apprenticeship as a printer, then mandatory labour service with Caritas (catholic welfare organisation). Military service 4 April 1934 to 30 September 1936 with 16th Infantry Regiment; discharged with the rank of *Unteroffizier*. Worker with the German state railway 1 October 1936 to 31 March 1937. From 12 April 1937 with the Security Police in Wilhelmshaven, promoted to *Oberwachtmeister* 1 June 1939. From September 1941 on active service with 18th Police Regiment. In spring of 1944 assistant detective with criminal police in Wilhelmshaven. Transferred to Reich Security Service 2 June 1944; served until end of war. On 30 April 1945 was witness to cremation of Hitler's body. Break-out from Chancellery on 1 May 1945 and escape to West. Arrested by British on 25 May 1945 and held until 26 August 1946.

69 Peter Högl, born 19 August 1897 in Poxau near Dingolfing (Bavaria). Learned trade of miller. From 1915 to 1916 miller in Landshut. Active service from 2 June 1916 to 18 July 1919 with 16th Bavarian Infantry Regiment; discharged with the rank of *Unteroffizier*. Joined Bavarian police. After three months' training at police school in Munich, worked as police officer. Transferred to criminal police on 4 June 1932. From 1933 with *Führer* bodyguard and entered SS 1 July 1934 with rank of *SS-Obersturmführer*. When *Führer* 'Special Command' was converted into the Reich Security Service in April 1935, Högl became Rattenhuber's deputy and Chief of Department 1 (protection of Adolf Hitler) with posts in Berlin, Munich and Obersalzberg. Promoted to *SS-Hauptsturmführer* 30 January 1937 and to *SS-Sturmbannführer* 1 March 1940. From 9 November 1944 Criminal Director with rank of *SS-Obersturmbannführer*. Witnessed Hitler's suicide and cremation on 30 April 1945. During the break-out from Chancellery Högl was seriously wounded in the head at Weidendamm bridge and died of his injuries on 2 May 1945, aged 47.

70 Ewald Lindloff, born 27 September 1908 in Stuba near Danzig (East Prussia). Engineering college from 1928 to 1933. Joined SS on 1 May 1932 and served with *Leibstandarte 'Adolf Hitler'* from 15 July 1933. From 5 May 1934 member of the *Führer* bodyguard. Promoted to *SS-Unterscharführer* 30 June 1934 and to *Hauptscharführer* 20 April 1938. On 4 February 1938 married Ilse Borchert, who had worked as a secretary for Hitler's adjutant Fritz Wiedemann. Promoted to *SS-Untersturmführer* 30 January 1941 and on active service 20 October 1942 to 10 May 1943. Promoted to *SS-Obersturmführer* 9 November 1943 and to *SS-Hauptsturmführer* 30 January 1945. Witnessed Hitler's suicide and cremation and was the man who scattered the few remains in the garden. Killed at Weidendamm bridge during break-out on 2 May 1945, aged 36.

71 Gerda Christian, née Daranowski, born 13 December 1913 in Berlin. After completing school, worked as a clerk for Elizabeth Arden in Berlin. Joined Hitler's 'personal chancellery' on 1 May 1935. In 1937, at age 24, became Hitler's third secretary in his adjutant's office. Worked in the various *Führer* headquarters during the war. On 2 February 1943 married *Luftwaffe Major* Eckhard Christian, who worked at *Führer* headquarters as adjutant of Military Command Staff. After a break, returned to 'Wolfsschanze' as secretary to Hitler in mid-1943. In Chancellery and bunker until 30 April 1945. After the break-out on 2 May 1945 managed to make her way to West. Arrested by Americans in early March 1946 and held until 19 April 1946. Now lives in northern Germany.

72 Nicolaus von Below, born 20 September 1907 in Jargelin near Greifswald (Pomerania). Trained as pilot in 1929 at German Commercial Pilot School. Service with 12th Infantry Regiment 1929–33, promoted to *Leutnant. Jagdgeschwader 'Richthofen'* in Döberitz 1933–36. From 5 March 1936 with *JG 26* in Düsseldorf. From 16 June 1936 adjutant of *Luftwaffe* to Hitler. Arrested early 1946 by British, held until 14 May 1948. Died Detmold 24 July 1983 aged 75.

73 Heinz Lorenz, born 7 August 1913 in Schwerin (Mecklenburg). Studied law and economics. Left university and worked as press photographer for the German Telegraph Office from 1 October 1930. Became junior editor with German News Service (DNB) in 1934. Frequent trips abroad. Transferred to Reich Press Chief *Dr* Dietrich late 1936; responsible for editing DNB reports on foreign policy. From late 1942 senior editor with DNB and at *Führer* headquarters until 29 April 1945. On 28 April brought Hitler information about Himmler's negotiations with Count Folke Bernadotte. Escaped to West, arrested by British in early June 1945 and held until mid-1947 (while in prison, copied out the notes from Hitler's briefings held during the final period). Died in Düsseldorf 23 November 1985 aged 72.

74 Erich Mansfeld, born 30 May 1913 in Bowallno near Oppeln (Upper Silesia). With state police in Bremen from 1934. Transferred to Security Police 1 October 1936 and to Reich Security Service 7 June 1944. Was witness to cremation of Hitler's body. Escaped to West and held captive by Americans from 14 July 1945 to 4 November 1946.

75 Franz Schädle, born 19 November 1906 in Westerheim near Memmingen (Württemberg). Trade school, construction technician. Joined SS 1 February 1930 and with Hitler's bodyguard from 1 March 1932. From 1 May 1934 on staff of *Reichsführer-SS* Himmler. Accompanied Hitler on all his trips and always present at *Führer* headquarters. Promoted to rank of *SS-Obersturmbannführer*. After Bruno Gesche was dismissed

on 5 January 1945 Schädle took over as Commander of the Bodyguard and was wounded in the leg by shrapnel on 28 April 1945. Even though his comrades wanted to take him with them, Schädle shot himself in the Chancellery before the break-out on 1 May 1945, aged 38.

76 Georgi K. Zhukov, *Erinnerungen und Gedanken*, Deutsche Verlagsanstalt, Stuttgart 1969, p. 607.

77 Michael J. Katukov, *An der Spitze des Hauptstosses*, Military Publishing House of the GDR, Berlin 1979, p. 388 *et seq.*

78 *Diary 1938–1945*, Putnam's Sons, New York, 1972, p. 763.

79 Microfilm T-84, Roll 22, National Archives, Washington DC.

80 Hans Baur, born 19 June 1897 in Ampfing (Bavaria). Secondary school and commercial training. Volunteer in 1915; served with *Flieger-Ersatzabteilung* in Schleissheim. Pilot with 1st Bavarian Air Squadron (artillery spotter and reconnaissance) spring 1916. Discharged as *Vizefeldwebel*. Pilot with Bavarian Air Mail 1920, Bavarian Air Lloyd and Junkers Air Service 1922, Lufthansa 1926. From 1932 frequently flew Hitler during election campaigns. Released to Hitler by Lufthansa in 1933 and assigned to build up a government air squadron. As Hitler's pilot, appointed *SS-Standartenführer* on staff of *Reichsführer-SS* Himmler 14 October 1933. Promoted to *SS-Oberführer* on 9 September 1934 and finally to *Generalleutnant* of Police and *SS-Gruppenführer*. In Chancellery and bunker until 30 April 1945. Following break-out on 1 May, was captured by Soviets on 2 May after having received several wounds (both legs, chest and hand; Baur's right lower leg had to be amputated in Posen on 10 June 1945). Held by Russians until 8 October 1955. Died in Neuwiddersberg on 17 February 1993 aged 95.

81 Wilhelm Keitel, born 22 September 1882 in Helmscherode (Lower Saxony). Joined Army on 9 March 1901 as cadet; *Leutnant* 1902, *Hauptmann* 1914 and active service during First World War. *1 Generalstabsoffizier* on staff of Navy Marine Corps 1918. Instructor at Cavalry School 1920–22. *Major* 1925 and from 1925 in Armed Forces Ministry (Organisation Department T 2); Department Head 1930. *Oberst* 1 October 1931 and Commander of infantry regiments in Potsdam and Bremen 1933–34. Appointed Chief of the Armed Forces Department in Reich War Ministry 1 October 1935. Promoted to *General* 1 August 1937 and Chief of OKW 4 February 1938. Keitel was Hitler's closest military adviser until 1945. On 9 May 1945 Keitel signed the unconditional surrender of the German armed forces in Berlin-Karlshorst. Arrested on 13 May 1945 in Flensburg, sentenced to death on 1 October 1946 during the Nuremberg War Crimes Trials and hanged on 16 October 1946, aged 63.

82 Alfred Jodl, born 10 May 1890 in Würzburg. Entered Cadet Academy in 1903. Senior Cadet 1910, then War Academy in Munich. Promoted *Leutnant* 1912 and from 1914 on active service in First World War. *Oberleutnant* 1917. After the war with the Mountain Artillery in Landsberg. Training for General Staff in Munich 1920. Promoted to *Hauptmann* 5 May 1921 and *Major* 1931. Transferred to Armed Forces Ministry (Department T 1) in 1932 . Promoted to *Oberstleutnant* in 1933 and to *Oberst* in 1935. Worked in Armed Forces Department of Reich War Ministry. When OKW was restructured, was appointed Chief of Home Defence on 7 February 1938. Commander Artillery in Vienna 1 October 1938 to 22 August 1939. Promoted to *Generalmajor* April 1939. From 23 August 1939 Chief of Military Command Staff in OKW and Hitler's adviser on strategic and tactical matters. Promoted to *General der Artillerie* in 1940 and to *Generaloberst* on 30 January 1944. On Dönitz's orders, Jodl signed the

partial surrender of the *Wehrmacht* to the Western Powers in Reims on 7 May 1945. Arrested together with the Dönitz government and interned on 23 May 1945 in Mürwik near Flensburg; sentenced to death in Nuremberg 30 September 1946 and hanged 16 October 1946, aged 56.

83 ZS 678, Institute for Contemporary History, Munich.

84 Percy E. Schramm, *Kriegstagebuch des Oberkommandos der Wehrmacht, 1944–1945*, Vol. II, Manfred Pawlak Verlagsgesellschaft mbH, Herrsching 1982, p. 1721.

85 'Die Vernehmung von Generalfeldmarschall Keitel durch die Sowjets', *Wehrwissenschaftliche Rundschau*, 1966, Vol. 11, p. 660.

86 Schramm, op. cit., p. 1716.

87 Heiber, op. cit., pp. 607–8.

88 Erwin Giesing, born 7 December 1907 in Oberhausen (Rhineland). Studied medicine from 1926. Doctor's degree 1932; ENT specialist at Virchow Clinic in Berlin 1936–39. Joined NSDAP and SS 1 August 1932 with the rank of *Sturmbannführer*. From 1939 military doctor in various field hospitals; promoted Chief Doctor (Reserve) 1 July 1940. Called to *Führer* headquarters 20 July 1944; treated Hitler's ear injuries caused by assassination attempt of 20 July 1944. Dismissed in September 1944 together with *Dr* Brandt and *Dr* von Hasselbach because of conflict with *Dr* Morell; subsequently served in military hospital in Hamburg. Arrested by British in June 1945 and held until March 1947. After release, practised in Krefeld where he died on 22 May 1977 aged 69.

89 Carl von Eicken, born 24 May 1874. Appointed *Professor* of 2nd ENT clinic at Charité in Berlin in 1922. After death of *Professor* Passow in 1926, 1st and 2nd ENT clinics were merged and von Eicken headed new clinic as director until retirement in 1950.

90 Hermann Göring, born 12 January 1893 in Rosenheim (Bavaria). Military Academy in Karlsruhe and Gross-Lichterfelde (Berlin). Promoted *Leutnant* in March 1912; transferred to Air Force 1914; pilot May 1915; *Oberleutnant* in *Jagdgeschwader 'Richthofen'* at end of war. After war lived in Denmark and Sweden. Returned to Munich in early 1922 and took over command of SA March 1923. Wounded during the *putsch* attempt in 1923, fled abroad. After the warrant for arrest was withdrawn on 14 May 1926, rejoined NSDAP 1 April 1928. Became Minister of Interior and Minister President of Prussia 10 April 1933. Appointed Reich Air Minister 28 April 1933 and 'responsible for Four Year Plan' 18 October 1936. On 19 July 1940, Hitler promoted Göring, who was CinC of the *Luftwaffe*, to *Reichsmarschall*. On 20 April 1945 left Berlin to go to country house on the Obersalzberg near Berchtesgaden. On 23 April 1945 dismissed by Hitler from all offices and arrested by SS. Interned in SS barracks in Salzburg, later freed by members of *Luftwaffe*. Gave himself up to Americans 7 May 1945. Tried by Military Tribunal in Nuremberg and committed suicide during trial by taking prussic acid on 16 October 1946, aged 52.

91 Albert Zoller, *Hitler privat. Erlebnisbericht seiner Geheimsekretärin*, Droste Verlag, Düsseldorf 1949, p. 229.

92 *The Bormann Letters*, edited by François Genoud, Weidenfeld & Nicolson, London 1954, p. 129.

93 David Irving, *Die geheimen Tagebücher des Dr. Morell. Leibarzt Hitlers*, Wilhelm Goldmann Verlag, Munich 1983, p. 277.

94 Karl Brandt, born 8 January 1904 in Mühlhausen (Alsace). Studied medicine; doctor's degree 1928, then training as surgeon in Bergmannsheil Hospital in Bochum. Joined NSDAP January 1932 and met Hitler in Essen in summer 1932. After Brückner's accident in August 1933, when he first came to Hitler's attention, he was appointed resident doctor to Hitler in summer of 1934. Joined SS 29 July 1934 with rank of *SS-Unterscharführer* and rapidly promoted, reaching the rank of *SS-Gruppenführer* on 20 April 1944. Always in Hitler's company at *Führer* headquarters until 1944. When he was away, his deputy was either *Dr* Haase or *Dr* von Hasselbach. Appointed *Professor* 5 September 1940 and 'General Commissioner of the *Führer* for Sanitation and Health' 1942, becoming 'Reich Commissioner for Sanitation and Health' 25 August 1944. After assassination attempt on 20 July 1944 and conflict with *Dr* Morell, was dismissed in September 1944. Successor was *Dr* Stumpfegger. Arrested 14 April 1945 on Hitler's orders because he had sent his wife to Bad Liebenstein and his staff to Garmisch so that they would fall into the hands of Americans; this was considered to be defeatism. Tried by military court 17 April 1945 and sentenced to death. Subsequently sent to Kiel, released on Speer's orders 2 May 1945. Arrested by British 13 May 1945, tried at Nuremberg in connection with 'doctors trials', where he was accused of having participated in medical experiments in concentration camps and practised euthanasia. Sentenced to death 20 August 1947; hanged Landsberg prison 2 June 1948 aged 44.

95 Hans-Karl von Hasselbach, born 2 November 1903 in Berlin. Studied medicine; doctor's degree 14 July 1927. Training as surgeon and then surgeon at Surgical University Clinic in Munich from 15 October 1936. Joined NSDAP 1 May 1933 and SS 13 August 1934. From spring 1936 was *Dr* Brandt's deputy as resident doctor on staff of *Führer*. Promoted *SS-Hauptsturmführer* 8 October 1939; from September 1939 active service with medical company. From September 1942 to September 1944 permanent resident doctor with Hitler at *Führer* headquarters. Appointed *Professor* by Hitler 20 April 1943. Dismissed in October 1944 in connection with the conflict with Dr *Morell* and Chief Doctor in field hospital in West until end of the war. Arrested by Americans 13 April 1945 and held until 2 August 1948. Subsequently practising surgeon in Bielefeld and Munich.

96 *The Bormann Letters*, p. 130.

97 Heinrich Himmler, born 7 October 1900 in Munich. Secondary school degree in 1917, then officer cadet and *Fähnrich* during First World War. Studied agriculture at Technical University in Munich. Joined *Reichskriegsflagge* organisation 1923 and worked as laboratory technician for fertiliser company. Took part in *putsch* attempt in 1923. Joined NSDAP 2 August 1925 on staff of Gregor Strasser. Joined SS in 1925 and became *Reichsführer-SS* 6 January 1929. Member of *Reichstag* from 1930. Chief of Police in Munich March 1933, took over leadership of political police April and became Chief of German Police 17 June 1936. Organised and built SS, *Gestapo*, Reich Security Service (q.v.) and *Waffen-SS*, installed and ran concentration and extermination camps etc. Appointed Reich Minister of the Interior 25 August 1943. Dismissed from all offices by Dönitz on 6 May 1945, arrested by British on 20 May 1945. Committed suicide by taking prussic acid 23 May 1945 aged 44.

98 *The Bormann Letters*, p. 137.

99 Ibid., p.151.

100 Zoller, op. cit., p. 204.

101 Irving, op. cit., p. 231.

102 Hugo Blaschke, born 14 November 1881 in Neustadt. Came to Berlin 1885; studied dentistry in Berlin and at University of Pennsylvania. Then training as dental surgeon in London. Opened practice in Berlin towards end of 1911. Military dentist in Frankfurt/Oder and Berlin 1914–18. Practice in Berlin 1919–1945. Came into contact with NSDAP through having treated Hermann Göring in 1930 and joined Party 1 February 1931. Hitler's dentist 1933 to February 1945. Joined SS 1 May 1935, appointed Chief Dentist on staff of *Reichsführer-SS* 31 August 1943. Promoted to *SS-Brigadeführer* and *Generalmajor der Waffen-SS* 9 November 1944. Arrested and interned by Americans in Dorfgastein (Austria) 20 May 1945 and held until 7 December 1948. Subsequently practised in Nuremberg, where he died on 6 December 1959 aged 78.

103 Linge Diary, Institute for Contemporary History Munich, sig. F 19/14.

104 Various authors, *Deutschland im Zweiten Weltkrieg*, Vol. 6, Pahl-Rugenstein Verlag, Cologne, 1985, p. 26.

105 *The Bormann Letters*, pp. 139,142.

106 Schramm, op. cit., p. 1721.

107 Heiber, op. cit., pp. 719–21, 724.

108 Churchill actually said, on 15 December 1944, 'Expulsion is, as far as we can oversee it, the most satisfactory and lasting means . . .' See Gotthold Rhode and Wolfgang Wagner, *Quellen zur Entstehung der Oder–Neisse-Linie*, Stuttgart 1956, p. 123 *et seq.*

109 Heiber, op. cit., p. 738 *et seq.*

110 *The Bormann Letters*, p. 152.

111 Heiber, op. cit., p. 742.

112 Nicolaus von Below, *Als Hitlers Adjutant 1937–45*, von Hase und Koehler Verlag, Mainz 1980, p. 398.

113 Heinz Guderian, born 17 June 1888 in Kulm (Chelmno) on the Vistula (East Prussia). Military Academy in Karlsruhe and Gross-Lichterfelde (Berlin). *Leutnant* 1906; assignments as field and staff officer from 1919. Promoted *Oberst* 1933 and Chief of Staff with Inspector Motorised Forces 1934. Promoted *General der Panzertruppen* 1938. Commander of a Panzer Corps in 1940 and promoted *Generaloberst* July 1940. Guderian is considered to have been strategically and tactically the best commander of armoured forces on either side during the war. He is credited with being the inventor of the *Blitzkrieg* envelopment tactics by fast armoured forces. Commander 2nd Panzer Army 1941. Appointed General Inspector Panzer Forces 20 February 1943. Chief of the Army General Staff 20 July 1944 to 1 April 1945 (replaced by *General* Hans Krebs). Arrested by Americans 10 May 1945; held for one year. Died in Schwangau near Füssen (Bavaria) 14 May 1954 aged 66.

114 Heinz Guderian, *Erinnerungen eines Soldaten*, Heidelberg 1951, pp. 346–52.

115 See testimony of Alfred Jodl in ZS 678, Institute for Contemporary History, Munich.

116 According to testimonies by Schaub, *Frau* Wolf and *Frau* Schroeder.

117 See *The Bormann Letters*, p. 163.

118 Ibid., p. 175.

119 Ibid.

120 Schroeder, op. cit., p. 199.

121 See Musmanno papers.

122 Ibid.

123 Schroeder, op. cit., p.197 *et seq.*; and Zoller, op.cit., p. 149.

124 See Musmanno papers.

125 Ibid.

126 Zoller, op. cit., p. 56.

127 Zoller, op. cit., p. 57.

128 Linge Diary.

129 Zoller, op. cit., p. 29 *et seq.*

130 Bergschicker, op. cit., p. 537

131 Guderian, op. cit., p. 388 *et seq.*

132 Jodl in ZS 678, Institute for Contemporary History, Munich.

133 The Ju 52 was a three-engine all-metal monoplane which, despite being slow, was justly famous for its toughness and dependability. By 1945 more than 4,000 had been built. The aircraft was officially approved for 17 passengers in the civilian and 20 in the military version.

134 Heiber, op. cit., p. 933 *et seq.*

135 Hitler's telex to Army Group Vistula, 30 March 1945.

136 Heiber, op. cit., p. 615 *et seq.*

137 Shorthand text transcribed in 1947 by Heinz Lorenz in *Der Spiegel*, 196⁄1, 3, p. 34.

138 Irving, op. cit., p. 278.

139 See Musmanno papers.

140 Irving, op. cit., p. 280

141 Ibid.

142 Musmanno papers.

143 Schramm, op. cit., Vol. IV/8, p. 1589 *et seq.*

144 Ibid., p. 1589.

145 *Deutschland im Zweiten Weltkrieg*, Vol. 6, p. 699.

146 Karl Dönitz, born 16 September 1891 in Grünau near Berlin. Joined Navy in 1910. Promoted *Leutnant* 1913. Served with Submarine Service 1917–18. British prisoner-of-war. Commander of submarine flotilla 1919, then commanded cruiser *Emden* with rank of *Korvettenkapitän*. From September 1935 again with submarine fleet, promoted *Kapitän zur See* 1936 and Commander of the submarine fleet being built up. Promoted *Konteradmiral* 1938, *Vizeadmiral* 1940 and *Admiral* 1942. Became *Grossadmiral* and succeeded Raeder as CinC of the Navy 30 January 1943. After Hitler's suicide, Reich President and Supreme Commander of the Armed Forces as Hitler's successor. Until 23 May 1945 head of a caretaker government in Flensburg-Mürwik. Arrested by British and sentenced to ten years in prison by Military Tribunal in Nuremberg 1 October 1946. Released from prison 1 October 1956 and died 24 December 1980 aged 89.

147 Joachim von Ribbentrop, born 30 April 1893 in Wesel (Rhineland). With his father in London in 1909 and in Canada in 1910. Trained in a bank in Montreal, later worked in New York and Ottawa. Served in First World War, promoted *Leutnant* 1915 and on an

Army staff in Turkey in 1918. After the war worked for a firm importing cotton. Married Annelies Henkel, heiress of the Henkel champagne company in Wiesbaden July 1920 and became champagne salesman for Henkel in Berlin. In 1925 adopted by an aunt whose father had been elevated to nobility. Joined NSDAP in 1930 and was Hitler's adviser on foreign affairs from 1933. Appointed 'Responsible for Disarmament' on 24 April 1934, von Ribbentrop conducted negotiations in May 1935 in London leading to the Anglo-German Naval Agreement. Ambassador in London 1936. Signatory for Anti-Comintern Pact between Germany and Japan, which Italy joined in 1937. Appointed Reich Minister of Foreign Affairs in February 1938. Arrested by British in Hamburg where he was in hiding in May 1945, sentenced to death by Military Tribunal in Nuremberg and hanged 16 October 1946, aged 53.

148 Speer, op. cit., p. 478.

149 See Federal Archives, Koblenz, File R 62/10.

150 Margarete (Gretl) Braun, born 31 August 1915 in Munich. Girls' secondary school in Medingen. Clerk in photographer Heinrich Hoffmann's publishing company from 10 April 1931 to 1943. From 1 September 1943 enrolled at Bavarian State School of Photography. On 3 June 1944, at age 28, married Hermann Fegelein in Salzburg, who was liaison officer of *Waffen-SS* to Hitler. At end of war was on Obersalzberg and travelled to Garmisch-Partenkirchen with girlfriend of Eva Braun. Now lives in northern Germany.

151 Käthe Heusermann, born 5 June 1909 in Liegnitz (Silesia). Girls' secondary school and from 1931 dental assistant in Berlin. Joined practice of Hitler's dentist *Dr* Hugo Blaschke 4 April 1937. Was present whenever Hitler was treated in Berlin or on Obersalzberg, as well as during operation on 10 November 1944 in 'Wolfsschanze' *Führer* headquarters. In Chancellery until 1 May 1945. Captured 13 May 1945 by Soviets. Identified bridge from Hitler's upper jaw May 1945. Brought to Moscow 29 July 1945 where she was held in various prisons and labour camps until 2 June 1955. Died in Düsseldorf 14 February 1993 aged 83.

152 'Die Vernehmung des Generaloberst Jodl durch die Sowjets', *Wehrwissenschaftliche Rundschau*, 1966 (11), p. 535.

153 *Führer* Order of 21.4.1945, 1750 hrs, to *SS-Obergruppenführer* Steiner, OKW War Diary.

154 Irving, op. cit., p. 277.

155 Ottmar Katz, *Prof. Dr. med. Theo Morell. Hitlers Leibarzt*, Hestia Verlag, Bayreuth 1982, p. 348.

156 Eckhard Christian, born 1 December 1907 in Charlottenburg (Berlin). Officer cadet with Navy 1 April 1926 and promoted *Leutnant zur See* 1 October 1930. Transferred to *Luftwaffe* glider school in Warnemünde 1934. Promoted to *Hauptmann* 1 April 1935 and from 1 July 1938 in Air Ministry and on General Staff. Promoted to *Major* on 1 June 1940 and from 15 January 1941 attached to Chief of the Armed Forces Command Staff at *Führer* headquarters. Promoted to *Oberstleutnant* 15 March 1942 and to *Oberst* 1 March 1943. Married Hitler's secretary Gerda Daranowski 2 February 1943. After death of Jeschonneck, appointed Ia of *Luftwaffe* Command Staff at Hitler's request and promoted to *Generalmajor* and Chief of the *Luftwaffe* Command Staff 1 September 1944. Left bunker in Berlin on 22 April 1945 to become Chief of the liaison staff of the *Luftwaffe* to OKW Command Staff North. Captured in Mürwik by British 8 May 1945 and held until 7 May 1947.

157 Olaf Groehler, *Das Ende der Reichskanzlei*, VEB Deutscher Verlag der Wissenschaften, Berlin 1978, p. 11.

158 See Musmanno papers.

159 ZS 678, Institute for Contemporary History, Munich; and Jodl in *Wehrwissenschaftliche Rundschau*, 1966 (11), p. 525.

160 Denazification Proceedings of Karl Koller, Special File S, Munich.

161 See Musmanno papers.

162 Ibid.

163 Ibid.

164 Denazification Proceedings of Karl Koller.

165 Testimony of Alfred Jodl, op. cit., p. 535.

166 Keitel, op. cit., p. 656.

167 See Musmanno papers.

168 Schramm, op. cit., p. 1454.

169 Ibid.

170 Karl Koller, *Der letzte Monat*, Bechtle Verlag, Esslingen-Munich, 1985, p. 59.

171 'Lagebesprechung Hitlers am 23. April 1945', *Der Spiegel*, 1966, 3, p. 32.

172 The Fieseler Storch (Fi 156), built by the Fieseler Works in Kassel, was originally used as a reconnaissance plane. Later on it became a much favoured all-purpose aircraft because it could take off and land on very short runways owing to its very low landing speed of only 38 km/h.

173 'Lagebesprechung Hitlers am 23. April 1945', p. 37.

174 Groehler, op. cit., p. 15.

175 Speer, op. cit., p. 485.

176 'Der Endkampf in Berlin (23.4–2.5.1945)', *Wehrwissenschaftliche Rundschau*, 12, Vol. I, 1962, p. 43.

177 Ibid., p. 44.

178 Ibid., p. 46.

179 Ibid., p. 47.

180 'Lagebesprechung Hitlers am 23. April 1945', p. 39.

181 Ibid., p. 34.

182 Ibid., p. 41.

183 Groehler, op. cit., p. 22.

184 Schramm, op. cit., p. 1457.

185 Ibid., p. 1459.

186 Robert *Ritter* von Greim, born 22 June 1892 in Bayreuth (Frankonia). Pilot and *Leutnant* 1919. Stayed in Army until early 1921 and then studied law for three years. In China 1924–27, where he helped build up an air force. Pilot with airline in southern Germany 1928–34. Re-joined Army as *Major* 1934. Promoted to *Oberst* and commander of a *Jagdgeschwader* 1935. Promoted to *Generalmajor* 1938; Commander of *V Fliegerkorps* 1940. CinC *Luftflotte 6* February 1943 to 25 April 1945. Flew to Berlin 26 April

1945 where Hitler promoted him to *Generalfeldmarschall* and appointed him CinC of *Luftwaffe* as Göring's successor. Flew to *Grossadmiral* Dönitz in Plön 29 April 1945 and then to southern Germany. Captured by Americans; committed suicide in Salzburg by taking prussic acid 24 May 1945, aged 52.

187 See Musmanno papers.

188 Groehler, op. cit., p. 23.

189. Lew Bezemensky, *Die letzten Notizen von Martin Bormann*, Deutsche Verlags-Anstalt, Stuttgart 1974, p. 230.

190 Schramm, op. cit., p. 1462.

191 Ibid., p 1461 *et seq*.

192 Ibid., p. 1462.

193 Groehler, op. cit., p. 29.

194 Bezemensky, op. cit., p. 230.

195 'Lagebesprechung Hitlers am 23. April 1945', p. 44.

196 See Musmanno papers.

197 *Wehrwissenschaftliche Rundschau*, 1966, 11, p. 655 *et seq*.

198 Ibid., p. 536.

199 See Musmanno papers.

200 Walter Lüdde-Neurath, *Regierung Dönitz*, Druffel-Verlag, Leoni 1980, p. 45.

201 Schramm, op. cit., p. 1463.

202 Testimony by telephone operator Rochus Misch.

203 *Deutschland im Zweiten Weltkrieg*, Vol. 6, p. 698.

204 Schramm, op. cit., p. 1466.

205 Groehler, op. cit., p. 31.

206 Speer, op. cit., p. 313.

207 Zoller, op. cit., p. 100.

208 Speer, op. cit., p. 313.

209 Groehler, op. cit., p. 32.

210 Schramm, op. cit., p. 1465.

211 Ibid., p. 1466.

212 Ibid.

213 Ibid.

214 Ibid., p. 1467.

215 Werner Naumann, born on 16 June 1909 in Guhrau (Silesia). Joined NSDAP 1928 and became *SA-Brigadeführer* beginning of 1933. Chief of Propaganda Office in Breslau 1937. Undersecretary and Chief of the Minister's Office in the Propaganda Ministry in Berlin 1938, where he was one of Goebbels' closest associates. State Secretary in Propaganda Ministry April 1944. In bunker with Goebbels in final days in April. Succeeded in escaping to West. Arrested by British 16 January 1953 and held until 28 July 1953. Died 25 October 1982 aged 73.

216 ZS 687, Institute for Contemporary History, Munich.

217 Trevor-Roper, op. cit., p. 184.

218 Karl Dönitz, *Zehn Jahre und zwanzig Tage*, Athenäum Verlag, Frankfurt-Bonn 1958, p. 432.

219 Ibid., p. 432 *et seq.*

220 *Wehrwissenschaftliche Rundschau*, 1962, 12, Vol. I, pp. 118, 170.

221 Ibid., p. 169; and Groehner, op. cit., p. 33.

222 David Irving Collection, ZS 2234, Institute for Contemporary History, Munich.

223 Transcripts of the IMT in Nuremberg of 3 July 1945, p. 12330 et seq. of the English text.

224 See Musmanno papers.

225 Hans Frank, *Im Angesicht des Galgens*, Munich 1953, p. 426.

226 David Irving, *Wie krank war Hitler wirklich*, Wilhelm Heyne Verlag, Munich, 1980, p. 129.

227 See Musmanno papers.

228 ZS 687, Institute for Contemporary History, Munich.

229 National Archives, Washington, DC.

230 See Musmanno papers.

231 *Journal of Forensic Medicine*, Vol. 5, 1925.

232 Ibid.

233 *The Stars and Stripes*, 3 November 1945, p. 2.

234 Ibid.

235 *Süddeutsche Zeitung*, No 216, 18 September 1992, p. 9.

236 Musmanno papers.

237 Günther W. Gellermann, *Die Armee Wenck: Hitlers letzte Hoffnung*, Bernard und Graefe Verlag, Koblenz, 1984, p. 180 *et seq.*

238 Schramm, op. cit., p. 1468.

239 Ibid.

240 Dönitz, op. cit., p. 434.

241 Schramm, op. cit., p. 1468.

242 *Wehrwissenschaftliche Rundschau*, 1962, 12, Vol. I, p. 170 *et seq.*

243 Schramm, op. cit., p. 1469.

244 Dönitz, op. cit., p. 436.

245 Schramm, ibid.

246 Lüdde-Neurath, op. cit., p. 46 *et seq.*

247 Dönitz, op. cit., p. 437.

248 Vassil I. Chuikov, *Gardisten auf dem Weg nach Berlin*, Militärverlag der DDR, Berlin, 1976, p. 513.

249 Hans Hofbeck, born 30 September 1909 in Mühldorf (Bavaria). With the Bavarian State Police 1928 and transferred to the Reich Security Service 28 January 1939. Hofbeck was a witness to Hitler's cremation. Captured by Russians during break-out 2 May 1945, held captive until 15 October 1955.

250 Erich Kuby, *Die Russen in Berlin 1945*, Scherz Verlag, Bern-Munich, 1956.

251 Harry Mengershausen, born 28 January 1915 in Bremen. Learned trade of basket weaver. Joined Bremen State Police 1935 and transferred to regular police 1936. Then active service and from 10 May 1944 transferred to the RSD. Witnessed cremation of Hitler's corpse. During break-out on 2 May 1945 was captured by Russians and taken to Russia, where held until 12 January 1956.

252 See Bezemensky, op. cit.

253 See Kuby, op. cit., p. 202.

254 Fritz Echtmann, born 24 July 1913 in Berlin. Dental technician and from 1 July 1938 worked at *Dr* Blaschke's practice. From 25 April 1945 in Chancellery together with *Frau* Heusermann. Arrested by Soviets 11 May 1945; required to prepare drawing of Hitler's dental status and to identify bridges from Hitler's upper and lower jaws. Taken to Moscow 29 July 1945 and held until 5 December 1953. Died in Berlin 7 August 1983 aged 70.

255 Musmanno papers.

256 Trevor-Roper, op. cit., p. 189 *et seq.*

257 General Staff, Military Intelligence, 20 June 1945, War Office Library, London.

258 Trevor-Roper, op. cit., p. 29.

259 Kuby, op. cit., p. 196.

260 Pierre Galante and Eugene Silianoff, *Voices from the Bunker*, Puttmann's Sons, New York, 1989, p. 162.

261 Musmanno papers.

262 Cornelius Ryan, *Der letzte Kampfe*, Droemer Knaur, Munich-Zürich, 1966, p. 49.

263 Reidar F. Sognnaes and Ferdinand Stroem, 'The Odontological Identification of Adolf Hitler. Definitive Documentation by X-rays, Interrogation and Autopsy Findings', *Acta Odontologica Scandinavica*, XXXI, 1973, p. 43 *et seq.*

264 Werner Maser, *Adolf Hitler—Legend, Myth, Reality*, p. 529n.

265 *BMA News Review*, November 1981, p. 20.

266 Chuikov, op. cit., p. 473.

267 Zhukov, op. cit., p. 604.

268 Chuikov, op. cit., p. 225.

269 Zhukov, op. cit., p. 607.

270 Ibid., p. 605.

271 Ibid., p. 357.

272 See Herbert Moore and James W. Barrett, *Who Killed Hitler? The Complete Story of How Death Came to Der Führer and Eva Braun*, The Booktab Press, New York, 1947, p. 134.

273 Ibid., p. 135.

274 Ibid.

275 See also *Pravda*, 10 June 1945.

276 Robert E, Sherwood, *Roosevelt and Hopkins*, The Universal Library New York, Grosset & Dunlap, 1950, pp. 887 and 892.

277 The White House Papers, 1949, p. 902.

278 *Krushchev Remembers*, Little, Brown & Co, 1970, p. 129.

279 James F. Byrnes, *Speaking Frankly*, Harper & Bros, New York, 1947, p. 68.

280 William D. Leahy, *I Was There*, McGraw-Hill Book Co, New York/London/Toronto, 1950, p. 396.

281 *The Stars and Stripes*, 3 November 1945, p. 2.

282 See *The Times*, 9 July 1945, p. 3.

283 See the *Sunday Express*, 5 July 1992, p. 15 (reprinted under the title 'Hitlers letzte Reise' in *Der Spiegel*, No 30, 1992, p. 110 *et seq.*)

284 See *Der Spiegel*, No 14, 1995, p. 170 *et seq.*

285 Angelika Raubal, née Hitler, born 28 July 1883 in Vienna, daughter of Alois Hitler by his second wife and Adolf Hitler's older step-sister. Married Leo Raubal 14 September 1903; he died in Linz 10 August 1910. From 3 June 1919 she again lived in Vienna. From 3 March 1927 managed Hitler's household in Wachenfeld House on Obersalzberg. After personal conflicts Hitler discharged her 18 February 1936. She then married *Professor* Martin Hammitzsch. Died in Dresden 30 October 1949 aged 66.

286 Heinrich Hoffmann, born 12 September 1885 in Fürth (Frankonia). Worked in father's photographic shop. From 1908 photographer in Munich. Joined NSDAP 6 April 1920. Hitler granted Hoffmann exclusive right to publish photographs and illustrated stories about him. Elected to *Reichstag* 1933 and appointed *Professor* by Hitler in 1938. Arrested by Americans 10 May 1945, held until 31 May 1950. Died in Munich 15 December 1957 aged 72.

287 H. A. Turner (ed.), *Hitler aus nächster Nähe. Aufzeichnungen eines Vertrauten 1929–1932*, Verlag Ullstein GmbH, Frankfurt 1978, p. 485.

288 Bormann letters, op. cit., p. 174.

289. Angela ('Geli') Raubal, born 4 June 1908 in Linz (Austria). From 1927 in Munich. Studied medicine but broke off to take up singing and music. From 5 November 1929 she lived with Hitler in his apartment at 16 Prinzregentenplatz. Was Hitler's step-niece and probably the great love of his life. Relationship suffered from Hitler's refusal to acknowledge it publicly due to the family ties, causing Geli Raubal increasing emotional problems. On 18 September 1931, after a quarrel with Hitler, she shot herself, aged 23.

290 Anni Winter, née Schuler, born 27 February 1905 in Pfakofen (Bavaria). From 1922 housekeeper for Countess Törring in Munich. On 1 May 1929 married George Winter, servant with *General* Epp. Employed by Hitler on 1 October 1929 as housekeeper in his Munich apartment, where she lived in two rooms together with her husband. Held by Americans from 8 June 1945 to mid-1946. Died in Munich on 17 October 1970 aged 65.

291 See Musmanno papers.

292 SS File Hermann Fegelein, Federal Document Centre, Berlin.

293 Ibid.

294 Ibid.

295 Ibid.

296 Ibid.

297 Marianne Schönmann, née Petzl, born 19 December 1899 in Vienna. Daughter of opera star Maria Petzl whom Hitler admired from his time in Vienna. Through her acquaintance with Erna Gröpke, who married Heinrich Hoffmann, she met Hitler and was his frequent guest at the Obersalzberg 1935–44. Here she met and became a friend of Eva Braun. Married Fritz Schönmann August 1937; Hitler guest at wedding. Committed suicide in Munich on 17 March 1981 aged 81.

298 Schroeder, op. cit., p. 167.

299 Galante and Silianoff, op cit., p. 110 *et seq.*

300 Schroeder, op. cit., p. 168.

301 Galante and Silianoff, ibid.

302 Testimony by *Dr* Karl Brandt: '. . . demoted to a parlour maid by Eva Braun'.

303 Galante and Silianoff, op. cit., p. 111.

304 Ibid.

305 Musmanno papers.

306 Schroeder, op. cit., p. 167.

307 *The Bormann Letters*, p. 155 *et seq.*

308 Ibid.

309 Ibid.

310 Ibid.

311 Testimony of von Loringhoven, ZS 254, Institute for Contemporary History, Munich.

312 Galante and Silianoff, op cit., p. 113.

313 Schroeder, op. cit., p. 168.

314 Statement by *Frau* Schroeder, 1983.

315 Nerin E. Gun, *Eva Braun-Hitler. Leben und Schicksal.* blick und blick Verlag S. Kappe KG, 1968, p. 192.

316 Trevor-Roper, op. cit., p. 161.

317 See Musmanno papers.

318 Ibid.

319 Galante and Silianoff, op cit., p. 9.

320 Otto Günsche testimony, David Irving Collection, ZS 2234, Institute for Contemporary History, Munich.

321 See Fegelein File, Munich Special File S.

322 Schroeder, op. cit., p. 286.

323 See Otto Günsche testimony.

Bibliography

Ainszstein, Reuben, *How Hitler Died: The Soviet Version*, International Affairs, XLIII, April 1967, 307, 18

Atlanta Constitution, 'Hitler is Dead, Say Nazis', 2 May 1945

——, 'British Foreign Office Believes Death Report', 2 May 1945

——, 'If Hitler is Dead, Good Riddance', 2 May 1945

——, 'Adolf Killed by Bomb', 3 May 1945

——, 'Hitler and Great Love Hinted in Death Pact', 4 May 1945

——, 'Hitler's Death Marks End of an Era', 4 May 1945

——, 'Hitler Not in Berlin. Pravda Says: Russians Push Search for Body', 4 May 1945

——, 'His Doctor Suspects Adolf Hiding', 7 May 1945

——, 'Lest We Forget', 10 May 1945

——, 'Hitler's Body Found, Russian Source Says', 7 June 1945

——, 'Burned Hitler, Eva After Suicide. Valet Liberated by Soviets Relates', 10 October 1955

Baltimore Sun, 'Hitler's Body Thought Found', 7 June 1945

——, 'Hitler and Eva Reported Safe', 17 July 1945

Baur, Hans, (trans. Fitzgerald, Edward), *Hitler's Pilot*, Frederick Muller, London 1958

Bayerische Staatszeitung, 'Hitlers Todeserklärung. Nicht der geringste Zweifel: Selbstmord am 30. April 1945' (Hitler Declared Dead. Not the Slightest Doubt: Suicide on 30 April 1945), Munich, 27 October 1956

Below, Nicolaus von, *Als Hitler's Adjutant 1937–45* (*Hitler's Adjutant 1937–45*), Hase und Köhler Verlag, Mainz 1980

Berchtesgadener Anzeiger, 'Amtliche Todeserklärung Hitlers in Berchtesgaden' ('Hitler Officially Declared Dead in Berchtesgaden'), No 169, 26/27 October 1956

Bezemensky, Lev, *The Death of Adolf Hitler: Unknown Documents from Soviet Archives*, Michael Joseph, London 1968

——, *Die letzten Notizen von Martin Bormann* (*Martin Bormann's Final Notes*), Deutsche Verlagsanstalt, Stuttgart 1974

Bild Zeitung, 'Hat Adolf Hitler den Zweiten Weltkrieg überlebt?' ('Did Adolf Hitler Survive the Second World War?'), No 105, Munich, 7 May 1993

Boelke, Willi A., *Deutschlands Rüstung im Zweiten Weltkrieg. Hitlers Konferenzen mit Albert Speer 1942–1945* (*Germany's Armaments during the Second World War: Hitler's Conferences with Albert Speer 1942–1945*), Akademische Verlagsanstalt Athenaion, Frankfurt/Main 1969

Boldt, Gerhard, (trans. Stern-Rubarth, Edgar) *In the Shelter with Hitler*, Citadel Press, London 1948.

Brockdorff, Werner, *Flucht vor Nürnberg: Pläne und Organisation der Fluchtwege der NS-Prominenz im 'Römischen Weg'* (*Flight from Nuremberg: Plans and Organisation of the Escape Routes of Prominent Nazis on the 'Roman Way'*) Verlag Welsermuehl, Wels 1969

Byford-Jones, *Berlin Twilight*, Hutchinson, London 1963

Byrnes, James F., *Speaking Frankly*, Harper & Bros, New York 1947

Casey, William, *The Secret War Against Hitler*, Simon & Schuster, London 1989

Chicago Daily Tribune, '56th Birthday Finds Hitler is Still Mystery', 21 April 1945

———, 'Hitler Believed Running War at Berchtesgaden', 22 April 1945

———, 'Europe Buzzes With Mystery: Where's Hitler?', 25 April 1945

———, 'Hitler's Love Life is Told by His Valet', 11 October 1955

Chicago Sunday Tribune, 'Tells of Hitler's Suicide', 9 October 1955

Chicago Times, 'Hear Argentina Hides Hitler, Eva', 16 July 1945

Chicago Tribune, 'Autopsy on Hitler Released by Russia', 2 August 1968

Chuikov, Vasily I., (trans. Kisch, Ruth), *The Fall of Berlin*, Ballantine, New York 1969

Connecticut Magazine, 'Whatever Happened to Hitler. A Bold New Theory', March 1983

Cosmopolitan, 'How Dead is Hitler?', 1946, 62–186

Daily Telegraph and Morning Post, 'Hitler's Death Officially Announced', 26 October 1956

Darmstädter Tageblatt, 'Hitler nicht in der Berliner Reichskanzlei verbrannt' ('Hitler Not Burned in the Chancellery in Berlin'), 27 May 1952

Deschner, Gustav, 'Interview mit Traudl Junge, Hitlers Sekretärin über die letzten Wochen' ('Interview with Traudl Junge, Hitler's Secretary, about the Final Weeks'), *Welt am Sonntag*, 28 April 1985

Die Ergebnisse des Grossen Vaterländischen Krieges (*The Results of the Great Patriotic War*) in Vol. 5 of *Geschichte des Grossen Vaterländischen Krieges der Sowjetunion* (*History of the Great Patriotic War of the Soviet Union*), German Military Publishers (GDR), Berlin 1968

Dönitz, Karl, (trans. Stevens, R. H.), *Ten Years and Twenty Days*, Weidenfeld & Nicolson, London 1958

Duffy, Christopher, *Red Storm of the Reich*, Macmillan Publishing Co., New York 1991

Evening Standard (London), 'Paris will Believe it When They See the Body', 2 May 1945

———, 'Last Throw to Save the Hitler Myth. May 2, 1945

———, 'Hitler not in Berlin', 3 May 1945

———, 'The Body They Cannot Find' 4 May 1945

———, 'Hitler Mystery' 4 May 1945

———, 'Hitler Took Poison and Died in Fire', 6 June 1945

———, 'Hitler was Married, May be in Hiding', 9 June 1945

———, 'Hitler Lives', 16 June 1950

Fabricant, N. D., *Hatte Adolf Hitler die Parkinsonsche Krankheit?* (*Did Adolf Hitler suffer from Parkinson's Disease?*), *Welt am Sontag*, 11 February, 1960.*

Fest, Joachim C., (trans. Richard and Clara Winston), *Hitler*, Vintage Books, New York 1975

Frankfurter Allgemeine Zeitung, 'Der bayerische Staat soll Hitlers Nachlass herausgeben' ('Bavarian State to Relinquish Hitler's Estate'), 4 December 1953

———, 'Entlassungen nach dem russischen Alphabet' ('Releases According to the Russian Alphabet'), 10 October 1955

———, 'Ermittlingsverfahren gegen Hitler' ('Investigation Proceedings against Hitler'), 20 February 1965

Frankfurter Nachtausgabe, 'Zahnprothese als Beweisstück' ('Dentures as Proof'), No 238, 13 October 1954

Fritzsche, Hans, *Hier spricht Hans Fritzsche (This is Hans Fritzsche Speaking)*, Interverlag AG, Zurich 1948

Galante, Pierre, and Silianoff, Eugène, *Last Witnesses in the Bunker*, Sidgwick & Jackson, London 1989

———, *Voices from the Bunker*, G. P. Putnam's Sons, New York 1989

Gellermann, Günther W., *Die Armee Wenck—Hitlers letzte Hoffnung (Army Group Wenck—Hitler's Last Hope)*, Bernard und Graefe Verlag, Koblenz 1984

Genoud, François (pub.), *The Bormann Letters*, Weidenfeld & Nicolson, London 1954

———, (ed.), (trans. Stevens, R. H.), *The Testament of Adolf Hitler: The Hitler-Bormann Documents, February–April 1945*, Cassell, London 1961

Gilbert, Felix, (ed.), *Hitler Directs His War: The Secret Records of His Daily Military Conferences*, Oxford University Press, New York 1951

Goodman, Anne, Review of H. R. Trevor-Roper, *The Last Days of Hitler*, in *New Republic*, CXVII, 22 September 1947

Groehler, Olaf, *Das Ende der Reichskanzlei (The End of the Chancellery)*, VEB Deutscher Verlag der Wissenschaften, Berlin (GDR) 1978

Guderian, Heinz, (trans. Fitzgibbon, Constantine), *Panzer Leader*, E. P. Dutton, New York 1952

Gun, Nerin E., *Eva Braun: Hitler's Mistress*, Leslie Frewin, London 1969

Haupt, Werner, *Berlin 1945: Hitlers letzte Schlacht (Berlin 1945: Hitler's Final Battle)*, Erich Pobel, Rastatt 1963

Hegner, Hans (pseud.), *Die Reichskanzlei 1933–1945: Anfang und Ende des Dritten Reiches (The Chancellery 1933–1945: Beginning and End of the Third Reich)*, 3rd ed., Verlag Frankfurter Bücher, Frankfurt/Main 1960

Heiber, Helmut, (ed.), *Hitlers Lagebesprechungen. Protokollfragmente seiner militärischen Konferenzen 1942–1945 (Hitler's Briefings. Fragments of the Minutes of His Military Conferences 1942–1945)*, Deutsche Verlagsanstalt, Stuttgart 1962

Heim, Heinrich, *Adolf Hitler, Monologe im Führerhauptquartier 1941–1944 (Adolf Hitler, Monologues at Führer Headquarters 1941–1944)*, Albrecht Knaus Verlag, Hamburg 1980

Heim und Welt, 'Ist Hitler wirklich tot?' ('Is Hitler Really Dead?'), Nos 26–34, 29 June–24 August 1952

'Hermes Handlexikon', *Synchronopse des Zweiten Weltkrieges (Chronological Synopsis of the Second World War)*, ECON Taschenbuchverlag, Düsseldorf 1983

Hillgruber, Andreas, and Hümmelchen, Gerhard, *Chronik des Zweiten Weltkrieges. Kalendarium militärischer und politischer Ereignisse 1939–1945 (Chronology of the Second World War: Calendar of Military and Political Events 1939–1945)*, Athenäum/Droste, Düsseldorf 1978

Hulme, George, *The Life and Death of Adolf Hitler*, Colin Smythe, Buckinghamshire 1975

Infield, Glenn B., *Eva and Adolf*, Grosset & Dunlap, New York 1974; and New English Library, London 1975

———, *Hitler's Secret Life: The Mysteries of the Eagle's Nest*, Stein & Day, New York 1979

International Military Tribunal, *Trial of the Major War Criminals*, Vols XVII–XXXV, Nuremberg 1947–49

Irving, David, *Wie krank war Hitler wirklich? Der Diktator und seine Ärzte (How Ill was Hitler Really? The Dictator and his Doctors)*, Wilhelm Verlag, Munich 1980

————, *The Medical Diaries: The Private Diaries of Dr. Theo Morell*, Sidwick & Jackson, London 1983

Investigator, The, 'Wanted Dead or Alive', May 1988

Katukov, Michael Jefimovitch, *An der Spitze des Hauptstosses* (*On the Point of the Main Attack*), Military Publishers of the GDR, Berlin 1979

Katz, Ottmar, *Prof. Dr. med. Theo Morell. Hitler's Leibarzt* (*Dr Theo Morell: Hitler's Personal Doctor*), Hestia Verlag, Bayreuth 1982

Kelly, Elsworth K., 'Adolf Hitler: His Dentist and His Dental Problems', *Journal of the California Dental Association*, No 41, October 1965

Kempka, Erich, *Ich habe Adolf Hitler verbrannt* (*I Burned Adolf Hitler*), Kyrburg Verlag, Munich 1950

————, *Die letzten Tage mit Adolf Hitler, erweitert und erläutert von Erich Kern* (*The Final Days with Adolf Hitler, Extended and Commented on by Erich Kern*), Verlag K.W. Schütz, Pr. Oldendorf, 1975

Khrushchev, Nikita, (ed. and trans. Talbot, Strobe), *Khrushchev Remembers*, Brown & Co., Boston 1970

Koelnische Rundschau, 'Hitler starb um 15:30 Uhr' ('Hitler Died at 15.30 hrs'), 26 October 1956

————, 'Hitlers Inferno in der Rille' ('Hitler's Inferno in the Slit'), 8 September 1959

————, 'Wann starb Hitler?' ('When did Hitler Die?'), 29 March 1964

————, 'Hunde-Freund und Henker' ('Dog Lover and Executioner'), 14 June 1964

————, 'Neue Sowjet-Version über Hitlers Ende' ('New Soviet Version of Hitler's End'), 13 July 1964

Koller, Karl, *Der letzte Monat. 14. April bis 27. Mai 1945* (*The Final Month: 14 April to 27 May 1945*), Bechtle Verlag Esslingen, Munich, 1985

Konev, I. S., (trans. Mishne, David), *Year of Victory*, Progress Publishers, Moscow 1969

Kuby, Erich, (ed.) *Das Ende des Schreckens: Dokumente des Untergangs Januar bis Mai 1945* (*The End of the Horror: Documents of the Downfall January to May 1945*), Süddeutscher Verlag, Munich 1956

Kuby, Erich, *Die Russen in Berlin, 1945* (*The Russians in Berlin, 1945*), Scherz Verlag, Munich 1965

————, 'Die Russen in Berlin' ('The Russians in Berlin'), *Der Spiegel*, Nos 9–24, 6 May– 9 June 1965

Leahy, William D., *I Was There*, McGraw-Hill, New York 1950

Le Tissier, Toni, *Berlin Then and Now*, After The Battle, London 1992

Lewis, David, *The Secret Life of Adolf Hitler*, Heinrich Hanau, London 1977

Life Magazine, 'The Last Days in Berlin', No XVIII, 21 May 1945

————, 'Did Adolf and Eva Die Here?' and 'Hitler's Last Stand Was in His Reichschancellery', No XIX, 23 July 1945

————, 'The Last Hours—and Some Last Words—of Hitler', No XIL, 24 October 1945

Linge, Heinz, 'Valet's Own Story: The Hitler I Knew', *Chicago Daily News*, 22–29 October 1955

Los Angeles Times, The, 'Hitler Believed Hiding at Berchtesgaden' 25 April 1945

————, 'Hitler Refuge Denied by Japanese' 27 April 1945

————, 'Britons Read Hitler Death Report' 2 May 1945

————, 'The Hitler Death Announcement' 2 May 1945

————, 'Hitler Body Found, Red Sources Claim' 7 June 1945

————, 'Hitler: "Wife" Reported Safe in Argentina' 17 July 1945

————, 'Argentina Investigates Story of Hitler Haven' 18 July 1945

————, 'Hitler Escape by Sub? No, He was No Sailor' 21 July 1945

Lüdde-Neurath, Walter, *Regierung Dönitz: Die letzten Tage des Dritten Reiches* (*Dönitz Government: The Final Days of the Third Reich*), 3rd edn, Musterschmidt-Verlag, Göttingen 1964

Mac, George, *La vie et la mort d'Hitler* (*The Life and Death of Hitler*), Editions Midicis, Paris 1946

McKale, Donald M., *Hitler: The Survival Myth*, Stein & Day Publishers, New York 1981

Maple Leaf, The, 'Hitler's Suicide Sofa Discovered Among Shambles', 6 July 1945

Maser, Werner, (trans. Ross, Peter and Betty), *Hitler*, Allen Lane, London 1973

Michalski, Peter, 'Hitler hat sich doch erschossen' ('Hitler Did Shoot Himself), *Welt am Sonntag*, 13 October 1968

Military Advisor, The, 'Flight of the Wolf—Berlin 1945', Vol. 4, No 1 , 1992/93

Moore, Herbert, and Barrett, James, *Who Killed Hitler? The Complete Story of How Death Came to Der Fuehrer and Eva Braun*, Booktab Press, New York 1947

Münchner Merkur, 'Hitler automatisch Kriegsverbrecher' ('Hitler Automatically a War Criminal'), 19 July 1952

————, 'Himmlers Putschpläne gegen Hitler' (Himmler's Putsch Plans against Hitler'), 26 April 1956

————, 'Hitler wollte sich im Flugzeug in die Luft sprengen' ('Hitler Wanted to Blow Himself up in an Aircraft'), 24 May 1994

Musmanno, Michael A., *Ten Days to Die*, 2nd edn., Macfadden Books, New York 1962

National Police Gazette, The, 'Hitler is Alive', No CLXXXII, January 1977

Neue Zürcher Zeitung, 'Hitler: Die letzten 10 Tage' ('Hitler: The Last Ten Days'), 6 October 1973

New Republic, The, 'Is Hitler Dead?', No CXI, 20 November 1944

News Chronicle (London), 'The Last Days of Hitler' 28–31 December 1945

Newsweek, 'Missing: The Corpse', XXV, 14 May 1945

————, 'Now You Find Him', XXV, 18 June 1945

————, 'Hitler: The Cremation', XXVI, 2 July 1945

————, 'Hitler's Last Gasp', XXVII, 7 January 1946

————, 'He Saw Hitler Burned', LVI, 17 October 1955

New York Herald Tribune, The, 'New Version of Hitler's Death: Himmler, Göring Killed Him'. 4 May 1945

————, 'Hitler's First Plan Held to Flee Berlin by Car', 21 October 1955

New York Journal-American, 'Chauffeur Tells of Burning Bodies', 3 July 1946

New York Times, The, 'The Bloody Dog is Dead', 2 May 1945.

————, 'The End of Hitler', 2 May 1945

————, 'Nazi Ruse is Seen in Hitler's Death' 2 May 1945

————, 'Just a "Fascist Trick", Moscow Radio Asserts' 2 May 1945

————, 'Cremation Report Predicted' 3 May 1945

————, 'Goebbels and Fuehrer Died By Own Hands, Aide Says', 3 May 1945

————, 'Truman Believes Hitler Dead', 3 May 194

————, 'Russians Find No Trace of Hitler in Berlin, Moscow Paper Reports', 4 May 1945

————, 'New Berlin Search Fails to Find Hitler', 8 May 1945

————, 'Hitler's Body Found, Russians Report', 9 May 1945

————, 'Goebbels "Virtually" Identified', 16 May 1945

————, 'Enemy Says Hitler Took Own Life', 16 May 1945

————, 'Hitler Kept Aide Ready to Kill Him', 20 May 1945

————, 'Says Hitler Died in Mercy Killing' 24 May 1945

————, 'Many Poison Phials Made by Germans for the Day', 25 May 1945
————, 'Hitler Body Proof Declared Fairly Certain by Russians', 7 June 1945
————, 'Zhukoff Says Hitler Wed Actress in Berlin. May Be Alive in Europe', 10 June 1945
————, 'Hitler Not on Spanish Soil, Foreign Minister Says', 11 June 1945
————, 'Hitler's Chauffeur Talks', 21 June 1945
————, 'Shaef Aides Sure Hitler Died May 1', 22 June 1945
————, 'Hitler Funds Reported', 12 July 1945
————, 'Hitler Reported Alive', 17 July 1945
————, 'Jawbone Claimed to be Hitler's', 31 July 1945
————, 'World-Wide Search for Hitler Goes On', 9 September 1945
————, 'Hitler Believed Alive, Eisenhower Tells Dutch', 7 October 1945
————, 'Eisenhower Didn't Say He Believes Hitler Alive', 13 October 1945
————, 'Hitler Plan to Flee to Japan is Reported', 16 October 1945
————, 'Abetz Says He Believes Hitler Still Lives', 29 October 1945
————, 'Text of British Report Holding Hitler Ended His Life', 2 November 1945
————, 'Hitler's Private Will Found. Affirms His Suicidal Plans', 30 December 1945
————, 'Interview With Dr. Morell', 22 May and 2 June 1948
————, 'Asks Hitler Death Proof', 26 May 1948
————, 'Hitler's Pilot Says He Saw the Dictator Shoot Himself', 9 October 1955
————, 'Valet Says He Set Fire to Hitler's Body', 10 October 1955
————, 'German Judge Confirms That Hitler Died as a Suicide in a Berlin Bunker in 1945', 26 October 1955
————, 'Re-Creating the Final Days of Adolf Hitler', 8 April 1956
————, 'Russian Writes of Hitler's Death', 22 February 1964
————, 'Soviet Report on Hitler Disputed by Historians', 23 February 1964
————, 'Hitler Took Cyanide, Soviet Inquiry Found', 2 August 1968
————, 'Hitler Valet Denies Account of Suicide', 3 August 1968
O'Donnell, James, *The Berlin Bunker*, J. M. Dent & Sons, London 1979
O'Donnell, James, and Bahnsen, Uwe, *Die Katakombe: Das Ende in der Reichskanzlei (The Catacomb: The End in the Reichs Chancellery)*, Deutsche Verlagsanstalt, Stuttgart 1975
Payne, Robert, *Stalins Aufstieg und Fall (The Rise and Fall of Stalin)*, Hans E. Günther Verlag, Stuttgart 1967
Recktenwald, Johann, *Wie krank war Hitler wirklich. Der Diktator und seine Ärzte (How Sick was Hitler Really? The Dictator and His Doctors)*, Wilhelm Heyne Verlag, Munich 1963
Reitsch, Hanna, *Fliegen mein Leben (Flying is My Life)*, Stuttgart 1956
————, *Höhen und Tiefen, 1945–77 (Ups and Downs, 1945–77)*, DSZ-Verlag, Munich 1978
————, 'Mein Erleben im Hitler-Bunker' ('My Experience in the Hitler Bunker'), *National-Zeitung Munich*, 28 July 1978
Röhrs, Hans Dieter, *Hitler—Die Zerstörung einer Persönlichkeit (Hitler—The Destruction of a Personality)*, Neckargemünd, 1965
————, *Hitlers Kankheit—Tatsachen und Legenden (Hitler's Illness—Facts and Legends)*, Neckargemünd 1966
Rosanow, German L., *Hitlers letzte Tage (Hitler's Final Days)*, Dietz Verlag, Berlin 1963
Ryan, Cornelius, *The Last Battle*, Simon & Schuster, New York 1966

Rzhevskaya, Yelena, (trans. Hanke, Werner), *Hitlers Ende ohne Mythos* (*Hitler's End Without Myths*), Deutscher Militärverlag, Berlin (GDR) 1967

San Francisco Chronicle, The, 'How Hitler May Have Died', 20 May 1945

———, 'Zhukov Sure Hitler Wed Eva and Fled', 10 June 1945

———, 'Hitler Legend', 12 June 1945

———, 'Hitler, Eva Suicides, Says Eyewitness', 21 June 1945

———, 'Hitler Pilot Says: "I Know He Died"', 9 October 1955

Schenck, Ernst Günter, *Ich sah Berlin sterben: Als Arzt in der Reichskanzlei* (*I Saw Berlin Die: As a Doctor in the Reichs Chancellery*), Nicolaische Verlagshandlung, Herford 1970

———, *Patient Hitler. Eine medizinische Biographie* (*Patient Hitler: A Medical Biography*), Droste Verlag, Düsseldorf 1989

Schlesinger Jr., Arthur, Review of H. R. Trevor-Roper, *The Last Days of Hitler*, *The Nation*, No 165, 20 September 1947

Schramm, Percy Ernst, et al., *Kriegstagebuch des Oberkommandos der Wehrwacht 1940–1945* (*The War Diary of the Supreme Command of the Wehrmacht 1940–1945*), Vol. IV, Bernard und Graefe Verlag für Wehrwesen, Frankfurt/Main 1961

Schoenberger, Angela, *Die Neue Reichskanzlei von Albert Speer* (*The New Chancellery by Albert Speer*), Gebr. Mann Verlag, Berlin 1981

Schroeder. Christa (ed. Joachimsthaler, Anton), *Er war mein Chef* (*He was my Boss*), Langen Müller Verlag, Munich-Vienna 1985

Seaton, Albert, *The German Army 1933–1945*, Weidenfeld & Nicolson, London 1982

Seifert, Paul, 'Studien zu Zyankaliumvergiftungen' ('Studies in Cyanide Poisoning'), *Deutsche Zeitschrift für gerichtliche Medizin* (*German Journal of Forensic Medicine*), No 44, 1952

Senior Scholastic, 'Clear Up Hitler's Death', LXVII, 20 October 1955

Sherwood, Robert E., *The White House Papers of Harry L. Hopkins*, Vol. II, Eyre & Spottiswoode, London 1949

Sondern Jr, Frederick, 'Adolf Hitler's Last Days', *The Reader's Digest*, LVIII, June 1951

Sognnaes, Reidar F., 'Dental Evidence in Postmortem Identification of Adolf Hitler, Eva Braun and Martin Bormann', *Legal Medicine Annual 1976*, Appleton-Century-Crofts, New York 1977

Sognnaes, Reidar F. and Stroem, Ferdinand, 'The Odontological Identification of Adolf Hitler. Definitive Documentation by X-rays, Interrogation and Autopsy Findings', *Acta Odontologica Scandinavica*, XXXI, 1973

Speer, Albert, (trans. Winston, Richard and Clara), *Inside the Third Reich*, Macmillan, New York 1970

Spiegel, Der, 'Hitlers letzte Lagebesprechungen' ('Hitler's Last Military Briefings'), 1966, No. 3

———, 'Buchbesprechung Besymenski', ('Book Review Bezemensky'), 1968, No 32

———, 'Adolf Hitler—Aufriss über meine Person' ('Adolf Hitler—Outline of my Personality'), 1973

———, 'Hitlers letzte Reise' ('Hitler's Last Journey'), 1992, No 30

———, 'Hitlers letzte Tage' ('Hitler's Last Days'), 1995, Nos 14 and 15

Stars and Stripes, The, 'Suicide Story Checked. Hitler Officially Dead', 3 November 1945

Süddeutsche Zeitung (Munich), 'Hitlers Tod endgültig aufgeklärt' ('Hitler's Death Conclusively Solved'), 14 September 1948

———, 'Hitler und Frau vor der Spruchkammer. Der Oberhauptschuldige/Einzug des gesamten Vermögens' ('Hitler and Wife on Trial. The Top Main Offender/Confiscation of all His Property'), 16 October 1948

————, 'Schwedische Documente zum Zweiten Weltkrieg' ('Swedish Documents on the Second World War'), 26 April 1956

————, 'Angebliche Hitler-Aufnahme bekannte Fälschung' ('Alleged Hitler Photo Well-Known Forgery'), 18 September 1992

Stevenson, William, *The Bormann Brotherhood*, Arthur Barker, London 1973

Sunday Express, The, 'How the Russians disposed of Hitler', 5 July 1992

Sunday News-Journal, The, 'Study Casts Doubt on Eva Braun's Fate', London 1981

Tabori, Paul, (ed.), *The Private Life of Adolf Hitler: The Intimate Notes and Diary of Eva Braun*, Aldus Publications, London 1949

Tagesspiegel, Der, (Berlin), 'Vor einem Jahr: Die letzten zehn Tage' ('One Year Ago: The Last Ten Days'), 3 May 1946

————, 'Akte II/52: Hitler endete durch Selbstmord' ('File II/52: Hitler Ended by Suicide'), 26 October 1956

Time Magazine, 'Adolf Hitler's Last Hours', VL, 21 May 1945

————, 'Legends Never Die', XXII, 12 November 1945

————, 'Historical Note: How Hitler Died', VIC, 9 August 1968

————, 'The Two Hitlers', C, 2 October 1972

————, 'What Happened to Hitler's Body?', No 19, 8 May 1995

Times, The, (London), 'Hitler's Visit to Oder Front', 10 March 1945

————, 'Jawbones Identified as Hitler's', 9 July 1945

————, 'Hitler's Fate', 16 October 1945

————, 'Last Hours of Hitler', 1 January 1946

————, 'Hitler's Will', 24 January 1946

————, 'Hitler's Chauffeur at Nuremberg', 4 July 1946

————, 'Hitler's Bunker Blown Up', 12 December 1947

————, 'Hitler's Last Pilot', 13 December 1947

————, 'Hitler's Confiscated Property', 10 April 1953

————, 'Hitler's Will Found', 12 February 1954

————, 'Hitler's Death', 5 August 1968

————, 'Hitler's Death Officially Established', 26 October 1968

Thomas, Hugh, *Doppelgänger: The Truth about the Bodies in the Berlin Bunker*, Fourth Estate, London 1995

Toland, John, *The Last 100 Days*, Random House, New York 1966

Trevor-Roper, Hugh, *The Last Days of Hitler*, Macmillan, New York 1947

————, 'The Last Days of Hitler', *Life Magazine*, XXII, 17 March 1947

————, 'Is Hitler Really Dead?', *Commentary*, XI, February 1951

————, 'Last Days of Hitler', *New York Times Magazine*, 24 April 1955

————, 'The "Mystery" of Hitler's Death', *Commentary*, XXII, July 1956

————, 'The Hole in Hitler's Head', *The Sunday Times* (London), 29 September 1968

Ueberschär, Gerd, and Müller, Rolf-Dieter, *Kriegsende 1945 (End of the War 1945)*, Fischer Taschenbuchverlag, Frankfurt/Main 1994

Various authors, *Deutschland im zweiten Weltkrieg (Germany during the Second World War)*, Pahl-Rugenstein Verlag, Cologne 1985

Watson, Peter, and Petrova, Ada: *The Death of Hitler*, W. W. Norton and Co., New York 1995

Weidling Helmut, 'Der Endkampf in Berlin (23.4.–2.5.1945)', ('The Final Battle in Berlin [23 April–2 May 1945]'), *Wehrwissenschaftliche Rundschau (Military Scientific Review)* No 12, January–March 1962

Welt, Die, 'Hitler auch amtlich tot' ('Hitler Now Officially Dead'), 26 October 1956

Welt am Sonntag, 'Hitlers Sekretärin über die letzten Wochen' ('Hitler's Secretary on the Final Weeks'), No 17, 28 April 1985

Weltbühne, Die, 'Hitlers enträtselter Tod', ('Hitler's Demystified Death'), No 40, 1 October 1968

Westdeutsche Allgemeine (Essen), 'Adolf Hitler schoss sich in die Schläfe' ('Adolf Hitler Shot Himself in the Temple'), 26 October 1956.

Work, Robert E., 'Last Days in Hitler's Air Raid Shelter', *The Public Opinion Quarterly*, X, 1946–47

Zeit, Die, 'So starb Adolf Hitler' ('This is How Adolf Hitler Died'), 6 August 1968

Zhukov, Georgi K., *Erinnerungen und Gedanken (Memories and Thoughts)*, Deutsche Verlagsanstalt, Stuttgart 1969

Ziemke, Earl F., *Battle for Berlin: End of the Third Reich*, Ballantine Books, New York 1968

Zoller, Albert, *Hitler privat: Erlebnisbericht seiner Geheimsekretärin (Hitler in Private: Experience Report by His Secret Secretary)*, Droste Verlag, Düsseldorf 1949

Index

Page numbers in italics refer to brief biographies given in the Notes.